Depression Anxiety
and the Child *of* God

Scott R. Kraniak

Depression Anxiety
and the Child *of* God
Daily Devotional
the companion to the book of the same title

YorkshirePublishing
www.yorkshirepublishing.com
Write Now.

ISBN: 978-1-947247-24-6

Depression Anxiety and the Child of God - Daily Devotional Part 2

Copyright © 2015 by Scott R. Kraniak

For permission requests, write to the publisher at the address below.

Yorkshire Publishing
3207 South Norwood Avenue
Tulsa, Oklahoma 74135
www.YorkshirePublishing.com
918.394.2665

To all of the silent screams of the lonely people out there who suffer with the worst kind of agony that no one seems to even want to hear

To my wife, Julie, who held my hand during the darkest days I can remember, who kept me focused on Christ, and whose unwavering faith in Christ never faltered

To Jesus Christ—the Mighty Counselor and Everlasting Lord. Thank You for Your grace and patience and for allowing me to go through it one more time so I would be motivated to write this book.

Good does come from bad, and the sun does shine after the storm.

Acknowledgements

I would like to take this time to thank those who
helped make this devotional a reality:

To my team of editors who spent a good part of a year on their
own time looking over my gibberish and making sense out of it

Lois Dipol
Linda Ziroli
Melodie Rubio

Heather Davis
Artwork and Photography

Lauren Ziroli
Cover Model

My family for allowing me to spend every free hour
writing when I could have been with them

Julie, Jacob, Aaron, and Luke

This devotional and additional book (sold separately)
is also dedicated to Jennifer Palagonia born January
13, 1982, and left this world on June 28, 2014

Jen was a dear young lady whom I counseled for many years; yet unfortunately, Jen gave up too soon and believed the lies of the destroyer. Jen was a beautiful and brave young lady. Through her passing and at her funeral service, many eyes were open to this silent monster called mental illness. So many people were moved to see what they didn't even know existed. Through her death, many are coming to understand and many are seeking God for the first time. As much as a blessing Jen was in her life, she is also being so in her passing. I will miss you, Jen, but your story will save countless lives so this never has to happen again.

—Scott R. Kraniak

What in the world is going on?

—Isaiah 49:13

January

January 1 - A What-If Day

He [Elijah] came to a broom bush, sat down under it and prayed that he might die. "I have had enough, LORD", he said. "Take my life; I am no better than my ancestors." Then he lay down under the bush and fell asleep. (1st Kings 19:4–5, NIV)

A new day begins. Yet sometimes we are not ready for that new day. What if I can't make it through this day? What if God's Word is not true? What if God's power isn't felt during this day? Lord, I just want to crawl back under the covers and sleep. The thought of another year of hurt is too much for me. Yet *what if?*

Dear friend, there is something about the starting of a new day. It can bring fear and apprehension or faith and excitement for what is unknown. I remember when my wife and I were expecting our first child. As a person of faith *clouded by fear*, fear always seemed to take the joy out of the moment. In my mind ran the thoughts of doubt. What if my child is born deformed? What if I lose my job and we lose our home? What if my wife dies on the delivery table? The *what-ifs* seemed to drown out every bit of joy the Lord had planned for that moment. My faith was strained again, and another day I let the enemy of self and Satan take what belonged to all children of God—*the joy of the Lord.*

Then he said unto them, go your way, eat the fat, and drink the sweet, and send portions unto them for whom nothing is prepared: for this day is holy unto our Lord: neither be ye sorry; for the joy of the LORD is your strength. (Neh. 8:10)

Dear fellow sufferer in Christ, yes, the negative can happen. Yes, the *what-ifs* can become reality, but for 99 percent of my life, and for most of us, they never do. What about all the times that the worst didn't happen? All the times when the day didn't end in calamity and pain? See, my child was born normal. In fact, so was my second and third. I didn't lose my job, my wife didn't die, the sky didn't fall. Oh for the joys stolen away. Can we ever get them back? Sadly we can't, and that is such a sad place to be. Now, in all fairness, maybe you are one who did lose a child or a job, or the worst did come to be. Has God left His throne or ceased being who He is? Pain is part of this world, but so is joy. So with that thought in mind, I leave you with this new thought to ponder:

What if today is going to be a good day? What if God chooses in His omniscience to do the amazing? What if all that you fear about this day never comes to fruition? Can we not trust God enough to at least give Him that?

Let's start today. Start this new year with the possibility that my what-ifs of fear can become what-ifs of blessings. What if God is going to start turning things around today? What if God has decided, *It's enough, my child, your season of darkness is now passed; and in this new year, I will begin a work in you so great that if it be told to you, you would not even be able to believe it.*

Friend, God is good, and He will do good! It is impossible for Him not to do good. What if we decide to accept that and decide to believe that as well? Besides, what is good and what is negative are all based on whose perspective eyes you see it through. Many of the things I thought to be the worst of times were actually the seeds for the best of times yet to come.

January 2 - Angry at God for How I'm Feeling Today

Wherefore, my beloved brethren, let every man be swift to hear, slow to speak, low to wrath, for the wrath of man worketh not the righteousness of God. (James 1:19–20)

I don't know about you, but January is not my favorite time of the year. In many parts of the world, it's cold and dark and dreary. A lot like what you're maybe feeling right now. In my darkest days, when anxiety and / or depression seem to be ruling and stealing my joy, the first emotions I feel are anger and downright bitterness at everything—at life and why it must be this way—anger at God Himself. Yes, I know it seems strange to be angry at God, but many biblical people and even many people serving God today have come to this place. I remember one time being so angry at God that I just laid it on the line. I said, "Lord, I have had it. I don't want to play this Christian game any longer. I might even switch teams and follow Satan."

Now, that might seem extreme for a Christian, let alone a pastor, but I have been there, and that's what depression and prolonged anxiety can produce.

Yet we must ask ourselves this question: If God knows all and sees all, then would He not also know where this trial of pain would take me? Yes, He does, and if He takes us there, He also has a purpose for bringing us there. I am thankful that the few days that I came to that place of anger didn't stay with me too long. I'm also glad that the Lord smiled and continued to love me, seeing in me what He had planned for me even before He created me. One thing about anger, even anger at God, is this: it should bring us just where He wants us, communicating with Him in an intimate way. He desires intimacy because He simply loves to be near us. So dear fellow sufferer of this dark gloom of trial, think it not strange concerning this fiery trial that is to try you (1 Pet. 4:12), but rejoice in that you are sharing in Christ's suffering, a suffering that does have an end and a purpose.

Set your mind on who holds your hand and let Him lead you through the valley, even if it's with a frown on your face. He still loves His children. Look to God our Father—as a child looks to his / her earthly father—as He holds our hands through scary days. Remember as a child how even in a scary place, there was peace because dad was holding your hand. Remember how you would glance up at him just to make sure he was still there at the end of that hand. We might have been angry at being pulled away from what we thought we wanted, but we were also glad to know that our father was still there.

January 3 - Remember God's Mercy

Like as a father pitieth his children, so the lord pitieth them that fear Him. For He knoweth our frame, He remembereth that we are dust. (Ps. 103:13–14)

Oh how good it is to know that God knows us. He knows how weak we are, how frail we are, how much we can take. Sometimes, in my days of depression and anxiety, I would forget this. I would often wonder if God knew what I was going through. Did He understand the pain and suffering that was pulling my soul apart? In Psalm 103:13 and 14, we are made aware of how much He does know. I like the wording *He remembers*, which reminds me of just that: He remembers me! Even more than remembering, He has mercy on us, which means He knows the pain, and the pain is a concern to Him. I remember when I first became a father how this really became apparent to me. For the first time I was able to see how God sees us through how I see my children. When my firstborn fell and would cry, it would be so real to me. I felt sad when he was sad. It even became more intense when my children grew to be teens.

I remember this one time in particular when my middle son had his first broken heart. His girlfriend said good-bye not only right before Christmas but on the day before his birthday, which also happened to be in December. It was the first time I really felt the pain of another person. To see my grown teen son weeping was something I would never forget. At the height of it all, he came home and just stood in the kitchen. My wife and I just hugged him, and we all started to weep. Tears flowed out like never before, and not just for his loss and pain, but for the fact that I could not do anything for him but share in his pain. I felt so helpless knowing that I could not bring her back, nor would it even be good if I could. No, it was God's lesson of gain and loss and learning to rejoice even when we don't feel like it.

After that day, I understood better how God must feel for us. Many times, pain and anguish must be had and must be endured for growth and better things to sprout. Dear friend, remember that our Heavenly Father is there weeping with us even though He has to bring us through this valley. Remember that God sees what we can't; He sees the future. Even though I told my son that day how God would carry him through and he would smile again, those words of comfort didn't do much for him as there is a time to weep and a time to rejoice (Eccles. 3:4). My son needed to feel pain that day as we may need to feel pain today, but joy does come in the morning (Ps. 30:5). His mercy is everlasting, and His truth endures throughout all generations. Praise Him daily so that mornings are filled with mercy if God be with us.

January 4 - You Will Make It

Thou shalt come to thy grave in a full age, like as a shock of corn cometh in, in his season. (Job 5:26)

There are some facts of life that cannot be disputed, things that are part of the circle of life that are preordained in God's plan. Summer will come, as well as winter, spring, and fall. In all of my years of living, I have not missed one. As a young boy, I would always get excited to see the crocus plants popping up in the very early spring. Even when the cool winter air was still in control, the little crocus plant would still push up through the hard cold frost-covered earth. In the part of the country where I grew up, these little plants were the heralds of spring when spring seemed so far away.

As you might be feeling down or disheartened today, remember the things that will always be a constant in your life. Some of them we wish were never a constant in life, but for the most part, they are. I don't think there was a winter when I did not have a cold or a summer when the pollen would not wreak havoc on my eyes and nose. As much as I looked forward to spring and summer, I also knew what came with it: sneezing and itching watery eyes, bugs and bees, fleas on my little beagle, Buddy, and gnats flying around my neck at the beach. Again, the idea and thought to remember is this—consistency in nature and consistency in life.

Dear friend, if you have fallen into a day of depression and fear, if your hands are sweaty and your heart is pounding for no reason but to make you feel miserable, remember this—you will make it, and you will always make it because God never lets us stay too long in a place where we can't produce for Him. Just as a cake can only be baked for so long until it is no longer worth eating, so the Lord won't shake and bake us to the point where we are decimated and / or destroyed. It would not be logical for our logical Creator to destroy His redeemed creation in flames. We will be okay, we will make it! We will come to the place and age that God has ordained for us, and no matter what the days seem to bring, God will bring something better. He must, or He would not be God; and evolution would then rule the hour, and decay would be the rule of life and not renewal. Imagine a world where summer would be the last, and all the trees that shed their leaves would never grow new leaves again. Oh what a godless world that would be, a world without power and purpose. Listen, dear child of God, you must go on because God goes on. We must complete our purpose because God must complete our purpose. There will be another day for you to be all that God wants you to be. And if He chooses to take us home today, then we are the better for it anyway. Remember we will all rise again in Christ. We will all do things for Him beyond our wildest dreams. We will come to where the Lord desires for us to be as long as all we desire is Christ. Good will come simply because God can only do good to those who are His and trust in Him.

January 5 - Needing Something to Hold On To

The lord is good, a strong hold in the day of trouble; and He knoweth them that trust in Him. (Nah. 1:7)

Ever have one of those days when you feel like you're falling? Well, if you're struggling with depression and anxiety, then that's every day. To fall is to not have control. In fact, I can't think of a time when we physically fall and are in control; for if we were, we would not have fallen. Funny thing about falling is we naturally grab on to something. What we grab on to is usually what is nearest to us, and not necessarily the thing that is most trustworthy to hold us up. In a free fall, we just tend to grab and thrash. When mental illness is what is making us fall, what we grab on to can be very dangerous. Sometimes it's illegal drugs, alcohol, sex, people—really anything that might just help even if for a minute.

Yet what I have learned in those free-fall grab fests is this—none of them are really able to do any good, at least not for a long period of time. They are simply just sand sifting through our hands as we grope to stay standing. It's like that persistent dream we have all had of falling or climbing up a flight of stairs, and our feet feel like lead. The rope that we grab for just keeps vanishing. Dear friend and fellow sufferer, we must learn some facts of life; and that is, though something looks trustworthy, it may not be. Though this or that looks like it might help us, it may be a deception. No, the only thing that really is rock solid and worthy of our grabbing on to and reaching up for is our Lord Jesus Christ.

Yes, I know what you're thinking. I have reached out for Him, and He too has left me falling. Well, it might appear that way, but it's impossible for God to lie. As our scripture in Nahum 1:7 says: "The Lord is good, He is a strong hold, and He knows them that trust in Him." Now, I know it's hard, for I too have reached out and felt as if God was not there; but emotions can deceive, and I am here to attest to this God is faithful, and He will hold you up when you are falling. How does He do this when we don't feel the immediate support from Him? Well, He is doing it by working "all things together for good to them that love God" (Rom. 8:28). He is working through your pain to bring you to gain. He is tearing down that muscle tissue only to make it stronger and bigger. Just like when at the gym, we feel the pain of lifting those weights but don't see the growth and new strength of those muscles right away. It simply takes time. As any bodybuilder will tell you, if you stopped lifting weights after a few weeks due to the pain, you will certainly walk away believing lifting weights does not work. Friends, lifting weights does build muscle and strength. It just takes time. So hold on to Christ even when you only see weakness. Trust that He is working even when it looks like He is not.

January 6 - I Have a Problem

By humility and the fear of the lord are riches, and honor, and life. (Prov. 22:4)

Well, it's still January, and it's probably still cold if you're living in the northern climates. Another day to face, and some of us are still facing that demon of anxiety and depression, which comes and goes. It fades away and then returns. I remember when I was going through my worst times and trying to figure it all out. I remember the secrecy I tried to live under for fear the world would find out my dark weakness. At my place of employment before I went into ministry, I remember thinking to myself: *Sooner or later I'm going to have to tell my boss that I'm struggling with this issue.* I remember trying to think of excuses for my struggle, even trying to blame my wife or family problems on what was overwhelming me. I remember when I found out that my issue was an anxiety disorder. I was hoping it was something else; even cancer would have been better as to not have to face the humiliation and stigma of mental illness.

When I first started feeling "funny" as I liked to put it, I remember going to every doctor under the sun to prove my issue was physical, not emotional. I wanted to be found sick with a disease other than mental illness. I would actually be disappointed when test after test came back negative. "Gee, Lord, can't I get one positive test result so I can tell everyone I have a sickness that needs surgery?" Well, as you know, it never happened; and there came that day when I had to say, "I have a problem, and it's emotional." That hurt to some degree until I also was able to say, "I have a problem that's emotional, and that's okay because God knows what He is doing."

Yes, it's not easy to say but very important in the light of scripture. See, until we can humble ourselves before the mighty hand of God, He won't do much to help us. There must be that breaking of the will and mind and heart for the Lord to begin rebuilding what has been exposed to His glorious light. I know it's hard now, but that day must come. Maybe for you it is today that you come humbly before Him and cry out, "Lord, I am broken, afraid, weak, ill-equipped, and unable to change what has befallen me. I am undone, beside myself, and completely unable to continue on unless you take the controls and steer me home."

You might not just be saying that to God but also admitting it to trusted loved ones so they too can see that God is all that is left, and you are turning to Him for maybe the first time in your life. Dear friend, it is only through true humility and flat-out faith in the living God that we can, and will see, the sun shine again. It will shine again as it did in my life, and as I know it will in yours. Let today be that day of letting go and letting God control you.

January 7 - Oh How I Hate Waiting

And let us not be weary in well doing: for in due season we shall reap, if we faint not. (Gal. 6:9)

As we go through another January day, we know and are certain of a few things. One is that spring will come, and two is that we will have to wait for it. Today, you might have a lot of things to accomplish and just as many fears to go along with that list, but we must also remember we have a God who has a word for us: be patient! Dear friend, one of the hardest things to accept while going through my seasons of depression and seasons of anxiety is that some things take time. In fact, many things that are worthy take time. Now, I am so grateful to the Lord that He never told me how long my trial of faith would last because if He did, I might become discouraged and give up. But praise His name He never does, and that's because He only gives us enough grace for the present day. If we choose to live in the next month or the next year with a what-if mindset, we would have to meet those times totally alone and devoid of God's strength.

This morning or evening as you read this devotional, I ask you to consider a very logical fact of life. Seasons always come, and seasons always go. Winter will always come to an end no matter how bad it is, and in the same way, this season you're going through will also end. If our Lord is true to His word and His creation, which He is, then as winter must end, so must your trial. The scriptures say clearly that pain might last for a night, but joy comes in the morning. Now, our job and duty is simply this: to say to ourselves, "This will not last forever, my Lord has promised me that." So on this day of waiting, we must set our sights on Jesus Christ and His unchanging words. Though we hate waiting, we must!

While we are waiting, we are not to just stand still as if at a red light but stay busy doing His work.

One of the worst aspects of emotional pain is that it tends to take all energy and focus off life and serving Christ, and turns its back on us. We become the center of our existence, and so God and His work and desire for us become nonexistent. If you are suffering, the best advice I can give is to never suffer while stagnant but suffer in service. It might sound odd or impossible, but watch what happens when we look away from our bleeding wound and focus on another person's bleeding wound. Suddenly we forget our pain, and before we know it, time has gone by, and our wound supernaturally becomes healed. Be patient, trust, wait, and serve the King. He never fails us—*ever*!

January 8 - Getting Our Ducks in a Row

The righteous cry, and the lord heareth, and delivereth them out of all their troubles. (Ps. 34:17)

Okay, it's a new day. Amazing, there will never be a day like this again. There will never be another January 8th (insert your year). Why this is important is because it makes this day very special. It makes this day unlike any other day that you have ever lived—past, present, or future. To me, that's exciting, and it should give all of us hope. What will the Lord do today? What will the Lord teach me, and where will He lead me? Dear friend, no matter what level your anxiety or depression is today, this truth still holds. Again, it is a new day, and it is up to us to find out what the Lord would ask of us as we try to reason out our emotional issues.

Well, for one thing, God has a question for us, are your ducks in a row? Are you where you need to be in Jesus Christ? I know in my life and in my struggle with fear, anxiety, and depression, I focused on all that I did right in the past and wondered why God would punish such a holy one as me? Well, I soon learned that I was way off on this one. I learned that besides finding God's will in my life through depression and anxiety I also needed to heed His correction. Many times we can't see the forest through the trees. We only see our pain and avoid seeing our sins. Now, I'm not stating that every case of emotional distress is due to sin, but I do know it is a good place to start. It is a good place to clean house and take spiritual inventory. To my surprise, I found that I did have many sin issues that needed to be confronted, sins that I would never have seen if my emotional state didn't bring them to my attention, such as lust, lack of love for others, selfishness, worry, and fear. These were things I never considered as much as I did while going through my days of darkness.

See, that's one of the many blessings of emotional pain. It makes us zone in so close to God that we see with clarity, not so much everyone else's problems but our own problems. Like Paul once said, "I am the chief sinner," and unless I start with me, I can never see what God is doing in me. Like Psalm 34:17 says, "When the righteous cry, their prayers are answered; God hears and delivers them from all their troubles." I have learned that I can moan and beg for God's working in my life and for deliverance from this pain, but until my sins have been confessed, repented of, and forgiven, I cannot experience the Lord's deliverance.

The point is this: unless we are right with our Creator, we can never be delivered by our Creator. First John 1:9 says if we confess our sins, He is faithful and just to forgive us our sins. Therefore, let us confess all of our sins, even those deep-seated private, hidden sins. You know, as well as I do, that they are there, the sins that only you and the Lord know. Maybe this is the reason for our pain, to bring us to a point of gain by simply cleaning house. Pray with me this day:

> *Lord, thank You for bringing to my attention my secret sins, and for those I don't see, please bring them to light so that I can see. I desire to confess them, repent of them, and turn from them once and for all. In Jesus's name, amen.*

Unless our ducks are all in a row, we cannot move on to the next step of healing. Sin must be the first duck to be dealt with.

January 9 - A Teachable Spirit

*For his God doth instruct him to discretion, and doth teach him.
(Isa. 28:26)*

One of the hardest things of going through this mess of emotional distress is this: I become very unteachable, as well as unreachable. Maybe today is one of those really bad days, a day when facing the fear of the day seems worse than what you will actually face. A day when you are filled with anger and bitterness, and you feel like saying, "Lord, I have had it with this fear and irrational worry. I am tired of it and feel like throwing in the towel." If that's how you are feeling today, I understand fully; but I also know this from many days in those trenches of bitterness, there is a major drawback, one that doesn't catch our attention until it's too late. The problem is simply this: we can't hear what God is trying to say if we don't want to listen.

Dear friend, I don't know where you are today in your struggle, but I am sure of one thing, you have been at the place where many voices tried to help you, yet you did not want to listen. Oh, how many well-meaning friends, family, and even coworkers have offered you scriptures, wonderful flowery emails, or lovely inspirational Facebook posts. They send you cards and pray for you, and when they ask you how you are doing for the ten thousandth time, you simply feel like screaming. You have thoughts like: *Stop sending me these things, stop sending me scriptures. I know them all, and I know how much Jesus loves me. I know that all things work for good, but you have no idea of the pain I am facing.*

Dear friend, if you have been there, you know what I'm talking about. But I also want you to hear what I'm saying to you right now as one who knows about fear. Please listen to me and understand the dangers of this mindset. Many times the Lord tries to reach us and teach us, but we are in no mood for the lesson. Well, what if one of those scriptures is from the Lord, one of those books on fear is from God? My point is this—God is always teaching us every minute and hour of the day. Through our pain and in our joy, He is molding and bending only to eventually heal. If we discard every note and prayer, we might be pushing away the actual answer that God has for us.

Now, not to be cliché, but that old joke about the drowning man and the boat, helicopter, and rescue plane really is not that far off the mark. Many times when drowning, we ask for help, and many times God sends it in varied forms, yet what if we are do not see His answers and only push them away? This is what I have found to be true in many trials of faith in my life. God is there and is answering prayers, but I simply will not receive it due to my pain. Please, dear friend, with as much strength as you can muster, listen for that still small voice of Jesus Christ. He is there; He is speaking. He is giving us the hope that we so desperately need, but maybe we are just too angry to hear it. Listen to Him today! Listen with ears that are willing to hear and obey.

January 10 - Embracing Your Thorn with a Vengeance

Then said Jesus unto his disciples, "If any man will come after me, let him deny himself, and take up his cross, and follow me. For whosoever will save his life shall lose it: and whosoever will lose his life for my sake shall find it." (Matt. 16:24–25)

Matthew 16:24 and 25 were always hard scriptures for me. What was Jesus trying to say? Why deny myself? Why take up my cross? Why must I lose my life to find it? What do these things mean, and how can I apply them to my situation if they are the answer? Well, the good and bad of it is this: they are the answer to our healing and victory in Christ, and yet they are hard to do. See, it all boils down to this one truth of living for Christ; everything that we encounter is part of God's plan. That means death, pain, loss, and waiting—they are from Him. If we don't believe they are from Him, then we deny the very nature of God in that He is always working in the affairs of men. God lets His sun and rain fall on all of us. Like the book of Ecclesiastes states: "There is a time for joy and a time for tears." And if that be true, then our tears are just as ordained as our days of joy and laughter. Yes, it's a hard one to grasp, but to reject it is to never embrace our thorn of affliction as from God Himself.

Did God allow Job's affliction? Did God allow Paul's pain? Did God allow David to wander in the wilderness, hiding out in caves from an enemy set on taking his life? Well, the answer has to be yes, and if so, then our depression and anxiety are also allowed by God. They are not some random accident of a haphazardly disconnected Creator. No—our Lord is aware of all things, and by His very nature, He is also designing all things for our good. You might be thinking, Right now, *this is for good? How can this torment be good?* Well, it is, but the problem lies not in our pain but in our understanding of what *good* really is. See, good in our eyes and good in God's eyes are not the same. He sees with an eternal vantage point, and we see only from a temporal vantage point. Guess which one is flawed? So with all of that said, where does it leave us? Well, it leaves us with a beautiful flower with pointy thorns. We see the beauty of the flower, but we cannot get passed those thorns. We try to separate the two, but we find very quickly that they are interconnected.

This is where carrying our cross comes into play as Jesus so wonderfully points out by divine example. Remember Jesus on the road to the cross. Did He not carry His own cross as an example for you and me today? Yet what is so wonderful is this fact: when that cross became too heavy to bear, even too heavy for Jesus in His humanity—what did God the Father do? He had that wonderful man come alongside Him and help Him carry that awful cross. Friend, He will send help for you and me also, but we must first be determined to carry our cross no matter what. Our cross must be seen as an honorable cross. One we are proud to carry for the Lord. One that the world can watch us carry and wonder how we are able to. It should ultimately bring glory to our Lord who is our true crossbearer.

Now, as to dying to self so we may live, it's the same thought. It's accepting all that the Lord has placed in our laps and saying, "Lord, if this is from You, if this is ultimately good for me, then I will praise You for it and die to all that I am if I must." I will die to self so I can live; yes, it is an odd duck, for sure, but one from our Maker. He knows what He is doing, and we must trust Him so much that we do the hardest thing we can ever imagine and embrace our depression, anxiety, and season of pain, with a passion, saying, "Lord, I trust you so much that if depression is good for me, then give me even more if I need it." Now, a small word of comfort: He will not allow more depression because He already knows the right dose we need, but our heart must be at least willing to embrace it with a vengeance of heart and will.

January 11 - It Will Be Okay—No Doubt

God is not a man, that He should lie; neither the son of man, that He should repent: hath He said, and shall He not do it? Or hath He spoken, and shall He not make it good? (Num. 23:19)

Today is a new day—don't you hate it when people say that? What if today is worse than yesterday? Well, it might be, but tomorrow definitely won't be. Listen, dear friend, I'm a realist, and this devotional book is one based on truth. People who don't know of mental illness don't know or have a right to give their opinion, but we do. We have been there, and we know. With all that said, I want you to hear me out as you may be facing a hard day. Yes, sometimes today is not what we have hoped. Sometimes there are setbacks in this battle of the mind. If people told me while I endured many a dark day that today was going to be wonderful and it turned out not to be, then that would have brought me deeper into darkness. Please don't tell me lies, and I won't tell you lies.

Friend, this cross to bear is not forever. If I knew that I would never ever see the light of joy, never see hope and peace of mind again, I would surely never have made it. My hope would be gone, and my will to fight would be dissolved. Well, I am here to tell you today two undisputable truths: 1) This might be a difficult battle, but 2) it will be a battle that will be over, and you will have joy not only in the eternal but joy in this life. Now, you might be asking yourself, how can I make such a claim? Well, it's easy because of this simple fact: God does not and cannot lie—end of story.

Psalm 30:5 says that weeping may endure for a night, but joy comes in the morning—well, that is either true or it is not. God is either a liar or He is not. Friend, if God is a liar, then He is not God. If that be the case, we are all dead in our sins and lost forever. We might as well burn this book, burn the Bible, and weep, for all is vanity. But God is true, He is the living truth, He cannot or ever would lie. Our Lord is sure and dependable, so fear not but instead rejoice.

Numbers 23:19 makes this point crystal clear, and here is why. God is not a man! Oh, does that bring joy to my ears as it should to yours. Friend, if God were a man, we are all in trouble, for we all know the error and weakness of man, but He is *not* a man! Say it aloud today with me. He is *not* a man! He is the Creator of man and the Healer of man. He, being the

Creator, knows His creation; therefore, He knows how to fix that which is broken. So be of good cheer. Face this new day with a positive hope of healing. Remind yourself of our Lord's words. He is not a man, and He cannot lie. Therefore, that which He says must come to be, and that includes the passing by of this cloud you and I face. Rejoice and praise Him, for salvation draweth nigh. It will be okay, there is no doubt.

January 12 - We Need Some Things—Amen?

And I will send grass in thy fields for thy cattle, that thou mayest eat and be full. (Deut. 11:15)

One of the lessons I have learned in my battle has been this: I need help. I need some things that I myself do not possess. If you are like me, then you also have come to this place; and if you haven't, you better soon. One of the blessings of emotional pain, when accepted with joy, is this: you place pride on the shelf and raise humility on high. This is just where the Lord wants us all to be, a place where self is useless and God becomes priceless—to understand that we don't have it all together and never will, for if we could achieve that, then we wouldn't need Jesus Christ. Friend, we need Jesus Christ and all that He offers. We need the Holy Spirit and all that He offers, which includes comfort.

See, comfort is something we don't come equipped with as sinful humans. It's like we are born with an empty tool belt, and once we come to Christ, the Holy Spirit then begins to fill that belt with tools such as power, wisdom, guidance, understanding, peace, and comfort. As humans, we don't possess those things, nor can we ever apart from our Lord's provision. One of the reasons why we fall into anxiety and depression is that we believe that *we* can fill our belts (so to speak). Look at yourself today as an electrician on his way to a job. The Lord is the dispatcher and tool provider. Now, we think that we can do the work with our own tools and methods, but when we get to that job site (life today), we realize the tools we possess are worthless. So we begin to panic, reaching for pliers and screwdrivers that we don't have. It is at that point that we must swallow our pride and cry out to our heavenly dispatcher and say, "I need what I don't have! Please, dear Lord, forgive me for thinking that I can tackle anything in this crazy world with only my own power and strength. Forgive me for not asking You for what You are so ready to provide for me."

Dear friend, the Lord has a tool chest full of tools, some of them *power tools*. They are tools like courage and fearlessness, boldness and wisdom. It's no wonder we have panic attacks when we face a complicated world with empty tool belts. Now, imagine facing this day with that belt filled with all the tools for the day's workload. No, not more tools than you need, not tools that you will need for next week's work, but only the tools for today. Oh, it is a sure thing that fear and worry won't have a place in our minds if Christ is the mechanic fixing the day. As our scripture says today in Deuteronomy 11:15, God will send us what we need. Our job is to realize that He is the sender and we are simply the receiver.

So yes, you will need some things for today. Is your tool belt full? The best way to achieve this is simply by asking God, "Dear Lord, I am facing a difficult day, and You know I don't handle difficulties well. Please fill me with what I need for what I will encounter, whether it be power or swiftness or a dose of wisdom and guidance." Friend, He will equip you for the day's trouble.

January 13 - Sometimes We Have to Simply Hold On

Watch ye, stand fast in the faith, quit you like men, be strong. (1 Cor. 16:13)

To hold on when there is no power or strength left in us is a very precarious place to be. I remember one particular day when this truth became very evident to me. My wife was away in California, and I was home in New York. I don't think you can place two people farther apart at least in regard to the good old USA. I was in the depths of a bout with debilitating anxiety. It was Sunday morning about 9:00 a.m., and normally I would be getting ready for my 11:00 a.m. sermon. On any other day, it would be a joyful time for me as preaching is what I live for. Yet on this particular day, my anxiety was so intense that sweat was pouring from my body faster than I could change my shirt again. I couldn't eat, and I had lost a lot of weight. Some people eat more when anxiety takes its bite, and some can't eat a morsel. I was the one who couldn't eat, and I had lost so much weight that my pants would not stay up. People were beginning to ask me why I was so thin, and it was easier to lie and simply say, "Oh, it's this new diet I'm on, don't I look wonderful?" Oh, the moments of do or die where the rubber meets the road. What was I to do? Fear had consumed every fiber of my being. Not fear of preaching but fear of living another day. Fear of fear as they say.

The clock was ticking, and I was alone. I frantically called my wife on the cell phone and said to her, "Babe, I can't do it, I can't preach today, I cannot move." Well, praise the Lord for spouses who are truly from the Lord Himself. She did what a good, godly pastor's wife should do and comforted me by saying, "It's okay, ask one of the elders to fill in. But I think it's the wrong thing to do. You can do this, and I will be praying for you." She hung up, and I stood alone looking at myself in our full-size bedroom mirror. I looked worn, tired, weak, and finished. At that moment, I had a choice to make, and one that I alone could make. I took a deep breath, put on another tie and dress shirt, got on my knees, and prayed for strength. I begged the Lord to carry me, and He said He would, but I had to take the first step.

See, so many times we want the Lord to simply lift us and carry us through the entire situation. He can and will, but only when we exercise our faith in Him being able to do it. It was truly an Abraham-and-Isaac moment. Well, I got up and marched over to church, and it was there that the Lord took over. I actually felt myself sit down on the sidelines and watch the Lord preach through me one of my best sermons. I say the best because it didn't include me and only included Him. The people that day didn't know how blessed they were to have their pastor sitting this one out and getting to hear the Lord God.

Now, I say all of this to make a point. Maybe today you are feeling how I felt that day. Maybe it's a do-or-die time for you, and it's time to get up and march and let God take over. Well, friend, you will never know what that is like until you do *get up*, pull up your pants, button your shirt, and say, "Lord, there is nothing left of me, so this must be all You. Today I need You to take over, and I know this can only happen when I flex my faith muscle and show that I truly do trust only in You." Dear friend, the good news for you today is that He will take over when we hand over all that we are. You can make it through this day while He molds you into something wonderful. Will you trust Him?

January 14 - Saying Thank You for Mud

I will bless the LORD, who hath given me counsel: my reins also instruct me in the night seasons. I have set the LORD always before me: because He is at my right hand, I shall not be moved. (Ps. 16:7–8)

One of the ongoing concepts you will hear throughout this devotional will be this: praise is central. If there is anything that ever changed me or moved me from one level of healing to the other, it was praise, praising God through the pain, the hurt, the sorrow, and yes, during times of agony. It was a very hard lesson to learn and one that would take many years to master. In this particular area, I wish to thank a dear sister in Christ whom I will simply call Jena. To know this dear sister would make one wonder why I trusted so much in her counsel. Well, like you are learning from my season of pain, I learned from her many seasons of pain. She is a dear sister who battled more with depression and anxiety than anyone I had ever met. In fact, I counseled her for many years never knowing that one day she would counsel me. Of all the things she shared with me, the greatest and most effective gift was that of praise. Sometimes I would text her and ask her how she made it through so much pain. She would always send me back the same text: "Praise Him, just keep on thanking Him even when darkness is all that you see." I trusted her words because her life lived out those words. I never saw a person suffer so much with emotional issues and yet do so much for Jesus Christ. She is truly an inspiration to me and should be to you.

Friend, there are going to be times when nothing is working, when medication isn't cutting it, when every trick up your therapist's sleeve is not doing it for you. When all you have to hold in your hands is dark damp smelly swamp mud. It will be at those times that the Lord will be waiting patiently for you to say the sweetest words to His ears: "I praise You, Lord, for this disgusting mud." Dear child of God, through faith in Jesus Christ, until you can say those words in the worst of times, you will never be able to praise Him in the best of times. Praising God is everything, praising Him for rain, pain, and emotional strain. It must become so reflexive that it becomes as natural as breathing.

Find a Christian who knows how to praise Him, and you have found someone important to God. Not simply hands up in the air during Sunday morning *praise-and-worship* time, but praising Him while stuck on the side of the road alone with a flat tire and the rain pouring down. Praising Him in sincerity and truth, not simply words of praise but true thankfulness to be sharing in the sufferings of Christ Himself. Get there, get to that place, and you'll be getting somewhere. Can you thank Him for how you are feeling right now? No, don't thank Him so He will bless you, but thank Him because you are truly thankful.

January 15 - Learning Something

That ye might walk worthy of the Lord unto all pleasing, being fruitful in every good work, and increasing in the knowledge of God. (Col. 1:10)

If what our Lord God says in His book is true, then we have a lot of learning to do as part of His plan. Well, the news is in. His book is truth, and we do have a lot to learn. In fact, one of the things I have learned through my struggles with emotional pain is this: everything happens for a reason. Now, don't you just hate that overused phrase? I know I do, and what makes it worse is that it's so true. Friend, this morning I want you to focus on one thought. I want you to contemplate one idea and biblical concept, which is this: What if every single pain and trial we go through is wrought with purpose? If every time you stub your toe or break down in tears is meant for something wonderful? Now, again, I know this is a well overplayed hand, and it is very annoying to hear it over and over again. But I must ask you the question again. What if it's very true and very real?

Well, it would change a lot. It would change everything, therefore changing many things for the good. To know that this season of depression or anxiety was designed by God Himself would certainly give me much comfort. To know that this season of lack is only so we can have a season of much. Case in point is this: for those of us who were ever able to purchase a brand-new car, you would have experienced this common phenomenon—horrible gas mileage for the first few thousand miles. Now, I bring this up to make this point about temporary setbacks and the blessings of knowing about them beforehand. See, new engines need to break in, yet if you didn't know about the break-in period, you would be angry at the car manufacturer. But because you know the truth ahead of time, you are not upset about it because you know your miles per gallon will increase over time. You know this because the creator of the car told you so.

Dear friend, this is the same situation that we must cling to, to know that our Creator has told us over and over again that there will be pain but only for the purpose of future gain. Over and over again we must tell ourselves that this is for a purpose; this has a lesson behind it, and this will make me better. It will bring me to a place that I could never reach without the pain. Now, if that isn't enough for you, I leave you with this: I would not be writing this devotional book if I had not gone through my own emotional pain. I would not be the man, pastor, husband, father that I am without the horrible pain I endured. I am better, and I must be thankful to the Lord for loving me enough to allow me to be trained. Dear friend, if you are not increasing in the knowledge of Jesus Christ, then you are not allowing God to do in you what must be done. Allow Him to train you, and in that training, seek what He is trying to teach you. The sooner we learn His lesson, the sooner this trial of faith will pass.

January 16 - He Fixes, We Are Fixed

He maketh peace in thy borders, and filleth thee with the finest of the wheat. (Ps. 147:14)

One of the reasons many people never come to Christ is that they never want to accept the fact that God must do the fixing. With all the atheists that I have encountered, the main underlying wall of refusal is that of pride. They will simply not accept the fact that they are broken and that only God can fix them. They want to be in control of their own destiny, and proudly they demand that they are. I remember reading about a famous writer who was known throughout the world. In all of his personal glory and wisdom, he could never come to grips with there being a god who controls all things. In his personal struggle with this issue, he ended his life at the bad end of a gun barrel. His reasoning was to show the world that he alone was in control, and if anyone would take his life, he would be the one to do it. It's a sad story, and one that points to the futility of playing God or even trying to fight Him. No, there is no virtue there, and there will never be any victory there. In the end, it will always be God who is in control, and it will always be us deciding whom we allow to rule our hearts and minds.

Friends, God wins simply because He is God. It is fruitless to try to fix what we can never fix. Our pain, depression, and anxiety can never be nullified by exerting our personal pride or our willpower. We can see counselors, therapists, psychiatrists, or whatever means we choose, but it is God who is ultimately the healer, the fixer. Now, I don't mean that we can't use those means, but that we must ultimately understand that only God can allow them to work. I will go over this in more detail in the chapter on medicationin the book (sold separately), but the long and short of it is this: God is the healer, and only He will allow those other means to work, and only when we understand that it's only God who fixes us. Whenever I would trust in a doctor or a herbal remedy, it would never work, not until I cried out, "Lord, allow your healing powers to work through this resource." When we do that, we are giving God what He desires and what He deserves—glory! We must always place God at the top of everything. It is He alone who fills our hoppers with wheat, and He alone who can bring peace to our borders. Today, fall into the hands of the Fixer so He can do the fixing. Cry out and declare for all the world to see and hear, "Lord, fix me, for I cannot fix myself!"

January 17 - My Security Blanket

But now thus saith the LORD *that created thee, "O Jacob, and He that formed thee, O Israel, Fear not: for I have redeemed thee, I have called thee by thy name; thou art Mine.*

When thou passest through the waters, I will be with thee; and through the rivers, they shall not overflow thee: when thou walkest through the fire, thou shalt not be burned; neither shall the flame kindle upon thee." (Isa. 43:1–2)

I have three sons, and one thing I remember about them is how they each had individual attachments to certain items of security. Even now, my youngest, being eleven, still has his little stuffed bear that he sleeps with. Please don't tell as it's a secret. Funny, isn't it, that if we need an item to give us comfort we are often ashamed of the fact that we need one? Like needing Jesus Christ, to our world today, is looked upon as a sign of weakness. Jesus is called our crutch, as if it is a bad thing to need one when we have a broken leg. Friends, I am proud to say that I am a *living broken leg*. I can't walk without my crutch Jesus Christ. As we would never laugh or mock a person with an actual broken leg needing a crutch, why should we mock ourselves for needing Christ?

One of the many areas where we need an aid to help us make it through our seasons of darkness is in the area of ownership. If we don't know who the owner of our soul is or even that He does own us, we will walk this earth as bastards with no family or father. But we are not without a lover of our souls. We are not without a Father who cares for us. No, we have One who knows us, knows us so well that not a tear falls to the ground without His knowing. Sometimes, we need to be reminded of who made us and who loves us. As Isaiah 43:1–2 so wonderfully declares, "I have called thee by thy name; thou art Mine." He will be with you. Focusing more on verse 2, we see what this promise really means—that whenever and whatever we must pass through, the lover of our souls is right there with us. Even more than being with us, the flames of that needed fire will not harm us but only make us better. Just as God loved and still loves His chosen people Israel, He also loves us, His called-out ones, the church. As He is not finished working on Israel, He is not finished working on us.

Friends, as long as the blacksmith holds the iron in his hand, that horseshoe is not completed. Now, you might want God to release you, but think again. Why would we ever want our Lord to be through with us? We need to be joyful that our Divine Blacksmith still bangs, hammers, and holds us under His controlling fire. Let us think on this for a moment more. If you ever watched a blacksmith holding that unformed iron in the fire, did you ever notice who controlled that fire? It is not the enemy but the lover of that work of steel. Watch how he pumps the bellows until the fire is not too hot or too cold. That fire must be hot enough to shape the iron, but it also must not be too hot as to harm the item being created. Dear friend, know today that your fire of affliction is under the control of the One who created you.

January 18 - I Should Never Feel Good Again?

And also that every man should eat and drink, and enjoy the good of all his labor, it is the gift of God. (Eccles. 3:13)

If you have struggled with emotional issues for a number of years, then you will be very familiar with this thought process: *Maybe I'm not supposed to be happy? If I feel too good today, then is misery waiting around the corner. How can I enjoy anything when there are so many people unhappy and suffering today?* This type of circular logic is a clever ploy of the enemy. It ensures that we will never ever enjoy another day in this life. When we are feeling bad, we are miserable; and when we have good days, we are miserable. We are guilty for feeling bad and guilty for feeling good. Guilt just hovers over us like a dark cloud. We can never be happy because there will always be some reason for us to feel guilty for feeling happy. Sad to say, "religion" has done a lot of this damage with laws and restrictions that were only made to bring bondage and never freedom from bondage.

Dear friend, if we are to ever break free from this bondage of glorious depression and gloom, we must be able to break free from the guilt of being happy. As Solomon states in Ecclesiastes 3:13, there is a time to enjoy the fruits of your labor. Though Solomon was battling with his own depression of sorts in Ecclesiastes, he also makes some good points. Life is vanity if lived only to self, but life can be wonderful if lived unto the Lord.

I remember one particular time when I was battling with never enjoying life. Each pursuit was always laced with condemnation. Whatever I did, I only expected God's wrath and anger simply because I felt I always deserved it. If I started to have a season of feeling well, my mind would always race toward the coming fall waiting for me around every corner. Life fact number 990, no one likes to be around a killjoy and perpetual pessimist. In that state, we cannot show our light to the lost of the world, nor can we please the Lord who sent us to bring that light. Instead of bringing people to God's wonderful glory, we only push people away from Him. People see us and conclude that God is only the bringer of sad and bad tidings. God destroys and crushes instead of bringing life and salvation. So as you start this day, please be ready for the joy and healing that God has waiting for you. If you feel good, enjoy it and let the world hear you sing praise unto our Lord. If the Lord blesses you with a season of prosperity, then enjoy that time; just use it wisely and let not the blessings become the god.

There are seasons coming when the air will smell sweeter and the flowers will radiate brighter. When they come, let all the world know that it was your Lord who made all things possible.

January 19 - This Is Too Big to Fight

And ye shall serve the lord your God, and He shall bless thy bread, and thy water; and I will take sickness away from the midst of thee. (Exod. 23:25)

So it's still January—"yuck" as my wife would say. It's another cold day or, at the least, another winter's day of limited light and warmth. But again, I live in New York, so January here might be a bit different than it is where you live. Be that as it may, it is still another day and maybe one where you might have to fight the dreadful demon of darkness. Funny, though winter is certainly a harder time to fight emotional issues, I also discovered that I could be in the wonderful sunshine in July and still be under a cloud. I even lived in sunny California for a while as the pastor of my first church, and even there where it's sunny every day, sadness can overpower you, and suicide can run through your mind.

Dear friend, as you contemplate what this new day will bring you, please listen to this small word of wisdom: *you can't do this alone*. Now, even though what you and I might be going through emotionally can seem like a million pounds of heavy lifting, the fact is that it is not ours to lift. When it comes to divine healing, it's also something that only the Divine One can do. Now, that alone should give you hope and excitement. Imagine someone showing you fifty yards of topsoil to move, and your first thought is using a hand shovel. Certainly your heart would fall. But what if they showed you a bulldozer parked next to that pile? Suddenly that huge mound of dirt doesn't seem so large. Suddenly it's not really you moving it but the machine that is provided.

In my life and in my struggles with depression and anxiety, each day seemed like a mountain of dirt to be moved only by me using a hand shovel. It always seemed overwhelming, and so it would always crush me. Today I want you to look at the day ahead not focused on that mountain but focused more on the machine the Lord has provided. The Holy Spirit of God is that bulldozer, and we simply need to sit in the operator's seat as God pulls the levers. As our scripture for today reads, it is God who takes away the sickness, not us. It is God who moves the huge mountain of dirt, not us.

Focus on the mountain, and the mountain will crush you every time. On my business card for my counseling practice, I have a favorite scripture that so wonderfully points this truth out: "'Not by might, nor by power, but by My Spirit,' saith the Lord of hosts" (Zech. 4:6). It is not by your strength, and it can never be by your own strength or your own power that these monstrous days can be met. It is only by the power of the Lord and His forces that they can be met. Jesus Christ is that bulldozer, our fear is that shovel, and the mountain of dirt is our enemy. Whom we choose to depend on to move that mountain is up to us.

January 20 - The Promise of a Certain Future

And this is the promise that He hath promised us, even eternal life. (1 John 2:25)

Focus—it's one of the issues that always destroys and crushes our forward momentum. As we described in yesterday's devotion with regard to mountains of pain or problems, our focus is always key. Focus on the mountain, and the mountain is all you will see. If we always focus on the mountain, we will never see the trees and flowers and all the wonderful blessings God has waiting for us. One of the problems that I have always faced was focusing all of my energy on the issue right in front of me. Be it my terror of the day's issues or the gloom that came with that terror and / or fear. I would cry out, "How will I make it today, Lord? How can this be good for me?" I would complain, "How can anything of worth come from such a dark time in my life?" My focus was always on today; therefore, I could never see the bigger picture that the Lord was focusing in on.

Again, that's the issue, not seeing things as the Lord sees them but as we see them. The Lord is an Eternal Being, and so His view is always on the things that are eternal. He doesn't see our daily struggle as we do but only sees their eternal benefits. Let's never forget that our Lord Jesus Christ always referred to this world and this life in the temporal sense. Abraham, spoken of in the book of Hebrews, spoke of focusing on a better country. He knew that this world was not his home, but he, like us, was simply passing through. We must never forget the focus of God's Word on eternal life. Really, if you look at God's Word, this temporal life isn't given too much emphasis. It's always about future things, future rewards, future peace.

Dear child of God, there is only one place that is problem-free and that is Heaven. To live looking for freedom from today's problems is a fruitless endeavor. All we are really promised in this world is peace to make it through, only to be able to get to the final resting place of joy. In this world, we shall have tribulations, of that there is no doubt, but be of good cheer. The Word of God cries out, "I have overcome the World!" Let us focus on His heavenly promises and leave this worldly pain in the hands of He who holds Heaven in His hands.

January 21 - Who's Your Teacher?

And all thy children shall be taught of the lord; and great shall be the peace of thy children. (Isa. 54:13)

I can't tell you how many times I have gotten advice from well-meaning yet ill-informed people about my situation. If you have struggled long enough with depression and / or anxiety, I'm sure you've had your share also. I'm sure you have heard things like, *"Just cheer up it's all going to be fine. You have so much to live for. Why are you so distraught?" "Read Romans 8:28,"* or the most painful and so insensitive—*You just need more faith.* Like I said, all of those words might be true, and all of those words might be well-meaning, but they are not what we might need to hear. Today might be one of those days when the advice on what you need to do overwhelms you. Today might be one of those days that you just feel like screaming if you get another inspirational card sent to you. In days like these, we need to remember two things: 1) we are to always respond in love and simply reply "Thank you for being so concerned about me," and 2) the only thing we really need to hear is the Word of God—from God.

When my days would grow long, and emotional pain overwhelmed me, sometimes the best comfort I received was simply from opening up my Bible and reading the Psalms. Other times, it was just listening to a Christian radio show that just happened to be speaking directly to me. Other times, it was simply getting alone with God and crying out my complaints to Him. One thing is for certain and that is this: what we need to hear is God's Word but also in God's timing and delivery system.

Dear friend, we don't need bigger emotional muscles but bigger ears to hear. God speaks in so many ways, and when it is truly from the Lord, it will bring peace to our souls. This day, as you enter school or work or simply deal with day-to-day chores, listen for that still small voice of the Lord. It might be through a bird you watch digging for a worm with all he has. It may be through a song that reminds you that God is always watching over you. Listen and listen hard, and you will hear.

One of the skills we must master is not of speaking well but of listening well. Show me a good listener to God's voice, and I will show you one who has peace in their heart. God is teaching you today, and it might be a message or lesson you don't want to hear. Please, with all that you are, ask the Lord to speak to you and that you might be able to hear and receive His word when He is speaking. Remember, we can hear and not be listening. To listen is to take what we hear into our hearts and put it into action. Are you listening to God today? His Word brings peace.

January 22 - This Must Be for Now

But godliness with contentment is great gain. (1 Tim. 6:6)

Waiting and accepting. Two of the things I hate doing. If I could only know when this would end, if I could only know that this is temporary, then I would be able to face what lies ahead. Friend, that's not how God works, so we must get used to it. In fact, I'm very glad that God never showed me what lay ahead and how long I would have to suffer. Knowing that back then might have not excited me but discouraged me. See, it was longer than I thought and at times harder than I ever imagined I could endure. Of being content, well that's another story and maybe even harder to accept. Friend, being content in whatever place or trial God has placed you is pivotal to victory. If you hate what you are going through, if you hate everything about it, then ultimately you hate God's plan, purpose, and methods, and dare I say, you might even hate God. If you know your Bible, then you know that patience is never optional but mandatory. If you don't know your Bible, then get reading.

Now, I know on this January day, the last thing you want to hear is about waiting and accepting. I know you want this over, done with, passed by, and forever forgotten. Yet it might be that the Lord has other plans, and that's not an excuse for God's seemingly inactiveness in your life but a fact of God's control over your life. Because He loves, He must lead; because He is the Good Parent, He must nurture.

When you were a child and going to school, what if your parents would have listened to your wishes and pulled you out of school, say at about nine years old? Now, to any nine-year-old, it would seem like Christmas every day, but would it really? Would you be ready for life, work, being on your own? As it is in that example, so it is with us today. We must go through the training that is needed as a nine-year-old must endure until high school and even on to college. We can't say as a nine-year-old, "I have no patience for this nonsense, give me the car keys, I'm going driving." We must stick with the program God has planned for us.

We all have to be trained, yet we all hate the training. Any career or profession requires training and patience. Would you go to a doctor who quit medical school because it was taking too long? Now, that's a lot of truth to accept on this January day, but there is good news. One day you will graduate, and the feeling will be amazing. Look forward to that day. Look forward to the wisdom that God has purposely implanted in you. Be excited that you were chosen for a special mission that requires specialized training. Rejoice and wait on the Lord.

January 23 - Getting Mine

And He said unto them, "Verily I say unto you, There is no man that hath left house, or parents, or brethren, or wife, or children, for the kingdom of God's sake, Who shall not receive manifold more in this present time, and in the world to come life everlasting." (Luke 18:29–30)

I remember an older man who started coming to church. He came from a very traditional major denomination and was intrigued by our little Bible church in the suburbs of Long Island, New York. For a while he would come, and tears would often run down that old worn face. One day, after a service that must have really touched him, he approached me ready to know more. I told him of Jesus Christ and the salvation He offers to anyone who believes. He thought that was all wonderful, but the words that followed gave me cause for alarm. I will never forget his pointed question: *"Now, when do I get mine? When is it my time?"*

I understood exactly what he meant, but I also knew he really didn't understand God's salvation plan. Now, I wasn't upset with him because I knew he was looking for the same thing we all seem to be looking for—our time. Getting ours is what everyone seems to want. Getting the good stuff is what we all really desire. Well, I'm here to say there is (the good stuff), but it is not for us to demand or even for us to order up as if we were placing an order at a restaurant. Funny how we wish it was that way—"Lord, I will take a life of ease, with a side order of money and maybe, for dessert, some sexual pleasure, and maybe if You are speedy with the order, I will give you a nice tip in the offering plate."

Now, don't deny it because we are all that way to some degree, but it's the mindset that God is most concerned about if we are to receive anything of Him. First of all, we must come to our Lord today as a servant, ready and willing to serve without expecting anything in return. Then we must come with the attitude of caring nothing for the things of the world but only for the things of Christ. We must come with a burden for the lost and downtrodden. We must come forsaking sin and sensual desires. We must come holding on loosely to our money and possessions, holding on loosely to our very sanity and physical conditions. Holding loosely onto all we are or ever hope to be simply because we love our Lord and King.

Friend, if you can come to Jesus Christ with that mindset, you can be assured of one thing—rewards of peace and blessing here and in the world to come. There are rewards to faithful stewards of God's ministry, but rewards as a by-product not as a goal.

> And He said unto them, "Verily I say unto you, There is no man that hath left house, or parents, or brethren, or wife, or children, for the kingdom of God's sake, Who shall not receive manifold more in this present time, and in the world to come life everlasting." (Luke 18:29–30)

This is a promise not made by me but by our Creator Himself; therefore, that promise of reward for all your suffering is a sure one.

January 24 - Why Are They Having All the Fun?

> Do ye think that the scripture saith in vain, "The Spirit that dwelleth in us lusteth to envy?" (James 4:5)

There is an old saying that says "misery loves company," and it is certainly true. It's amazing how we can suffer a loss or a pain, and suddenly it doesn't seem so bad if another is suffering that same loss. In this age of a falling economy and massive layoffs, it doesn't seem as bad if you lost your job when you know that everyone else at work got laid off too. What's so sad about this phenomenon of the human heart is this—it's sin and very evil. It's a selfish and unloving way to process the affairs of this life. It's not a picture of what we should be as a Christian.

I remember years ago when my second church suffered a great split. Because the split was mainly due to me and some people not liking my style or what have you, those who left secretly were hoping for me to crash and burn. For a season, we suffered an exodus of people leaving, and those who left secretly licked their paws as if a great vindication was achieved. I don't fault them as that is what we are as people. If that is not the case, then Jesus would not have had to have gone to the cross for our sins. Yes, we are sinners, and all of our good works in the flesh are as filthy rags unto the Lord. Sinners do what sinners do, and maybe if the circumstances were reversed, I would have felt the same way. Be that as it may, the point is this: we are sinners, that is true, but that is no excuse to sin. Because we are saved through faith in Jesus Christ doesn't mean we have license to continue in the flesh. No, we must be above reproach, and we must strive for Christ-likeness even in our season of pain.

Friend, there will be times when everyone around you is doing well. The neighbors are flourishing, and your church friends are prospering. There will be times when you will see others laugh and go on wonderful vacations, and your heart will boil. Envy during strife and trial is not unusual and, in fact, is all too common. Many times while in my pain, whether emotional or even spiritual, I would let that dark troll of envy steal whatever joy I had left. There were times when simply watching another family enjoying a day of fun would only bring me deeper depression. To go even deeper and darker, I might even say that there were days when I wished others could feel my pain. Days when I wished the whole world would simply burn so I wouldn't feel so alone in my season of painful blessing.

I know people think they aren't supposed to be that honest, and maybe this brutal honesty is too much to bear. Maybe so, and maybe it's just me who can be so evil, but I do know one thing: we are not to be such a person. So today, if envy of another's season of joy is making your season of trial seem so much worse, don't let it! Don't let the sun go down upon your evil and wrath. Yes, even in our pain, we are still asked to be holy and set apart unto the Lord. Depression and anxiety are no excuses for sin and evil intentions. If we are ever to be free, certainly we must first begin with getting our hearts right with our Lord. Repent of your envy and whatever sin lies in your bosom and give it over to our Lord. At the foot of the cross, all our sins must be placed.

January 25 - Desire Takes Diligence

The soul of the sluggard desireth, and hath nothing: but the soul of the diligent shall be made fat. (Prov. 13:4)

Getting up in the morning is not always the greatest joy in living, but it is a part of living. We can't enjoy a day unless we get up to face it. When a person begins to hate living, they also begin to hate life. It's like the domino effect—once one falls, they all seem to fall. When depression and anxiety rear their ugly faces, other things begin to take place. Sleep becomes your best friend, and climbing under the snugly quilt becomes your favorite stomping ground. Now, they are all wonderful, but they are not good. Here is what I mean: if things that were designed only for certain times become the only thing you do, then they can become bad—like the old adage "everything in moderation."

Too much sleep, food, leisure, TV, or anything else is never good, and these patterns develop with depression and anxiety, as well as letting our minds wander into dark places. We must try to keep them in control and within reason.

Dear child of God, let us remember God's rule and remember it well. If we desire to do nothing, then nothing will happen; and yet if we are diligent to please the Lord, He will bless us abundantly with things happening. Now, I have mentioned before the bad advice and prodding of loved ones and friends and how they can be your worst enemies. But the truth also is that sometimes they can be your greatest asset. Case in point would be my wonderful wife who would push and encourage me when I need it the most. When I say encourage, I don't simply mean her saying things like, "You can do it" or "God loves you, so be happy." No, she was there in a more real and conventional way. It was at those times when fear would grip me, and words of defeat would emanate from me like sweat from a truck driver. It was at those times when I needed the strong yet loving words that would ultimately push me to move on. I must say she never gave up on me, and even more, she never gave up on God.

Friend, if you don't have a person like that in your life, the Lord will provide one. And when they are laid at your present place of need, please praise the Lord for them. See, we need to understand that healing from this dreaded blessed affliction is best beaten by action. Inactivity is the fuel to the fire already burning, and activity is the water that puts it out. Simply put, we must be active, moving, striving, pushing ourselves if there is no one else there to do it. If today is one of those days when you just want to sleep, don't do it! If today is one of those days where you just want to curl up in a ball and hide, don't do it! Yes, it will take will and strength like no other, but you must make yourself fight. There is never healing in sleeping, at least with regard to depression. Depression and anxiety feed off sleep like a leach feeds off a person's blood.

Get up, get going, and with all that you have, push harder and watch what the Lord will do. To not get up and move is to give up and give in. Know for certain healing won't take place in that bed. Today, say, "I must live, for Christ lives in me, and I wish not to suffocate Him."

January 26 - Give Me More Faith

So then faith cometh by hearing, and hearing by the word of God. (Rom. 10:17)

Faith is an interesting thing. We want much of it yet never seem to have enough of it. We desire to live by it yet don't know how to attain it. I'm amazed at how many Christians don't understand where faith comes from, at which I shouldn't be amazed since it's simply so common today. When we are faced with any trial, faith is what we need; yet when we are faced with the trial of our minds, we simply don't just need it, we must also thirst for it. Faith is the key, but faith in a mind that is upside down and sideways is hard to achieve. I know because I have been there. Mental illness seems to kill faith as a bug zapper kills moths.

Now, because faith is killed off so easily by emotional trauma doesn't mean it can't coexist within us. If this morning your faith is at its end, or maybe it's at bedtime and your faith level has been depleted through the day's struggles—either way, faith is still the answer, and the goal should still be getting more faith. Filling up that faith tank is a place to start, but how do we fill up our faith canister? Well, filling is one thing, but knowing where to get the fill is another. Again, I go back to the common Christian. They pray for this filling, they desire this faith, they ask people to pray for their faith, and yet they never received faith because they ask amiss.

Dear child of God (through faith in Jesus Christ), please listen and listen well. Faith comes from only one source, one place where its bounty flows like a river. Faith is attainable, but it cannot be prayed for. No faith comes from a most unlikely place. Faith comes from reading God's Word. Faith comes from hearing God's Word preached. Faith comes from no other place, and of that we must be clear. Let's read again Romans 10:17: "So then faith cometh by hearing, and hearing by the word of God." Now, if you have never heard this before, it might appear as a shock, but not so when you look at your faith gauge and finally understand—"Oh, that's why my faith is so weak."

So this morning or evening, get out that Bible and start reading God's Word. Go to church, go to Bible studies, find a good Bible-believing church, and plug yourself in hook, line, and sinker. Funny—I'm always amazed at people who are going through very hard times. Their first thought is to stay away from church until they get their act together, until things clear up. I scratch my head and think, *So you are staying away from God when you need Him the most?* Please, this day, run into the arms of God's Word and there find faith.

January 27 - When You Fall Down

> *Though he fall, he shall not be utterly cast down: for the* LORD *upholdeth him with His hand. I have been young, and now am old; yet have I not seen the righteous forsaken, nor his seed begging bread. (Ps. 37:24–25)*

Have you ever run, tripped, and then fallen? If you have made it past the age of two, then you know it's part of life. When we are children, this falling-and-getting-up exercise seems to fill our every waking moment. When we reach ages five through ten, it starts to subside. Yes, by that age, our knees have been cut, bleeding, and bandaged many times, but praise God the falling-down part stops. The tears and running to Mom slowly fades away into past history.

See, falling is part of living, and yet if we would have never fallen, we would also never have learned to get up. Think about it—if we never fall, we will never learn to get back up. When we are children, sure Mom and Dad help, but in time, they'll want us to get up on our own. The tears must stop, and the humiliation of falling must be put to rest. Falling is not a sign of weakness or deficiency of some sort. No, falling is part of living, and the sooner we embrace it as fact, the sooner we can move on, fall down again, and pick ourselves up.

My point for today is this: emotional stumbling is not much different than physical stumbling. Everyone faces it in one form or another. I don't know anyone who has never been sad, down, afraid, and nervous. Even just starting a new job brings the best of us to bouts of anxiety; it's just that some of us hold on to that anxiety longer than others. It's simply how God made us.

Dear friend, please try to understand a few things about falling and getting up. We will fall, and sometimes it will be a big one. Whether it is depression, anxiety, or agoraphobia, we all have to face them in this life; and if God allows them in our life, then they must have purpose. So like the lesson of falling as a child to help us learn to get up, why can't bouts of emotional pain be lessons to help us get up from that? I don't know about you, but I have never fallen as a child and been left there for dead. If I couldn't get up myself, soon enough there was an adult or friend there to help me. If this week has been one with many trip-ups, or maybe even this month or year or the last ten years have been filled with falls, doesn't that mean we should be experts in getting back up from them? Doesn't that mean that maybe we are better equipped and trained to help others who fall?

Dear hurting soul, there is virtue in everything God allows in our lives. Why do we not include emotional issues then as part of those virtues? So the next time you have a spiritual or emotional trip-up, remember how you got up last time and apply it to today. Or even better, look out for another who falls and help them up with all your years of experience. It is not all about us, but it is all about Him. If the Lord is putting so much effort into us in this area, then maybe it's only because He has so many people He wants us to help. So get up and help others get up also.

January 28 - When Rest Is Needed

Come unto Me, all ye that labor and are heavy laden, and I will give you rest. (Matt. 11:28)

As we have spoken about before, sleeping and doing nothing can be a very dangerous drug of sorts to the person battling emotional issues. Sleep can become an addiction and more of an escape. It's amazing how similar drug addiction and sleep addiction can become. Hiding from our problems and hiding from our life can be very appealing, and if not kept in check, it can become destructive. But that's not to say that rest doesn't have its place. When fighting the daily struggles of life and placing on top of them emotional trauma, it can almost be too much for the human body to endure. Sleep does have its place in emotional healing, and sometimes it's downright mandatory. The problem with sleep and emotional unrest is trying to find the happy medium between the two. In these cases, it's sometimes good to consult your mental healthcare provider to find that sweet spot. If life finds you in a season of emotional pain, and you are working full-time plus a full schedule to boot, it might be time to plan that elixir of rest.

Now, sleep doesn't always equal rest, and rest doesn't always mean a five-thousand-dollar cruise or even an island vacation. I have found my best rest in just being alone on the beach, walking or sitting outside on a sunny day. I have a bench swing in my yard that has given me more peace and tranquility than the fanciest vacation I could take. The fact is that vacations can have their own stresses and fears. If anxiety is pushing you over the edge, then why would you want to add to your situation a vacation laced with traffic and airports and confusion? In this day and age in which we live, we have confused God's picture of rest and mediation with party-filled extravagance. I don't recall Jesus and His disciples doing much party hopping other than the wedding reception where Jesus turned water into wine. And even there it was simply a time to lie back and sit at Jesus's feet.

As we read scripture more and more, we see that rest was always filled with quiet times of introspection, times of being alone with the Lord and away from the cares of the world. David found his peace gazing at the stars as he shepherded his family's sheep. Noise and crowds don't bring us to that place but only being alone with our Creator.

Speaking of creation, a good place to meet Him is in His creation. The mountains or a quiet beach is a great place. What if you don't have that luxury of having nature to rest with? Maybe you are living in a busy city tenement. In that case, climb those stairs to that rooftop and pull up a chair. Even with the noise of the city below, the stars above can give you rest. The key is getting alone, alone with our Lord. Jesus promises us rest. It's up to us to claim and find that rest. Rest doesn't always mean sleeping, and sleeping isn't always resting. If your mind and soul need rest, ask the Lord to provide it, and somewhere, somehow, He will.

January 29 - Not Always a Hammer

For My name's sake will I defer Mine anger, and for My praise will I refrain for thee, that I cut thee not off. (Isa. 48:9)

When I first became a Christian, I, like many other new believers, had a lot to learn. I remember in my early days of salvation thinking that I had God all figured out. At one particular time, I made the grave error of boldly proclaiming that God was like a genie in a bottle. I said this because of the honeymoon the Lord often gives to baby believers. In that honeymoon phase, I would ask for anything in prayer, and it seemed the Lord answered me. Before I knew it, I felt I had come up with the secret formula to blessing. I gave the right amount of money to my local church, for which I was all too quick to pat myself on the back as I was a big giver, so I thought. I had my church attendance perfect, making a point to never miss a Bible study or a morning or evening service. I had God just where I wanted Him, and as long as the formula stayed on track, life was certain to be a dream.

Well, that worked for a while until the Lord hit me with my first case of anxiety and depression. Now, what's interesting is this: when I felt the first blows of emotional illness, when *my* plan stopped working, the first thought that came to mind was God's hammer of judgment. *What went wrong?* I thought. *God must be angry, and as soon as I find out why, this dark horror will be lifted.* Friend and fellow sufferer, please understand this: God does get angry, and He can slap a trial or two on us, but that is not always the case. In fact, I have found the Lord to be very slow to anger and of great mercy. He is truly a loving Father, and we must not always assume that His hammer of judgment hangs over our heads waiting for one slipup.

See, sometimes pain and sorrow and trials are not judgment but simply training. Sometimes our trials are a loving Father correcting a child whom He loves. So dear friend, do not be angry or discouraged but rejoice in that the Father is not seeking to destroy us but rather to renew and heal us. In the meantime, praise Him in the storm, praise Him in the fire, and praise Him in the pain. He cares enough to do enough and to get enough out of us. That is simply an amazing truth of God, and the hammer we sometimes feel is only the hammer of our imaginations.

January 30 - We Will Be Defended

Then shalt thou lay up gold as dust, and the gold of Ophir as the stones of the brooks. Yea, the Almighty shall be thy defense, and thou shalt have plenty of silver. (Job 22:24–25)

I remember my first bout with depression and anxiety. I wanted so much for someone to tell me it was all going to be okay. I wanted someone to come up and say, "No worries, I got this all taken care of, and I promise you it will all be okay." Oh, to hear those words and to know without a doubt that our Lord is faithful and will come through with what He promises. See, that is a major problem for those of us in these dark times. Do I really trust God enough to let Him take me where He will? Do I trust Him enough to lay me down in peace and give rest to my soul? I think a major problem is that Christians today are simply not being honest with themselves or with one another. I make it a point in my ministry as a pastor to always be brutally honest with my sheep. I tell them of my doubts and fears. I let them know that it's okay to not have to put on a happy face all the time, to say it's okay that Christians are not always happy and jumping for joy.

When people come for counseling, I will often say right off the bat these odd words—"I cannot help you or do anything for you, but God can." That is the truth, friends, and we need to understand that. We need to accept the fact that people, friends, family, and the best doctors cannot help you unless Christ is behind them. Christ must be centralized in all of our thought processes. Christ must be all whom we depend on. Christ must be the goal we are running to. No, not just running to Him to get healing, but running to Him because we want to know more about Him. See, many Christians only look to Christ as a celestial servant. One that we are running to simply because He can help us. This is a wrong reason to ever come to Christ, and so many times Christ *doesn't* work simply because we come and run to Him for the wrong reason. We must run to Christ because we want Christ, because we want to apprehend His glory and learn more of Him.

Whether He chooses to heal us or not is irrelevant. What is relevant is coming to Him because we love Him and want to know Him more. Jesus says we will find rest for our souls, and He says this with these important words that follow: "Learn of Me." Therefore, today, as you cry out to God for healing, also cry out to God for wisdom. Cry out and say, "Lord, I want to love You and not simply use You." I tell you this. When we come to Him this way, then and only then can we be partakers of the promises He gives. Then we can claim the *Almighty* as our defense, the lover of our soul and the healer of our mind.

January 31 - Forever?

> For the Lord will not cast off for ever:
> But though He cause grief, yet will He have compassion according to the multitude of His mercies. For He doth not afflict willingly nor grieve the children of men. (Lam. 3:31–33)

Well, today is the last day of the month. I bet when January started, it felt like it would never end. It's a lot like mental illness. It has no recuperation time. No set amount of healing that we can look forward to. In my life of having various ailments, some bad and some not, what made them endurable was knowing how long they would last. When I had my first surgery, I knew that I had four weeks until I could go back to work, six weeks until I could drive, and eight weeks until I could lift something again. Though those sounded like long times, they still had a definitive end. Even when I get a bad stomach flu, which is one thing I dread the most and to me is one of the worst things to go through, what keeps me going is knowing that it will usually only last one night.

I remember one time being on vacation with my family. I had gotten food poisoning from a local burger joint. I tell you, of all the pain and suffering in my life, those forty-eight hours seemed like an eternity. Yet it did pass, and I knew it would, and so I had hope.

Now with depression and anxiety and such, one thing they do not have is a set duration. There is no standard recuperation time. There is no one—whether it be a doctor, professor, or pastor—who can tell you how many weeks, months, or years it will take to pass. That, my friend, is one of the hardest truths of this mental pain to accept. With mental illness, one of the most common questions that go through our minds is how long this will be with me. "Lord," we cry out, "will this be *forever?*" That word *forever* is like a knife struck deep into our souls. If I was to know it would be forever, I don't think I could have ever gone on. To know there is no reprieve is almost too much to bear. To know that anxiety might be with me "forever" seems like a life sentence of pain. One that makes us even question if living is worth it.

Well, I have very good news for you today, news that you can take to the bank, as well to heart. Your pain will not last forever! Doesn't that sound wonderful just to hear? This will pass, and you will be restored! Oh, to hear those very words. In 1997, I heard them when I was first hit with this ugly friend called anxiety. My pastor at the time said those words of hope: *"This will pass one day, and all will be well."* They were life to me, and they were the hope I so dearly needed to hear. And I clearly remember meeting with my pastor and asking him, "Will this be forever?" and hearing him say, "No, it will pass. That is certain." Well, that day I left his office with my heart a little bit happier than it was when I first came in. To know that this too will pass meant more to me than a pound of pure gold. Now, did anything change in my struggle? No, but what did change was my ability to fight, knowing that there was an end.

Friend, forget *forever* and focus on Christ's promises. Even the suffering of Jesus Christ didn't last too long but just long enough to accomplish what God intended to accomplish. So please, this day, remember that your season of pain is just that, a season of pain. Seasons always change, and a new one appears. Your pain will pass, maybe even today or, if need be, next year. But it will pass, and since God cannot lie, so we know that it's true. Rejoice and wait for Him to part the red sea of darkness in your life.

February

February 1 - Learn of God, Find Healing

The lord is gracious, and full of compassion; slow to anger, and of great mercy. (Ps. 145:8)

Well, it is a new month with so many new possibilities waiting for us. It is a new month of hope, healing, and changes in our lives. With the new month, we also need to learn anew of the wonderful mercies of our Lord. We need to focus on what He can do and why He will do them. We need to be excited and even begin praising Him simply because He can only do good to us. Now, maybe you are saying that this is just all wonderful but that it can never apply to you. Maybe you are thinking that this great news might apply only to others because your situation is so grim and bound for destruction. Well, dear friend, it does apply to you, and if you're a child of God by faith in Jesus Christ, then our Great God will do great things for you also. Now, if you are not buying it, I totally understand, but I also understand why you are feeling this way. It's simply because you do not understand the divine character of God. You do not understand who and what He is. You, like many of us, have let the world, circumstance, and the enemy confuse you about our God. We have listened to the lies for so long that the lies become truth to us. Dear sufferer, please hear me and, more importantly, hear what our Lord has to say.

The lord is gracious, and full of compassion; slow to anger, and of great mercy. (Ps. 145:8)

Did you just hear what those words said? Did you understand what wonderful promise God has made? Look at the character of God. He is full of compassion, which means He has compassion for us. He knows our pain and would not do anything that would not be good for us. He is slow to get angry at us, and He is of great mercy. Wow, that's a chock-full of promises that can't be denied. Friend, instead of starting this day and month looking for answers to our emotional pain, let's start looking deeper into our Lord

51

and learn of all the wonders He has waiting for us. Today He is telling us, "Learn of Me, search Me out, love Me, long for Me. Desire all that I am, and in that searching, you will find two things: a) *wisdom of the Holy One* and b) *healing for your hurting souls.*" It is well worth the search. It is well worth the effort. Seek Him, learn of Him, and in doing so, you will certainly please Him. Remember, it's not about God pleasing us, but us pleasing Him. Read Revelations 4:11 for it says much on this matter.

February 2 - A Sound Mind

For God hath not given us the spirit of fear; but of power, and of love, and of a sound mind. (2 Tim. 1:7)

Many of us have a favorite scripture. Second Timothy 1:7 is one of mine. During a very hard time in my life, I would keep that scripture taped to my dashboard and also a copy of it in my wallet. It was a scripture that I would often meditate on and read to myself. In this particular scripture, the Apostle Paul is training young Timothy to be the man of God he was called to be. It is believed that Timothy was not the bravest of men and that fear and anxiety often troubled him. It was for this reason that Paul penned these words and why they are so helpful for us today. If you are struggling with anxiety today, if fear and worry have you so turned upside down, then memorize this scripture. Some points that jump out in this scripture are how it points out the sources of certain things.

In verse 7, it tells us what God gives and does not give. Of fear, this is not from God. This type of fear spoken about is irrational fear. See, some fear is good. Fear of falling and of getting burnt by fire. Those are good fears that the Lord places in us. Yet this fear is more like anxiety. It is fear of things that might happen but most likely never will. It is like being afraid that your roof will fall on you when you sleep. Can that happen? Sure, but it is very unlikely that it will. So to worry about it is something the enemy and our minds conjure up. Moving on in the scripture, Paul tells Timothy what God gives us instead of fear. He gives us power, love, and a sound mind. Now, why does Paul say that? Well, because he knows his scriptures and he knows that love cast out all fear.

There is no fear in love; but perfect love casteth out fear: because fear hath torment. He that feareth is not made perfect in love. (1 John 4:18)

In this scripture, we see clearly what irrational fear can do versus what love can do. Fear left unchecked can torment us, yet love, God's love, cannot dwell where fear controls. One of the two has to go, and if we don't hold on to God's love hard enough, then fear will destroy us. Back to 2 Timothy 1:7, we see the promise of God's indwelling Spirit within us. We see that a sound mind is the goal, and a goal that is certainly attainable. A mind that is focused and balanced. That is God's will for us. God promises these things, and so we should be excited to know that even in our state of a compromised mind, a sound mind can be had. When it speaks of power, it means that we have the power through Christ to achieve this, yet noting that alone we can't. Remember this scripture and cite it often. Claim it as truth and watch for the salvation of the Lord and be of sound mind!

February 3 - Let Them Have It

For where envying and strife is, there is confusion and every evil work. (James 3:16)

If you're a sinner like me, you have been to that ugly place where you wished another could see your pain. Yes, I know it is an ugly truth to accept, but it's human. In my struggles with depression and anxiety, there have been times when it hurt so bad that I wished someone else could see it for themselves. It was not so much that I wished it on another, but that so others could better understand it.

See, this little dark monster is so frustrating simply because no one can understand or see it. Oh, I wished so many times that I had a broken arm so others could see my plight and understand my pain. So many times people would comment on how well I looked. "You don't look sick," they would say. Or how many times would people say, "Gee, I never would have guessed that you suffered with that." Or to really make you feel like dirt, they would say, "You, I always thought you were a rock, a happy-go-lucky person of faith." Yes, thanks a lot for that, friends.

See, not seeing a hurt makes the hurt so much more complicated. Sometimes people think you are faking it to get attention. They say this in all honesty because they only hear our complaints and see no wound. It is hard for our loved ones and fellow church family to comfort us, so it becomes awkward to them. Sometimes they even become angry at us for not getting better when they see us as having so much. Sometimes they are frustrated because their lives are so much harder than ours and they seem to deal with it with ease. In their hearts, they also say, "Spend a day in my shoes and you will have something to be depressed about." Yes, it is ignorance, but understandable ignorance, and the reason why we should never envy those who are doing fine.

Unfortunately, envy and anger follow mental illness. We do get angry at those who do not understand, and we envy those who seem to be so strong. If I can offer you some hope today, it is this: Do not be so quick to envy sinners, as well as brothers and sisters in Christ. When our hearts fall into envy and bitterness, we also fall into sin. Sin left unrepented or unconfessed leaves us separated from our Lord. The last thing we need in our situation is to be separated from our Healer. So confess and get right with God. Envy not, lest we become the ones guilty of sin.

February 4 - Full of Joy?

These things have I spoken unto you, that my joy might remain in you, and that your joy might be full. (John 15:11)

Being full of joy is sometimes the last thing you think of when facing a day of emotional struggles. Hearing a scripture like John 15:11 sounds so good but also so far way from where you are. *Full of joy*, we think. *I'm lucky if I can be full of air to breathe for this day.* We think of joy gone by and wonder if it will ever come again. We see people happy, and it makes us sad. Watching people enjoying life becomes a curse, and we end up staying indoors so we do not have to watch people being happy. Dear friend, as you face this new day, face it trusting the One who created us to be full. Trust the One who created us to experience a wide range of emotions. As it says in Ecclesiastes, *"There is a time to mourn but also a time to dance."*

As no one can live sleeping twenty-four hours a day, so too no one can live awake twenty-four hours a day. We need a mixture of all things. We need to weep, and we also need to have joy. If today is a day of weeping, rejoice in that soon there will be a day of rejoicing. In my life of struggling, I have come to live circumspectly. I live looking around in all places searching for that silver lining. I learn to accept my times of sorrow as well as my times of joy. We need to live always expecting highs and lows. See, if I am in a time of joy, I should be careful that I do not become obsessed with it, and I need to also understand it is just the part of the ebb and flow of life. Rain comes then sun comes. Winter comes then summer comes. I cannot hate the one and love the other, for to do so is to hate what season God has placed us in. Yes, great worth can come from seasons of joy but also from seasons of sorrow.

Of all the things and thoughts that have run through my brain, most of the beneficial ones have been learned through sorrow. Yes, sorrow is a great teacher, and we should not think it bad if the Lord brings us to that valley, for it is only there that we can find Him in His fullest form. So today seek the joy of the Lord. Understand the blessings of that joy, as well as its fullness. Praise Him that our Lord Jesus promises us that our joy will be full, not just joy given but joy in the fullest form.

February 5 - To Never Be Ashamed

For the scripture saith, "Whosoever believeth on him shall not be ashamed."
(Rom. 10:11)

Good day, my friend, and may this day be that day you have been waiting for. May today be the day when the Lord says, "Today I release you from the crucible of purging. Today is the day when those long-sought prayers are answered. Today is the day when the rain subsides and the clouds begin to part." This day of deliverance will come, and you will walk again. Yes, that's a certainty, and one we should long for. Now, dear friend, as you wait for that day, we must also understand that we must wait in proper heart. We must live boldly for Christ enduring that particular storm until it has passed by. How we endure that storm is of great importance to our Lord. As it is of great importance not to be ashamed of the Lord we serve, we should not be ashamed of the trial He places us in.

Yes, it is of great worth to smile at the storms of life. Not so much great for us at that particular time, but for those who are watching us, weather that storm. Here we go back to the issue we must never forget. The issue of God's plan and God's will through us, not for us. See, God is seeking to save the lost. He is doing all that He can so that not one soul might perish. That is His will, and so it should be ours. So if the Lord calls you to face a great loss or sorrow, look at it as God's gift to another while it appears like a curse to you. Understand that we are being watched in how we endure such contradiction of heart.

What if this present struggle has nothing to do with you at all? What if all that you face today is for a dear friend to see Christ working through you for their salvation? It is such a difficult thing to understand in this world today. To understand that Christ came to save sinners and nothing more. To know that Christ came to redeem a creation lost in sin. Not just so they could live happily ever after, but so we could live happily with Him throughout eternity. We need to see through God's worldview and not man's worldview. We need to praise Him and never be ashamed of Him. Anxiety and depression seem to carry shame with them as a traveler carries luggage. This should not be, and we should quickly learn to drop and leave our shame at the cross. No, instead of embarrassment, may we find joy in being counted worthy of suffering for Christ's work of redeeming lost souls.

February 6 - Sometimes It Is Because of Them

In God have I put my trust: I will not be afraid what man can do unto me. (Ps. 56:11)

In regard to depression and anxiety, there is no doubt that it is an internal battle. It is a battle that is fought within the confines of the mind, soul, and spirit. Yet with that being said, sometimes it has nothing to do with our inner man but the outer world in which we live. If you have lived long enough to get tripped at school by a foot blocking your path, then you have been alive enough to know that people are evil. When we read the accounts of David, we find that none of his depressions and fears were from within but from without. There *were* people trying to kill him. There *were* people who hated him and wanted to do him harm. King Saul was real, and his anger for David was real. There were no paranoid delusional thoughts here. It was a real problem with real consequences.

In cases like his, being happy is hard to achieve if not impossible. When people are trying to get you, it is okay to feel down and gloomy. It is normal to feel fear and anxiety if a person in a fit of road rage is trying to run you down. The point for today is this: what ignites our emotional trauma doesn't really matter. Be it a chemical imbalance in our brains or a person dead set on making your life miserable on the job, the end result is the same. When these moments of testing come upon us, let us remember the psalmist's encouraging words: "In God have I put my trust, I will not be afraid of what man can do to me." Though you may not feel as brave as these words proclaim, they are still truth, and they are still promises. David was able to pen many psalms about his very real enemies, but he was only able to do so because he had past experiences of victory in Christ from them.

My dear friend, we must remember this system of our Lord's. His system of using past pains turned to victory to strengthen us for future pains waiting to be turned into victories. David could say these words with authority and passion simply because he knew they were true. He knew they were true because he knew the Lord always delivered him in the past and would be faithful to deliver him in the future. Let us say it together today, "I will not be afraid of what man can do unto me, not any man or enemy, for I know that God's Word is trustworthy."

February 7 - But It Is Just Too Big

For by thee I have run through a troop; and by my God have I leaped over a wall. (Ps. 18:29)

"It's too big," my ten-year-old son said as he tried to lift the trash pail. My little guy has been trying to throw the trash pail into our church Dumpster for many years. He sees me doing it, and it frustrates him that he can't. Each time he helps me take out the trash, it's the same routine. He drags the very large pail and brings it way out to our Dumpster area, and with all that he has, he tries and tries and tries. I must admit I am impressed by his persistence, and it even makes me feel a bit sad for him. I know one day he will be able to lift that pail, but for now, he cannot.

Now, what happens to that pail? That is the question. Do we leave that pail full of trash there to rot and smell up the neighborhood? No, that would be silly, but the fact remains that there is a pail that needs to be lifted but cannot, and that is where the Father comes in. In this case, the father is me, and I say, "Son, let me do that for you. One day you will do it yourself, but for now, you can't and that's okay." Friends, in life, there are going to be things that are just too big to lift. There will be times when we just can't get out of the hole we have found ourselves in. Something needs to be done, and yet we know not how to do it. Well, like I came to my son's rescue, so the *Father* comes to our rescue. He is there ever willing, ever able, and ever ready to help, heal, and deliver.

Now, you might be thinking to yourself, *Well, that's all fine and good, but how do I get the Father to help me?* Or maybe you are saying, "I have been praying for help for years, and still nothing happens." Friend, listen to me and heed this word of advice: God is waiting to heal and deliver, but we are not so ready to let Him do that according to His way and will. This is what I mean: As my son couldn't lift that pail and I had to for him, so too does God have that choice to make. Meaning, not only if we should be helped in the lifting but also in how He chooses to lift that pail for you. That is His call and not ours. It is His call to choose the means that would best accomplish the task. Yes, whatever way He chooses will be an answer to our prayer and faith, but after our prayer is made, it's His sovereign *will* to bring it to fruition.

With my son and the pail example again, I could get another person to lift it for me, which would still get the job done, or I can do it myself or even get a forklift to do the lifting. Now, we in our human minds might think it odd that God chose a forklift, but it is still an answer to prayer; and at the end of the day, that's all that really matters. Now, why do I say this? Because many people demand God answer their prayers in a way of their choosing, but that's not always God's way. I say this because sometimes with emotional issues such as depression and anxiety, God may choose many ways to heal and help you lift. He can choose a scripture to give you hope, a godly friend or counselor to give you guidance, or simply, He can give you the Holy Spirit's power to overcome it.

But what if God chooses to use medication? What if God chooses a way we don't approve of or other Christians don't approve of? Friend, to question how God heals is a very dangerous place to be and why many Christians make improper judgments of what is or is not proper for God to use to heal. At the end of the day, remember this: a prayer was made, God heard that prayer, and the answer and help were given. Shame on us if we refuse the help we simply don't like simply because of our pride. Friend, through my God, I have leaped over a wall. By my God, I have run through brick walls. If the answer comes—take it in any form. Amen

February 8 - My Maker

O LORD of hosts, God of Israel, that dwellest between the cherubims, thou art the God, even thou alone, of all the kingdoms of the earth: thou hast made heaven and earth. (Isa. 37:16)

So what do you have to face today? If you are like most people, I can make an educated guess. There is work, school, or maybe a doctor's visit, maybe an appointment with a person you really don't want to talk to or maybe you have to face something today that is a little bit scary. A new job, a new bunch of people you must get to know. Whatever it might be, rest assured of one thing—God knows all about it! He is on the case, and even before you ever thought of today and its challenges, He already knew about them before the foundations of the world. We must understand as we face each day who this God is. If we do not understand Him and His might, then all else will always appear bigger.

Over the years that I have been a pastor, I have learned to get used to calling God the Creator. In the beginning, people at church thought it strange that I would refer to Jesus and God the Father in this way. Yet in time they learned to appreciate it, for it truly placed a new emphasis on *who* this God is. He is the Creator, the Creator of time, space, and all of the cosmos. He created and holds our DNA strands together. Before we knew about string theory and quantum physics, He already was there. Before we heard the term *space-time continuum*, He was also light-years ahead of it. Our Lord is not just a religious figure or a man in a long robe with a beard. He is more than an idol or a statue made by the hands of men. He is not a good-luck charm or a token we hold in our hands. No, this is thrice Holy God, Creator, Redeemer, Planet Builder, Star Breather, Galaxy Former. He gives life to cells and created the amazement of procreation. He forms a child in the womb and gives life to its heart. This God is the only God. He is the first and the last, the beginning and the end. Before Him, there was no other, and before time began, He was there.

Now, the reason I spent so much time on this is the same reason why car dealers spend so much on advertising to sell their new sports car. We can see a car and say, "Wow, that's a fast car," but we won't know it is fast unless we read the stat sheets on its engine or of its advance traction control and complex six-speed automatic transmission. We need to know these things or we will never trust in these things. Dear friend, whatever you must face today, know this—God (the Creator of you and me), He is big, real big; and boldly I will say He is more than big enough for you and me. Enjoy this day knowing He has it all under control.

February 9 - Significant

There are, it may be, so many kinds of voices in the world, and none of them is without signification. (1 Cor. 14:10)

Significance is something we do not often think about. I thought it was odd when my oldest son said to me, "Dad, my only fear is that I will die without being remembered." I think we all feel that way to one degree or another. We might not say those exact words, but we know deep down that we want to know we were important in some way. Today, as you go through what life has waiting for you, as you go through your routine of the mundane, remember that there is One watching you. There is One who cares about your every move and every thought. Sometimes in Christian circles, we Christians make the mistake of focusing so much on us being sinners that we forget our significance. As a pastor, I have taught on man's sinful nature and his total depravity. I have spoken of our good works as filthy rags, and yet one day, another thought entered my mind. That was of our significance.

Sure, we can focus on our evil apart from Christ saving work on the cross, but was Christ a fool? Friend, if we were of no worth at all, then Christ went to the cross in error. God the Father didn't know what He was doing when He sent His son of infinite worth to be sacrificed for worthlessness. Well, I hope you agree that, that simply cannot be. Friend and fellow Christian, we must be of some worth or we would not be worth saving. God the Father loves us so much that He gave His only Son. We are loved, and if loved, then of great worth. If we are of great worth, then we are significant, and so significant that He has our name written down in the Lamb's book of life. Imagine that—God has my name written down. He has a record of me and a place where He looks upon and thinks about me.

Dear friend, if you're feeling alone and worthless today, please don't. If you feel that your living or dying would not change a thing in this world or matter to anyone, well, think again. You and I, all of us, have great purpose and significance. To be significant to the world might be your goal, and you may or may not ever achieve it. But to be significant to the Creator of time and space—well, that is the greatest significance of all, and that can be achieved. Dear friend, remember that you matter today. That your life here on planet earth has purpose. Please remember that if you are significant, then your pain and sorrow is significant also. God cares. He knows, and He will bring you through. Come to God the Father through faith in Jesus the Son. Have your name also written down in the Lamb's book of life.

February 10 - Those Inner Flaws

The LORD will perfect that which concerneth me: thy mercy, O LORD, endureth for ever: forsake not the works of thine own hands. (Ps. 138:8)

Don't know about you, but I have many flaws and imperfections. I have many areas in my life that are well below God's standard of perfection. I have fear, doubt, lust, anger, and a lying heart that I must battle each and every day. Through my some thirty years of being a Christian, these battles have become easier, and victories have been won. I have been in some dark places but never so dark that the Lord couldn't find me. In these years of dark and fierce battles, there have been some wounds. I have been cut, beaten, and battered. I have been left a bloody mess by the enemy's rusty jagged sword. It has been a hard road, and sometimes that road was so uphill that I thought I would surely faint.

Dear friend and tired, weary one, if this story sounds like your story, then please listen to the wisdom that I have gleaned through these battles for the soul. The Lord knows that we are but flesh, and in knowing that, He knows our weak and easily defeated nature. He knows what sin we will fall into even before we fall into it. He knows our valleys and mountaintops. Yet with all His knowing and watching, He is still loving. He is still there looking past what we are and only focusing on what we will be one day. Forget your past and even today's losses and focus on tomorrow's victories. Understand that our Lord is already working on our weaknesses, already fighting for our futures. If we have an area where we lack, He knows about it and has a plan. If we have an area where we often falter, He already has a plan in place.

We must remember the Lord's mercies and how they are new every day. We must remember that the One who made us with His own hands also knows how to sustain us. That our Lord is concerned with our pain and also is concerned with the way He will approach us. In my counseling practice, I do not use the same approach for each counselee. I look at the entire person and seek out their areas of weakness. I then try to incorporate the best tactic for that person. Now, I put a few hours into making that decision, and I can be wrong. But the Lord, knowing all things, places an eternity in making that call, and He will never be wrong. So today, as you face your own unique struggle, know that our Lord knows that special struggle and already has a plan to combat it.

February 11 - Big-Boy Pants

Yea, and all that will live godly in Christ Jesus shall suffer persecution. (2 Tim. 3:12)

Well, today is a day with some heavy news. No matter what you are facing today, we must face this one truth first. There are going to be days when life is hard. To deny this fact is to deny God's Word. Friends, life is hard, and no matter what some TV preachers might promise you, Jesus says the complete opposite. Sure, the Lord promises us peace, joy, and hope, but nowhere did He say it was going to be easy. As I write this, immediately what comes to mind is my dear wife. She was and is a very important component in the healing plan the Lord had in store for me. When I was in that fetal stage—you know, that curled-up-in-the-bed-hiding-under-the-covers stage—it was her strong words and strong actions that the Lord used to push me through. After being compassionate and loving, there came a time when she had to get rough. At those times, she had to get angry and say words I didn't want to hear: "Get up, get out of bed, you are not the only one with troubles. People need you. God desires to use you, and this defeatism is pure selfishness!"

Wow, that surely hurt, and there were other pointed words that she added to that spirited tongue-lashing. Now, some might say it was harsh, but truth and life says otherwise. Friend, today you are going to hear what you don't want to. God will say things that you don't want to hear. Facts will be tossed at your feet, which you must come to grips with. As 2 Timothy

3:12 says, "Yea, and all that will live godly in Christ Jesus shall suffer persecution." Notice it doesn't say you might suffer persecution, but you will. "Life is hard but God is good." I have those words hanging over the entrance way to the church sanctuary where I pastor at present. It is a fact that this might turn some away seeking a church with a better message, but if it is the truth, then what other message can there be?

My middle son at age nineteen had many dreams. He longed for a full-time position in music ministry. He longed to be a rock star and live off his music. He desired many material things and toys. He met a wonderful young Christian lady, and marriage was also tickling his ears. Yet with all of this to be desired, he did not like the hard truth that we presented him. Truths like, "You can't get to B until you go to A." God's plan has many roads, but they all start with that first step of faith. While we wait, we must also act; and many times, that means getting a little dirty, feeling a little pain, breaking a little sweat. My son had to be humbled, and in his anger and misery of a life not being as easy as he thought, he had to bite the bullet and take a laboring job. He didn't like this idea, but it was what the Lord had provided at that time.

Friend, right now the Lord might be telling you the same thing. Today might be hard, and your answer of deliverance might be delayed. What are we to do? To sleep and hide under those covers, or get up, get out, and fight with all we have looking unto Jesus, the Author and Finisher of our faith? Forgive my inconvenient truth this day. They might not be the words you hoped for, but they are surely the words that are true. I made it through those dark days, and as the Lord carried me, He will also carry you. So carry on, pull up your big-boy pants, and serve Christ—when you can and even when you feel you can't.

February 12 - God Shall Get You Through

But my God shall supply all your need according to his riches in glory by Christ Jesus. (Phil. 4:19)

One of my favorite scriptures is found in the book of Philippians chapter 4, verse 19. I love the power and confidence that Paul expresses when penning those now famous words. Yes, it is true we have needs, and yes, it is true that our needs seem to be bigger than our supplies. That being the situation does not mean that it is a fact and the end of the story. Our God is simply much bigger than our needs, and until we understand this, we will never find the peace that He has promised us. Today might be a good day for you, or maybe today is not; but regardless of what this day brings, there is nothing bigger than what our God can provide. He is bigger and greater and stronger. He is higher than any other, and in that height, He is able to see more than any other. Today I present to you this question, If God promises to supply all our needs, then why isn't He supplying yours? Well, I pose a few suggestions, and it is up to you to discover which one applies to you. Find the right one, change your position in that place, and find deliverance. So let us begin with the number one reason why God is not supplying all your needs.

Number 1, God is providing for your needs, but you are not accepting what He is offering you. You do not like His choice of provision, and so you choose to stay in that place of suffering. Number 2, You know God, but only in a religious sense. You are not His *child by faith* in Jesus Christ. If this is your case, then repent of your sins, confess Jesus as Lord and only King over your life. Forget your attempt at goodness for your salvation and come to Him completely by faith in His redemptive work on the cross. His work of doing what we can never do through His resurrection power. Number 3, He wants you to trust Him at this time while He is preparing your deliverance at a later date. Number 4, You are living in sin, and because of that sin, He cannot work or heal until that sin is confessed and atoned for. If that is the case, then search your heart and find what the Lord is trying to expose in your life and confess it in Jesus's name. Number 5, What you are going through has nothing to do with you but with those around you. In this case, the Lord wants you to praise and trust Him in your trial so that those around you will see your faith in God, and then they will turn to Him in faith. Or number 6, Jesus is trying to teach you something about faith, trust, and growing into a deeper relationship with Him. If this is the case, then learn quickly and be ready because he has something special planned for you. Those, dear friends, are the six facts we must face. The six answers to our current situation.

While you wait and seek out the one that applies to you, praise Him and remember His sure, steadfast words of provision: "The Lord *will* supply all your needs according to His riches in Glory through Jesus Christ our Lord."

February 13 - Great News for You Today

Therefore take no thought, saying, "What shall we eat? or, What shall we drink? or, Wherewithal shall we be clothed?"

(For after all these things do the Gentiles seek:) for your heavenly Father knoweth that ye have need of all these things.

But seek ye first the kingdom of God, and his righteousness; and all these things shall be added unto you. (Matt. 6:31–33)

God knows! Oh, how I love to hear those wonderful words. He knows me when I put my head on my pillow, and He knows me when I get up in the morning. Dear friend, what does your day have waiting for you? Is it something that scares you and sends you off in hiding? Is there some news that you are dreading and only wish to delay its results because you feel you cannot bear it? Do you look at yourself and feel saddened about dreams that seem too distant and far away? Well, if you feel this way, I have some very good news. Not just some feel-good news or some fortune-cookie news but real news—the Good News. Listen. Before you and I were ever born, there were greater saints than us fearing these same things or worse. Worry and fear of having help and comfort have been around since the beginning of time. Uncertain futures are as old as the stars. Yet the answer to these fears and concerns has always been the same. Jesus Christ is that answer, and His promise is what we need to hold on to. In the gospel of Mathew chapter 6 verse 31 to 33, we see the old worries of man and the same answers from our God.

Will we have a roof over our heads? Will there be clothes on our backs and food in our bellies? The Lord Jesus our Creator knows of these needs, and He is ready to provide for those needs, but we first must adhere to His rules. Seek Him first! Did you just hear that? Seek Him first, and not for those needs to be met, but *seek Him to find Him*. Desire to know God. Desire to love Him and learn all about Him. Desire with all that you are to understand His righteousness, and in that seeking, understand how unrighteous you are. Let this news bring you to your knees. Let this news bring you to worship and fear our Lord. Do this and understand all of this and *then* all these things shall be added unto you.

We cannot put the cart before the horse, so neither can we put provision before devotion. For where your heart is, there will be your treasure. If Christ is not your treasure, then how can He be your Lord of all? If He is not your Lord of all, then how can He meet your needs?

February 14 - No Battery Bars

He giveth power to the faint; and to them that have no might he increaseth strength. (Isa. 40:29)

Cell phones, what would we do without them? It is amazing how they took over our life, and we can barely think of life without them. My kids often laugh at me as I refuse to let go of my outdated model. It works, so why should I get rid of it? But yeah, I do hate change, and even learning a new cell-phone model frightens me. It is kind of like us. Change is never something that we embrace, unless it's a change for the better, that is. Anyway, while thinking about my cell phone, I often find myself keeping my eye on one thing, the battery bars. You know those four little bars that let you know how much battery life you have left. The bars that signify your power or lack of it. I tell you, all of these modern conveniences do not take away worries and anxieties; they add to them. The point being this—now I have "low battery" anxiety. If I am out, and my phone is not charged, I start to panic. "What if my phone dies? What if I am left stranded?" I have become so cell phone dependent that I am amazed that I ever lived without one or can even remember that time. It almost seems like we were born with a cell phone attached to our hips.

Now all that being said, my point is this: we are like cell phones. We need to have our battery bars on full all the time, or we might be caught in a situation when we need them full, and they are not. As we remember to plug in our cell phones at night so they are all powered up for the next day, we also need to make sure our spirit is all charged up so we can face all that we must on the next day. For our cell phone, we use a charger that gets its power from the wall socket. For us, as humans, we need Jesus Christ to be that car charger to funnel all the power of the Godhead into us. See, it is the Lord alone who gives us power. It is the Lord alone who gives strength to those who are weak. Yet if we don't understand this spiritual need, we will never seek to fill that need. If you are tired, if you are weak and overburdened, remember the filling of the Holy Spirit. Call out to God, read His word, pray and meditate and watch those power bars of the soul begin to appear.

Dear friend, we are not a powerless people, yet why do we choose to live that way? Being powerless is a choice, as well as walking around without a charged cell phone is a choice. When trouble comes and trials overtake us, it is only us to blame for our powerless hearts and no one else. This morning or evening—plug in, fill up, feel powered for the day or night ahead. Feel the peace of knowing that you are equipped and filled for all that the day has to give us. We are in constant communication with our Father because our spirit is filled with His Presence.

February 15 - Get Off My Back

I am not able to bear all this people alone, because it is too heavy for me. (Num. 11:14)

Responsibility, it is one of those things you do not understand until you are faced with it. As a teen, we often laugh at life because we do not understand that dreadful and rotten word. To be responsible for anything places a new pressure on you that you never had before. I even remember feeling its dreaded curse as a milk monitor back in the fourth grade. I remember this one tough kid Chris who demanded his milk for free. I remember the fear and anguish of that situation since I wanted to be the milk monitor so badly, and now this pressure took all the joy away from it. For now I had responsibility, and I would be held accountable for the milk sold and money taken in. So that bully taught me my first lesson of responsibility, and one I would never forget. Now as an adult, that burden of responsibility takes on new meaning. Now I have debts to pay, bills to pay, a family who depends on me.

Maybe you are not married but simply on your own for the first time. There is also responsibility there. At work, you wanted to be the boss but now you are simply a shift leader. The money is better, but again the responsibilities are more. The car is making a funny noise, and the cell phone bill is due. You need a tooth fixed but do not have adequate insurance. Everywhere you go, someone needs something from you or expects something of you. No wonder anxiety is a problem with all of these loads dropped on your back each day. If you are there right now and the problems keep piling on your back, then I know that you feel like screaming, "Get off my back!" Ever feel like that? Ever feel like one more straw is going to push you over the edge?

You even long for childhood when the summer meant no school and beach parties. No more pressures of testing and homework. You think about those days and wish you had a summer off again. Now you're an adult; summer is just another season of bills and trials to face.

Dear friend, do you not think that your Lord knows all of this? Do you not understand that He understands? Today, with all the loads being placed on you, remember this: He is the Burden Bearer. He is the One who comes up along side us and says, "Hey, throw some of that on my back." Come unto me if you are overloaded, and today I will give you rest. Rest of soul, mind, and body. He will, and we simply have to ask Him to take that load, and in Him taking it, we need to release it. Release your loads today and tell everyone who is lining up with more loads to "take a number. I can only carry so much." Today, do not look at how strong your back is but how strong God's back is. It is unbreakable.

February 16 - You Don't Know Me

> *But Job answered and said,*
> *"Oh that my grief were thoroughly weighed, and my calamity laid in the balances together!*
> *For now it would be heavier than the sand of the sea: therefore my words are swallowed up." (Job 6:1–3)*

How many of us today understand the loneliness of fighting depression and anxiety? How many of us wish other people really understood what we are going through? It is hard, darn hard, and not having people understand who you are and what you are going through makes it that much harder. People think they understand; they think they know, but you know they never could. Sad to say, this is very true of our world today. Most people do not understand depression or anxiety. They think of depression as simply a bad day where things don't work out. They think it's like a day when you are bummed because your team lost the game. Depression to them is simply getting into a car accident and having to deal with getting your car on the road again. Well, those might be some things that bring you down, but it is certainly not depression in the clinical sense.

They simply have no idea what this heavy heart of sorrow really feels like. The feelings of simply wanting to break into tears and crawl under a blanket and die. To feel so overwhelmed that nothing brings you joy, and if there was a sunny day, it would simply make you sad simply because you know that you could never enjoy it. That is depression, and of anxiety, well, it is kind of the same thing. It is not just being nervous about a job interview; it is not simply feeling apprehensive while driving to work in a blizzard. No, anxiety disorder is a debilitating monster of crippling fear. It controls and possesses you to the point of emotional paralysis. It is an all-consuming fear of everything.

So yes, people do not know us nor do they have any idea what a day in our life is like. But God does, Jesus does. He has been there and felt all that a human being can feel. In the garden, Jesus sweat as it were drops of blood. Sounds like a panic attack to me. He was left by his friends all alone. Being separated from the Father for the first time took Him to a place of despair. See, Jesus felt all that we could ever feel, and yet He did it without sin. In feeling these things, He also beat them at the same time. When Christ defeated death on that cross, he also defeated all the sins that go along with it—fear, depression, loneliness, and despair. Jesus felt them all and defeated them all at the same time.

Dear friend, today understand that there is One who knows us better than we know ourselves. There is One who faced these monsters and defeated them. Be encouraged knowing that they are beatable, and if we climb onto Christ our Lord, we can defeat them too. Climb onto Christ today as a solider climbs onto an army tank and fights what he could never fight alone in the flesh. Climb on and ride over those demons of destruction and find peace, safety, and new hope. Hope for a person like you and me. Hope because someone does know what we are feeling and what we are facing. Climb on and climb out of the darkness.

February 17 - We Are Not Dirt!

What? know ye not that your body is the temple of the Holy Ghost which is in you, which ye have of God, and ye are not your own?

For ye are bought with a price: therefore glorify God in your body, and in your spirit, which are God's. (1 Cor. 6:19–20)

So it is still February, and spring seems a long way off. Maybe so, but we are closer today to spring than we were yesterday. Oh, spring and with it comes all the hope of a new start and a new beginning. Let us pray that this spring will see you laughing and thriving like never before. Spring with its flowers and birds chirping. Grass growing and flowers to be planted. When I think of spring, I think of all that is holy and alive. God's creation springs from its dormant winter's hibernation and explodes into vibrant new birth. Now, imagine not having to wait for spring. Imagine having that new life in us every day. Imagine feeling that divine presence of our Lord trying to burst through from every nerve ending of our being. Sounds too good to be true, but it's not.

Dear friend, if you are a child of God through faith in Jesus Christ, then you have that Spirit Divine waiting to explode. In Christ, we are the temple of the Holy Spirit, the dwelling place for God's water of life. If you do not know Christ, then find Him today, and if you do know Him as Lord, then find Him again and understand what 1 Corinthians 6:19–20 really means. To know we are of worth, that we are not simply dirt evolved into life. No, we are a purchased possession, meaning that we are of great worth to God. Our bodies and souls are of great value to Him, and He lives and breathes within us. Imagine that—God dwelling in human form. Imagine the Creator of His creation inhabiting His creation. That is exciting and powerful. It is the good news you and I need so desperately today. We need it to have purpose, virtue, and reason for going on and fighting. Hold on, dear friend, and understand this Lord who loves you so much to embrace you. Grab a hold of this promise and cry out to Him to experience Christ in you and the hope of what that all means to you.

We are a royal priesthood and a blessed people. We are his adopted children waiting to be nurtured and hidden under His wing of protection and care. Rejoice, for you, me, and anyone who has breath is of great worth. Not dirt, not an evolved animal, but a human being made in the image of our God and Creator.

February 18 - Take It Away

And he said, "Abba, Father, all things are possible unto thee; take away this cup from me: nevertheless not what I will, but what thou wilt." (Mark 14:36)

So Jesus is facing something we can never imagine. True, we do not really understand what Jesus had to face in its totality, but we really do not have to. It is like with us, you, and anyone. We all face struggles that many times are unique to us and us alone. Your battle with anxiety is not completely like mine. Your battle with depression is not the same as mine. Whoever you are and whatever you face, to some, it may seem like a cakewalk; to others, it is a mountain. As a Christian man, my particular struggle with lust and pornography was very intense. It was so intense that I wrote my first book about it, *Spiritual Living in a Sexual World.* But that's just me; to some men, it is no struggle at all. If you're a woman, maybe your struggle is with eating too much; but to another, it is spending too much. Maybe it is gossip. See, it doesn't matter what it is; what matters is how much it controls you. That is the key, my friend, and that is what really concerns the Lord. The control of our soul by God or by our flesh. The walking in the Spirit's power or in our own power.

Jesus, when in the garden, prayed that the Father would take the cup of crucifixion, separation, and death from Him. Jesus, in His humanity, showed us the weakness of our flesh. Praise God that Jesus went to the cross for our sins, or we would really be in trouble. Praise Him that He obeyed the Father's *will.* Likewise, in your case and mine, our cup of pain or fear might not be taken away. Sometimes we have to go through the fire of trial. Sometimes we have to endure so others can see our faith in our pain. Sometimes when we cry out, "Lord, take this pain away," sometimes He says, "Not now, My child, for I have still much to do in you through it." Again, back to Jesus, through His enduring pain and agony we can never imagine, His loss is our gain. Him enduring our pain so we don't have to is what saved us from an eternity of hell and fire.

Yes, sometimes good comes from bad, but if you think of it, if good came from bad, was it really bad at all? It is one of those principles I want to instill in each of you reading this book. If our emotional pain ultimately brings about change and good in our lives—was it really ever bad at all?

Like pulling a nail out of your foot—wow, it hurts, but I could never walk again unless that nail is removed. When pulling nails out of a 2 × 4 of lumber, I cannot use that beam unless the nails are pulled out. It is hard and even leaves holes to remind us of that pain, but they still have to come out, and only when the Master Carpenter says it is time or expedient. There is good in broken vessels if they are assembled in a way that makes them better than they were before.

So yes, we can pray, "Lord, take this from me." It is okay to pray that prayer, but it also must be okay to accept God's timetable and purpose in that removal and delayed prayer.

Today, wait on the Lord as He decides when it is time to take it away.

February 19 - Whose Fight Is It Anyway?

And he said, "Hearken ye, all Judah, and ye inhabitants of Jerusalem, and thou king Jehoshaphat, Thus saith the lord unto you, 'Be not afraid nor dismayed by reason of this great multitude; for the battle is not yours, but God's.'" (2 Chron. 20:15)

Fighting, who likes to fight? Well, some people do, but I never did. I remember being back in grade school, there was always a fight after school *at* (the gate).

Toward the rear exit of the school leading off the school property, there was this chain-link fence with a makeshift exit in it. It was the place where two young males duked it out. It would always draw a crowd of people as people always love to see someone else's pain and suffering. In my life at that grammar school, I only met there once to fight, and I am glad to say the fight never happened. I stood up to a bully, and being a skinny bag of bones, that was no easy task. But I did meet him there, and through words and standing for truth, somehow the Lord got me out of it, and I ended up being best friends with that bully.

It reminds me a lot of dealing with emotional pain. It's a battle, a fight, a struggle. Anxiety runs high, sweat is shed, and stomachs get butterflies. What's different about emotional battles is that there is no actual enemy to size up. There is no physical foe to look in the eyes. Sometimes we desire to actually see God and touch Him. Sometimes we also desire to see and touch what our emotional opponent looks and feels like. If I only knew his weakness and where to kick him. If I could just see how really big or small he was, then maybe I could outrun him or push him down. Sadly, in our emotional battles, we cannot do that, but what we can do is what the scriptures tell us to do—give the battle over to the Lord. To remind ourselves that in any battle we face, at the end of the day, it is God who is really standing with us. We are not alone, and our victory is not based on our ability to fight or the size of our muscles, but it is based on the size of our God. When little David fought the giant, it wasn't David's strength and wisdom that defeated him. It wasn't David's bravery either. No, it was David's love for his Lord. Remember his words to the giant: "Who are you that you defy the armies of the living God?"

Wow, to be a man like David. We read that account and marvel. We yearn to have such faith and boldness. How did David do it? How was he so brave? Dear friend, it is really nothing more than this, knowing God more than we know ourselves. It is really loving God more than we love ourselves and trusting God more than we trust anyone or anything. It is knowing that God is with us and reminding ourselves of His love for us. It is first being bold about our love toward the Lord and then Him teaching us to use that boldness to face any monster or enemy.

Friend, to say the battle is the Lord's is easy, I know, but it is also true. Learn about Him and His faithfulness from thousands of His children throughout history. Read about the Christians who endured torture and imprisonment for the gospel's sake. Who really carried them? Who really fought for them? In human strength, they would all have crumbled. No, it is only through God's power that they always had the victory.

February 20 - It's That Simple

All scripture is given by inspiration of God, and is profitable for doctrine, for reproof, for correction, for instruction in righteousness. (2 Tim. 3:16)

Reading the Bible is not always what we want to do. The Word of God is a funny thing. We say we love it, believe it, and it is all that we live for, yet why do we find it so hard to endure reading? Enduring the Word of God—just saying that rings wrong somehow. If I love the Lord with all my heart, then why do I run faster to watch my favorite TV show over running to His Word? My wife and I try to read the Word every morning and every evening before going to bed. We read a few devotionals and the Bible. We know it is important, and we know it is biblical; but to be honest, we have to make ourselves do it. What is even stranger is that we are more prone to read God's Word with enthusiasm when we are going through a hard time than when things are going well. Oh, how selfish and wicked we are. We say we love the Lord with all our breath but find it hard to love His Word.

Sometimes I feel like we only look at God as a celestial servant or a divine butler. We look at him as one whom we call on to fix things up and then send away when we no longer need Him. I wonder how the Lord feels about that. I wonder how He feels about running to our aid yet having His Word buried under a bunch of old magazines gathering dust. Dear friend, I have this simple but true word of wisdom to give you. Pertaining to depression, anxiety, and any emotional problem, before we start looking for the deeper causes, the underlying root, before we start taking medication or even seeing a counselor or therapist, why not first look into our owner's manual? Wouldn't it be amazing if all that stood between a healthy, happy heart was God's Word? Maybe before we increase our dose of this medicine or this vitamin or that herbal supplement, maybe what we need all along is the Word of God.

Now, here is the key before you open up that Word for healing. See, before it can do anything, our motivations for reading it must be placed in check. See, if you are hearing what I'm saying right now and you are thinking, *Great, I'm going to read my Bible today and get healed*, then you are missing the whole point. We are not to go to God or His Word to use Him or it for our benefit. No, we are to run to His Word and to Him simply because we love Him and want to know Him more. Too many people in the church today are simply using God for what they need. Like putting on a seat belt because you don't want to get killed yet having no concern or care for the seat belt itself. God is not a seat belt or a life jacket; no, He is thrice Holy God and Creator of our universe. He is lover of our souls, and as lover of our souls, He desires to be loved back.

Dear friend, healing of our minds always begins first with the healing of our souls. That starts with caring about other people's souls. Do we truly love Jesus Christ? Do we truly care about the lost He came to save? I believe Psalm 37:4–5 really says it best: "Delight thyself also in the LORD; and he shall give thee the desires of thine heart. Commit thy way unto the LORD; trust also in him; and he shall bring it to pass."

February 21 - Hope

Be of good courage, and he shall strengthen your heart, all ye that hope in the lord. (Ps. 31:24)

Hope, it seems to be a very popular word today. Everyone is offering us hope. From politicians to used-car salesmen, hope is being offered. They tell us to trust them, to have hope that all is going to be well. Hope for a better tomorrow and a better today. Even some fancy TV preachers sell us this hope. They tell us that life will be good to you and that you deserve a better future. Funny thing is, the only ones who have a better hopeful future are the politicians and television preachers. We send them both our money, and they both promise us their hope. Well, I'm not a rocket scientist, but I look around and I don't see *their* hope doing anything for us here on planet earth. I see wars, terrorism, the falling economy, natural disasters, and sickness of all sorts. I see neither very little hope for the future of man nor any hope for my own future. Now, I could stop there and leave you feeling more depressed than you were before you started this day's devotion, but I won't because there is something more to this word *hope*. It is in the person who promises it to us.

See, if any man or woman promises you hope, that hope is only as sure as their ability to make it happen. In case you didn't know, man cannot stop sickness and wars. Man cannot even solve traffic problems. Man is what man is; that is human and, by that humanity, very limited. So that being the case, his hope is of no value nor should it ever be trusted. Trust in that hope and rest assured you will be disappointed. "It is better to trust in the Lord than to put confidence in man" (Ps. 118:8).

Now, let us talk about *true hope*, hope that is real and hope that is sure. That is God's hope. His hope is a hope of a new life, a better tomorrow, strength for today, and comfort for our trials. Now, being that we live in a terrestrial world, our ideas of certain words can be corrupted and so is the case with this word. See, to the world's system, the word *hope* is just that—hoping that things get better. It is a hope that is not any surer than gambling at the casino. It is all a fifty-fifty shot with odds leaning more to things turning worse than better. I think they call that Murphy's law, whoever he was. Yes, that's true of the world's hope, but of God's definition of hope, it is miles apart. See, hope in God's Word is a positive expectation of things turning around. It is a certainty that (in Christ) things will turn for the good, life will have purpose, our pain and suffering will have meaning. It is God's hope in all of God's glory. It is sure, steadfast, and certain. It is a better future and a future where God walks with us through every trial and pain. Dear suffering friend, today stop hoping in man's promises and start trusting in God's certainties. His hope is real, and His hope will not fail you.

February 22 - To Thy Own Self Be True

Ye shall not steal, neither deal falsely, neither lie one to another. (Lev. 19:11)

Well, it is still February. I am sad to say, but it is what it is. See, truth has that two-edged-sword effect. It does cut both ways, and sometimes it really hurts when it cuts where you wish it would not. Now, I could tell you it is the first day of spring. I could tell you that it is going to be a balmy eighty degrees today, yet all too quickly, you would uncover my deception. Now, I am glad that you are able to spot those lies as I know that God is also. He warns us about following shepherds who are really wolves in disguise. Most of us understand these truths, and all are not fooled by the lies of man, but where we are fooled and destroyed is in the truths about ourselves. In this quest to find answers to our emotional pain, there must be one place that we do not overlook. That is in the truths about us.

When I first felt the twinges of anxiety and depression back in 1997, I was in complete denial. I was certain my odd symptoms were of the physical sort, and so I sought out physical treatment and testing. I went from one specialist to another. I went from an endocrinologist to a cardiologist. When people started suggesting that my symptoms were more in line with anxiety, I refused to accept it. Test after test came back negative, and my options became less and less. I remember the day when it hit me like a ton of bricks that my problem was anxiety. I was so disappointed with my discovery. I would have been so much happier if I simply needed a surgery or physical treatment. Again, denial was an ugly monster as the truth of my pride screamed out. Mental condition, oh Lord, not a mental or emotional condition. Anything but something that makes me appear weak and less than others. Oh no, dear Lord, not anxiety and depression. Doesn't that mean that I'm living in sin? Oh no, dear Lord, not an ailment that will make me look as a failure for Christ.

Friends, if you have ever been down that road, then you know all too well these prideful emotions. We can fight it all we want, and we can deny it all we want. But like cancer—deny it all day long, but the facts are in, and you have it. Then there is the next stage of denial. It is the stage after you have prayed, trusted, asked the elders to pray over you. After you have been anointed with oil, after every sin is confessed. After you have fasted and prayed and begged God for healing. Still it abides. I tell you, it is at those times where looking deep inside is the hardest thing to do—to accept that maybe this is your season of trial, to understand that for now, the Lord chooses to have you pass through the fires.

Today I bring you this painful truth, a truth that sometimes we must accept; that is, right now, your thorn in the flesh must stay as is, and in its staying, you know there also must be contentment. See, when the Lord says to be content in any state you are in, that's exactly what He means, and that's exactly what true faith is. To thy own self, we must be true. Lord, I have a problem, and if it must stay for now, then I will praise You for it until the time as You deem it proper to remove it. That, my dear friend, is faith in action.

February 23 - It's That Anger Again

He that is slow to anger is better than the mighty; and he that ruleth his spirit than he that taketh a city. (Prov. 16:32)

There are going to be some topics that we need to deal with more than others. Anger is one of them, and unfortunately, it will be a difficult one also. Anger is another one of those companion emotions. It partners well with self-pity and anxiety. If you are a person like me who suffers from obsessive-compulsive disorder, then you know how anger feeds off it like a leach feeds off our blood.

Today might be one of those days for you, a day when you are just angry at the world. You are angry at your family, friends, coworkers, and anyone you come into contact with. Even down in your own private cave of that inner mind which is you, even there, you are angry at the Lord. See, it is okay, people. Get angry at God if you must, but don't think that He doesn't know it. I will go as far as to say, you haven't been in the belly of the beast of emotional pain until you've been tried by God to the point of being angry at Him.

In my many years of serving Christ, I have had my moments. I have had moments when I would be ashamed to let you in. I have had moments when I said some nasty things to our Lord, moments when I even gave Satan the green light to take me. "Just come and destroy me because I hate all that I am, and I hate what God is allowing in me." Yeah, it's a bold, nasty thing to think about, but I did promise you brutal honesty. See, I'm a realist, and to just write about all the lovely flowers of life and how just having faith turns everything up roses would be a blatant lie. It would not be true because I am not always filled with faith. I am not always filled with joy. Sometimes I want to scream and throw things. Sometimes living this life for Christ can seem like too much to bear. If you are suffering with depression today, then you know where I am coming from. But, and I love that word *but*, the fact of the matter is also this other truth, the truth that anger comes—and yes, it takes hold of us—but "greater is He that is in us than He that is in the world." Meaning that God the Holy Spirit, which dwells in me, can also control me.

God and the Spirit of Truth have not left us to ourselves. Our dear loving Father is Abba Father, meaning He is the Dad of dads. We can be angry at Him and even curse Him at times, but He cannot change His position as Father and our position as child of that Father. Simply put, our anger might rule our hearts at times, but God dwells in our souls all the time. He is patient, compassionate, and full of grace. His mercy is everlasting, and His love is all-consuming. So if you are angry today, well, get it out of your system and realize it never changes one thing of your condition. Just let it out and then fall back quickly into God's loving arms. Arms that are always waiting to take us back even when we think we aren't even worthy to be taken back. His love wins every time. His love never fails even when we do.

February 24 - But It's True!

For God so loved the world, that he gave his only begotten Son, that whosoever believeth in him should not perish, but have everlasting life. (John 3:16)

John 3:16—yeah, everyone knows it or knows of it. Sad how something so precious can become so overlooked simply because it is so overused. Today, as we look into this scripture, let's get excited about how it even applies to those struggling with emotional issues. Now, I know I might get some complaints from the theologians out there, but I believe that God's Word is alive with purpose, and to place any scripture in a box takes away the Holy Spirit's power. With that said, let's dig into this old scripture and see if we can glean virtue for us today. For starters, we notice that God loved the world. He loved it a lot and still loves it today even with all of its faults. Now, unless you are from Mars, you are part of this world too; and if so, then that means He also loves you. Let's never forget this fact.

Okay, moving on, sometimes when I read scripture, I like to personalize it for fun. In this case, take out the word *world* and replace it with your name. Make it read something like this: For God so loved _____ (place your name there). Notice how it changes the whole dynamic of the scripture. Friend, God loves *you*! Yeah, you've heard that all before and wonder how that helps you. Well, it does when we continue on with reading this scripture. Okay, so God loved (*loves*) you so much that He gave what was most important to Him for you. Doesn't sound like much until you put yourself in that place. Imagine giving away your child or spouse or parent—whatever it is that you value the most. Giving it away to die a horrible, painful death and doing it for a person who hates you and cares nothing for you. See how that changes things even more?

God loves us even when we are angry and hateful. He loves us even when we are overcome with sin or overcome with pain. His love never changes or fails. Next is the *whosoever* part, which is my favorite. That means that God loves all of us. No matter what you have done, are doing, or will do, He still loves you. Even if today was a nasty day and you are not proud of yourself and your sin, yet He still loves you. Next is our part and our job. We must believe that He is, that He is real, and that he can do anything. We must believe in His power and His resurrection power over death. Now, so far we have learned about God's love then God's actions then our responsibility to believe and trust. But next the reward, that we should never *perish*. That by trusting in Jesus's work on the cross, we will never perish. Now, here is where the theologians might get upset as we know this is speaking of salvation and eternal life in heaven. But doesn't it also mean that in our depression and anxiety, no matter how far we fall and how upset we are, Jesus still loves us, and we won't cease to be?

As a person who has felt the grips of paralyzing anxiety, I know the feelings of losing control, losing my mind, feeling like I might explode from the inside out. That my heart won't keep beating, that my lungs won't keep on breathing. See, all of those fears are wiped away with God's Word in John 3:16. Because God loves us and we love Him, we will never stop being. That's God's job, and that should give us peace and rest even during the worst panic attack. In fact, even more than not perishing, we will even have eternal life. We will have a life of peace on earth, as well as in Heaven. It's a promise, my friend, that cannot be broken. Yes, it is true. Now claim it.

February 25 - Reaching Further

I press toward the mark for the prize of the high calling of God in Christ Jesus. (Phil. 3:14)

Have you ever ridden on a merry-go-round? You know, the old-fashioned type with the wooden horses that go up and down. In the little town about an hour's drive from where I live, there remains one of the last of those original ones. It was restored wonderfully, and I'm happy to say that all of my children have had the simple pleasure of riding it and reaching for the golden ring. Now, in case you don't know about the golden ring and the history of merry-go-rounds, the ring part is the biggie. See, as the wooden horses go up and down, as the merry-go-round goes round and round, one of the greatest joys of being a child on this ride is to reach with all of your might to the person or machine that holds out a golden metal ring. If you are lucky enough to grab the gold one, as some are silver, then you win a free ride or some type of prize.

So what's the point? Well, the point is this: in order to get the golden ring, you need to reach. If you just let life take you round and round, up and down, it will be one boring ride. In fact, to me, the merry-go-round is a boring ride to some degree, but the golden-ring grab makes the ride exciting. Truth is, life does feel like a merry-go-round, and sometimes people actually call it so. It can get boring; it can become monotonous. Add to it the pain of depression and anxiety and it becomes downright agony. Even with us knowing of Jesus Christ's love and salvation, even there, it simply seems like it is not enough. What's the point we sometimes cry out? Why bother trying to go another day? I would rather just fall asleep and let the horses go up and down until my life is over. Hate to break it to you, but that's never the life that the Lord has planned for us. As Christians, we are to live life to the fullest. We are to have a peace about us that passes understanding.

But what if you are dealing with emotional issues? Well, even there those promises stand true, and what is missing is our part in this ride of life. It's the reaching part. No matter how hard this day might seem to you, we still must reach for Jesus Christ. Reach for His promise and purpose for your life. In Philippians 3:14, we read Paul's words of pressing toward the mark for the prize of the high calling of God in Christ Jesus. Our deliverance is found not in simply fighting but in reaching for that prize. Our prize is our renewed hope and renewed mind. In can happen, and it will when we do our part and reach with all we have for that golden ring of hope.

Please, dear friend, don't give up until you have reached up. Jesus is there, and His answer is there, whether it is through divine healing, a good Christian counselor, or even a season of proper medication. See, God won't reach down with the solutions until we reach up in faith. Reach up today and grab that golden ring.

February 26 - He Will, He Will, He Will

The lord thy God in the midst of thee is mighty; he will save, he will rejoice over thee with joy; he will rest in his love, he will joy over thee with singing. (Zeph. 3:17)

Some days we need to just walk out on the tightrope of faith. We need to say,

"Lord, I cannot see You, but I know You are there. My problem is very big, but You are bigger. I know you *will* save me." Yes, that is hard to do, but that's what faith is all about. See, sometimes there is nothing left to do, no other place to go. Sometimes there is no answer and no way out. Simply put, sometimes you just have to know that the Lord *will* save you.

I remember one particular time when my depression was at its zenith; the thought of taking my life had come and gone. There was simply nothing left to try. Medication wasn't working, counseling wasn't working, nothing was working. There was no place to turn to for relief from this agony of agonies. I knew that taking my life was no longer an option, and all that was left to do was simply believe against all odds. It was one of those times when all meant fail. *Nothing* was left but God alone. I will not lie and say that it was easy. No, it was not, but it was a place that I needed to get to. I was even past the point of questioning God's very existence as I knew He was real but simply not working on me, so I thought. I read my Bible until I could not read anymore. I was prayed over and prayed out. If I had any more anointing oil on me, I would slip off my bed. It was a time of gathering my thoughts, getting out of bed, and standing. I had to stand and say, "Lord, Your creation tells me You are there, and all I can do now is move forward trusting that somehow somewhere there is a plan and purpose." It was one of those days when all I could keep on repeating was, "He will, He will, He will," "He will save me from this hour of darkness," and "I will be okay again because God loves me and will not fail me." Though tears were flowing down my face and there was no strength in my soul to even breathe, I knew I must go on!

Now, I don't know what you are facing today, and I hope it is not what I faced way back when. But if it is, I have some really good news for you. In fact, I have some amazing news for you: God never left me, and so He will never leave you. Never, ever, ever. He will get you through this, and it might take every fiber of your being to achieve it, but He will save you from destruction. Psalm 30:9 says, "What profit is there in my blood, when I go down to the pit? Shall the dust praise thee? Shall it declare thy truth?" David is saying to the Lord, "Lord, if I go down to the pit, how can I praise your name?" If we crumble and die and the unsaved is watching, it is the Lord who looks bad. See, it behooves God to deliver us, for it is His faithfulness on the line, not yours or mine.

Now, some may disagree with my theology here, but it is what I used to get me out of the pit. I simply said, "Lord, if I die or commit suicide, what will become of all the souls I led to You, all the people that I talked to about You, all the people who were watching to see if my God was really God? Lord, I cannot fail because You cannot fail." Praise the Lord He never failed, and I'm here today because of His faithfulness.

February 27 - Sometimes It Is Us

I will heal their backsliding, I will love them freely: for mine anger is turned away from him. (Hosea 14:4)

If you ever had a chance to hear me preach, you probably would not like it. I tend to preach just as the Bible reads, and not too many people enjoy that type of preaching, at least not in this day and age. What I mean is, I preach not with kid gloves because God does not preach with kid gloves. Sometimes the problem needs to be pointed out, even if that problem is me. Of all the years of counseling that I put in, the one main reason for lack of deliverance has been a refusal to accept fault. In marriage counseling, this is bar none 85 percent of the reasons those troubled marriages will never be healed. No one wants to admit that they are the cause of the problem. It is always another one's fault.

Take automobile accidents as proof of this point. How many people do you know who have ever admitted fault? I tell you in all my years of living on planet earth, I have maybe heard one person confess that they were totally at fault. Even our insurance companies tell us that if we are ever in an accident, don't admit fault! Well, what if it was my fault? Should I still deny it before the Lord? It is sad to say that the answer is yes in the world that we now live in. It is sad to say that not accepting fault for anything is what our modern world is all about. It is a "who, me?" mentality. Now, my point for today is this, be it a painful one: sometimes God is trying to teach us something that we simply do not want to hear.

In my battles with depression and anxiety, there was never a time when the Lord was not teaching me something about myself. It was either a sin that I needed to let go of or a mindset that needed to be changed. Each and every time, there was always a lesson. I do not think that there was ever a time when I had depression or anxiety where the Lord just allowed me to suffer for nothing. See, the fact of the matter is, pain and sorrow are good at one important thing, and one thing that we always have a problem with, which is paying attention to God's leading. Pain and sorrow are very good at getting our attention, and until there is a better way, the Lord will continue to use it. Now, I am not stating that depression and anxiety are always a result of sin, but that they can be used by God to get our attention to where we need to be tweaked so we can hear Him.

Yes, sometimes emotional issues are caused by outside forces, chemical imbalances, family struggles, financial struggles, loss, and / or trauma, but sometimes they are caused by a God who is trying to get us to focus on Him. Now, why would a loving God do that? Well, simply because we are not focusing on Him. Did you hear what I just said? Focusing on *him*! It is always about Him, and if our life becomes only about us, then because He loves us, He must change that. Read Revelations 4:11 when you have time. This verse always gets my focus back in check.

So today, this might not be what you wanted to hear, but what if it was what the Lord wanted you to hear? What if our attention is what the Lord wants all along? I know when my season set in, I was all ears. He got my attention, and if He ever loses it, He might need to tap me on the shoulder one more time. In closing, let's never forget this one thing also: though we backslide and fall into wrong living, He will always love us and will quickly turn His anger from us. We just need to pay attention and return to Him.

February 28 - He Does the Keeping, and That's Good

And the peace of God, which passeth all understanding, shall keep your hearts and minds through Christ Jesus. (Phil. 4:7)

Well, it is finally here. February is almost over, and a new month is ready to begin. Winter is almost over, and before we know it, the days will be longer and the nights shorter. It is good news and good news that we need to hear. Dear friend, one of the great things about being a child of God is that good news always comes. Sooner or later, the sun will shine again. The clouds will part, and the blue sky will appear. Yes, rainy seasons and rainy climates are not too conducive to people with depression, but sometimes we just have to be content in whatever state we are in. Sometimes that's literal.

I live in Long Island, New York, and it tends to be a rainy place with more days of clouds than of sun. The winters are not too harsh, but they are long. Yet even with that being the case, there is one fact that never changes: even though it rains for a long time, the rain must end. It simply does not rain forever, and that's good news. Now what makes the rain and stops it should be of concern to us. I'm glad mankind doesn't control the rain, for then I would be worried of it never stopping. But we do not, and God does, and that's a very good thing. See, it is the Lord who keeps the rains at bay or allows them to fall.

Remember Jesus on the boat with the storm raging? Remember what He did and how He did it? "Peace, be still," he said. Friends, it is God alone who controls the rain and the winds, and so it is God alone who controls our lives. As the Lord controls all the seasons of nature, He also controls all the seasons of life. Seasons must end, and new ones must begin. Though we are in a season of sorrow, sorrow cannot live forever in the life of a child of God.

In our scripture today, Philippians 4:7, we see a few important facts. One is that God does the *keeping* of our hearts, and that is done through Jesus Christ. It is God who will give us peace, and a peace that is unlike anything that this world could ever imagine. It is a peace that passes *all* understanding, meaning that we can have God's peace even when the rain is falling. I'm living proof of this as I lived in sunny California and was sad, yet I could be happy in rainy New York. See, it is not the weather, situations in life, or anything else that keeps our minds in a place of peace but the Lord Jesus Christ and His indwelling in our hearts. God will keep your heart if we but let Him have it.

March

March 1 - Dying to Self, Key to Living

And they that are Christ's have crucified the flesh with the affections and lusts. If we live in the Spirit, let us also walk in the Spirit. (Gal. 5:24–25)

There are many things that we come upon in scripture that really dumfound us. Dying to self is one of them. In our walk with the Lord, it is one dynamic that we must come to grips with, or never come, to true life in Christ. Now, the dying of anything never sounds like a good thing. Dying, no matter how you say it, brings up negative thoughts. Then comes the Word of God, where up might appear down and down might appear up. Take Paul's words about being weak when he is strong; that's another odd one but nonetheless a truth also worth understanding. Now, back to this dying to self, if you are struggling with emotional issues, it might be the last thing you want to hear about. Yet what if it's the key to all of your suffering?

See, living in Christ is a lot like having your house remodeled. You don't remodel your kitchen and then put the old sink and rotted flooring back in. No, you rip everything out that is old and replace it with new. For those of you who have done this yourself, you know what you often find under that old floor or sink. There is mold and rot and pipes just hanging on by a thread. That sink-trap pipe under the sink is filled with all kinds of nasty things. It all needs to go, and yet to really remodel it all and leave in the old drainpipes would not be a remodel at all but simply a spruce up. Friends, if we are struggling with emotional pain, we don't need a spruce up but a remodel. Everything must go, including the kitchen sink.

In our lives as Christians, we also need everything to go. We need all of our lusts, fears, weaknesses, and demons to be removed. Yes, I know that we can't be indwelt by demons as Christians, but we can certainly be oppressed by them. Cast them off and begin rebuilding, except in this case the Lord does the rebuilding; we just need to allow Him to do so. Like our kitchen example again, the carpenter can't begin the remodeling until we allow him access into our homes. Until we sign the contract to release him to throw out and destroy what must be destroyed.

Funny, but one of the first tools in remodeling is the hammer. Smashing and ripping are two of the things that must happen first. It's a mess, and it's ugly. Sometimes we peek in to watch, and we see our kitchen looking worse than it did before they began reconstruction. That's how our lives might even look when God begins remodeling our souls. Pride might be lying on the floor with some nails sticking out of it. Jealousy is in the Dumpster outside. Fear is in a dusty pile on the floor getting ready for the trash heap.

Yes, it all must go, and a spring cleanup of the soul just might be what the doctor ordered. Today let us let go of our emotional mess and allow the Lord full access to our emotional soul. Confess and then rest, tear down, and wait for the building up. To get the pretty new life, sometimes, if not always, requires daily remodeling. Let Jesus do what needs to be done. He desires to remodel your body, mind, and soul. Let us allow what needs to die, to die, and then watch what comes alive in us.

March 2 - Money and Depression?

For the love of money is the root of all evil: which while some coveted after, they have erred from the faith, and pierced themselves through with many sorrows. (1 Tim 6:10)

Talking about money while you're going through depression might not seem like the most logical thing, but in many ways, it is. Sure, losing all their money in the stock market has led many to take their own lives and / or fall into depression, but that's not what I'm talking about. I'm talking about trusting too much in our money for that peace that only God can bring. In one of my bouts with depression, I remember thinking this crooked thought: if I had enough money, I could then afford to lie in bed all day and not worry about life any longer. Sure, it's a silly idea, but being depressed makes us do and think silly things. Much like being under the control of alcohol changes our critical thinking skills, so does being under the power of depression inhibits our rational thought processes.

I use money as an example because it's so misunderstood and also thought of as a joy maker. To most of the world, money is the key to happiness, success, and joy forevermore. That's what we are told, so that's what we think. To be a movie star and rock star is the goal of many. To win some lottery is also the goal of many. Now, if we are really honest with ourselves, we must conclude that at every attempt to gain money, happiness is the real goal. Now, if that is true, and it is, then we believe that money is the source of all peace and not God. Friend, that is so far from the truth, and I can prove it.

Take people in third-world countries; they have nothing and have no hope of getting anything. Now, check out the rate of depression there as compared to the rate of depression in the USA. Next, look at celebrities in the entertainment industry; check out their rate of depression and anxiety. One would think that there should never be an unhappy person as their money and fame is the secret to their happiness. Something is wrong as all the answers to those surveys are not what we might think. Those in third-world countries have a very low depression and suicide rate as opposed to the affluent USA. Look at all the young movie stars who are strung out on drugs and facing jail time. Depression and suicide are high on their list, and joy is very low.

Someone is lying to us, people, and it's certainly not Jesus Christ. Money does not bring joy unless Christ is central first. In fact, I have seen happier Christians with nothing than with a lot. The more we have, the more fear we have of losing it. With that fear comes anxiety, and with that anxiety comes depression. Connect the dots, and it's plain to see. Christ alone brings peace to our souls; nothing else can or ever will. Sure, money can make things easier for a time, but in the long haul, money's staying power is short-lived. Money can be taken away; Christ never can. Trust in Him, and we can watch the economy fall and smile at the storm.

In my current church, there was a dear brother who went home to be with the Lord. I would often refer to him as the happiest man I know, and what's odd about that is he was bound to a wheelchair for life. He was paralyzed by a motorcycle accident, yet his love for Jesus Christ was like nothing I have ever found. I would ask him if he was ever depressed, and to that he would reply, "No, because Jesus Christ is my joy." Need I say more?

March 3 - In Times of Trouble

But the salvation of the righteous is of the lord: He is their strength in the time of trouble. (Ps. 37:39)

Where would we be without the book of Psalms? If there is any part of my Bible with the most tears staining the pages, it is there. I often recommend the psalms to people who are hurting, and not just because there is much healing there, but because there is a picture of one who hurt and made it through. Think about this: if King David never went through trials and struggles, then we would not have the book of Psalms to lean on. As you read the book of Psalms, you quickly notice that people have problems, people have pain, people are sad, but God brings them through. That is why you will see me use the book of Psalms so much in this devotional. There is not a better place to find help in times of trouble. But again back to David who was no stranger to trouble, I find it hard to understand how one could read the book of Psalms, as well as most of the entire Bible, and not understand that life is hard and filled with troubles.

I listen to some of the famous preachers out there today and marvel at how they promise us a life of smiles when the Bible promises us a life of trials. Maybe they are reading the NUV, the New Utopia Version? I say that with tongue in cheek in case you didn't get my sarcastic humor. All through the Bible we read of tribulations; we read of people betraying us, people hurting us, lives leaving us, and sickness overcoming us. It is truly a symptom of the universe to have troubles, but dear friend, our God is a help in those times of trouble. And more than a help, He is deliverance, salvation, and peace of mind.

In Psalm 37, we read of the Lord's strength in times of trouble. The Lord doesn't just take our hand and help us cross the street. He becomes our strength to cross that street. Notice also that this strength of the Lord is for the righteous, which means we better make sure our hearts are right with our Lord in order to get that strength. Today be thankful that our Lord is our strength. He is our God and our King. More than that, He is able, able to do what He promises to do. Today embrace your day with His strength and leave yours at home. We simply need to believe that He is, and He will enable us to do the rest.

March 4 - Don't Forget to Keep Loving Others

Beloved, let us love one another: for love is of God; and every one that loveth is born of God, and knoweth God.
He that loveth not knoweth not God; for God is love. (1 John 4:7–8)

Today, as you embrace this new day, you might be inclined not to be too loving. Meaning that loving others isn't the first thing on your mind. I know this well as going through emotional trauma tends to keep our focus on the self and not so much on anyone else. I remember this well as I tried to counsel others while I needed counsel myself. I found myself quickly annoyed at other people's issues when mine were so much worse. To love the brethren was not on top of my to-do list but rather buried way beneath the deepest, darkest hole I could dig. Praying for others became hard to do; praying even for my own family became hard to do. I became shut out from all that was going on in the world, and for the most part, I didn't really care. There could be news of hurricanes and earthquakes, but until my little storm passed, I had little sympathy for much else. Now, maybe I was just a wicked person—and you are able to love other people more than yourself—but I was not, and it became such an issue that the Lord had to call me on it.

See, if we are to claim the position of child of God, then we better act on the condition of a child of God, which is to love one another. God is love, and if we are to be *of God*, we better have love. One of the practices I started to incorporate into my life during my emotional days was praying for others who needed help. It wasn't easy, but it did take my mind off myself and placed it on another. In the beginning, it wasn't very real as I was just going through the motions, but after a while, when I realized that my selfishness was also sin, then I began to see the purpose of it all.

It's amazing how all sin has one common denominator: the centrality of self. We are all basically selfish beings, and our hurt always seems to be first in getting our attention. If you are taking a walk with a friend and you both stub your toes at the same time, watch whose toe gets rubbed first. So for today, I challenge you to rekindle your love for others even when you are hurting more than they are. You might be surprised at what happens as the Lord sees our proper direction and begins to heal our affliction. If Jesus loves us, then we must love one another. That means loving the mean, the nasty, and the unsaved. Love them all as Christ loves, and we begin to take on Christ-likeness. Until we do, we are only self-absorbed and can never be of Christ.

March 5 - Learning to Live in Both Worlds

I know both how to be abased, and I know how to abound: everywhere and in all things I am instructed both to be full and to be hungry, both to abound and to suffer need.

I can do all things through Christ which strengtheneth me. (Phil. 4:12–13)

Over and behind the pulpit in my New York church, I have hanging Philippians 4:13. I like how it looks as the center of the scripture is Christ. It just falls perfectly across the back with very large letters at about fifteen-feet long. It's a reminder to me that Christ is central to anything that I must face and a reminder of His strength being used in an earthen vessel like me. In our struggles over any problem, but even more through emotional ones, Philippians 4:13 is a constant reminder of how we can and will make it through this thing called life. If I need strength, it is Christ's strength that I must call on, and if I need to have victory over anything, it is Christ again and Christ alone who will bring it to me. What's even better about the verse is the first part where it says, "I can do all things." *All things* means all things including depression, anxiety, OCD, bipolar disorder. *All things* means everything, and that is, and should be, great news to us all.

So Philippians 4:13 is a great scripture, it is true, but any good Bible teacher will also take you back a bit to see if there is more to glean from a particular passage. In this case, let's go back to verse 12.

I know both how to be abased, and I know how to abound: everywhere and in all things I am instructed both to be full and to be hungry, both to abound and to suffer need. (Phil. 4:12)

Paul here declares something that most modern-day preachers fail to proclaim: there will be times when we will have to succeed even when the tide is not favorable, to not change who we are when things are good or when they are bad. This reminds me of Sunday-morning Christians versus Monday-morning Christians. It's the all-show-and-no-go trend that seems to be prevalent in our world today. We are all on fire for Christ with our hands waving in praise, but only as long as our life is peaking on a ten.

Yet when the tire goes flat in the rain, when sickness comes our way, when emotional issues overtake us, we become a different Christian. This should not be, and it could be exactly what the Lord is trying to show us through our depression and anxiety. Can we still praise Him as much in the valley as we do on the mountaintop?

Speaking of mountaintops, another thought entered my mind: mountain tops are deceitful and a dangerous place to try to live on. In my counseling practice, I came up with a number-gauge process in which to realistically measure each day. A ten is fine but not probable or even likely. A zero is unacceptable but probable in some cases. What is probable and acceptable is a five. It is there that we must strive to live, and it is there that we will find true peace. So like Paul, let's live at level five even when it's a zero or a ten day. Get into that groove, and you will never fall out of it.

March 6 - Got to Break a Little Sweat to Get a Little Rest

Come unto Me, all ye that labor and are heavy laden, and I will give you rest. (Matt. 11:28)

Today we come upon another amazing scripture, but again one that we take for granted and pass by too quickly. It is Jesus speaking of His rest and offering us a temporary rest from our labor. As we read this scripture, we must not pass up some important points, one being, what comes first? Notice how we can't have rest unless there is labor. Now, before we go further, let's just dig quickly into a few important words and their actual meaning in the Greek: *Labor* in Greek means to "feel fatigued," *heavy-laden* means to "load up or spiritual anxiety," *rest* means "to refresh." Now, when we incorporate them together, we get a better picture of what the Lord is trying to tell us. 1) Those who feel overtired and exhausted, whether from physical or emotional stress; 2) those who have too much placed on them to the point that they can't carry anymore, so overladen with burdens that it's causing spiritual anxiety—3) the Lord will give you refreshing, a new breath of air, not to escape the cares of this world but to get back into battle and carry more.

Friend, this is good news and bad. Good in the sense that God will give us rest from our labors and trials, but only so we can be refreshed to bear more. See, God does give us rest. He will give you a second wind from this battle of the mind, but there might be more battles to face. They might not be of the emotional kind, but rest assured they will be of some kind. In this world, you will have tribulation, that is a certainty, but Jesus is bigger than the world. In Christ, we can go through anything, but that doesn't mean we won't have anything to go through—we will!

Some might say that this is negative news, but it is neither. It is simply the truth. God's Word says that all things work together for good to those who love the Lord and are called according to His purpose. This means then that everything is eventually good if you are in Christ. It won't always seem that way, and when it does, rest assured that Christ will give us that temporary rest you and I both desperately need. Today lay your burden on the Lord's shoulders, and (together) you can carry the world.

March 7 - For the Children

> Lo, children are an heritage of the lord: and the fruit of the womb is his reward.
> As arrows are in the hand of a mighty man; so are children of the youth. (Ps. 127:3–4)

Ever been to a place where you are looking for an out, and yet it alludes you?

I remember one particular time when I was in the depths of despair, and suicide was grasping deeply. It became an obsession as I tried in my mind to plan out the most painless and perfect plan. Suicide can be like that, a controlling force that haunts you day and night. As pain continues to build and relief is nowhere in sight, it can become a very viable yet deceptive option. Now, before I continue on with the suicide solution, I want to explain some things about suicide. Taking one's life actually crosses many people's minds in one form or another. Who has not said or thought, "I have had it, and I just wish the Lord would take me or a big truck would run me over." That, my friends, comes close, but is not a true suicidal thought process, but I will tell you what is.

It's to come to a place so dark and so low that life seems unbearable for one moment more, and suicide becomes so appealing that you begin to plan it out in your head. If you have gotten to that place, if you have crossed that line, then you need to run to a safe place, a friend, or the police for help and safety from yourself. It is a very bad place to be, and I am saddened to say I have been there twice in my life. Praise the Lord I never took it to the extreme, but I will tell you what stopped me from going there. I remember this one time; it was the second time I came to that place. I could not get the thought out of my mind, and every scenario I could imagine was rushing through my mind. On this particular day, I was driving to see a dear associate about my depression. It was on that day that I was listening to a Christian radio station where I heard a story about (of all things) suicide. Yes, God knows us well, and His divine appointments are nothing short of supernatural. On this particular broadcast, they were talking about children and what devastation suicide places on them. How a father who took his life left a trail of carnage that forever devastated the family for generations to come. How that one little boy whose father took his own life had to go on with pain and baggage, which he was never able to get over.

Friend, it was that word from God through that perfectly timed radio broadcast that turned me forever away from that horrible thought, the thought of the ultimate selfishness that is suicide. God clearly spoke to me about my children and, more directly, my youngest son. He forced me to picture my son's life without me—hearing the news of Dad's grizzly demise, the scuttle that would follow, and the radical change of life that he would have to endure. It was a place where God wanted me to think of others more than myself, to think of my wife and people whom I loved and who loved me. Yet again of my son, my children, and all the children that knew me well. The effect on them would never go away and that was a pain I could not bear.

Dear friend, if you are in that wicked, wretched place of self-destruction, please don't go any further. Please realize the consequences that will follow—the finding of your body and the hurt you will cause. And not only to those around you but even to our Lord Jesus Christ who lived and died so we could live and die and be forever with Him. Suicide is never a solution but the greatest lie of Satan. Hold on one day more, for His salvation waits for you.

March 8 - Not There Yet, But You Will Arrive

And the angel of the lord appeared unto the woman, and said unto her,
"Behold now, thou art barren, and bearest not: but thou shalt conceive, and
bear a son." (Judg. 13:3)

Whenever we read the Bible, we notice one thread running through its many pages; that is, of the impossible becoming possible. A woman who cannot bear a child but then all of a sudden she can. A mass of water that cannot be crossed but then it can. A body that is dead but then it is not. It is the picture of the mighty, all-powerful Lord whom we serve. He is the God of the impossible, the God of salvation from destruction. Today you might be at a place where it seems impossible. I have been there too, so I know that place, and yes, I know that yours seems worse than anyone else's. Maybe it is; maybe it is the worst set of circumstances anyone could imagine. No job, money, friends, health, and on top of that, a debilitating depression and anxiety.

How can your circumstance change, you ask? How can even God turn this around? There is no scripture I can read to you or prayer I can say for you. It is over, done; you are at the bottom of the bottom. There is not a fragment of energy or hope left in you. Well, if that's you today, then I will say a very strange thing to you—*that is the best place to be.* You are where God wants you to be and where He has been trying to get you for years. To the place of *nothing*, nothing but the clothes on your back and whatever air is left in your room. See, at that place, when God delivers you, there will be no way for you to explain that deliverance but by God alone. It's a place where only God can get the glory for saving you, and no one else can claim that prize.

Dear friend, we need to get to those places so God can deliver and deliver us alone. It's the places of the impossible, the places where it could only be explained by the supernatural. Please, right where you are, call out to the Lord, confess your sin, and you, being at the complete end of self, cry out to God and say, "Lord, You are all I have left, there is none left to save, and there is no plan of man that can turn this around." Say it and believe it and wait in faith. Today might be that day or maybe tomorrow or maybe even next week, but certainly soon, there will be an answer. There will be that knock on the door, that phone call, that letter in the mail.

In God's own way, He will give a child to the barren and sight to the blind. Look for it in any form, maybe even in the form of that still small voice of the Lord. The voice that says, "Child, I love you and have not forgotten you, I hear your cry." Hey, for all you know, this devotion you are reading today might be the answer to your prayer yesterday. Maybe these words are God's words. You will rise again, dear child, fear not.

March 9 - What Are You Doing to Me?

Wherefore do I take my flesh in my teeth, and put my life in mine hand? (Job 13:14)

Poor Job, he truly went through more than we could ever imagine even on our worst days. We talk about him much and use him as the picture of suffering. I remember the first time reading the book of Job and having to go to my pastor at the time and asking him, "Hey, what's up with Job? This is pretty depressing." I also remember his words: "Finish reading the book!" So I did, and I learned more from that book about the character of God than any other book. I love the book of Job for its science and also for its depiction of the majesty of God. It is truly an *all-in-one* book: science, friendship, God, Satan, creation, and most of all, deliverance.

When I read the book of Job, I also try to place myself in the mind of Job. He must have been so confused, so taken by surprise to have so much and then to have it taken away so quickly. To love the Lord with all your heart yet have that same Lord allow the enemy to have at you. Do you ever feel like Job? Maybe today you are feeling like the offspring of Job? Maybe you are questioning all that God is doing and scratching your head about it. "Lord, why are you doing this to me?" If you have been at that place, don't feel bad; even the best of us question God's motives at times. Truth is, He does do things not as we would do things. He does blindside us at times, yet at other times, He pulls a rabbit out of a hat when we least expect it. As the scriptures declare, His ways are certainly not ours, and His thoughts higher than our thoughts. It's one of those things we just have to accept, or let it cultivate anger toward God.

When it comes to being angry at God, I have one word for you—don't go there because He is always right, and we will always be wrong. He is God, and because of that, He knows what He is doing *all the time*. There is not a single time that He is not in control of all things. If you are at a place today when you feel like pounding your head against the wall in frustration trying to figure out what God is doing, well, stop it! Sometimes it doesn't make sense; sometimes it seems crazy. Sometimes the thing you fear the most is the thing that the Lord lets come into your life. Sometimes that's what He does, yet all the time, we must accept it and obey it full on, 100 percent. If we don't, and if we let it fester, it will destroy our fellowship with God; and instead of healing us, it will weaken us. Allow the Lord full access to your mind, body, and soul. Let Him do what must be done, and in the process, praise Him for it. As Job learned, there is no direction in trials but one direction—complete submission.

March 10 - Who Me?

> But the lord said unto Samuel, "Look not on his countenance, or on the height of his stature; because I have refused him": for the lord seeth not as man seeth; for man looketh on the outward appearance, but the lord looketh on the heart. (1 Sam. 16:7)

David's father learned a thing or two about what makes a man and how God views a man. When Samuel was searching for the new king, he thought he knew exactly what God was looking for. David's father also thought he knew, but he did not. I think we can learn a lot about how God looks at us from this account. David's dad assumed God was looking for a mighty man of valor, one of large stature and one of boldness and attitude. Well, he had the boldness part right, but he just never dreamed his youngest son would be that man. When I read this story, I can't help but feel encouraged by it. God surely does look at the heart, which gives a lot of hope for people like you and me.

I have never been much to look at, especially as a youth: skinny, weak, and not good at much. I had a great speech impediment, which all but crushed any dreams of me publicly speaking. And speaking of public speaking, I would be the last person to stand in front of any crowd as I was also petrified to speak to anyone. I was the hide-behind-the-last-row guy. I had no self-confidence and always thought of myself as not too bright, which was proven by my low grades in school. So when the Lord called me later in life to leave all that I knew and become a pastor in the far away land of California, it was an absurd idea. When I was called to counsel those with anxiety and depression, that too was an even more absurd idea. Well, like God's sense of humor with young David, He also had a sense of humor with me. Friend, this trial of trials that you are enduring might bring you to a place of failure and weakness, but what if God has instead plans of greatness through those weaknesses?

He does prefer to choose the lowly and despised of the world to confound the wisdom of the wise. See, it's not a great thing if a person with a PhD becomes a great doctor, but it is if that person was once a high school dropout, strung out on drugs, and living on the streets. Don't we applaud more those who come from meager backgrounds to go on and live extraordinary lives? Let us not forget that God is in the miracle business, and He knows that a person of weakness whom He has made great can only praise Him as they know it could never be of themselves.

So be of good cheer. No matter how low you are today, the Lord, our Lord, can raise you higher than you ever dreamed. Now, that's a good way to start your day—with endless possibilities.

March 11 - How Long?

The burden which Habakkuk the prophet did see.
O lord, how long shall I cry, and thou wilt not hear! Even cry out unto
thee of violence, and thou wilt not save! (Hab. 1:1–2)

How long? is a question that we will see scattered throughout this devotional. It will be brought up often because we ask it often. I know in my struggles with depression and anxiety that question would be asked on a daily basis. "Lord, how much longer must I go on in this pain?" It was one thing to feel this way for a day, a week, or a month, but what if it never went away? Oh, that was my greatest fear, but even a more real fear was—"Would it be gone today?" I needed to know this, and every day I would beg Him for an answer. Every day, everyone would tell me, "It will all be fine. Just hang in there, and in just a few more weeks, the cycle will break." That was fine, but that also became old when weeks turned into months. How long, Lord?

I think all of us, in one way or another, have asked God that question, whether it was over the sickness of a loved one or being unemployed for an extended length of time. Even during those short but *nonetheless* nasty stomach flues, we asked, "Lord, how much longer?" as that nasty nausea hung on for what seemed like an eternity. In our scripture for today, the prophet Habakkuk was asking the same question. He was asking about his tears and crying. He was complaining about the Lord not answering. He was even getting a bit irritable by saying, "I even cry out violently," and still I get nothing.

Habakkuk was a man like you and me (human). Male or female, we get impatient. We get angry at the delays to move mountains and hills for us. In this case, Habakkuk was a bit more virtuous than you and me as he even cried out for the evil he saw in the land. The injustice he observed kept increasing, and yet God sat silently by doing nothing. Friends, even when God appears to be doing nothing, He is doing something by doing nothing. That's God for you, the most efficient power source in the universe. So for today's devotion, the tactic is to stop complaining and begin to wait. Wait and trust on what God has up His sleeve for you and me. Tomorrow we will see a little bit clearer.

March 12 - When Our Nasty Comes Out

Why dost thou show me iniquity, and cause me to behold grievance? For spoiling and violence are before me: and there are that raise up strife and contention.

Therefore the law is slacked, and judgment doth never go forth: for the wicked doth compass about the righteous; therefore wrong judgment proceedeth. (Hab. 1:3–4)

Today we are continuing from where we left off yesterday. We are back with Habakkuk, and it is getting ugly. His nasty is beginning to show, and when it does, all love, faith, and trust go out the window. See, after our patience wears thin, the next emotion to pop up is that of frustration, and from there it's downhill until aggravation. In our scripture today, Habakkuk was even past aggravation and crossed over into condemnation. Can you imagine that, mankind yelling at God and putting Him in His place? Doesn't seem like the best course of action, but sadly enough, and given enough time, any of us can get to that ugly place where our nasty comes out. Listen how the prophet lays into God, how he feels he has to explain to

God what's going on—as if God didn't know. But still, the prophet feels he needs to school the Lord here.

> *Why dost thou show me iniquity, and cause me to behold grievance? For spoiling and violence are before me: and there are that raise up strife and contention.*
>
> *Therefore the law is slacked, and judgment doth never go forth: for the wicked doth compass about the righteous; therefore wrong judgment proceeded. (Hab. 1:3–4)*

Wow, poor Habakkuk seems to really have had it with his struggles and complaints. He loses his cool and says things he will probably regret one day. Can any of us out there place ourselves in his shoes? Have you been there when it's just too much to bear and God seems like a good target to shoot at?

Friend, as we read these scriptures, notice what Habakkuk complains about: some things of life that can't be changed. There will be wicked people; there will be those who don't follow God's laws. The righteous will lose sometimes, and the wicked will appear to win. It does stink, to put it plainly, and the world doesn't always go the way it should. But is this anything to be surprised about, to be shocked about? Ever since the fall of man, pain and sorrow have been a part of living. Since sin entered, death followed. Disease and sickness are not always punishment but simply results of the fall, and nothing more sometimes. Cancer comes, terrorists blow up innocent people, and tribulation goes on, but—let's not forget the *but* part—God is bigger and stronger, and He can take this rotten world and do amazing things for His children. Let's see what one more day brings.

March 13 - When God's Blessings Come Out

> *Behold ye among the heathen, and regard, and wonder marvellously: for I will work a work in your days, which ye will not believe, though it be told you. (Hab. 1:5)*

Wow, Habakkuk 1:5, it is a very special scripture to me. It is *the* scripture that turned the tides of my time of depression and anxiety. When I was at the lowest and waiting like Habakkuk to see God do something big, God did just that. It's amazing how little we need to break the chains of pain and set us on a new road. Sometimes we think it's winning the lottery or getting a new car or even a new love in your life, but rarely does the Lord turn the tides in such a trivial way. He doesn't need to give us money or toys (though He can), but so often the best catalyst to break the spell (so to speak) is simply the Word of God. One scripture cleverly placed is enough to ignite our world and life again—like planting bombs. After the terrorist attacks of 9/11, the first thing the highway department did was to restrict picture-taking while going over New York bridges. I thought that was odd until I learned that a terrorist who knows what he is doing can take one small bomb, and if he knows engineering and structure design, he can place it and take down an entire bridge. Now, if a man can think that technically, why would we not think that our Creator God also can?

So getting back to the scripture that saved my life, it wasn't a big famous one. It wasn't a vision I had or revelation from God. It wasn't a faith healer who came and laid hands on me. No, it was God's Word telling me (directly) that it was going to be okay and that one day something real big would come my way. Now, keep in mind this all happened before I wrote my first book, before I was called to be a pastor, and before I really started Christian counseling. Finally, my pain would have purpose, but until I had that shot in the arm to keep going, I didn't see the purpose. Anyway, it was about 3:00 a.m., and I went to bed after another day of struggling with depression and anxiety. I was praying like I never prayed before, praying and waiting for an answer, something supernatural. Well, that's what I received. To you, it might seem like nothing at all, yet to me, it was everything.

Anyway, at 3:00 a.m., I woke up from a sound sleep with a scripture in my head. What was odd was that it was the book of Habakkuk, a book which I didn't know much about nor ever really read. So when I woke up with that, I said to the Lord, "If this is from You, well, it better jump out at me right in chapter one and the first few verses"; He gave me no other clue but that book title. So as fast as my little feet could take me, I ran to my Bible, tried to find where Habakkuk was, prayed, and then opened to chapter 1, verse 1, and began reading. Verses 1–4 were all me, all about me, and how I felt toward God and about my situation. Then verse 5 came, and it would be the verse that would change everything. God simply said, "I have something waiting for you. I know you are angry, but hang on, it will be worth it, and it will be so big that if I were to tell you, you wouldn't even believe it" (my paraphrase). Now, I know my understanding of that scripture is not particularly scriptural, but it spoke to me, and I heard by application what I needed to hear that day.

Friend, I believe the Lord is saying the same thing to all of us. So don't give up. Move.

March 14 - We Are Not Alone in There

Nevertheless I tell you the truth; It is expedient for you that I go away: for if I go not away, the Comforter will not come unto you; but if I depart, I will send Him unto you. (John 16:7)

God dwelling within us—after all the years that I have been saved, I still need to be reminded of that. God the Holy Spirit takes up his abode within us. If you're like me, then you need a reminder too. When we become a child of God through faith in Jesus Christ, we are then baptized in the Holy Spirit and forever sealed and indwelt with Him. Kind of odd, I know, but it's something we need to really and truly embrace: God in us, God forever abiding in our very being. Where we go, He goes. What we look at, He looks at. His power is there, yet only squelched by our sins. That's when we grieve the Holy Spirit. It might just be that the grieving is the pain we feel within us, that agony of separation from God and His Holy Spirit being suffocated by our wretchedness. We can look at this indwelling of God a few different ways: as a blessing, knowing that God is with us everywhere we go, comforting, guiding, instructing, convicting, loving, and showing us the way home every day! Or we can see this as a hindrance to our sinful desires. It's our choice to embrace this amazing blessing or reject it and bring pain to our God. Ever think of that, pain to God?

I don't think we ever think of God ever feeling pain or disappointment or sadness. Well, we know that Jesus wept over Jerusalem, so why can't He weep over us? People often say, "You are not alone in this," and they mean well, but they can't be with us all the time. It's a comment wrought with impossibility, but Who can be and is with us all the time is real. He is God the Holy Spirit, and when Jesus ascended, He also promised us the Comforter.

Today, as you face the sunshine or the rain, clouds or flower gardens, remember the words of Jesus Christ: If I go, I will not leave you alone (my paraphrase). As you go off to work, school, or play, constantly remind yourself of this abiding presence of God within you, His very dwelling and companionship traveling with you and meeting every trial and enemy with you. Like David said in the twenty-third psalm, "Though I walk through the valley of the shadow of death, I will not be afraid." Why? Because You are with me! Who is with him? God is with him, yet even in that, we have so much more than David could ever imagine. Our indwelling can never be shaken off by sin nor just simply snuffed out a bit by our sins. But it's all good, my friend, as even in our sin, He is still with us, still loving, watching, and guiding. When panic comes, He is there. When depression flows over us like a wave, He is also there. Our God is with us—can we say amen?

March 15 - One of Those Days

Heal me, O lord, and I shall be healed; save me, and I shall be saved: for Thou art my praise. (Jer. 17:14)

Well, today is a special day. It's special because you get to hear a word of encouragement hot off the presses. As I write this devotion for March 15, I do so in pain and sorrow. See, there is no magic pill or happy place to hide where every arrow of the enemy can never find. Life being life means that there will be days when it all goes south. There will be days when trouble comes, and the highest hill looks like a good hiding place. Depression and anxiety can be cured, but that doesn't mean you will never face depressing or anxious times ever again.

Today was a rough one for me; running a small church is very hard at times. Fighting among the boards and the congregation is commonplace. Being accused of this or that is par for the course. Today I took a lot of hits from dear, well-meaning Christians, and no matter how tight I wear that armor of God, little darts always seem to find a way to sneak in. No, they're not knockout punches but ones that bring you to your knees just long enough to scrape those knees up real bad.

Now, in that place of pain, hurt, and anguish, we have a few choices. We can get nasty in return. We can give up and say, "What's the use?" or we can do the hardest of them all: get up, dust off our dirty knees, and live to fight another day. It's not easy, I know, but there is no other choice that is God-approved. As to our deeper emotional sickness, well, God says He will take care of those. In Jeremiah 17:14, we see it's His job to heal and save, and it's our job to praise Him for it. But of the daily pitfalls and attacks, we simply can't avoid them. To live in a world without pain and sorrow is to not live on planet earth. Sometimes we like to excuse our situations due to our depressions and anxieties, but sometimes, no matter if we have them or not, life still happens.

I wish there was a way or place to avoid them, but since Adam and Eve fell in that garden all those years ago, that place of nirvana exists no more. Only in Heaven with the Father will that place of peace and problem-free living ever be found. For now, like I must also do, we must move on and let the Lord put the daily pieces back together again.

March 16 - One of Those Days

The lord is good unto them that wait for Him, to the soul that seeketh Him. (Lam. 3:25)

If there is one thing we must pound into our heads, it is this fact: the Lord is good. If He is not, then we have major problems with life, the Bible itself, and ever finding deliverance from our emotional battles. But the Lord is good! He is good every day and in every way. Once we start to see Him in that light, then the dark corners of our souls will also feel His light. Now, I know it is truly hard to grasp this concept of *everything* that happens to us as being good, but it must be. If we are a child of God by faith in Jesus Christ, then God being our Father can only do good to His children. As earthly parents, we could only think of doing good to our children; yet being sinners at heart, we can make a mistake here or there. But God is not a sinner, and even more, He is perfect righteousness. If that is the case (and it is), then He can only do good. Again let's say it together, "My God can only do good to me." In the pain, He is there working good; in the sadness, He is there working good. In the loss and suffering, He is there working good.

Now, the question that is always in our celestial minds is this: How can this be good when it hurts so bad? Well, that's where scriptures like Lamentations 3:25 step in. Notice it says, "The Lord is good unto them that wait for Him." That's the first step, to wait for Him to reveal His goodness. Yes, waiting is hard, and you might believe that you have waited for Him, but this waiting is waiting in faith. It's knowing that He will show us good from our pain. Then notice the next part: "to the soul that seeketh Him."

If we are going through a hard time and we only assume that bad is the result, then we are not seeking Him. Instead we are seeking the bad. We are seeking and expecting only evil to result in our struggle.

Let's read our scripture one more time: "The LORD is good unto them that wait for Him, to the soul that seeketh Him." If this is not true, then the entire Bible is a lie. God is good, and though it was hard to see during my darkest days of depression, it still remained a fact though I didn't believe it at times. It's like not believing in gravity anymore. My belief in it doesn't change it one way or another. Gravity is working, and that I cannot change. God is good too, and that fact we cannot change either.

March 17 - I'd Rather Just Sleep This One Out

But he that shall endure unto the end, the same shall be saved. (Matt. 24:13)

Today our watch word is *endure*. I don't think there is a positive way to look at this word without thinking about being tired. I remember one particular time while my little church was going through another great battle. I remember saying to my wife and the Lord, "I don't think I can go through this again." It's bad enough to go through a major ministry struggle once, but to go through it again is often the straw that breaks the camel's back. I kept hearing the word *endure* as I sized up what this new battle would entail. Endure to the end, keep going, run the race set before you, look unto Jesus, the author and finisher of our faith.

Yeah, I knew those scriptures well, but the fact remained that I would have to pull up my droopy pants and fight the enemy that lay ahead. When I think of the word *endurance*, what comes to my mind is sweating, labor, strife, pain, and sorrow. What I always tend to block out is the victory. See, sometimes even as Christians, we tend to be glass-half-empty kind of people. We see the traffic jam ahead and never consider the accident that we might have been spared from by being late. Our first knee-jerk reaction is to the negative and to failure. Since when has God ever been the author of failure? Since when is that the endgame for those who serve the King? In Christ, we cannot fail. In Christ, we will be victorious no matter what odds are against us. Sure, our natural inclination is to say, "I'd rather just sleep this one out" or "I'd rather just sit this next battle out." Maybe you've never said that, but I have, and many times, in fact: "Time to quit, time to throw in the towel and let the enemy win this round."

I remember one time that was so bad: problems at church, with my family, with money, with everything. I was hit on every side in such a short period of time that I actually said out loud, "Okay, Satan, you win, I cry uncle." Praise God He wouldn't let that ever happen, and as always, He called in a legion of angels and worked the supernatural. It's amazing that I always seem to cave in, and God always seems to keep saving me. As my wonderful wife always says when the next battle rages on, "We have been through worse, and the Lord has always delivered us, every time!" She is right, and so is our Lord. If we endure, we shall be saved from all and any foe.

Now, again that leaves us with the endurance part. What if we can't endure? What if we don't have the fight in us? Well, it is at those times when the Lord picks us up and carries us. Our mission is to simply not give up in soul and spirit. We need to be okay with physically losing steam but never with spiritually losing steam. We need to read our Bible, pray even when we don't see any end to the pain, and blindly trust in God to carry us when we can't carry ourselves. That, my friend, is enduring—it is to *never* say die.

March 18 - Why Keep Fighting?

Be ye strong therefore, and let not your hands be weak: for your work shall be rewarded. (2 Chron. 15:7)

So we spoke about enduring yesterday. It seems virtuous and wonderful, yet why endure if it's so painful at times? It seems this problem of intestinal fortitude or lack of it is not simply for adults but for children too. It goes right back to childhood. When we are raising our children, we are always telling them to clean up after they have taken all the blocks out. When they get a bit older, we tell them to put the laundry away; and even in those wonderful teen years, we tell them to take out the trash. Now, what's so amazing in all three cases is the response we get: "But, Mom. But, Dad." We get the grumbles, the looks, and the sluggish labor. It's as if we were asking them to drag a fifteen-hundred-pound sack of horse meat to the trash bin.

As children, we simply don't like doing things that require work; and as we grow up, that never seems to change. My eldest son is great for this example. He, when asked to carry in the groceries or carry out the garbage, always has the same picture in his head: make as few trips as possible, and, if at all possible, make only one trip. It all sounds great until he tries to carry everything at once and always manages to drop something. Normally it's the eggs or a glass jar that shatters.

Sure, we get angry, but we also know the heart of man: man needs motivation to do just about anything. We go to work because we have to. We go to school because we have to. And at the end of the day, we do what we must for this one reason—to get something back or not to get punished for not doing what we had to. Be that all as it may, what we must understand is this: there are rewards for sticking with it. There are rewards in the eternal, as well as in the temporal. Now, even if it's really not a good idea to reward our children for doing what they are told to do, we do it anyway because we love them. It's the same with the Lord.

We should always do what God called us to do, and never for reward. But being the children we are, it doesn't hurt to get us moving. So today, with all of that in mind, "be strong and let not your hands be weak." There is a purpose and a reason. God is watching all we do, and being the great parent that He is, He is always waiting to give us that celestial bear hug we all desire. So today again, fight, push on, be strong in the Lord, and ye shall be rewarded.

March 19 - How to Be Lifted Up

And whosoever shall exalt himself shall be abased; and he that shall humble himself shall be exalted. (Matt. 23:12)

Wow, do I hate the sin that rules over me sometimes. I often wonder what life would be like in the *sinless*, glorified body that awaits us on the other side of eternity. I can't even imagine how my mind would function without sin. All I know is that it will be a glorious weight lifted off my shoulders. Now, the reason why I say this is because like Paul, I have a sin problem as we all do. Sometimes I let people know this all too often as I like the reaction I get when, on a Sunday morning from the pulpit, I proclaim, "Your pastor is a sinner." People don't know if that's a good thing or a bad thing, and I do get complaints from people about it. From my church in California to my church in New York, I have heard the same thing, mostly from leadership: "You know, pastor, you should keep that *sinner* thing to yourself. We are concerned if people hear it too much, they might think you are a sinner,"

Say what? But I am a sinner! And as Paul so wonderfully and boldly put it, "Christ came to save sinners of whom I am chief." Hey, if it's good enough for Paul, it's good enough for me. Now, I'm not saying that we brag about sin as a badge of honor—no, not at all. I always make sure I show them my shame in that I fight a daily struggle to be Christlike, but every day I fail. Sin is a part of what we are; though it is an unfortunate part, it is nonetheless who we are. So what's the point of proclaiming my sinful nature? Well, it's so people know I'm like them. It's so people know I still have a battle to fight. I am better than yesteryear but still a long way from the perfection of Jesus Christ. In Matthew 23:12, Jesus Himself brings the mandatory rule of humility to light. He lets us know that there is a cause and effect, so to speak, in denying our sin or admitting it. To boast of how righteous we are versus to admit how weak we are.

Dear friend, to struggle with depression and / or anxiety is not something that we should hide, and it's not something that we should lie about. Interestingly, in a survey taken about ailments in the church, the least excepted ones are those of the emotional type. We will ask for prayer about our broken leg, diabetes, and every other sickness, but we will rarely ask for prayer about our depression or anxiety. I tell you, if we don't come clean with who we are and what we suffer with, we are ultimately denying it before men; and of that, the Lord can never bless.

I have willingly made many public announcements of my struggles with depression and anxiety. In fact, whoever comes to my church, know—"Oh yeah, Pastor Scott struggles with depression and anxiety." Was that easy to admit? No, not at all, but I felt the Holy Spirit convincing me to share so others would see my good works and likewise do the same.

My admissions at numerous venues have helped an untold number of people feel a little better about themselves and more prone to ask for the help and prayer they need. And in case you didn't catch it, I just boasted a bit so it proves I'm a sinner, but it also proves that God still loves even me, despite all my sins. As I pray for victory over these and other sins that trip up my walk for Christ, let us each pray for one another's ability to be honest and truthful about it also.

March 20 - Gladness Comes from God Alone

Thou hast put gladness in my heart, more than in the time that their corn and their wine increased. (Ps. 4:7)

In the world we live in today, it is a common misunderstanding that joy comes from external sources. Sources such as the type that only mankind can provide. Things like sex, drugs, money, and power. The idea is that to have joy, we must have those *things*! Well, we do live in a world of things. We have accumulated more things than any other generation before, at least in the USA. I would even venture to say that there has not been a people who has walked this earth with more *things* like we have today. Things on every shelf, things in every corner, so many things that we need more shelves, more space, and now we even have to rent storage facilities outside the home just to keep them in. We are truly surrounded by things, so many things that we no longer have a fear of not having enough but a fear of losing what we have. Worse than that, we look at the world in envy for what they have.

We become angry at their success, and so we fail in living for Christ. The enemy of the cross beats us over the head again and again with this lust for things. Nicer cars, nicer homes, nicer husbands and wives. Pornography tells men that their wives are never going to give them the joy that they should. Our women look at their bodies and clothes and compare them to the supermodels and movie stars, and they feel that they could never be the women their husbands want. It's a four-squared attack, and we are crumbling under the pressure. At the end of the day, the sad truth is that we all wanted and still want the same thing—joy! What's even sadder is that most will never know that true joy is never found in those things but in Christ.

It is Christ alone who gives us that joy and everlasting peace. Sure, things are neat to have. I like Jeeps and have restored a few over the years, but every time I get one, I soon lose the joy of it, and I want another one, a better, newer one. I have come to the point where I finally understand that joy only comes from Him. Now, if you doubt me on that, then that is wise as you should doubt men but never God. Yet as we see in our scripture for today, it is very clear: only God can put gladness in my heart, even more joy than when the wicked have their most prosperous time. Only Jesus, only Jesus, *only* Jesus can bring us joy.

March 21 - Step Two to Joy

A sound heart is the life of the flesh: but envy the rottenness of the bones. (Prov. 14:30)

Yesterday we spoke at length about where true joy comes from. I say this because the world does offer joy and sin does produce joy in some carnal way, for if it didn't, then sin wouldn't be a problem. Worldly joy also is a real thing as I stated yesterday about my love affair with old Jeeps. Sure, if someone bought me a new one, I would probably get excited. If my wife surprised me with one for Father's Day, yeah, I would feel all gushy inside but only for a while. I would soon be convicted by God of purchasing something that I could not really afford. Even if I could afford it, the joy would pass, and a 2013 model would not be good enough as those 2014 models look even better. Oh, by the way, I just fell in love with a 2015 Jeep. See, I told you.

Now, what's interesting about us humans is the next step in our desire to find joy: it is in seeing another's joy and being envious of it. It's the old adage of, "If I can't have it, then no one should be able to." We see our neighbors with a new boat, a new child, or whatever it may be that we don't have, and right away that green-eyed monster starts to form. We begin to say things like, "I work so hard and do so much for the Lord, and yet my non-church-going neighbor gets the new inground swimming pool."

For those of us who are struggling with depression and anxiety, this fuels the fires even more. We look at what others have, even simply peace of mind, and we question God's motives. We think of all our suffering while the wicked enjoy a day of golf or gardening. Everywhere we go and wherever we look, envy cooks and boils within our blood. Forget about having things, we would even take the joy of being able to sit outside and watch the birds eat. Envy—it is an evil that kills us daily.

As Proverbs 14:30 says, "It is rottenness of our bones." It digs in deep, and like a tapeworm, it works its way into every fiber of our being. From there it evolves into anger, and from anger into hatred, and from hatred into self-righteousness. Everyone becomes wrong, and we become right—since we must be if we are suffering so for Christ. We then assume that anyone who is doing well must be in sin, for truly the righteous must suffer. Well, that can be true and not true. The righteous will suffer, but having things doesn't also make you a sinner either. No, it's where you find your true joy. Remember, money is not the root of all evil, but the love of it is. Friend, in your season of pain, do not envy, for it only wounds our own souls and no one else's. Seek Christ, find joy and find peace.

March 22 - Help, There's a Monster Following Me

For Thou art my lamp, O lord: and the lord will lighten my darkness. (2 Sam. 22:29)

I remember as a child growing up with this one vivid fear: having to go down my basement. It was damp and dark, yet it wasn't so much the going down that frightened me but the coming back up the stairs. Now, this might sound odd, but as a child, going down those stairs, though it was dark, I could still see in front of me. I knew where I was going as I went down there many times before. I knew I had to reach way up high to flick on the light switch, which happened to be at the bottom of the steps. This made it even worse as I had to walk down into the dark until I could get to that darn switch, reach up, and flick it on. Yet again, it wasn't as bad going down as it was leaving because when I had to go up the stairs, I had to shut off the light and then go up the steps without knowing what was behind me. I tell you, every time I would run up those steps, I was certain that there was some creature ready to grab at my heels. I would swear that I actually felt his hot monster breath behind me.

Now, that's a child's silliness and innocent fears, but do we really lose all those fears of the dark? I don't think we ever do even as our Lord speaks about the battle between darkness and light. Darkness is truly a creepy place to live when you are a child, that's true, but when an enemy such as depression or anxiety overtakes you, it feels just as creepy even as an adult. Now, I could focus this devotion on the darkness we can't see ahead of us, but I want to do something different and focus on the darkness that lies behind us. To a person who has never dealt with depression or anxiety, this would make no sense; but for those of us who have, we know it all too well. It's the fear of that darkness past coming back to get us. It's the fear of feeling good and worrying that the old monster will reappear. "What if it comes back?" is as much of a reality as going through it. Many a time that fear of past darkness would steal the joy of my present light.

Dear friend, I would present this word of hope to you today: As much as God is the Lord over future darkness, He is also the Lord of past darkness. If He lit your path in the past and is lighting your path in the present, He will certainly keep that light turned on. Sure, there will be days when it feels like that monster of darkness is at your heels again, but remind yourself constantly: "For Thou art my lamp, O LORD: and the LORD will lighten my darkness". He is the same yesterday, today, and forever. And yes, God is even bigger than the boogie man.

March 23 - Help, There's a Monster Following Me—Again

For by Thee I have run through a troop: by my God have I leaped over a wall. (2 Sam. 22:30)

March 23 and summer is calling your name, not only seasonal summer but spiritual summer. A place where the air will be sweeter and the days longer. Hold on, my friend, it is coming. Sure, we must go through spring to get to summer, but at least we know summer always follows spring. Okay, now for those who are paying attention, you might have noticed that we have used this scripture, 2 Samuel 22:30, before. But that's okay because the Word of God is new and fresh every day, and today it will speak even brighter than it did before. What I like about this scripture is the focus on the past tense. "I *have run* through a troop, by my God I *have leaped* over a wall."

See, David could sing such praises to the Lord because He knew what God has done for Him in the past. Now, I would note something very important: the Lord's provision from scary monsters didn't mean David will never face them again in the future. David knew that monsters were a part of this present evil world, and if the Lord was with David in past battles, He would be with Him in future ones. Also notice how David says, "By my God have I leaped over a wall." Notice it was still David doing the leaping, but that the Lord was just giving him a leg-up. Notice also what David was able to fight in the Lord's strength—a *troop*, a company of people, a band of robbers. David was able to face monsters much bigger than himself. He did it in the past, and so he knew it would work the same in the future.

So yes, monsters are part of life, and they do tend to follow us as they are always hungry. We must be careful not to do the victory dance as if we have beaten every foe because there will be more to face. Yes, let's dance about this present victory, but also think somberly about the future ones to come. They will be defeated, of that there is no doubt, but nevertheless, they will keep coming. As to a time and a place where monsters no longer live, well, that is only heaven. Get used to monsters. Know where to kick them and know who gives you the strength and wisdom to kick them.

March 24 - The Dragon Slayer / Monster Killer

As for God, His way is perfect; the word of the lord is tried: He is a buckler to all them that trust in Him. (2 Sam. 22:31)

Sorry, more monster talk again, but it's simply how things are. Today I wish you to focus on the monster slayer more than the monsters. Over the last few days, we have spoken about where they live and how persistent they are. We have spoken about how the Lord helps us to defeat them. Today I want to focus on the Lord and how He is able to defeat them. See, if I were to tell you about the monsters in our lives, you would agree. And if I were to tell you that God can defeat any monster, you would also agree and say great! But what if I told you about God and that He is really an ice-cream man who does monster fighting only on weekends? It's His hobby and that's about it—I think all of a sudden your countenance would drop, and all hope would be gone.

It's like learning for the first time that your dad can't really beat up everyone. It's a sad day in any child's life, but praise be to our God it will never be a sad day in ours because He can defeat any monster. It's a 100-percent guarantee of victory every time. Now, how do we know this about our Lord? Well, David explains it to us again moving on in 2 Samuel 22:31: "As for God—His way is perfect," meaning His methods and weapons are tried and true. Next, David speaks of the Lord's Word—"It is a tried word." It is a word that you can always count on; if the Lord says it, it is as good as gold. Notice also that David uses the word *LORD*—*Yehovah* sounded out (yeh-ho-vaw'), *the* Self-Existent or Eternal One.

I like *Yahweh* myself. Using this name for God gives us all the kick we need. David is simply saying by using this name that this is the real deal, the big McCoy. My daddy can beat up your daddy any day or time. My Abba Father can do this because He is the maker of all things, even the maker of Satan himself, and the Creator can always destroy the creation. Next, notice how David places a clause here or a small print disclaimer. God is a shield and protector but only to those who trust Him to do so.

So today, if you're facing those emotional demons and monsters, remember who can defeat them. Also make sure you trust in Him to defeat them. We can't face a sniper and expect to live if we don't put on our bulletproof vest. We can hold the vest and carry it around all day. We can believe in the vest and even show it off to people, but if you don't put it on, it won't stop one single bullet. Put on Jesus and stop the monsters.

March 25 - We Need to Stand on Solid Ground

For who is God, save the LORD? *And who is a rock, save our God? (2 Sam. 22:32)*

For those of you who have ever been stuck in the mud or snow, you know the feeling of helplessness. This past year in the northeastern part of the country, we had the biggest snowfall in history—well, at least in my history. We had three feet of snow, and it hit us by surprise. One lady from my church ended up stranded for close to nineteen hours. She was on a main road but simply couldn't keep moving anymore. All forward momentum was lost, and the snow just piled around her and all the other cars caught in rush-hour traffic. She ended up sleeping there overnight. While stranded, she would call me every few hours, and I would call her. It was frustrating because I had a big four-wheel drive truck plus my little but mighty Jeep, but even they could not move. The problem was simple—no traction due to unstable footing. Even if you could get on top of the snow, you would quickly sink back down. Even the snowplows were stuck. It was a scene out of an apocalyptic movie.

Now, snow is one thing, and mud is another. There are some tires better for mud, and some made simply for snow. Yet in the end, no matter what type of tires you have, no matter if you're even operating a bulldozer, lack of solid footing will stop you cold. Now, in the spiritual realm, it's somewhat similar. There are our fears and emotional mud. There is the place at which we wish to arrive at—*a sound mind*, and the obstacle is *lack of spiritual footing*. See, even if we have money, the right medications, the best counselors and doctors, if we have not spiritual footing, we will sink and never move forward.

In 2 Samuel 22:32, David describes who God is. He uses a terrestrial term to describe a celestial being. Certainly God is not a rock, but He is like a rock. He is strong, unmovable, and solid. Our Lord is a place where we can rest all of our hopes and cares upon. David had been followed by Saul for a long time, and he was not a figment of David's imagination. No, he was a real enemy with real swords and real hatred. David couldn't rely on earthly weapons all the time. David needed not spears and arrows; he needed the Lord God. David made it through the dark times because he had his feet on what always got him through the dark times. No, not sand or water but on a mountain of power and stability.

Today, dear friend, as you depend on many things to deliver you—I'm not saying that they can't or won't—but if your trust is only in them and not in Christ, then they will not work. When we talk about medications in the companion book (sold separately), you will notice my warning about medications, though I am not opposed to them in certain cases: but they will only work if God allows them and only if you have faith in Him and not in them.

March 26 - I Don't Know the Way Today

God is my strength and power: And He maketh my way perfect. (2 Sam. 22:33)

Each day that we face is a new day. Sounds silly to point that out, but it is a simple truth, meaning that each day needs new approaches. Some days are easy with little or no obstacles and are over and done before we know it, yet for the most part, most days are not like that. Those "normal" days are usually hard days, days where people hurt you, accidents surprise you, and complications confuse you. Add to that day the feelings of anxiety and / or depression, and it's a bad day to the tenth power. When these days happen, what are we to do? Where are we to turn? Panic starts to set in, and the fear cycle begins. It's not a pleasant place to be, yet it's a place we must be in order to live another day.

My dear friend, I wish that I could grab all the sad and depressed people and lock them away safely and then deal with all of their problems for them. Sounds nice, doesn't it? As you heard me say those words, a fleeting yet very real lightbulb went off. "Oh, if someone would tuck me under their arm, rock me off to sleep in a warm hammock. And while I lay sleeping, that person would make all my appointments, pay all my bills, and feed me when I get hungry." It's an interesting thought and not as silly as you might think. See, there was a time when that was your day. It was when you were an infant, a child, even while in your mother's womb. As a child, you could laugh and enjoy life as "another" was dealing with the pains of real-world living. What's funny is that as that child, all you dreamed of was being the adult and having freedom.

So we grow up, and all of a sudden, Mom and Dad can no longer rock us to sleep and deal with our problems. It is normally around the age of thirteen when we start to feel that comfort slipping away; some, even sooner. I believe the solution to all of this might be as simple as *transference*, the *transference of dependence*. That is, replacing Mom and Dad with Jesus Christ, our Heavenly Father. It is climbing into His papoose and saying, "Jesus, take me where you will." I know it sounds too simple, but it's really not, especially if we understand this one fact: being in that spiritual cocoon does not spare you from the weather of the world. If it's cold outside, you might feel some of it too. Even a child in the womb feels the jarring of a car accident or the g-forces of a carnival ride.

So today accept the fact that you must feel life, but you don't have to feel life. Makes no sense, you think, but what I mean is this:

God is my strength and power: And He maketh my way perfect. (2 Sam. 22:33)

The way of life we must travel is inevitable, but what is not is how it affects our spirit and soul. Cry out to the Lord and ask Him to carry you through this day. Ask Him to teach you to rest in His control and provision for the day. Picture Him with you as you go to the bank, deal with a mean coworker, and drive in a bad snowstorm. No, it's not a trick because Christ is there with us just waiting to carry us home. Will you let Him? That is the question.

March 27 - Walking on Shaky Ground

He maketh my feet like hinds' feet: and setteth me upon my high places. (2 Sam. 22:34)

If you have ever been hiking in the mountains, you know how difficult it is to keep from falling down. Try climbing up a rocky cliff or mountainside. The first thing you notice is that you slow way down. No longer are you skipping about, but you take very careful steps. You even watch where you place each foot like a novice guitar player watches his fingers on the fretboard. Each one is thought out and strategically placed in position. Well, that's all fine and dandy for mountain climbing, but what if your daily walk is like a mountain climb, a spiritual mountain climb? What if each day you step out the front door is a day of cliffs and dangerous slopes? We can't creep along at a snail's pace praying over each step. We can't tiptoe as if walking on glass; we have to progress and get things done.

Well, you are absolutely correct in saying so, and that is why the Lord gives to those who love Him—"feet like hinds' feet." The term *hinds' feet* can mean a few different things: a deer's feet, rear feet, a female deer's feet, or a young deer's feet. Either way it's okay as it points to one important fact. Deer and animals like them are excellent at walking on rocky and shaky ground. They can leap around sheer mountain cliffs without even giving it a second thought. Rocky Mountain rams excel at this.

Now, how does this all apply to you and me? Well, it applies perfectly as we look at life (in Christ). When in Christ, we are able to walk where others trip and fall. In Christ, we can walk in dangerous places and still do it with ease. In 2 Samuel 22:34, we notice that it's not something that we can learn in a hiking class but something that the Lord does. It is He who "makes my feet like hinds' feet." It is a transformation of who we are. It's making us into something that we weren't before. It's becoming a new creation in Christ. From a clumsy three-legged dog to an agile mountain lion. Then notice what happens in that place of agility—"and setteth me upon my high places" (2 Sam. 22:34b). Notice again who does the work. It is the Lord who places us up above the places of fear and gives us a holy vantage point.

Yet this vantage point can never be reached unless we get those *hinds' feet*. It's understanding that we can't put the cart before the horse. It's trusting in Christ, letting go of those training wheels, then heading out full-on and doing it without fear and without the training wheels. Life is rocky. Life with anxiety is even worse, but no matter what the state of our mental health, we can still climb up and over those rocks. We can and will walk on shaky ground and do it well.

March 28 - But There Are Mean People Out There

He teacheth my hands to war; so that a bow of steel is broken by mine arms. (2 Sam. 22:35)

I remember being a teenager in junior high, probably the worst part of my youth. I was one of the unpopular ones: being pushed into lockers, picked on, and made fun of. It was a living hell for a quiet, introverted person like me. I simply didn't know how to process mean people or how to deal with hurtful words and personal attacks. Not that I could have physically fought off anyone as I was a skinny little thing, but at least I could have intellectually fought back. It was hard, and I was so grateful when I grew up and bullies were a thing of the past. Well, that's partially true; though I didn't run into bullies anymore, I certainly ran into hurtful demeaning people all over. On the jobsite, at the office, just about everywhere, there is a person who lives off making you feel belittled. It's the perfect picture of the sinful heart of man. It's ugly, real ugly, but it is life. As I grew, these people didn't stop; they just mastered their game. In the business world and even in the church world, those (people killers) were always there. You know the ones—just seeing their face at church or at the local store sends shivers down your spine, the people who simply hate you, and yet you cannot understand why.

As a pastor, you try to get used to it, but it's never easy. No one likes to be hated without a cause, yet that is exactly what Jesus was—hated without a cause. They spat at Him, mocked Him, ripped off His beard. Yet through it all, how did He deal with them? He did it in the Father's might and power. He did it in peace and meekness. He used a type of warfare we have never seen before: strength under control and knowing that you could destroy your enemy with the whisper of your words and instead return their barbs with love, compassion, and forgiveness. It's like giving us a supernatural, superhero status, making us a *solider of the cross*. Our weapons are not carnal but spiritual.

In 2 Samuel 22:35, we learn of this superhero-type, unarmed warfare. "He teacheth my hands to war; so that a bow of steel is broken by mine arms." Now, could David break a bow of steel by his arms? No, and neither could I, but what can be broken are the powers of darkness that so easily beset us, those powers that we meet every day out in the streets, people who love to see us fail, people who don't understand our fears and make fun of our weaknesses. We don't want them destroyed, but we want to be able to stand up to them. We desire God's power through our weakness, and that is what the Lord offers us, to fear the enemy no more. Not just to have a defensive plan but also an offensive one. God will teach us how to fight these spiritual and emotional battles. We only have to be good students of His Word.

March 29 - Being Great

Thou hast also given me the shield of Thy salvation: and Thy gentleness hath made me great. (2 Sam. 22:36)

Rock and roll—not a proper way for a Christian devotion to start off, but I have to admit, I'm still a closet rock-and-roll fan. Sure, the words can be nasty and the themes evil, but I stay away from those. In fact, I'm not really into modern music at all, but I do remember the classic rock I grew up with in the late seventies and early- to mid-eighties. When I was in high school, I really started to get into music, and I began playing in your typical garage band. Some of them were pretty good, and one of them was real good, and my dreams of becoming a famous rock star were flamed.

I remember running into this man who later turned out to be dishonest, playing on the dreams of young, unsuspecting musicians. He was a make-believe record producer, and he told us that by next time this year, we would be playing Madison Square Garden in New York City. Talk about pouring gasoline on a fire. The band members and I spent a summer telling all our friends that we were going to be famous. Guess you figured out what really happened—I grew up a little wiser and a little less excited. My dream of being famous was not to be, and stardom would have to be left only to nighttime dreams.

That is why I am so happy I found Jesus Christ. Jesus reignited that simmering flame. Yet this time, not so I would be known by the world but to be known by God Himself. See, to be admired by our friends and families is okay, but it's fleeting and, at the least, disappointing. I can only be so good of a dad, a husband, a pastor, a friend, and a person, but in Christ Jesus, I can be great. Dear friend, being great and loved might seem like the furthest thing from your mind. You might think of yourself and say, "Forget about doing anything worthwhile in my life, I am just hoping I can make it through another year." I know how you feel as I too felt that way and sometimes still do, but the Lord has news for all of us. He can make us great! Not great in the world's sense of being a celebrity, but great in the sense that you will have purpose and reason and hope.

God will take you just as you are and create in you a new and wonderful creation. A creation that will be great because God is great, and God doesn't make dummies He creates wonders. In 2 Samuel 22:36, it reads, "Thou hast also given me the shield of Thy salvation: and Thy gentleness hath made me great." I love that wording, "thy gentleness hath made me great." The word *gentleness* in Greek is not what you might think; in fact, it's really completely the opposite. *Gentleness (anah)* in the KJV is "abase self, afflict self, chasten self, deal hardly with." Now, though some might disagree, I believe that it simply means God's *tough love* has made me great. I read once that great faith requires great trials. Well, to become great Christians, we need a heavy hand of discipline laced with God's love. Friend, we can be great in Christ, and God might just use this season of depression to make you great.

March 30 - Anything Can Be an Enemy

Thou hast enlarged my steps under me; so that my feet did not slip.
I have pursued mine enemies, and destroyed them; and turned not
again until I had consumed them. (2 Sam. 22:37–38)

In the day and age in which we now live, enemies have not gone away; they have simply changed. Back in the day, an enemy of the nation was a distinct army with uniforms and tanks. They were from a certain country that declared war on us and us on them. Well, that was then, and this is now. Our enemies wear no uniform, carry no flag, swear allegiance to no country. They are in everyday clothes, living right here with us. They work with us and walk among us in all areas of life. If anything, it has made modern warfare harder, not easier. It's no longer a bigger tank we need but better technologies, firewalls for our computers, and high-tech medical vaccinations for our bodies.

Enemies may change, it's true, but what's at the core of an enemy is the same. They hate us, want us dead, and would love to see us left useless. In the spiritual realm, it's clear to see that also. Our enemies there are sin and the world. Depression and anxiety, temptation and lust, they are our enemies. Greed and corruption camp about us. They have plans of attack and stealth, high-tech infantry. As in any war, our approach to winning is always the same no matter how the enemies of man have changed. We must win. They must be defeated and the least personal damage done.

In 2 Samuel 22:37–38, we see a small picture of this battle. We see how the Lord fights for us (through us). We see how the Lord gives us the footing we need so we don't fall, how we must still pursue our enemies and destroy them but do it in a way that they don't turn back on us and destroy us. David was a good solider and king, but he was also a good follower. He knew that any enemy should be viewed as a formidable one and should not be taken lightly. He also knew that the Lord was the real commander in chief, and at the end of the day, all battle plans should first go through Him.

Friend, yours and my emotional issues, fears, depression, and so on—they are enemies of the cross, as well enemies against us. We must look at each one sometimes as a terrorist set on blowing up our peace and purpose in Christ. We must walk circumspectly because the days are evil. Yet most of all, we must walk knowing that we will always win no matter what or who our enemy is. Jesus will defeat them, and we will be victorious. There is no defeat in God's army so there should be no spirit of defeat in our souls.

March 31 - Thank Him Today

It is God that avengeth me, and that bringeth down the people under me, And that bringeth me forth from mine enemies: Thou also hast lifted me up on high above them that rose up against me: Thou hast delivered me from the violent man.

Therefore I will give thanks unto Thee, O lord, among the heathen, and I will sing praises unto Thy name. (2 Sam. 22:48–50)

Throughout this devotional, you will see a few threads running through it. One of them is the power of true praise unto the Lord, thanking God during the worst of times and waiting with faith for His deliverance. I tell you, until you can do that, not much will change in your spiritual struggles. Sure, it's great to praise God after a major deliverance and victory. It's great to let the world know that your God has made you glad. Yet is it not just as important, if not even more important, to God to thank Him in the very fire of affliction? Imagine the Lord's pleasure if at the Red Sea the people would have praised God before the waters parted. If they would have given thanks as Moses delayed his time coming down from the mountain. To thank God for how a situation will turn out before it happens is the greatest form of worship you can ever muster.

I often watch what goes on at different churches, and I'm amazed at how much time is spent in worship and praise yet, at the same time, how little the people are grateful to God. Many of them don't even know why they are raising holy hands unto the Lord. They don't know why they are praising God. They don't understand the real heart of worship. Now, I don't care if you're singing hymns or jumping to a full worship band, what I am concerned about is what is truly in the heart. I've seen just as dead praise in quite reserved hymn worship as I have seen in full-blown modern worship. So it's not the style of your worship but the heart of your worship. Are we praising God in hopes He will do us good? Are we praising God for the good that He has already done? Or are we praising Him in a nasty trial when all says fail but we still trust Him full-on, all the way?

That last type of worship is the greatest: to praise God in the storm, on the boat, in the hospital bed, at the doctor's office waiting for test results. Of all the Lord looks for in worship, it is my belief that *preemptive praise* is His favorite. Today, as this month comes to a close, I ask and suggest that you start the new month with a heart of thanksgiving, saying to the Lord, "Lord, I am in a pickle here, but I want to thank You right now for how You will get me out of it." It's not easy, and we must be sure we are not just mouthing the words to get the blessings. But if we do master this *true faith* in Jesus Christ, we will be opening up ourselves to a newness of life like we have never tasted before. So try it, you'll like it. Praise Him now.

April

April 1 - Believing in Hope

Who against hope believed in hope, that he might become the father of many nations, according to that which was spoken, So shall thy seed be. (Rom. 4:18)

Praise the Lord it is April 1. To the world, it is a foolish day, but to us in Christ, a new day. See, any day is a new day and a gift from the Lord. To call any day foolish is to call God's Word foolish. Psalm 118:24 says, "This is the day which the LORD hath made; we will rejoice and be glad in it." Today is the day that the Lord has made, so let's enter it with hope. Winter is past, and spring is blooming. Darkness is fading, and the sun is rising. Now, I know those are just words, and if you are going through hell today, they will only be words. But, dear friend, these are not my words but God's words. To say it is just words is to say that God's entire Bible is just words. They are all true, or they are all lies. I know you know the truth to that, so let's not even go there. No, let's believe in hope: God's hope, which is not the world's hope.

Think of Abraham who was promised a seed, an offspring, that through it, God would bless the entire world. What if Abraham said to God, "Yeah, those are nice words, Lord, but I don't believe it"? What if all the promises that God made throughout the entire Bible were not believed and were laughed off as just nice words? Moses wouldn't have done what Moses did. David wouldn't have done what David did, and so on and so on. It was because of those who hoped in God's Word that God's Word became real in their lives.

I often read many nice and uplifting quotes on the Internet. So many are so sweet and encouraging, but they can really do nothing because there is no power behind them. They are just the words of man saying nice things about man. Man's words have no authority, so man's words mean nothing. But God's Word is different; by it, the heaven and earth were formed. The galaxies were stretched out, the planets were placed in orbit, and the DNA strands in our bodies were set in order. See, God's Word is the Creator's Word, and if He says that it is worth hoping for, then it is!

Today you might be facing the hardest day of your life. Hope might sound like a foolish child's nursery rhyme to your ears, but today listen with a different ear. Listen to God's Word and know it is true, it is real, it is positive, and it is ready to rock your world. April 1—we would be a fool not to embrace it and ask the Lord to bless it. Better days are ahead because God makes the future, and God can only do good.

(Ps. 91:11)

April 2 - Not Alone When Alone

For He shall give His angels charge over thee, to keep thee in all thy ways.

It's a nice thought to think of angels watching over us, but it's another thing to see it in action. Today I am here to share with you the facts of God's spiritual army and the reality of it on full display. First of all, His heavenly hosts are not little babies with cupid arrows; if so, I would be afraid. No, His angels are mighty beings of war, fighters, and servants for our Lord. They are dressed in full holy body armor with strength and power enough to slay the enemy at the Lord's command. Remember when the soldiers came to take Jesus and one of His followers lopped off an ear. What did Jesus say to them in so many words, but that if He wanted, He could call down the entire heavenly hosts? He could call an army as *if He even needed one.* Jesus was just making a point of His authority and power over all circumstances of life.

Friend, there is a real spiritual battle going on around us, and our very soul is the target. Yet be at peace. God has our back, even when you feel like you are all alone and no one is there to help. All your contacts have left you down, and your little black book has no more numbers to call. Even then when alone, you are not.

When I had my first battle with depression, I will never forget this one particular situation in which I actually saw how real the battle was. I was able to realize the ever-present power of God and His mind fixed on my little world. I was working at my secular place of employment before I went into ministry. Thoughts of suicide were running full speed ahead. A strange man stopped by and seemed to be following me around. He came up behind me and with a creepy, evil voice said, "Scott wants to kill himself." I kid you not. I turned around and said, "What did you say?" He just smiled, and I ran off to another part of the building in a state of anxiety. A full-blown demonic attack was upon me, and it was coming down to the wire. I was barely functioning at my job, and holding it together was stressing me to the limit. This last attack was too much, and I cried out to God, "Help me, Lord, please."

One half-hour went by, and another person stopped by, a woman whom I knew was a Christian. She said she was driving down the road, and she felt this strong feeling to stop by and visit me. When I told her what had just happened, she was not surprised. She prayed with me for a few moments and left. I was strengthened and made it through the day. Was my battle over? No, but I knew better than ever that it was a real battle and also that God knew it was a real battle. I understood that day that God is aware of every situation, and He will send another Christian or angel if need be. I have met some of those angels too, but that's for another day. So, dear friend, hold on. The Calvary is coming, and not a moment too soon.

April 3 - But Do You Love Him?

Because he hath set his love upon me, therefore will I deliver him: I will set him on high, because he hath known My Name. (Ps. 91:14)

There is a famous account in the scriptures of Jesus asking Peter this interesting question, "But do you love me?" It is found in John 21 and a worthy read, no doubt. Peter is perplexed and, toward the last request, a little angry. Why would the Lord ask an apostle if he loves Him? Would Jesus even question such a thing as Jesus knows our hearts anyway? I believe it is because He wants us to see what He already knows. Many times we don't love Jesus as we should, and without that full-on, sold-out love for Jesus Christ, nothing really matters.

In my own life, I would question my devotion for the Lord. I know I love Him, but do I really love Him? Odd sentence, I know, but I also know how I can love my wife while at the same time love myself more. I know there has been more than one occasion when my wife would want to spend money on something for herself, and I would get all upset about it. Yet there were other times when I needed a new part for my Jeep and wouldn't think twice about spending that money. It was in those situations that the Lord would show me where my true passion was. At the end of the day, my life was built around me.

As we read in Psalm 91:14, let's notice this same emphasis on *us loving Him*. Notice the word *set*. We must set, lock on target, focus on the Lord. Like setting our clocks to the atomic clock which all time is set on, we must also use Jesus as our true north. He is our standard in all that we do, say, breathe, and think. It all must be focused on Him. Next, notice the results of *setting* our love on God. Because of this love, God delivers us. Now, it is true that before we loved Him, He Loved us, even when we were dead in trespass and sin. But we still need to fall in love with Christ.

Many times in my counseling sessions, a young lady would describe her desire to meet that man of her dreams. "I feel so alone and need to meet that man. Why won't God bring this man to me?" Well, the answer is simple: until you fall in love with Jesus, all other loves are only distractions from us loving Him. That is why we need to first find peace in Christ alone. It is being at peace while in the middle of depression, poverty, and loneliness, still satisfied with (only) Jesus Christ. Until you get to that place, nothing will release you from your fears because your trust was never really in God but in everything else.

Please, today, fall in love with our Lord. Desire to know Him, and not so He will do things for you but simply so you can know Him better. We need a no-strings-attached love for God; meaning, we love Him regardless of what He does or doesn't do. Do you love Him? Do I love him? We must, or we will surely perish.

April 4 - Wipe the Tears and Stand

And he said unto me, "Son of man, stand upon thy feet, and I will speak unto thee." (Ezek. 2:1)

As a parent who has three boys, I know a thing or two about broken hearts. I know of little souls who fall down and just could do nothing more than throw a pity party for themselves. My two youngest boys are what I like to call my drama queens. Complaining and crying over a broken toy or ruined day was very common to them. When my little guy would have a bad day or something gone wrong with his plans, he would throw himself into this inconsolable place of weeping. We couldn't speak to him to calm him because he didn't act rational enough for him to hear you. My wife and I would literally have to drag him into his room and tell him to come out when he stopped crying. It might have seemed mean, but it always worked. We couldn't hold and hug him in that crazy state, nor could we give him words of explanation to why this or that happened. We could only speak to him to comfort him when he regained control of himself.

Now, my middle child, as he grew older, carried this into his young adult life. Not that he would cry uncontrollably, but that he would always assume it was all doom and gloom. The sky is falling, and it is all over. God hates me, and my life will never be good. These would be common words from his mouth when life at nineteen didn't pan out the way he hoped. My wife was always better at dealing with him than me. She would just tell me, "Let him alone and let him pace and moan until all his complaining and irrational thoughts are passed." He would have plenty of them as silly things always seemed to come out of his mouth. "That's it, I am quitting," "God doesn't want me happy," "I am never talking to that friend again," "I'm moving to Montana, and I've got to get out of this house." On and on it would go yet always with the same result. He would calm down, we would ask him if he was through complaining, we would console him, pray with him, and let him know that God will take care of him and his issue. God always did, and the sky never fell.

My middle son reminds me of us all who are having a meltdown. Depression has set in, anxiety is building, crying and complaining are moving in, and then anger begins to manifest itself. Through all of those emotions, we wait for the Lord to come in and save the day, but He doesn't. We are surprised that with all of our threats and moaning that God doesn't send down the angels to whisk us off our feet of sorrow onto mountaintops of joy. My friend, He doesn't do that because God is not moved by tantrums but by silence. It is only when we calm down, clear our minds, confess our sins, and listen that God can speak. We simply need to wipe our tears, get out of the bed, and say, "Lord, okay, I am ready to listen." Many times it is when we are the most silent that God does the most speaking. God is God, and He won't try to get a word in edgewise until we leave the spot for Him to interject it.

April 5 - God Says Go, We Must Go

And the angel of the lord said unto Elijah, "Go down with him: be not afraid of him." And he arose, and went down with him unto the king. (2 Kings 1:15)

One of the hardest things in this life of fear and anxiety is the fear of riding without training wheels for the first time. Anxiety and depression are a lot like that and even more. It is very much like riding a bike *with* training wheels. Notice I said with training wheels. I don't know about you, but riding a bike with training wheels isn't that easy. In fact, if you were to try to ride with them now as adults, it would be downright dangerous. If you can remember back that far, you would remember the bike wanting to go straight even when you turned. The feeling of falling over then stopping as the training wheels would catch. They would do so with a jerking motion, and it was never a smooth ride. In a lot of ways, riding without the extra wheels was much easier and much more enjoyable.

I can remember riding without my training wheels for the first time. It was a nail-biter yet oh so sweet a transition. If you could remember back then, you would also remember that it was never your choice to take the training wheels off but your parents'. Why did they push us so to get the wheels taken off? Didn't they know that we could fall over and get hurt? Didn't they know how dangerous life could be without those extra wheels? Well, maybe they did, but they also knew how much better the ride would be in the long run. They knew that you could not ride on training wheels forever. It is a hard place for a parent, and maybe so too with God.

God always wants us to grow and take the next step. He loves us so much, and if He could choose to only say one sentence to us, I believe it would be, "Be not afraid." Now, I make this point to bring us to the place where the Lord really wants us to be. He doesn't want us tied down with crippling fear. He doesn't want us balancing on a tightrope forever. There must be a time when we take off the training wheels. There must be a time when we look unto Jesus and start pedaling toward Him.

Now, what does it mean to take off those training wheels? Well, it could mean taking that next step of faith and simply getting out of bed, or maybe it's taking that job that has always scared you. Maybe it's talking to that person who has always frightened you. Maybe it's time to try a day without the anxiety medication you have been depending on for so many years. I don't know what's right for you, but I do know it has everything to do with leaving your comfort zone and stepping out into God's zone. If anything great is going to happen in your life, it will never happen in the comfort zone. We must let go and, with shaky legs, begin walking toward our Lord.

April 6 - He Knows

And God heard the voice of the lad; and the angel of God called to Hagar out of heaven, and said unto her, "What aileth thee, Hagar? Fear not; for God hath heard the voice of the lad where he is." (Gen. 21:17)

If you have ever been accused of something that you didn't do, you know how painful that can be. Imagine being placed in jail for a crime you didn't do. It happens all the time, and to me, it seems like a bitter place to be. As a pastor, sometimes you get accused of things, misquoted, or misrepresented. It is not my favorite dilemma, of that there is no doubt. What's worse is when other people start to believe the accusation, and you find yourself having to defend yourself for something you didn't do. In such times as those, I have often found comfort in the fact that at least God knows the truth. As fleeting as that comfort is, it is still the truth and really all that should matter. When it comes to our emotional struggles, I find the same pain. People don't know what we are really feeling. Friends don't understand; some outright don't believe us and secretly declare that we are faking it for attention. If you have been there, then you know that pain. Yes, our pain is a hidden one, which makes it so much worse.

Recently, a childhood friend of mine was diagnosed with leukemia. He has been posting his daily struggles on a popular Internet social media site. Every day he posts his setbacks and his accomplishments. People post back and give him kudos and words of encouragement to keep his spirits up. I also do and pray that he pulls out of this horrible place. As I have been following his daily progress wrought with nausea and pain, I also was thinking how much we need the same encouragement from our loved ones, but we seldom get it. The reason is clear and yet oh so sad. For mental illness is the hidden pain, the unacceptable sickness. There are no tubes and IV drips; there are no hospital beds and blood to show. Sure, in some extreme cases you might end up in the hospital, but no one really has the same sympathy or the same desire to visit you. It is all a hush-hush moment, and your family is not quick to tell the world where you are.

In Geneses 21:17, we get a word from God about such situations. Those situations the world and family may not know about, but God does. That is the peace we all need, the peace in knowing that God *knows*. When Hagar was forced to leave with Ishmael, it was a lonely pain and a confusing one. No one really cared, and it was all a hasty change of life. Imagine being Hagar—alone, cast out, and responsible for a child. I'm sure she felt the pain of being alone in her distress, but as we read, she was not, and God made sure she knew it. Dear friend, if today you are facing this lonely pain, remember you are not alone. God reached out to Hagar and Ishmael (where they were). And as God reached out for Hagar and told her not to fear, God is telling us the same thing. "I have your back, dear child. I know."

April 7 - Irrational Fear

Deliver me, I pray thee, from the hand of my brother, from the hand of Esau: for I fear him, lest he will come and smite me, and the mother with the children. (Gen. 32:11)

I come from a long line of worriers. My grandfather was a nervous Nellie as was my father. No matter what people say, fear and depression are sometimes in our DNA, and there is nothing we can do to change that. My grandfather suffered the worse and actually had shock treatment back when that was all they knew. Even my children are affected by it as my middle son really has my worrisome nature. Now, I know some will disagree and declare that faith should eliminate all of our fears, but bear in mind that faith can't change our old sinful nature. If you are from a gene line that is prone to cancer, the odds are you will get it also. Recently, a famous female movie star had a double mastectomy knowing that her chances of getting breast cancer were high due to her family background. Be that as it may, some weaknesses are part of who we are. They are part of the fall of man; they are what we see in society today. It's a corrupted gene pool, no doubt, and in my case, being afraid has been a part of me since birth.

Now, not all fear is bad as the Lord placed fear in us for our good. Like the fear of falling is a good one if you like to play on rooftops. Good fears keep us alive, and the fear of the Lord keeps us right with God. But what of irrational fear? In Genesis 32:11, Jacob had some fears. Some were good, but some were irrational, and it was the irrational ones that caused him the most pain. Jacob lived for many years afraid of his brother. He lived wondering if his brother would ever try to get back at him and smite him. Interesting thing here is that Esau never killed Jacob, and things never turned out as Jacob thought throughout all the years of worrying.

Sometimes when we pray, we must understand not to ask God to remove the things we are afraid of but rather ask God to remove the fear we have of the things that will never happen. Of all the things I have worried about in my life, maybe 10 percent of them even came to pass. That means that 90 percent of my fears were hours and years that were stolen from me. They were years that I gave up by my own irrational fear. So no, I cannot change my molecular makeup, but I can (through Christ) have my *old nature* become a new creature in Christ. One that trusts in the Lord more and one that stops worrying about things I could never change even if I tried. In the end, the Lord controls your destiny and mine. To think that our fears and sobbing can change that is to put ourselves in the place of God.

Dear friend, if you suffer with fear, please instead learn to see God more clearly. When you begin to see and remember God's faithfulness in your past, you will have less to fear in your future. Remember, most things that we fret and worry about *never* happen. As they say, worrying is like a rocking chair; it gives us something to do but never gets us anywhere.

April 8 - Sin Is to Be Considered

And Moses said unto the people, "Fear not: for God is come to prove you, and that His fear may be before your faces, that ye sin not." (Exod. 20:20)

I've been a Christian now for close to thirty years. In all of those years, I have learned, watched, and seen the many ways of Christians and how we all think. We are an odd lot sometimes, and as I have often said, "Some of the oddest people I have ever met are Christians." Yet God loves us all, and He loves to use the despised of the world to do the mighty things for Himself. I'm not an exception to that rule as I often wonder why, with all of my weaknesses and hang-ups, the Lord uses me at all. His grace and love are certainly amazing.

Now, through those years of being and watching Christians, I have found that we have a few shortcomings. One of them is to always assume that every problem and difficulty in life is always from either one or another place. One we will often declare is from Satan. "Satan is causing me harm and out to get me," which is true to some degree, but not every single stubbed toe or stomach flu is from the cloven-hoofed one. Then there is the other place where we always assume our trials come. That is, we are being persecuted for righteousness's sake: "People are out to get me because I'm a Christian." That too might be the case, but again, not all the time. Not unless you live in some third-world country where Christians are being killed for their faith. So far, as a citizen of the good old USA, I have not had my life threatened for following Christ.

Well, that leaves us with the third possibility of our trials and problems. And that is divine discipline. Now, in all my years as a Christian, I have watched Christians, and I must declare I cannot remember a single case where a Christian said, "I'm being chastised for my sins." Now, the reason we don't hear that often is because we really don't think sin is a big thing, and two, we don't think or believe that God really corrects His children for sin. Well, the Bible is pretty clear that any good father corrects his children, and so God, being the perfect parent, better be laying the belt to our hide once in a while.

How do I know this? Well, I know this, for one, because the Bible says so, but also because I have learned it in my own life. I remember one particular time when I forgot about this loving Father's divine correction. I was going through a difficult time in my life, and everything was going south. I assumed all of my problems were due to other people as I was doing everything right. Then one day, the Lord spoke to my heart and said in His still small voice, "Ah, wake up, do you not remember the sin that you are constantly in? Do you not know that I cannot bless until this is confessed and, even more, until this area is removed from your life?" I got the message and said, "Oh, that sin. Okay, Lord, you're right, and I have just been confessing and committing the same thing over and over without ever planning on changing that area in my life."

So, dear friend, I'm not saying that your struggle today is the result of sin or that every problem is the result of sin, but it may be. So ask the Lord to examine you and point out where you might have a hidden thorn giving you all that pain.

April 9 - Now Go Get It

Behold, the lord thy God hath set the land before thee: go up and possess it, as the lord God of thy fathers hath said unto thee; "fear not, neither be discouraged." (Deut. 1:21)

Peace of mind, joy, happiness, and reward. Those are conditions that we with emotional issues such as depression and anxiety feel we will never experience. Often we see our lives as one of never-ending pain and sorrow. A life of fleeting mountaintops and then back into the trenches. We watch other people and see their joys and blessings and assume that, that's just for the *other* guy. "My life is one bent on sorrow, and that's just the way it is." What's amazing is how fast we can fall into that thought process. With regard to depression, one bout of it leaves you feeling that it will never pass. Anxiety is the same thing, and while you are fighting it, it feels like an eternity of agony. One hour of depression, one hour of anxiety is just too much to bear, and if it happened once, it will happen again. It is just who you are, and any dreams of doing something big for the Lord is just not in the cards. Well, I'm here to tell you that it is just not true. God can still use us, take us, and place us into places where we would have never thought possible.

I will go as far to say that it was because of my two bouts with serious depression that God was able to use me. It was with my first bout that I got my call to become a pastor. I wrote my first book and entered the first major growth spurt in my walk with Christ. Through my second bout, I really started to understand the need for more dialogue about depression and anxiety. This devotional that you are reading now is somewhat an offshoot of my last bout—not to mention the many, many years of remission that I enjoyed and where I served the Lord, leading many to Christ and becoming a Christian counselor specializing in depression and anxiety. I was able to host my own radio call-in show about emotional issues and also write a newspaper column helping people with their walk with the Lord. I moved from New York to California and took over my first church. All of these amazing things would have never have happened if it were not for those very difficult times of darkness and pain. It made me more compassionate and understanding.

As a pastor, I learned to be humble and never trust in myself but in the Lord alone. And not only did those times of pain and weaknesses open the doors for amazing opportunities, they also empowered me to endure a church split, personal struggles, and very challenging times that I could never have made through in my own strength. Please, if today is a day that has you thinking it is all over, please change that thought to—it is all just beginning. A new chapter in your life is starting, and it will be amazing. The Christian life has never been boring for me. God is good, and God is so faithful. No matter how old or young you are or what disability you might have, God can still use you.

April 10 - Longer and Better

> That thou mightest fear the lord thy God, to keep all his statutes and his commandments, which I command thee, thou, and thy son, and thy son's son, all the days of thy life; and that thy days may be prolonged. (Deut. 6:2)

What we spoke about on the April 9 devotion, we will also speak about today. Yet today we will focus more on time instead of circumstance. Yes, the Lord can and will bless you and use you where you are. But also, He can lengthen your days so that your life will be a full one as well as a productive one. Now, for a person who may be dealing with depression today, living a long life might not be on your top list of things. I know that feeling, and I know that desire to have a shorter life than a longer one. But for those who look to the Lord, we must remember that He can change our whole outlook in life so that besides doing more, you will actually desire to live more.

See, if the Lord has a plan for you, He also needs to make sure you are up to keeping that plan, able to perform what He has called you to do. If the Lord is calling you to a place of service, would He not then also make you able to serve? Like the old adage, "God doesn't call the equipped, He equips the called." That's His job, and so we should not fear if we have enough skills or talents. We need not look at our shortcomings and declare ourselves ill-fit to serve. Life can be better and longer, and at the end of the day, it might be that depression and anxiety were the catalysts to it.

I cannot tell you how important it is to understand what the Lord can do. How one day we can be living in New Jersey in a dead-end job, depressed and alone, and in one year we are living clear across the country and serving

God in amazing ways. God does the impossible, and we are only to follow His power over the impossible. Climb in and aboard and see the salvation of the Lord.

April 11 - No Use Dead

And the lord commanded us to do all these statutes, to fear the lord our God, for our good always, that He might preserve us alive, as it is at this day. (Deut. 6:24)

I love the words of David in Psalm 30:9: "What profit is there in my blood, when I go down to the pit? Shall the dust praise thee? Shall it declare thy truth?" David, for all the fear he had, had ten times more boldness and faith. I love his attitude as he declared to the Lord, "Hey, if I'm dead, I can't do much praising of you." I believe that was one of the many characteristics that the Lord loved about David. He loved David's brashness and zeal, his fear of the Lord but also of his trust of the Word. Sometimes we need the zeal that David possessed, the state of mind in bringing attention to God what God promised to him, to be able to declare to the Lord His own word.

I know some people feel my approach on this is wrong, but I truly believe that calling God on His own words excites the Lord as we are simply showing bold faith in His Word. To say to the Lord, "You said you would never leave me or forsake me. Lord, I'm calling you on that scripture. I need that to be true right now for me." I have used this approach many times, and I always feel the Lord's approval and, if I may, His smile at this type of faith. Sometimes we must remember that it is here on earth that souls are saved. It is here on earth that ministries are raised. If souls are to be converted for ministry, it is on earth that they will be transformed.

Friend, to take our life is to make us unusable to the Lord. To end our existence before its time is to shortchange what the Lord has in mind. We need not fear death, this is true, but we should never also be hasty to go there while work still needs to be done. Remember we are here for God's glory and not our own. It is for God's pleasure we are and were created, not our own. To end what God has created to live is to slap the face of our Creator. We must live, go on, live on, and serve on. As Paul once said, "Sure, would be better to be with the Lord in Heaven, but it's more important that I stay and serve here on earth."

Dear friend, if that dark place of taking your life has grabbed hold of you again, please don't let it. Push it away, knock it out and over. Declare whose child you are and to whom you owe your allegiance. Satan surely wants your premature, death but the Lord desires your lifelong service. Now, some of us might live many years, and some might live less. But in the end, it is only God who appoints the day that men die. So fight on, move on. Better days will certainly come if we but hold on.

April 12 - Hang On Tightly

Thou shalt fear the lord thy God; Him shalt thou serve, and to Him shalt thou cleave, and swear by His name. (Deut. 10:20)

I remember when my boys were very young, the days when we had to hold their hands to simply help them walk. At that age and time, their hands clung so tightly to ours. Every scary noise or situation provoked an even tighter clasp. I remember when we had our first son; we were the ever overprotective parents. For a short time, my wife was convinced that holding hands was not enough, and one of those child leashes was purchased. I don't know, but I never took too well to walking my firstborn on a dog's leash. Time went on, and we let go a little more. Those years raising young children were special times, but times that also tested our heart muscles.

One day, my firstborn, Jacob, was walking around an in-ground pool and fell in. A good friend was near and grabbed him out so fast it was like he never even touched the water. In all of those circumstances, holding and grabbing were important dynamics. Not letting go no matter what came between us. There is something about a child's hand and a parent's grip that is hard to fathom, and the bigger question is—who is holding on tighter?

I remember this one story I heard that happened down in Florida. A little boy was playing in his backyard near a swamp when an alligator grabbed him by one leg. As soon as he screamed, his father was there pulling him in the other direction by his arms. The boy was pulled free and rushed to the hospital. It was a big local news story, and all the local reporters were at the hospital. One reporter was determined to see the boy's legs and observe how damaged they were. As the reporter persisted in seeing his legs for a photo, the boy exclaimed, "Forget my legs. You need to see the marks in my arms from where my dad would not let go."

The point is this: God is holding on to us, but we also need to let Him. In our scripture today, we see a formula for staying close to our Heavenly Father.

In reading this scripture, the one word that jumps out to me is the word *cleave*. It says we are to cleave unto our Lord. The word *cleave* in Hebrew is better described as "to adhere to, to catch by pursuit." It is a picture of willful adherence. A mind set upon holding on to what we see we need. It is like the grip we automatically take when slipping off a high area and grabbing on to a rope nearby. It is not a casual grip or a gentle reaching. No, it's an instantaneous powerful, sustained holding-on-to.

Dear friend, this is the kind of clinging we need to have as we hold on to our Lord. If we hold on to Him loosely, we might slip away through trial or doubt. No, He won't ever let go of us as a dear father would never allow. But we might compromise His grip by our lack of cleaving. Hold on to God with all you are, for it is there that safety is found.

April 13 - Walking Alone Is Risky

And thy life shall hang in doubt before thee; and thou shalt fear day and night, and shalt have none assurance of thy life. (Deut. 28:66)

God's people from ages past to present day all seem to make the same mistakes, and worse is, we make them over and over again. How many times did Israel turn from the Lord and then turn back? Oh, to be blessed and forget where the blessings came from and then only to run back into God's arms again. Friend, this is a dangerous game we all play. We run far from the Lord and wonder why God seems so far away. I see this scenario played out over and over again in the church today. We as people seem to have an odd way of dealing with pain. When things get bad, we run from God. We run from church, and we hide in our little worlds. I know this to be true as I have observed it many times. If I don't see a person or family at church for an extended amount of time and I ask them if things are okay, without fail the response would be the same: "Well, we have been going through a troubling time, so we decided to back away until things get worked out." Talk about pouring gasoline on an out-of-control forest fire.

Why do we do such a thing? Why do we run from the One who is waiting for us? God knows our ways, and He knows our hearts. He is deeply hurt by this running and warns of its consequences. When sin and doubt and fear and depression rule our day, if we run from God, He has no choice but to be far from us. As our scripture for today says by application, "Our lives will hang in doubt, we shall fear day and night, and there shall be no assurance of thy life." If that is not a picture of us in our rebellious hearts, I don't know what is.

Also keep in mind that it is not really God punishing us as much as it is the result of God being far from us. It is never His choice but ours. For people who suffer with depression and anxiety, this running in anger from God is all too common. I have done it many times, yet only for a very short time. In our desperation, we yell, whine, and complain. We feel that somehow we can spite God by our absence from Him, that by some way, He might be so hurt that we could force Him to cave in and deliver us. It's a silly game to play, yet one we play all too often. God does not play games, nor does He work in such a way. He is not forced to move by the playing of our hand. He is the potter; we are the clay. Dear friend, run back to the Lord—stop the spite game. Confess, repent, and call out to Him again. He is waiting.

April 14 - God Will Never Forget You

Be strong and of a good courage, fear not, nor be afraid of them: for the lord thy God, He it is that doth go with thee; He will not fail thee, nor forsake thee. (Deut. 31:6)

The Lord, through Moses, gives Joshua in Deuteronomy 31:6 a send-off like no other. Talk about a pep talk. Imagine having the Lord Himself telling you, "Be strong _____ (your name here). Fear not nor be afraid of them, for the LORD thy God, it is He who will go with you, and He will not fail you or forget you." I bet if you heard that directed at you today, your day would be a whole lot different. Well, the truth is the Lord did just say that to you as He said it to Joshua. God is with you, and we do not have to be afraid. Gee, I wonder if Joshua was ever afraid again after that send-off. Know what, I'm sure he was, as man has a very short memory, especially when it comes to the promises of God.

If you notice one thing in scripture, it is that the Lord is in a constant state of reminding us of things. Even with such an event like the crucifixion and Christ's sacrifice for our sins, the Lord still has to remind us: "Do this in remembrance of Me." Remember Jesus's body being broken for us and His blood being shed for us. How could we ever forget such an event? An event that is central to time and space. Well, it is simply because we forget, and just as we in the USA celebrate Memorial Day to remember our fallen soldiers, so too must the Lord remind us of His ever-abiding presence. God is with us; He will never ever, ever, ever forsake us. No matter how far we fall or how deep we sin, no matter how deep our depression or how crippling our anxiety, listen. Our Lord is the living mind. He is the essence of eternal being, and so He cannot forget. It is simply impossible for Him to forget, and even more when it comes to His promises.

Again, let's listen to His words to Joshua: "Be strong and of a good courage, fear not, nor be afraid of them: for the LORD thy God, He it is that doth go with thee; He will not fail thee, nor forsake thee." These are not simply words that sound good, feel good, or look good. They *are* good. They are the truth, and being truth, they cannot lie. No, the only liar there is Satan, and if you believe Him, you will surely perish. But our Lord, His Word is true and dependable. So, dear friend, move on this day with an assurance that no matter how hurting you are today, the Lord will deliver you—of that there can be not a single doubt.

April 15 - Car Shopping

And the lord, He it is that doth go before thee; He will be with thee, He will not fail thee, neither forsake thee: fear not, neither be dismayed. (Deut. 31:8)

It is kind of funny. I've been a pastor for a while now, but my secular trade through my father was auto mechanics. My father owned his own shop for years and my father in law was also a mechanic. Guess you could say it is in my blood. From there I went to a training position as the Lord was preparing me to stand in front of people and teach. Well, all things do work together for good, and as that classroom teaching experience helped me in my preaching, so did the training I had in fixing things. As a pastor, I soon learned that people had other needs besides spiritual, and before you knew it, I was working on people's cars at church—some who couldn't afford repairs and, sadly, some who could.

That couldn't go on for too long, but one thing that did continue and still does even till now is helping people buy a used car. It is an easy thing for me, and I don't mind. It would simply entail me finding out where the car was that they were going to purchase and getting there before them, in some cases, and checking over the car. This way, when the person who was buying the car got there, I would have the car pre-inspected with my thumbs up or down. All they had to do was say, "I'll take it." Now, why would a person want me to check out a car before they bought it? Same reason why we would want the Lord to go on ahead of us in life and prepare the path that we should take. As I gave much comfort to those people in buying an expensive item, so too does the Lord offer us much comfort in going before us and paving the way for our lives. I think it is sad that the Lord does offer us this "service," so to speak, yet we never take advantage of it.

In Deuteronomy 31:8, we see our Lord doing just that. He is going on before us, getting to that scary place that maybe we must face today and taking care of all the issues even before we have to face them. He goes on ahead and only allows the trials of that day He feels will best benefit us and train us. It is like the Lord saying this to us, "Okay, dear child of Mine, I went ahead to where your day would lead you, and I have approved all the difficulties and blessings that you will encounter. They all get my thumbs up, so march on knowing that I was already there." What peace that should give us, amen?

Now, with me preapproving cars for people to purchase, the one problem was, I could make a mistake. I could tell a person it is okay to buy this automobile and still have it be a lemon. Sometimes I couldn't see everything like the inside of the engine. I couldn't see the pistons and crankshaft, the internals of the transmission. I could only approve them via an educated guess through my years of experience. Praise God I never made a bad call until my first son purchased his first used car. Ironic that my only bad call was my own son's. But be that as it may, our Lord cannot make a bad call. He goes on ahead, and He never makes a mistake in His choices of what we must face. Amen!

April 16 - Forever

That all the people of the earth might know the hand of the lord, that it is mighty: that ye might fear the lord your God for ever. (Josh. 4:24)

If you are having a bad day today, one thing that would make it seem worse would be to know that it is forever. Imagine waking up to a day of rain, clouds, and a pain in your lower back. Next, imagine God telling you that it would be like that forever. The rain would never stop, and the clouds would never part. That pain in your back would follow you to eternity. I remember as a young adult working as a landscaper on a very hot August day. I remember thinking to myself, *Am I going to be doing this forever?* One particular day, we had ten yards of topsoil to move and spread by hand. It was a very long and painful day, and if someone told me I would be moving that pile for eternity, my enthusiasm would have been pretty lacking.

Forever is a very long time, and anything that lasts too long will eventually become a problem. Even good things, if they are all you get, can become too much. When I lived in California for a short time, I remember how great I thought it would be to have the sun shining every day. Well, that got old real fast after ten months of blue skies and baking sun, which took their toll on me. I started praying for a cloudy day. Imagine that, praying for a cloudy day. Funny, living currently in Long Island, New York, that seems kind of strange as most days are cloudy and rainy. So we can see that anything that is *forever* can be a downer.

When it comes to emotional issues like depression and anxiety, the thought of them being a part of your daily existence for all eternity is downright bone-chilling. In fact, that was one of the thoughts that would often flood my mind: What if this never goes away? Sure, I can bear it if I knew it would just be a few hours or even a few days, but to know it would be forever is too much. Friend and fellow sufferer, I can offer you one amazing word of encouragement and thought for today, and that is, this will not be with you forever. As sure as I am here today and as sure as I went through those dark nights of depression, I can attest that it goes away. Sure, it might reappear now and then, but it surely is never with you forever.

Forever can frighten us in the realm of human reasoning, and I can think of only two places where they should. One is of hell; it is forever, and you don't want to be there forever. Please turn to Christ and come to know Him as all-forgiving, saving Lord. The second is God. He is the only forever being, meaning that He has no beginning and no ending.

We are eternal in the sense of going forward in time, but God is forever both in the past and the future. Other than that, nothing should scare us into a spiritual coma. No scheme of man or plan of any devil can hurt or destroy what God came to earth for to save. So this day won't last forever, and neither will your pain or sorrows. But God will, and with Him, there is joy forevermore.

April 17 - Come Clean with God

Now therefore fear the lord, and serve Him in sincerity and in truth: and put away the gods which your fathers served on the other side of the flood, and in Egypt; and serve ye the lord. (Josh. 24:14)

Playing games is one thing we all do well. Manipulating people and things for our own benefit is a skill that we all seem to be born with. Today, as you face a new day and a new chance at peace, remember who it is that we serve. Remember the Lord God. Remember His abiding power over land, air, and sea, His all-knowing and ever-presiding personality. If you are dealing with a personal struggle, tell Him! If you are battling a difficult fear, let Him know. If you are in pain due to a past relationship, run to Him with its history. And in case you didn't know, He already knows about them all, but He still wants to hear it directly from you.

Sometimes in counseling, I would be working with a person for weeks and yet getting nowhere. It would be frustrating as I could not understand the lack of breakthrough. Well, over the years, I learned this one thing: people need to come clean, completely clean. So many people would share many things with me, but not that one thing that was key. I would often say to them, "Are you sure you are telling me everything?" Sure enough, it would come out, and it would be the catalyst for forward movement. Not all people come clean, and those few, as far as I know, never gained victory over their pain. Now, I know what you are thinking because we all think the same thing. If God already knows everything about me, then why must I come clean? The answer to that is simple, and one that we find within ourselves as we deal in the matters of the heart.

Take for example a person that you are dating with the intent of marriage. You find something out about them from a reliable source. Now, because you know this about them, don't you still desire for them to come clean with you? Many relationships fail due to this problem as they go on for years with a bitterness knowing that the person they love is keeping a secret. With the Lord, it is somewhat the same. Because He knows all about us doesn't mean we have told Him everything about us. He desires the complete trust that comes with complete honesty. He wants you to trust Him with every part of your heart and soul.

I remember when first being married. It was kind of awkward changing or being nude in front of my wife. We were in love, but we didn't feel that openness that only comes with time and honesty. Now we have no shame at all of being completely exposed before each other as we have nothing to hide.

Dear friend, we all need to get to that place with God where we feel completely comfortable being alone and spiritually naked before Him. He can check every drawer in our dresser, and He can check every file on our cell phone or computer. We have no fear because we have complete trust. Come clean with Jesus today and watch your relationship take a new step in the right direction.

April 18 - They Are Nothing

And I said unto you, "I am the lord your God; fear not the gods of the Amorites, in whose land ye dwell: but ye have not obeyed My voice." (Judg. 6:10)

So April is going by quite quickly, and before we know it, May will be here. With that hope of a new month and new beginnings also comes a warning. Don't let the monsters in your life become monsters in your life. By monsters, I mean the things that are of the world. The ways of the people we must deal with each day that are not the ways of God. I remember being at one place of employment where we would all meet for lunch at a lunch table. The newspapers would come out, and before you knew it, the horoscopes were being read. "What's your sign, Scott?" they would ask. You know what I am talking about as the world has its gods, and we have *the* God.

There are many gods out there today, yet we don't look at them as gods. Alcohol, street drugs, pornography are all gods. Spending our money and time on things that are not of God, like hanging at the bar and having a beer after work, can become a god. Going clubbing, spending time on the Internet looking at things we should not be looking at, posting comments on social networks on things we shouldn't be posting, flirtations with people, and joking of the sexual nature should not be a part of the Christian's life. Many of these things actually can open the door to our anxieties and emotional struggles.

If we play with the world's fire, we will get burnt by their fire. There are some things that we as children of God simply should not do. Even how we dress and carry ourselves. Are we addicted to the world's styles and ways? Are we being corrupted by TV shows and movies that push us away from the Lord and toward the darkness? I'm amazed at how many Christians enjoy a good slasher movie, a movie with occult themes. Nudity and perversion in what we listen to, read, and watch. All of these things are doors to the other side, the demonic side, and the Lord won't have them as a part of you and bless you at the same time.

What we don't understand is this: when God says do not fear these gods, He means don't let them control you. There is only one God we should have reverential fear for, and that is the Lord our God. Fear Him only and no others. Yet we toy and play with these things and feel that we are spiritually strong enough to resist their pull.

For all the people I counsel who struggle with depression and anxiety, there are these similarities that go along with 90 percent of them: drinking, street drugs, sexual activity outside the marriage bed, social flirtations, occult influences, and a party-focused mindset. People come for healing, yet they first need a cleansing. Today let's check our gods at the door and leave them outside where they belong. Let us worship only the Lord, or we risk being under His chastening hand. Run from this world and run deep into the heart of Jesus Christ.

April 19 - I'm Having a Heart Attack

And the lord said unto him, "Peace be unto thee; fear not: thou shalt not die." (Judg. 6:23)

For those of you who suffer with panic attacks, today is your day. If anxiety has reached its apex in your emotional state of mind, then you know what comes next. Anxiety attacks or panic attacks—they are the culmination of many factors all converging at one time. One of the most prominent complaints during a panic attack is that of dying. People will say things like, "I thought my heart was going to stop, I felt I couldn't breathe." I remember one young lady many years ago who battled with horrific panic attacks, yet like most who suffer these little monsters, her greatest obstacle to healing was denying she was having them. She would insist she had a heart issue or maybe a thyroid issue. She thought she had a brain tumor, a blood clot, or a stroke. She was dead-set on making sure her attacks were not from an emotional issue as her pride ran over reason.

When I first encountered her, I gave her my opinion of these episodes being clearly panic-oriented, but she resisted. It would be over a year of suffering before she went for the treatment I recommended. Like most people, it was a hard road as her pride caused her to fall into depression. So what's the point of this word for today? Well, it's simply this: If you suffer from these attacks and desire to be freed from them, you must then understand what they are and what they are not, what they can do and what they cannot do. Understanding these two dynamics will quickly point you in the right direction. It sounds too easy, I know, but in reality, understanding them is the first step to getting through them. Notice I said "getting through them." See, in order to overcome them, you must first get through them.

So what are these two important factors? First, a panic attack cannot kill you. This sounds too simple, but it's true, unless of course you do have an underlying heart or health issue. Panic does not kill; your heart won't explode nor will your body stop functioning. Second, at the worst, all they will do is a) make you sweat, b) make you panic, c) raise your blood pressure, and d) cause you to hyperventilate. Not fun things, I know, but if we understand what our body is doing, we won't be so prone to let it scare us. Panic attacks pass. We sleep, and in time, our body recovers. If you are a sufferer of these (little) monsters, then focus today on these facts. Again, you will not die, for the Lord controls that. It is only the Lord who can take your life. Fear doesn't kill; it just messes up your day.

Please, dear friend, understand that it is a little monster and that the Lord is the monster killer. Medication can help with these panic attacks and getting them under control so you don't fear them as much. When you master them and control them, then they will no longer control you and your life. Seek counseling, get medical help if need be, but remember who controls all things—yes, even panic attacks.

April 20 - When You Want to Run

And Jotham ran away, and fled, and went to Beer, and dwelt there, for fear of Abimelech his brother. (Judg. 9:21)

Funny thing about running, it can only take you in one direction at a time. We cannot be moving closer to God if we are running away in fear. I bring this up today because I know too well the thought of running. It always seemed like the first solution to enter my mind when panic or fear would come upon me—running to another job, another state, another church, or another woman even. Fear has a way of taking all that is logical and stomping on it like an old cigarette. Suddenly, rational thinking is out the door, God and His wisdom are no longer desired, and selfishness becomes king. All of a sudden, it is self-preservation in tenth gear. Your family, your Lord, your own testimony in Christ are all tossed aside. It is suddenly all about me, me, and me. It is the trinity of me. Hours will be spent lying in bed, pondering ways and schemes to escape this emotional pain.

Dear friend, sooner or later, you will face the fact that you don't want to face, the fact that running is not the answer and all the people and places you thought of running to can't really help you anyway. I remember my first emotional breakdown, and I remember what came so natural to me, to call Mom and Dad. Well, that's fine if you are nine years old, but not when you are thirty-four. I remember sitting with my parents and having this emergency family meeting. "Mom, Dad, I'm having a breakdown, and I need you two to help me get out of it." Now, certainly, they wanted to, but in reality, what could they do? I had a full-time job, a home, a mortgage, a wife, and children. I guess in my mind I reverted to childhood, and I was hoping (foolishly) to climb back on their big bed, pull the covers over my head, and have them fix everything. They told me they couldn't. I tell you that rocked my world. Who then could I run to? What else could I do? Well, I had one thing right, and that was going to my Father. I needed to go to my Heavenly Father. I needed to run to Him.

See, in all my confusion and fear, I was running everywhere except to the One who could really help. Running everywhere but to God is always destined for failure because running everywhere has one major downfall: when we run away, we are in reality running away from God. We can't run to things and people for help and run to God at the same time. It's like running when your car is on fire. You can either run away from it or back into it. You can't run in both directions at the same time.

Please, today, if you feel like running, stop, look unto the Father, and run to Him first. Seek His wisdom and direction. Ask for His guidance and clarity of mind to know how to make the important choices this fear sometimes forces us to make. Sure, family can help and friends can pray, but in the end, the only one who will guide you to the right place is our Lord and King Jesus Christ.

April 21 - Looking Back

Only fear the lord, and serve Him in truth with all your heart; for consider how great things He hath done for you. (1 Sam. 12:24)

Today is today, and that seems to be our greatest focus when dealing with the fear of today. We do not care about yesterday because today and tomorrow have us paralyzed. Dear friend, if you are in a place of questions and indecision about life, remember this one simple trick. Remember where you came from and what the Lord has done for you so far. The fact that you are reading this today proves that you are not dead. The Lord has carried you this far. He has gotten you through tough times of pain, sorrow, and deep struggles. He has been with you even before you knew Him. When it felt like you couldn't go on, He kept you going on. Let's not forget the good days too; things were not always bad. There were happy times and laughter. There were those times when life was a pleasure.

Time goes by quickly, and we forget the mercy and grace of our Lord. Remember the blessings that fell upon us that we often never take the time to appreciate or praise Him for. He is a good God even when we are not so good. Think on the times when you could have been dead, yet He spared your life. When looking back on my life, I now can see His divine hand watching over me, knowing what I would become despite what I was. So many times I could have been in jail or dead being with the wrong crowd, yet the Lord was there. Sickness passed by, and mercy overshadowed my sins. Friend, if you are here today, then God brought you here. It means that you have purpose, and purpose always means hope. He has kept you alive, not to fall apart but to fall into Him and find restoration to your soul. Look back and remember.

Remember when you couldn't go on and all hope was lost. The heartbreak that you swore you would never get over. The great loss that seemed unforgettable. Yet you still moved on.

His mercy is new every day, and today still falls into that category. Don't let the enemy take from you what God has given; today is a day that the Lord has made. It's His day as much as it's yours for the taking. Like our scripture today states, "Consider how great things He hath done for you." *Consider* means "to think upon and ponder." Marvel at how He carried you and pushed you when you needed to be pushed. Remember when He stood with you when no one else would. He is still that same God, and He will still carry you through this day. Trust Him. Believe Him once more. He is faithful in bringing you to the climax of this day. Of tomorrow, well, He will do the same again. But His mercy is only for this day. Embrace it now and make it through another day in Him.

April 22 - Never Outnumbered

And he answered, "Fear not: for they that be with us are more than they that be with them." (2 Kings 6:16)

If you have been a Christian for a number of years, you would have learned this one thing: sometimes it seems like our side is losing. We watch the news, Hollywood, popular culture, and it all seems bleak for those in Christ. The times are truly changing, and the powers of darkness seem to be gaining ground. Being a Christian isn't respected as it once was; standing for God's Word now has a greater cost to us than it did only a few years back. Friends don't seem to understand you, and your family thinks you are strange to be so in love with this One called Jesus Christ. It is beginning to really be a challenge to live for Him, and it seems that some Christians are even beginning to cave under the pressure. The politically correct movement has all but taken away our rights to pray and soon our right to read our Bibles. These are truly interesting days, and as many believe, they are the last days of the church.

When we read about these last days of the church, we also read about the pressures and those who will depart from the faith. Now, add to the mix our fears and phobias, and it seems even worse. It is hard enough being a Christian, but now we have to stand against tyrants even when we feel like tiny worms with the added load of anxiety and depression. It truly does feel like we are the Davids against the Goliaths. We are the weak and fragile against the bold and arrogant. It really can be a scary world out there, and again, for us, it's a bit harder. It is one thing to put a prizefighter up against a champion kickboxer, but to put a bunny up against a rattlesnake is a whole different ball game. A lamb up against a lion. So what are we to do as the frail and frightened? Well, the same thing as any other children of God should do—walk by faith not by sight, for the battle is the Lord's.

Friend, we must never let the enemy convince us that they are bigger and stronger, that we are too weak and frail. That might be the case, but they are not fighting us; they are fighting the thrice Holy God. And let's not forget David against Goliath. Who won that battle anyway, and how did they win it? Was it David's strength and power or God's wisdom and might? There's an old sci-fi movie floating around out there where the captain of the spaceship says, "Never give up and never surrender." That is true, but not because we are so mighty, but because our Lord is. Like I shared with you a few months back, when I was out numbered and the enemy was on the attack, what did the Lord do? He sent me another child of God to encourage me. If there are no Christians around, He will send angels; and if there are no angels, the very rocks will cry out and defend us if God commanded them to.

In our scripture for today, we are reminded of this hidden backup team waiting to jump into the rumble for us. 2 Kings 6:16 says, "And he answered, 'Fear not: for they that be with us are more than they that be with them.'" Isn't that great? Those who are with God are always more than enough than those who align with the enemy—be it angels or men or, dare I say, the Lord Himself and the heavenly host at His command.

April 23 - Not Just Some Things

But the lord your God ye shall fear; and He shall deliver you out of the hand of all your enemies. (2 Kings 17:39)

So today is a full day for you, and the things on your plate are more than you can handle. The problems to deal with are more numerous than the hours in the day. Your boss is on the rampage, you are fighting a bad cold, and the kids are driving you crazy. Just then, you hear an odd noise from the basement, and the washer is on the fritz and pumping water all over the floor. The dog ripped up your child's report card, which needed to be signed, and it's only 9:00 a.m. Did you ever have a day like that or worse? Ever have a day when there is so much going wrong that your capacity to evaluate and coordinate the damage and what needs to be repaired is more than you can handle? Those are tough days for anyone. Add anxiety and depression, and it's a five-alarm fire. Hey, if you didn't have anxiety and depression, you do now.

Friend, that type of day is happening all over the USA, but what about the rest of the world? Those in the parts of the world where there is no water to drink today, your child hasn't eaten since last Tuesday, your local village is filled with violence, and you can hear the gunfire getting closer. Now, that's a bad day, and yes, it's all how you look at it. To the woman in that third-world village, she would love to have the washing-machine problem; heck, she would love to have water to wash her clothes. Again, how we see things and how they actually are, are never quite the same. Now, those two examples are simply that—examples of one person's nightmare compared to another's. Yet in the big picture, they are as big to the one as the other person's problem is to them. So the point is this: we all have enemies of the heart, those things that tear us to shreds and leave us weeping. Yet both women can still call upon the same God five thousand miles away from each other and still have that same God answer them. It is the same God saying the same words of comfort to both women.

In 2 Kings 17:39, our Lord says the same things to all of us as well as to those two women: "But the LORD your God ye shall fear; and He shall deliver you out of the hand of all your enemies." Not just out of the hands of some of these problems, but out of all of them. Does that mean God will fix all of those issues? No, but He will deliver you out of the torment that they are putting you through. Doesn't matter if they are knives or nerves, the same Lord is lord over all of our enemies. Trust Him and cry out to Him knowing that He is big enough to cover you here in the USA as well as you over there in Haiti.

April 24 - You Can Be Great

And the fame of David went out into all lands; and the lord brought the fear of him upon all nations. (1 Chron. 14:17)

So many people today are seeking greatness. They long to be famous, rich, and leave a legacy of who they were. I was reminded of this truth by my eldest son, Jacob. He, to my surprise, expressed this one concern about his life, that when he left this earth, he would not be remembered. He wanted to have a career that people would respect and a position in life that people would look up to. It is interesting that we all desire this in one degree or another. I think what is even more important is why we want to be *great*, why we want to be rich, famous, and well-known. Well, on the surface, being rich, famous, and well-known is easy to decipher. Being rich is simply so you won't have to work. Being famous is so people will love us. And as to being well-known, it is so we won't be forgotten. They are all root emotions, but even more, they truly reveal what we really are. We are small people who want to be big. We are powerless people who want power. We are ungodly people who want to be gods.

Dear friend, you may be upset and disappointed with who you are and what you feel you can't ever be. You may look at your struggle with anxiety as an even greater wedge to anything great being done through you. I know how that feels as I have been right where you are. I too looked often at my weaknesses and wondered how I would make it, let alone become great. It is a depressing thought, especially in light of our current worldwide economic downturn. Yet the answer is not found in our smarts, wealth, opportunities, and strength. No, the answer lies in harnessing ourselves to the only one who is truly great—Jesus Christ.

Friend, being significant is only found in being part of something that is significant. If we look at past history, we would be surprised to find that many of the real significant people were not rich, famous, and well-known. They were people who really changed the world around by themselves, people who really affected the people they encountered. Now, you might be thinking who these people are or if you have ever heard of them. That is true because they were more focused on getting God's attention than yours.

See, to be truly significant is to have your priorities straight. It is to live so God alone is glorified and the people you know and meet see God through you. It might also surprise you that the Lord is not impressed with your worldly fame but your work for Him. The Bible says that the angels in Heaven rejoice over one sinner that repents. That's what gets the Lord excited, not your 401(k) or your popularity. It is the parents who impacted affected their children for Christ, the churches that sent out missionaries for Christ. It is the businesses that used their prosperity to affect the world for Christ. Notice the wording—*for Christ*! It is motivation, and if our motivation is right, then God will take care of the rest. He will make us great despite our anxiety. He will make us great and feared through His blessing. Keep Christ great in your life and you will also be great.

April 25 - Just Do It!

> *And David said to Solomon his son, "Be strong and of good courage, and do it: fear not, nor be dismayed: for the lord God, even my God, will be with thee; He will not fail thee, nor forsake thee, until thou hast finished all the work for the service of the house of the LORD." (1 Chron. 28:20)*

Getting up in the morning versus going to sleep at night. There is a major difference in how we view them. When I am feeling great and life is going along fine, the morning wins hands down; yet when anxiety is peaking and depression is in control, the tables are turned upside down. In my personal struggles with these emotions, the mornings were a living hell. To face another day of fighting and struggling was simply an exhausting thought in itself. Nighttime was my favorite, and going to sleep was like candy to a child. Sleep would become my god, and when sleep wouldn't come, I ended up medicated with all kinds of sleeping pills and tranquilizers. It was not a pretty picture and the one place that was hard to get out of. Breaking that cycle of hating mornings and loving sleep is not easy, and to do so requires a strong mindset.

In 1 Chronicles 28:20, we wonder if young Solomon had an issue with fear. Apparently, he did, and his father, David, gave him some great advice about this. He told him to be strong, be of good courage, and don't be afraid. Then he adds, "Don't be dismayed," which is the result of prolonged fear. It is what happens when anxiety controls us; life then becomes a depressing place. But notice next what David says. He proclaims this fact that "God, my God, is with thee." It is not a hopeful wish but a fact, and one that Solomon needed to hear. Then David tells his son what this God promises: "He will not fail you, or forget you, because you have work to do." Notice that last part; it is not Solomon-based but God-based. It is about serving God, not serving self; and if we are set on serving God, then it is up to God to move us and not ourselves.

Friend, God has a plan for you and a purpose. We must finish what God has begun in us, and He will help us through it and to it; but it is up to us to do one thing: get up and out of bed and trust Him. We cannot complete what the Lord has prepared for us if we are sleeping all the time. Yes, it is hard to start, but once we do, the Lord will take over the rest. It is taking that first step of faith. It is fighting against the odds of fear and reaching for Christ's strength with all of our strength even if we have little. So today we must embrace this command. Just do it!

April 26 - When It Is Time to Fear

Wherefore now let the fear of the lord be upon you; take heed and do it: for there is no iniquity with the lord our God, nor respect of persons, nor taking of gifts. (2 Chron. 19:7)

Sometimes it amazes me how little people know about God and how often they misquote His Word. Take for example, "Money is the root of all evil." That's a lie, and the Bible never says that. What it does say is this: "The love of money is the root of all evil," which is a major difference. The next example is the misunderstanding with regard to "the fear of the Lord." Many people don't understand what God means by this, and those who do don't follow it. Friend, if we are ever to break out of the cycle of emotional trauma, we must first understand our Lord. Too many times people who teach about God paint a picture that is only partially true. They tend to focus on one true character of God yet avoiding the other. To do so makes the complete picture of God false and then, in turn, a lie.

Even though the one character trait you are taught is true, it still must be negated because it leaves out the other. In this case, it's the teaching that "God is Love," which He is, and of that there can be no question. He is Love, and not just a quality that He possesses, but is His actual divine essence. Now, that is all wonderful but only partially true, for the other part of God, which is equally who He is, is *justice*. God is a just God, and just as He is Love, He is also just. We cannot paint Him without these two traits. Now, I bring this point out today so we don't make the mistake of living too much in His love without also fearing His justice. This is where the *fear* of the Lord comes in. Yes, we are to fear Him, but not in the sense that you are afraid of Him (who He is) but that you fear His justice. We never seem to have a problem loving His love, but we do have a problem fearing His justice. It is like only loving your earthly father but not fearing his authority as your father. To only love him is to dishonor him.

So for today's thought, I lay upon you this important understanding: we must fear His justice in the fact that His laws and commands must be obeyed. We can't simply lie in bed and depend on God's love to carry us through the day if we don't also fear His justice that says, "Get up and serve Me," "Go out to all the world and preach the gospel," "Be a fisher of men, and if I call you to it, I will enable you to do it." These are commands that are not just for other people but for us too. For all those who are strong and for all those who are weak. If we are going to get out of this emotional tourniquet, we need to obey the Father's voice even while we are afraid and weak. We might have many fears, and we know what they can do to us, but if we have not the fear of God's justice, then we are placing this world's fears above God's work and call. We must honor Him, and that comes with fearing Him. We want to obey Him because He is our Father, and we show that we want Him pleased with us. So yes, we can rest in His Love, but we must also be motivated by His justice, justice to get up and get moving. So let us *let* the fear of the Lord be upon us.

April 27 - Faith Enough to Follow

And he charged them, saying, "Thus shall ye do in the fear of the lord, faithfully, and with a perfect heart." (2 Chron. 19:9)

It is almost here. May is just around the bend and, with it, the smell of spring flowers. Just a few more days and it can all turn around, and the blessings will begin to flow. I say this to make a point as I don't know if in May your struggle will be over, but I ask you, if you knew it would, would you be able to hang on till then? You know I bet you could because what are a few more days when maybe you have been struggling with depression for years? Imagine any problem being removed in a few more days. I don't think there is anything we couldn't endure for a few more days if we knew for certain that relief and joy were on the other side.

I remember when I was struggling with depression and anxiety my wife would always say, "It's going to be over soon. Just a little while longer and it will pass." I never believed her with my head, but my spiritual heart did. In my human reasoning, it made no sense that just waiting would turn the tides in my life, but in Christ, I knew that all things were possible. I knew that God has never forgotten me before, and He wouldn't forget me now. Sounds impressive, doesn't it? But I was rarely in the spirit during those days, which means more often my logical mind saw no end in sight.

Dear friend, if there is no end in sight, then the future does look bleak, and living in that state of mind will surely wear you out quickly. What's needed is to live with a faithful heart and to serve the Lord despite all odds and faithfully move toward the north. To trust Him when everything points to failure, to praise Him when pain is all you can see. Oh, does the Lord love that kind of faith. He loves the before-the-Red-Sea-parting faith more than the after-the-Red-Sea-party-praise faith.

We must move on through this day trusting that we are one day closer to healing than we were before. We are to move on serving Him as if May does hold the key and the removal of our pain. Sure, anyone can praise God after it is over, but to praise Him in the fire is what He desires. Faith enough to follow—it is what we all truly need, especially in these trying days in which we live. To say, "Lord, I am in pain today, but I will move ahead in that pain because I trust your power to change my future." Faith enough to follow, do you have it? Do I have it? We must!

April 28 - Sometimes He Does It All

Ye shall not need to fight in this battle: set yourselves, stand ye still, and see the salvation of the lord with you, O Judah and Jerusalem: fear not, nor be dismayed; tomorrow go out against them: for the lord will be with you. (2 Chron. 20:17)

We have been speaking a lot about fighting and standing fast through the hardest of times. We have spoken about pressing onward with all the strength you can muster. Yet what happens when you are at that place when you simply cannot, when you are so weak that you physically cannot move your body, let alone your mind?

Dear friend, this is a fine line we cross here, and I wish not to let you lie on one side of it more than the other. If you are fighting and hurting, you still might have to fight and hurt some more before deliverance can break through. I understand this and have lived it out many times. For the most part, I had to move onward and upward in order to break through the darkness. I had to get up, get dressed, and complete the task that the Lord had planned for me that day. I remember performing funerals and weddings and ministering to depressed people all the while going through my own hell. I preached and presided over business meetings and town-board meetings. I even led people to the Lord, and none was the wiser of my true emotional state.

I can truly say that the Lord did carry me through those days, and I just kind of existed. He moved me when I couldn't move at all. I would come home, fall to my knees, and weep. I would weep knowing that tomorrow I had to endure it all again. It was a hard time but also a supernatural time. That was what most of my life was like, yet there were the times when I could not do anything. I'm talking about complete breakdown and fatigue. During one bout, I could not eat and lost close to thirty pounds. I was living on one banana a day and water. I was so weak that even moving my body was a task. It was during those days when the Lord truly did tell me, "You don't have to fight this one today. I will fight for you." It was during those days that I could only lie in bed and moan in agony. My family and children had to be placed on a back burner as I simply could not minister to anyone's needs; I couldn't even minister to my own.

Dear friend, I pray this is not where you are today, but if it is and there is no other place to turn, I ask that you would simply turn to Him in faith and cry out, " Lord, fight for me today because I can't even fight to keep air in my lungs." Friend, He will! He will fight for you today because He knows all the good that will be raised in you tomorrow. Good will come, new life will spring forth, and you will praise Him again.

April 29 - Why We Really Love God

Then Satan answered the lord, and said, "Doth Job fear God for nought?"
(Job 1:9)

In the book of Job, Satan asked the Lord a good question, "Why does Job follow and obey God so much?" What Satan says leads us to believe it's because God does so much for Job. Job is blessed and wealthy and doing fine. This one question by Satan is one that we must ask ourselves today. "Why do we follow the Lord Jesus Christ?" We will get back to Satan's question and the right answer, but first we must ask ourselves why this is even a question. Today many people are very confused about why they follow God. Ask people on a Sunday morning and you might get a very varied response. Even as we are discussing this, start asking yourself that question, why do you follow Jesus Christ? The reason this question isn't as cut-and-dry as it should be is because so many are teaching the wrong answer.

Just watch your typical tele-evangelist and see what they say, and you will be thoroughly confused. The problem, dear friend, is this: 90 percent of the USA believes that we serve God so He will do for us what we desire. Be good so we can get. Obey the Father so you can get the ice-cream cone you so desired. If you haven't understood this yet, I pray that you would today. Friend, we do not serve God to get, we serve God because He is *God!* Getting a blessing or a toy in return should not even enter our minds.

If you are serving God this way, watch how it can play havoc in your life's situations: 1) You serve God to get but then you develop anxiety and depression. 2) This does not compute, so you decide to give more money and study the Bible more, yet your depression and anxiety still remain. What then are we to conclude from this experiment other than God doesn't work and / or God is a liar? Being that, that's impossible, it must be something else. And what could it be but us being mistaught all these years? See, if you get this concept wrong, God will never act in a logical way. Get it right, and it will be easier to understand why God does what He does.

John 3:16 is a quick way to diffuse the confusion. God loved the world so He gave His Son so we would not perish but have what? That is the question. Why did Jesus die? So we could have an easy life on earth or a place of dwelling with Him in Heaven? Jesus died so we could be forgiven from our sins and gain eternal life, that's it. Even Satan didn't get it, or at least made-believe he didn't get it. Job didn't serve God to get; he served God for the same reason Paul did—because he was grateful for his salvation.

Today, in order to understand what the Lord is doing through our battles with problems, let's first understand why the world has them. *Sin* is the reason as since the fall of man, sin came in and death reined. It's a fallen world, and there is nothing to do about it but let the Lord use these issues of this fallen world to bring us closer to Him.

So our problems are not always due to a lack of holiness but also due to the nature of our world. At the end of the day, let's make sure we serve God simply because we love Him. We love Him because He first loved us. Start there and watch what happens.

April 30 - One Last Time

> *The fear of the lord is a fountain of life, to depart from the snares of death.* (Prov. 14:27)

Well, it is here, the last day of April. May, with all of its wonders, is waiting to bring upon us new things, unexplored things, and amazing things. That might sound like an exaggeration, but if you think about it, it can be true. We do not know what May 1 will bring, and for that reason, it is filled with wonder and mystery. It is exciting, and one thing you learn as you live this Christian life is it is anything but boring. Today, what will you do? Well, let's close off this last day of April by concluding our heavy month of devotions focused on the fear of the Lord. It is not something you would think to lift a person with, but in all actually, it is. It is central.

In Proverbs 14:27, we read about this holy respect and honor for God's justice. It can be frightening to fall under it but also a mighty blessing to obey it. Again, Proverbs 14:27 begins with the fear of the Lord but then segues into what it accomplishes: "The fear of the Lord is a fountain of life." It enables us, when followed correctly, to escape the snares of death. Isn't it interesting that the teachings of the fear of the Lord, which we have been taught incorrectly to shy away from, is where the answer is really found?

Life is what we want here, life to the fullest that Jesus promises. Yet that life in Christ is not found only in His love but also in fearing His justice to send us where we really deserve to go. Dear friend, as we finish out this heavy month, let us not lose all the blessings of these heavy teachings. God is love, and in His love, He will carry us through the worst of times. But let us also not forget that if we don't fear His justice with regard to our judgment, we would never come to Him in the first place. Fear of hell and knowing we can be spared from it through God's love should have us on our knees worshiping this God as king and not commanding Him to bless us as if He was our servant.

As we end this month, I hope your struggles are winding down, and even if they are not, I pray you understand that they will. Remember, serving a god who has no power is something to feel hopeless about, but following a God who is divine justice is a God who has the power to accomplish what He promises. When in a court of man, remember what makes that human judge so powerful. Is it not the fear that we have of him and the power that he has at his command? His word goes, and so does God's. When it is time, our God of justice can say, "It is over, your trial of faith is finished. Now go and rejoice in Me for what I have done for you." That day will come when we reach the place of worship that God desires. In the meantime, His love covers all until we get there.

May

May 1 - If I Only Had Money

Better is little with the fear of the lord than great treasure and trouble therewith. (Prov. 15:16)

Well, it's May 1. It finally arrived, and with it, all the newness of a new month with new opportunities. Will this be it, the time I have been waiting for? Will this be the day that my *ship* comes in? I have said that many times before, but truth is, sometimes it was not the new day I had hoped for. Sometimes it was a trying day with some setbacks. I remember going away on a short three-day trip, just me and a friend from church. It was to be a "guy" trip doing guy things. It was after a long hard year of struggling, and I was feeling great and thinking that my healing had come, and all was behind me.

So I went away. Yet to my surprise, it wasn't all that great. I had an anxiety attack that lasted the whole trip, and what was worse was that I didn't want the other person to know as it would be embarrassing. I remember being mad at God and thinking things like, *Lord, I worked so hard and suffered so much, and all I asked was a short day or so away to have some fun.* But no, the anxiety came back, and I had to fight the whole trip. There were a few times of fun sprinkled about, but for the most part, it was the reward trip I thought I deserved yet didn't get. I came back confused and upset: "Why, Lord? Why couldn't I have a good time? Why isn't this over once and for all?"

What a setback. As I let my mind slip back into rumination again, I started to reason what the problem was. "If I only didn't have to worry about so much, if I only had a better job, if I only didn't have to be concerned about performing on the job, if I only had money, then I could live happily again." It was the same old trap that I fell into, thinking that I could control my situation by my own mind. It was forgetting God and focusing on myself again. It was complaining about my life situation and finding a million reasons why I deserved better.

Now, I don't know why that little trip set me back, and I don't know what the Lord was trying to show me, but I do know this: the first thing that always jumps into my head when I encounter a setback is escape. Forget God and find money, for in money and security, there is truly peace. Well, that's a lie, and finding peace in anything else but God is never the answer. That weekend, I popped tranquilizers like they were going out of style. I didn't want to hear and listen to what God was trying to show me, but instead I wanted instant release and peace. I wanted an easy life with many things so I could find rest in "them" instead of Him.

Friend, sometimes we get confused, and we don't know what we are to do, but rest assured that in that seemingly confused state, there is actually order. God is doing something. He is always working something for the good, but it's up to us to find it. If today you are confused about why things aren't turning your way, about why God isn't doing what you desire, and you have little patience to find out and wait, please listen to me. Move ahead even in your confusion and praise Him. Look not for an escape or for money to save the day. Only look for Him. He is there.

May 2 - Alone with God and Satisfied

The fear of the lord tendeth to life: and he that hath it shall abide satisfied; he shall not be visited with evil. (Prov. 19:23)

May 1 wasn't the devotional uplift you were looking for, I know. It kind of set you back and made you think to yourself, *This devotional just gets me going then it sets me back into despair.* Friend, I know what you're feeling, but you must remember what I promised you in this book: honesty, truth, and reality in Christ. See, I could write a book that promised you a happy day every day if you just followed my simple twelve-step program. I'm sorry, but I can't do that, and I can only speak truth. I pray that you will trust me as I don't sell here what you desire but what is truth and what is truly Christ. Life is hard, friend, and someday when you are ready for a blessing, a seemingly heavy one may come upon you. Sometimes things don't go as we think they should. There will be days when we doubt the very existence of God Himself, and yet we must keep going, keep fighting.

Yes, good days do come, and deliverance is real, but first we must remove from ourselves all that we are until all that remains is Him. It's finding peace with God alone and nothing else. It's having a setback and praising Him the same way as when you had a victory. It's being alone and being okay there. I believe sometimes that God is testing us to simply see if He is really all we need. He wants to be sure we are not simply mouthing the words yet inwardly we are bitter and angry toward Him. It's getting a toothache on a cruise-ship vacation, which you waited all year for, and still thanking Him and loving Him the same way as when all is going well at home.

In Proverbs 19:23, we are handed a truth, a truth only lived out if we truly believe it. Does the fear of the Lord really offer us life to the fullest? Can we truly be satisfied with God alone and find all that we desire in Him? Paul did, and in worse circumstances than we could ever imagine. Dear fellow sufferer, I'm not trying to build temporary happy faces through this devotional book but long-haul truckers for Christ, people who will stand tall through the worst of the worst, the hardest of the hard. This world is rough, and if a person is going to make it, they will have to be tough. Cry out to the Lord today and ask Him to create in you not simply a smiling Christian, but a content Christian. Ask the Lord not to simply make you okay for today's battles of the mind but a warrior for the long haul of life. Nothing less will do; nothing else can do. It's all for Jesus or all for nothing. Which will it be for you?

May 3 - Does God Really Get Mad?

The fear of a king is as the roaring of a lion: whoso provoketh him to anger sinneth against his own soul. (Prov. 20:2)

It's a pity-party day, and you're all invited. I will share my complaints, and you can share yours. Hum, let's begin with me since I'm all that really matters. I hate my life and everything about it. I can't get happy, and I'm tired of fighting this battle of the mind. Everyone else seems to be doing so well and better than me. They have everything going their way, and I don't. Even when they are going through hard times, they seem to deal with it so much better than me. Lord, why are you allowing me to go through this? Why won't you bless me and turn my life around? I hate this so much I just want to scream, but in the end, it doesn't change a thing, so what's the point?

Do any of my rants sound familiar to you? Have you ever been in a place like that? Maybe you are feeling that way right now and are at your wits' end. If so, then read my rants again and see if it reminds you of someone else besides yourself. See if it reminds you of a child who is just pouting and on a rainy day with no friends to play with, a child who is just pouting and stamping his feet over a situation he hates yet cannot change. Next, place yourself as the parent of that child, a parent who must explain to that child the whys of their life. Think of how you would feel if that child made those complaints every day. If you are like me, then I'm sure you would be angry. You try to comfort them. You even try to encourage them, but for the most part, nothing really works. You know by your life wisdom that things will turn around, but no matter how much you try to convince your child, their rants go on. Sooner than later, compassion turns to anger, and anger to deaf ears. You have just had it, and instead of compassion, you turn to correction. You say things like, "You think you have it bad, I will show you bad, I will show you a bad day." You give your child a hundred different examples of people with real troubles, and if you could, you would show them a life with real troubles.

Now, that's us as humans running wild, but not too far from the mark when it comes to the Lord training us to be like Him. Sure, He doesn't lose His temper like we do, and sure, He doesn't act in irrational ways, but one thing He does do is get angry. Friend, the Lord gets angry, and though He never stops loving us, He can start punishing us. He can show us real troubles and real issues. He can turn away, if even for a moment, simply to show us what a life without Him is really like. In all my ups and downs, I have also seen God's anger at me and His disappointments with my attitude. But because He is a perfect Father, He knows when to correct us. Let's not push God too far with our threats and complaints.

May 4 - Singing with a Stubbed Toe

> *And David spake to the chief of the Levites to appoint their brethren to be the singers with instruments of music, psalteries and harps and cymbals, sounding, by lifting up the voice with joy. (1 Chron. 15:16)*

So these children of the Levites bore the ark upon their shoulders just as Moses commanded them. Having the glory of God in your possession is amazing. It was a time of celebration and rightly so. That being the case, David commanded the Levites to appoint people with musical talent to really get the joint rocking. Praise was in order, and a loud praise at that. I don't think it was too hard to get the people to celebrate just as it's not too hard to get people after a winning game to celebrate. To celebrate after a big victory is what we love to do and what comes natural; it's one aspect of humans that transcends cultures all over the world. People seem to be ready and willing to celebrate right from the womb, so we know it is surely an emotion that comes directly from God.

In the modern church today, we have taken this celebration to new heights. Where once we had a pipe organ, now in its place stands a five-piece band. We have amplifiers to even push it up higher and bigger. Celebrating and Jesus Christ do have a lot in common. We celebrate the resurrection and the victory over sin and death. We celebrate the powers of darkness being overtaken by the powers of light. There are certainly many things to celebrate today, and we certainly do it well. Sometimes I wonder if our celebrating is a little overboard and if it's truly a real celebration for the right reasons. Like our Fourth of July celebrations in the USA, I often wonder if anyone really knows what they are celebrating anymore, or is it celebrating for the sake of celebrating? Well, one thing that needs to be decided today is, can we celebrate in all things? Can we raise such a fevered pitch when it comes to a day with negative circumstances running rampant?

I know in my life, it's truly easier to celebrate the good and cry over the bad, but that's where I always get tripped up. If all things work together for good to those who are in Christ, if God can only do good to His children, then aren't even bad days actually good days? Hard, I know, but nonetheless a fact, one we need to embrace or forever miss the point of life in Christ Jesus.

Friend, every day is to be celebrated as if we had won the royal robe itself. Days of tears and mourning, days of stubbed toes—they all need to be celebrated as the mighty working of God in all circumstances. This is the truest form of worship and one that Satan hates and the Lord loves. Never forget that Satan's desire is to have us hating God. Simply by invoking such feelings leaves us serving Satan by default.

Hard as it might be, we must muster the same level of celebration for God through the painful days as we do in the wonderful days. Yes, it's a supernatural thing.

May 5 - People Watching

Wherefore David blessed the lord before all the congregation: and David said, "Blessed be Thou, lord God of Israel our Father, for ever and ever." (1 Chron. 29:10)

I have always been a people watcher. One of my favorite things to do is to go down to the local boat-launching ramp and watch people back down their boats into the water using their boat trailers. Some are better than others; some have trouble backing down the long steep ramps. People argue and fight. Families quarrel about who is holding the rope as their boat drifts away. As I would sit back and watch this live show, I also became convinced of the fact that it's easy to watch people screwing up. It's kind of fun, but fun that I don't think the Lord appreciates in the heart of a believer, let alone a pastor. I don't think Jesus would be there watching and silently laughing at the people struggling to launch their boats. Then I started thinking and placing myself down there, launching those boats. Could I do any better, or would I even want to try? Would I want people watching me as I hit the dock with my boat trailer?

Now, the point today is that people like to watch people. Just watch what happens on a highway when there is a fender bender. Why does traffic back up on the other side of the road? It's because people like to watch. Now, as I was drawing this conclusion about our tendency to watch others, I was also reminded of this: if I desire to watch others, then others probably desire to watch me. This fact can be looked at two ways. See, it's positive knowing that people are watching everything I do if I'm always bringing glory to God. "All the world is a stage," a famous playwright once said. If that's true, then why not use it for God's glory?

Take another example that is happening even today: people are fussing and complaining about the government eavesdropping on cell calls and emails, but what if we look at it as an opportunity to promote God's Word? See, if we are going to get caught talking about someone or something, why not get caught talking about God? Then there is no fear if we know our words are always seasoned with grace and love. As David says in our scripture for today, "Lets bless the Lord before the entire congregation." Praise God for all to hear, even while we are not in a praiseworthy place. Praise Him because people are watching.

May 6 - Start Planning Your Victory Dance

Then they returned, every man of Judah and Jerusalem, and Jehoshaphat in the forefront of them, to go again to Jerusalem with joy; for the lord had made them to rejoice over their enemies. (2 Chron. 20:27)

You know, it's funny. We always seem to be picturing our lives forever in an unhealed position. We always assume that this is always as we will be. Health and new beginnings are simply too far out of the picture to even look forward to. When I think about this, it makes me think about the future promises the Lord has for us. Promises like we read in Revelation when evil will be defeated once and for all and God's children will be vindicated. It will be a day of rejoicing, and if you're wondering what you are going to be doing for all eternity in Heaven, well, here's a heads-up: worshiping and celebrating! Get used to it today because you're going to be doing it for all of your tomorrows. Some of you might have no problem with planning that future celebration in heaven, but how about your future celebrations here on earth? The celebrations over demons that will be beaten and fears that will be overcome. Depression that was dark but will be turned to light. Why is it that we aren't planning those celebrations other than we really don't believe it will ever be?

Friend, believe it will never be, and it won't. We must claim God's Word and not let go of it until we hold His mighty victory in our very hands. We have enemies out there, and not all of them are the flesh-and-blood types. We have enemies of the soul: lust, fear, worry, bitterness, anger, doubt, greed, envy, and confusion. These are all enemies if they succeed in separating us from our Lord, and if our relationship is severed, then all is lost. The only thing we should fear is losing touch with God. Today we need to start planning our victories over these things, to celebrate while we are still on this side of the victory. We must plan the day that we will rejoice in front of our enemies. To tell depression that it will not rob us of our joy anymore. To tell anxiety that it will not be allowed to control our living anymore. To prepare the victory dance over the dead corpses of our inanimate fears.

Picture those famous football players who dance around the end zone when they make the winning touchdown. Sure, it's silly, but it sure feels good. In real terms, plan that day to go out for dinner when you once were afraid to leave your home and to sit and eat ice cream at the ice cream parlor as a personal victory for all the days that anxiety kept you bedbound. To the world, they will be insignificant victories and may not seem big at all, but to us, they will be mountaintop experiences. Trust me, those small victories will feel like major accomplishments.

I can remember simply riding bikes up to the local Italian ice place with my youngest son and having a wonderful day of joy because the year before I couldn't even leave the house. It's big, and God's victories should be celebrated big.

May 7 - How Can Joy Make You Strong?

Then he said unto them, "Go your way, eat the fat, and drink the sweet, and send portions unto them for whom nothing is prepared: for this day is holy unto our Lord: neither be ye sorry; for the joy of the lord is your strength." (Neh. 8:10)

I don't know about you, but sometimes I read scriptures, and they make me scratch my head in confusion. Like "being strong when we are weak," and from our scripture today: "the joy of the Lord is your strength." What does that actually mean in relation to everyday living? I'm always amazed how Christians like to throw scriptures around like this one and just assume you know what it means when they don't really know. To have a friend who is suffering with anxiety or depression and then to simply say to them, "The joy of the Lord is your strength"—well, it's all good and fine, but what does it do for them? Too often, we as Christians know more words of God than their meaning. We must stop throwing His sacred words around like fortune-cookie fillers and more like the precious words of truth they are. That only comes from knowing God's Word, and knowing God's word only comes from studying God's Word.

Friends, we can read devotionals (even like this one), and we can read online inspirational quotes, but without reading and knowing the Word of God, we have nothing. Today let's stop the scripture tossing and start understanding the scripture meanings. In Nehemiah 8:10, we hear these last two comments: "Neither be sorry; for the joy of the LORD is your strength." What is the joy of the Lord? Does God have joy, or does it mean the joy we have knowing the Lord? Let's look at an example, be it a *weak* one, to help clarify this question. Say you're on a sports team. You love that team with all that you are. It's the championship game, and you have been on a winning streak. When you go out to play that last game, you are on fire with enthusiasm. Why? Are you any stronger, faster, or smarter than you were for the past season? No, but your zeal and love for your team has given you a momentum that is hard to stop. You are like a Juggernaut barreling full speed ahead simply because the joy of the moment and the team have fallen upon you.

Being a Christian isn't being on a team, and I don't mean to belittle what being a child of God is, but in a way, our past success in Christ, our knowledge of our salvation, and redemption that we know we possess—they do raise in us a certain zeal and joy that give us strength. This also is good news for us, friend, for if we never have success in the Lord, it would be hard to cleave unto the joy of the Lord. God does deliver, save, redeem, and prepare for us a place with Him in the heavenly realms. That's an exciting possession, and one that we need to feed off. So if you're struggling today, try to embrace the joy of the Lord and think upon on all that it is to be a blood-bought child of God. Rejoice in what God has done, celebrate His power, and feel the strength of God through experiencing His joy.

May 8 - Joy in the Process

Behold, this is the joy of His way, and out of the earth shall others grow. (Job 8:19)

If you have ever made a cake, you know that it is a process. Like building a house, there is also a process. Find a carpenter who enjoys the process and not just the completed home and you have a well-built building. The process of things is very important to the outcome of things. I like watching how a skyscraper is built, how the foundation is laid, and how the steel begins to be raised. Before you know it, it's complete, and they are cutting the ribbon for the grand opening.

Here in New York where I presently reside, we are seeing the completion of the Freedom Tower, which was raised after the World Trade Center buildings were destroyed. It was a long process, but it's just about done as I pen this book. The lights are turned on, and it looks wonderful. They had the construction workers on the news, raising the last beam and flag. You could see the pride in the completed project. To them, it was more than a building; it was a statement. To have worked on that building is something to be remembered, and they all knew each step was a process toward the goal of finishing it. We here on the outside see only the finished building, yet the ones who were part of the process knew of the sweat, tears, and cracking hammers; the hours of long, hard labor during hot days and cold days; the welding and drilling; the bolting and cutting of metal. Each floor was a mess with dust and dripped piles of cement. Yet the work went on floor after floor.

Dear friend, to find joy while there is a messy project in the works is a hard thing to do. The process God puts us through isn't always pretty; the side effects and debris don't always look nice. If someone was to see us under construction, they might be appalled at what we look like. In a way, we kind of understand them because we too don't like what we see as the Lord is molding our clay hearts. Sometimes we look in the mirror during those dark days, and our faces look like a jackhammer was let loose on us. It's scary and hard to endure at times, and we wonder if we will make it until the process is complete.

Well, like those mighty men and women building that Freedom Tower, we too must focus on the finished product. We must find a joy in the process knowing that the process is as much a part of the building as the completed project. We, like the ironworkers, must take pride in what God is doing in us, getting excited about how we are going to turn out when this is all over. In my life, two of my greatest achievements came after the two worst spells of my depression. Without the depression process, I would simply not be where I am today. I certainly would not be writing this book on depression. True, the process is often not fun at all, but oh for the completed project ceremony.

May 9 - Two Outcomes

> *But let all those that put their trust in Thee rejoice: let them ever shout for joy, because Thou defendest them: let them also that love Thy name be joyful in Thee. (Ps. 5:11)*

Ever wonder why two different Christians have two different outcomes in their lives? Both seem to love the Lord. Both seem to be faithful to God. Yet one seems to be blessed, and the other—well, he is not. We see this a lot in how our children turn out. Parent A does all they can in raising that child, yet that child turns toward the world and darkness. Parent B does seemingly the same thing, and their child is a shining beacon for Christ. Careers and jobs are flowing, and God's blessings are clearly seen. I have noticed this when I look back over my high school alumni. I'm amazed at how so many different people turned out in so many different ways. Some of them just didn't make sense, yet some did. We all knew that dark Joe Jones would end up in jail, but not pretty Jane Jerkins. It's one of the mysteries of life at least to us humans, but is it a mystery to the Lord our God?

In Psalm 5:11, we get a small picture of how the Lord sees things and how He determines outcomes. Remember now—the Lord doesn't see as we see, and His ways are not our ways. Remember also that He sees what we don't see, as in what's really going on in someone's life. All that glitters in not gold, and the grass isn't always greener on the other side of the fence. These are all factors of life that must be placed into the mix, but just remember to let the Lord judge the outcome. I say all that as a disclaimer so we do not make the mistake of reading Psalm 5:11 and then plugging in person A or B and saying, "Hey, it didn't work." No, that's the Lord's wisdom knowing what really is in the heart—we are to simply just follow the rule and scripture.

"But let all those that put their trust in Thee rejoice: let them ever shout for joy, because Thou defendest them: let them also that love Thy name be joyful in Thee." In this psalm, we can clearly see that two people can choose two different roads. One person puts their trust in the Lord, and the other doesn't. We see a lot of stipulations in this psalm, and we would be wise to make sure we fulfill all of them and not just some before we complain that God is not doing His part. Friend, you might be suffering with depression, and another person you know is suffering with the same thing. They may come out of it before you or after you. Their deliverance might be a completely different one. One might have taken the faith-medication route, and you chose the faith-without-medication route.

No one is better or wiser, more spiritual or less; it's just how the Lord chooses to deal with person A and person B. Some things are not ours to know and certainly not ours to judge. I had to choose the medication route to get me out of my pit, and many accused me of not having enough faith. They were able to beat it through their faith, but I could only beat it through my faith in God through medication. To judge the two outcomes is to play God. Let's leave that up to Him.

May 10 - Crying Time

> *And it came to pass in process of time, that the king of Egypt died: and the children of Israel sighed by reason of the bondage, and they cried, and their cry came up unto God by reason of the bondage.*
>
> *And God heard their groaning, and God remembered His covenant with Abraham, with Isaac, and with Jacob. (Exod. 2:23–24)*

As of the writing of this devotional book, I'm fifty years old. Wow, seems like I was just thirty years old. My body today feels a bit more tired, and the joint pains and aches seemed to kick in right after I turned fifty. Maybe it's a warranty issue. One thing I do know about my life is how many times I have cried. As a man, we keep a record of these things as it's much more of a stigma with us than with women. I would say of my crying that, apart from being a child and maybe a broken heart at seventeen, I don't believe I cried too much. Not that I wasn't sensitive but that I just didn't cry.

Well, that was all to change in 1997 when I encountered anxiety and depression for the first time. I tell you I have never cried like I cried when I faced the battles of depression and anxiety. When I say crying, I'm not talking about simple tears. I'm talking about on-my-knees sobbing like I have never sobbed before. Sometimes it was outright moaning with a few moments to catch my breath. When not on my knees, I would be rolling or rocking, holding my knees tightly in some corner, hidden and alone. With those moans were words of desperation and crying out to God, begging and pleading for my very life: "Lord, please help me, for I cannot go on one more moment." There were only two seasons in my life where I was brought to that point, and I pray never again.

Now, were they wasted tears? Were they futile attempts to call out to a god who wasn't listening? Certainly not, for He heard every moan and felt every teardrop. What was worse was that God had to also endure watching me suffer just as He had to endure watching His Son suffer. We never think of that when we are in the boot camp of faith. We don't see how it hurts the Lord more than it hurts us. He knows we need to go through this, but He also knows it will be over, and we don't. That's what's hard for the Lord, to know it will pass when we are ready and wishing (for lack of a better term) that we could see the end outcome that He sees. He knows that if we could only see that future product, we would not cry so much.

Be that as it may, it's one of the unfortunate things in life. We must cry, and God must wait for us to listen. Crying is a part of our purging process; it's a place of humility where growth can be accomplished. It's like watching our child learn to ride a bike for the first time. We know they will crash at least one time and tears will fall, but they must crash and fall if they will ever learn to ride a bike.

Dear friend, if you're at the crying stage of your journey, please don't hold it in but let it out. Even let people see you as it moves people in powerful ways. I think it was only once or twice during my struggle that I actually cried while I was preaching. I was listening to the worship music before I went up, and I was so overcome with emotion that I had to wait for what seemed like an eternity to stop. It passed, the sermon was preached, and my life in Christ continued on—so will yours.

May 11 - What to Be Happy About

Happy art thou, O Israel: who is like unto thee, O people saved by the lord, the shield of thy help, and who is the sword of thy excellency! And thine enemies shall be found liars unto thee; and thou shalt tread upon their high places. (Deut. 33:29)

Feeling like a fool yet being a king. Imagine if you were randomly selected to be a king of a small country. You found out that your distant relative was royalty, and now the crown is passed unto you. Upon arrival, you are greeted by a red carpet and a marching band. The people are cheering you on and waving flags with your face on them. As you enter the castle and court of your new kingdom, you are directed to your throne. As you sit down and the crown is placed upon your head, you think to yourself, *This must be a dream.* Being the skeptic that you are, you insist on seeing the legal documentation for all of this. To your amazement, it's all true, and you are sovereign over your own little kingdom.

Now, stop for a moment and ask yourself a few questions: Now that you are king by bloodline, are you a different person than you were before you found out you were king? Is your anxiety and depression still a part of you? Are you the same frightened little kitten you were before? The answer must be yes, but for some reason, you don't feel as sad and afraid. Why is that? Why is it that you are the same person, but you're not having the same feelings? The answer is simple: you found out that you are of much more worth than you thought and that you're an important person to many people. You found out you are royalty, and being royalty, you are forever secure in your kingdom.

Friend, happiness is not so much getting things or having things your way but understanding who you are. Many times we have feelings of depression and hopelessness simply because we don't know who and what we really are in Christ. We have been lied to for so long by the enemy that we start to believe his lies about us. We become hopeless because we believe we are hopeless. We feel like worms because we have been convinced that we are worms. Listen to me today and read again our scripture in Deuteronomy 33:29. Notice what makes Israel happy. Notice where they find their joy— not in who they are alone but in what God has done for them. They become happy because *God* has saved them, protected them, set them apart, and defeated their enemies. They are told the truth about themselves and the truth about their fears.

Please, today understand who you are in Christ Jesus and walk in that newness of life. Walk knowing who you are to God. Remind yourself that you are saved, sanctified, and set apart. You are ones worthy enough to God to be called His children. Then understand that worthiness comes not from within but from without. It comes from God making us righteous through Jesus Christ's work on the cross. Now, that is something truly to be happy about.

May 12 - Play in Pain

Happy are Thy men, happy are these Thy servants, which stand continually before Thee, and that hear Thy wisdom. (1 Kings 10:8)

One day I was hit with so much negative news that I just felt like crawling into a hole and weeping. Everywhere I turned I could only think of negative things and worst-case scenarios. I was a true downer to be around, and feeling sorry for myself was my only source of joy. Call me the pity-party man because that was what I was. Woe is me, and no one else better try to top my pain and situation. Oh what a childish game I was playing, and what an immature state of mind I placed myself into. I felt alone in my pain, but in reality, I was not. Every devotional I read, every scripture I picked up, all seemed to say the same things: "Days will be hard, and enemies will be many. Nevertheless, we must keep moving on even if we must play the game in pain." I say "play the game in pain" because that's what I read in one of those devotionals. It was a story of a famous Christian ballplayer who was in severe pain but was able to help with the game for his team simply because he clung onto those words: "Sometimes you must play in pain." It's not pretty, nor an idea to jump up and down about, but one that is still true.

Sometimes in life, God doesn't remove the thorn. He doesn't stop the hurt. He doesn't fix the problem but instead commands us to *play in pain*, to keep going, not so much because the day is a happy day but because God says we must. Because God says that through this pain, there is growth, and through that growth there is future victory waiting for you. Did those words and directions from God change my lousy day? No, the day went on ahead with all of the same issues and ills that made me distraught in the first place. But I know one thing for sure. I must go on to fight through another day. God is with me, and that needs to be enough. God knows the truth about me and the lies thrown at me, but I must stay and play in pain. End of story. And that's all there is to do sometimes. Yes, it takes faith, but isn't that what we are called to walk by?

May 13 - If God Says It Again, So Should We

Happy are Thy men, and happy are these Thy servants, which stand continually before Thee, and hear Thy wisdom. (2 Chron. 9:7)

Our scripture for today basically says the same thing that our scripture said yesterday. It's a picture of cause and effect. Do this and that will happen, which is what most of the Bible really states. We notice the first few words, as they jump right out at us: "Happy are Thy men." We like that part, and we focus on it, but we seem to turn our eyes away the minute we come to the next few words, the words that say, "Happy are those who [*continually*] stand before Thee and that [*hear*] Thy wisdom." That word *continually* really jumps out yet is hidden at the same time.

As humans, we always want the cake without having to bake it. We want the meat without slaughtering the cow. Joy and happiness are things that we can obtain, not so much in regard to the world's picture of happiness but that of the Lord's. It's a peace and a place of mind. It's a joy in knowing that God is with us and that He is all we need. For those of you who have tasted that place, you know what I'm talking about. There is not a dollar amount that I would trade for it. But again, back to getting to that place, how do we arrive there and stay there? Our scripture again for today says it clear: it is to continually stand right with the Lord, not for a weekend, not for a Sunday service, but all the time, every day striving to please the Lord. It's not an idea but a way of life. Also notice what the last part of that scripture says: "And that [*hear*] thy wisdom."

We can listen all day to preachers on TV. We can go to church every Sunday and read God's Word through the Bible and devotions, but not until we hear what He is telling us will anything change. To hear means to take that information and apply it to our lives. It's to read "Do not commit adultery" and then to not commit it. It's to read about loving the Lord with all of our hearts and minds and then living that way.

So many times we complain to God about our issues and why He isn't doing anything about them when the one who is causing the issues is ourselves. We are not causing them in that we are making trouble come to us, but we are missing the blessings of joy through those trials because we are not obeying God's Word in living it out. To have a servant's heart, you must enjoy being a servant, not only to others but to God first and foremost. Be a servant to the Lord because you love Him, asking nothing else in return. And watch what happens.

May 14 - Not That Way, Lord

> For thou shalt eat the labour of thine hands: happy shalt thou be, and it shall be well with thee. (Ps. 128:2)

My nineteen-year-old son started a new job. He is doing manual labor for a landscaper. He had the choice of college and / or a trade school, but he chose to just make money. Though I have shared this story before, it's worth sharing again as it's a picture of getting out what we put in. So many times when going through emotional trauma, we pray that the

Lord would simply lift it. I have been there many times in one degree or another, and I waited for the Lord's deliverance, and yet none came (when I wanted it). Deliverance came eventually, but it was never on demand. See, we are an on-demand society, and that's how we feel that the Lord should work. We have a problem, we put in our request, and the Lord jumps to attention and fixes it for us. That would be nice, but it would not be good, and here is why.

My son Aaron wants many things out of life as most nineteen-year-olds do. He wants to be famous in his music band. He wants to have a lot of money so he can buy all the toys and guitars he desires, plus he wants to marry the girl of his dreams and have a wonderful home to live in—not to mention the motorcycle he has his eye on plus the around-the-world trip he dreams of. They are all fine dreams, and some may be even noble, but there is that process again. Right from the garden, we learned of that process as Adam and Eve ran the whole world into sin. From that day forward, the process began: work to eat, labor to attain, sweat and agonize to achieve what you desire. And in the process, expect woodchuck holes, roots, dust, and baking sun. At the end of the day, your back will ache, and your hands will blister; but as the Lord says, "It will be good." Good for our character and for our soul.

My son soon realized that making so much money an hour might sound great until you have to labor for that money. His first few weeks on the jobs revealed a lot of inner truths about us all. We don't like to labor if we don't have to, and it's easier to be handed things than to work for them. But this is not good! In our scripture for today, the Lord tells us this truth and explains it this way: "Labor for what you need, and it will be good for you." Sad that this concept is almost entirely lost today, but it's a truth nonetheless.

Again, with regard to emotional issues, I have found this also to be true. If I want the fruits of healing, I must endure the pain of laboring to get there. If the Lord was to simply lift every burden, then I would expect Him to do it all the time and would only look to Him as my servant. Sure there are times when the Lord will lift and carry our burdens, but for the most part, we must do our part in trusting, believing, and having faith in Him. Other than salvation, sanctification is a work of the heart and mind. Faith without works is dead as deliverance without faith in action is dead. Get up, trust God, and move on no matter how hard it becomes. It will be good.

May 15 - Finding Out What to Do

Happy is the man that findeth wisdom, and the man that getteth understanding. (Prov. 3:13)

In your search for answers and relief, you must first find wisdom. Now, there are many types of wisdom that are up for grabs, but the only wisdom that will lead to true wisdom is God's wisdom. Maybe you're confused by that statement, but let me explain. We all go through life with problems and trials. We all know that the Lord may use different means to achieve His will in our lives. The problem is that we run to the world's wisdom for solutions before we run to the Lord's. Take for example the Lord's amazing work in King Solomon and the account of the two ladies fighting over one child. One mother was the real mother, and one was not. The solution was a practical one given out by a wise king, but where did that king get his wisdom? We know clearly through scripture that Solomon got his wisdom from the Lord Himself. When he followed it and made tough choices, things went well; but when he didn't, things went wrong.

I make this point to bring attention to a much debated question, and one that this book was partially written to address. That is with regard to the options in dealing with some levels of anxiety and depression. I have been speaking on this issue for some time now and keynote speaking at various venues. On top of that, I have been counseling people through their trying times of anxiety and depression. It has been a blessing for me, but it has also placed me at odds with many "Christians," from pastors to counselors and lay people in the church. For the most part, I stand alone on this; but regardless of the opposition, I stand on God's Word. The taboo here I speak of is medication for treating clinical depression and anxiety disorder. Most, if not all, Christians believe it is never the answer and faith alone is. Well, I disagree, not in the faith alone part but in what you're doing with that faith. See, I can look at faith as a separate animal from God's wisdom. I can say that faith will heal me, but what if faith in God's wisdom tells me to do something else? What if having faith in God's wisdom is doing just that—having blind faith in whatever the Lord tells you to do even if people tell you otherwise?

In my struggles, I trusted in God's wisdom, wisdom that God decides, not wisdom that I choose to interpret. In my case, God's wisdom told me that it's time to use medication lest you die. Didn't Jesus answer His betwixt disciples about the possessed person saying, "This one comes out *only* by prayer and fasting." There is the wisdom of God for each situation, and His directions to you in this regard might be different than mine.

Friend, if you are in a place where you don't know what to do, a place where everyone is telling you something different, and all you feel is confused, then seek out God's wisdom above man's. When the Lord leads you to that place, jump in by faith and find peace there.

May 16 - Good Enough for God, Good Enough for Me

The lord by wisdom hath founded the earth; by understanding hath He established the heavens. (Prov. 3:19)

Today is a day that the Lord has made. This is a scriptural truth, and one we quote quite often. It's a truth we accept yet a truth we don't truly understand, nor do we have to. Wisdom, as we spoke about yesterday, comes about in many forms, and the world has some of its own. When I think of the world's wisdom, not all of it is evil or bad; some, in fact, are really amazing.

Take computers and how they operate. To this day, I have no idea how my typing on these keys are making words appear on my screen. I don't know how moving my mouse makes that little arrow float around. I certainly don't know how I can go online and click on an icon, and a world of information appears before me. To me, it's an amazing kind of wisdom that I use every day, yet what's even better about it is I don't have to understand it to use it. Did you hear what I just said? I can be blessed by wisdom and not necessarily understand it. Why is it that we can't give God's wisdom the same credit? Just because I don't understand how God could make all the worlds and hold the planets in orbit doesn't mean He can't exist. Just because I don't see Him doesn't mean He is not working. I don't see what goes on inside my computer, nor do I want to, but I know it works.

Today, as you try to understand what and why this day might be so hard, as you try to put your mind around what God might be doing in your life, don't worry so much about how He works but simply know that He is working. In Psalm 3:19, it states that the Lord by wisdom (His wisdom, if I may) has built the earth, and by His understanding (meaning I don't have to understand it), He has set in order the heavens. Today we need to embrace these truths even if we don't understand them. We must say to ourselves, "I don't know why I'm going through this, but God does, and if He holds the worlds together by His wisdom, then He must be able to hold mine together."

As you are reading this devotion this morning, take a glance down at your hands, fingers, and arms. Marvel how they all function and how, together with the rest of your body, they complete the task your mind commands them to. Find peace in knowing that this same God who created you also keeps you going. If He keeps your physical functions working, so can He then keep your emotional functions in order. Do we get physical ailments and broken bones? Sure, but somehow we keep living until He calls us home. Even in major illnesses, the body that the Lord created is fighting to live, to survive. Only the Lord can stop that heart and only the Lord can keep it beating. God's wisdom is exciting. Trust in it and see His Salvation.

May 17 - When Anger Rules

Happy is the man that feareth always: but he that hardeneth his heart shall fall into mischief. (Prov. 28:14)

Anger is an interesting emotion; it can motivate us toward good or toward evil. It can raise great strength within us and also bring us to a place of knee-jerk reaction and poor judgment. I have noted in my life of dealing with anxiety and depression that anger always seems to be hiding out somewhere behind the cobwebs of my mind. Either I'm angry at God, the world, or everyone who is trying to help but doesn't understand. With anger comes frustration, and with frustration comes short-temperedness. Mix all of these emotions up in a bowl and turn on the mixer and you have the makings of an ugly cake.

Now like I said, all anger is not bad, and anger over sin and this world's feelings toward our Lord are a great motivator for fighting for the Word and the truth. That is truly righteous indignation, things like anger over countless children killed by abortion and the mocking of God's name in movies and popular culture. Jesus was even angry when He turned over the money changer's tables. So anger can be good, but we all know what anger turned bad can do. In times of great trials, it's all too common for anger to take control and run the ship of our souls. Anger can break fellowship with God and with other believers. Sinful anger, being sin, can break communication lines down with the Lord. Families can be hurt, churches can be divided, and the mission of the gospel misunderstood. Anger misdirected and out of control can even harm us physically through high-blood pressure and stress. Hurtful words can be spoken in haste, which can never be taken back.

I heard it once said that anger is like toothpaste. Words that come out are easy but, like toothpaste, try getting it back in the tube, not so easy. I remember one particular time while newly married, my wife and I had a bad fight. In my anger, I through my arm up, hit our wall unit, and knocked over one of our wedding gifts. It was a set of engraved wine glasses with our names and the date of our wedding. Her glass broke, and we both stopped and felt the sadness for our foolishness. The glass was never replaced and left us a sad reminder of anger unchecked.

In my times of depression and especially in anxiety, anger would often run me, anger at God, friends, and family, anger at my life and where it ended up. Anger at other people just because they were happy and I was not. Anger taken to the tenth degree can lead to irrational thoughts, thoughts of suicide and violent behavior, thoughts of revenge and evil imaginations. In a state of anger, the lines between right and wrong can be hard to distinguish. We have seen that in our recent history with terrorists who, through anger, were led to kill thousands of people, some even claiming they were doing it in God's name. And the worst and last stage of anger is a hardened heart, one that can no longer hear or feel the things of God.

May 18 - On the Verge of a Miracle

Where there is no vision, the people perish: but he that keepeth the law, happy is he. (Prov. 29:18)

Proverbs 29:18 is a popular yet often misquoted scripture. A local secular newspaper uses it as a heading for their editorial section. I once wrote to them asking why they used that scripture when they don't even believe in God's Word. In Proverbs 29:18, what's amazing is that no matter how you interpret it, it still brings great wisdom and truth. As it is most applied, it means that when we stop looking forward, when we no longer have a dream or a hope for the future, we will perish. The drive that moves us forward, once gone, leaves us motionless. To be excited about tomorrow helps us get through the struggles of today. These are all true, and I have kept that word in my heart for difficult times. Yet to properly understand this scripture, we must understand what it really means and why it was written.

It was written at a time where prophets of God often spoke, and through those voices, God's people were directed. Elijah and Isaiah and so many more, it was through their words from God that God's people knew where to turn and what to do next. It was through their visions of heavenly things that earthly people could see God. Read the visions of John on Patmos and Ezekiel's extraordinary experiences, and you could see how God's people lived and waited for those men's words and visions. But what happens when the visions and instructions from God stop? What happens when our celestial map book is closed, and we are lost in the dark? It is there that true darkness and despair come in. It's such a place where we might perish for lack of direction.

It reminds me of driving through New York City, a place I despise, especially when my GPS is on the fritz. Without my GPS, I am totally lost, and panic sets in. I can truly say that without a vision in my GPS screen, I will perish in New York City. Now, that's a silly example but a simple and vivid picture of what Proverbs 19:18 really means. In our times of emotional struggles, we too can feel like we might perish if we don't hear from the Lord, and if we are waiting to hear from God, we just might have to wait a long time before we ever see a vision or hear an actual voice. But as the scripture continues, we have no need for a vision as long as we have the Word of God.

Today, though many follow visions and signs, the scriptures are clear that to do so is foolish as the days of prophets are past. All we need to hear from God is found in His Holy Bible, which gives us all the information we need to move on and continue in this life and the life to come. So, dear friend, fret not about the future or of not hearing a direct voice from God. We can hear all we need if we read His Word and listen through His Spirit. And from what I see and hear in God's Word, it's all thumbs up for His children, and we are all on the verge of a miracle. Just wait a moment longer. The breakthrough is coming with or without a vision.

May 19 - Excuse Me, Lord, But How About Me?

Righteous art Thou, O lord, when I plead with Thee: yet let me talk with Thee of Thy judgments: Wherefore doth the way of the wicked prosper? Wherefore are all they happy that deal very treacherously? (Jer. 12:1)

One of the things that get under my skin is how the Lord knows me so well. Like King David said, "There is nowhere to hide from His knowing. He knows every little detail of my inner soul." I'm glad He does, but sometimes it gets to me, like when He sees me angry over another person's blessings. Sure, many will deny that they have ever felt that way, but when I'm honest with myself, I must come clean with the Lord and repent of this wicked way in me. This anger or confusion about how the Lord works is nothing new. People from eons past have asked the Lord the same thing: "Why do the bad people seem to be doing well, and I'm not?"

In Jeremiah 12:1, I love how the prophet gently tries to question the Lord's actions: "Oh Lord, you are so great, but may I ask you something? May I have a minute of your time? Why do the wicked prosper? Why are the bad people so happy?" Notice that he never actually says, "Why am I sad even though I am so good?" No, he doesn't say that, but we sure know it's implied. Now, is the prophet out of line to ask this? Maybe, but it is a good question. Dear friend, if you are suffering through another day with anxiety or depression, whether it is clinical or just mild, you may feel that God is overlooking you while He is blessing your sinful neighbor. It's not unusual to feel that way, so don't beat yourself up.

I remember the worst pains of being depressed were seeing others who were happy. It reminds me of my wife and myself when we first got married. Before we knew it, we were ready for children, but God was not. For years we waited, and her womb was still closed, and what made matters worse was that all of our friends were starting families. Our church was filled with pregnant mothers, and every baby shower my wife went to secretly ate at her. She felt horrible because she wanted to be happy for all the others, but her old sinful nature was still alive and kicking. Jealousy and bitterness were eating her alive. Sure, it makes one look like a monster, but that's what we are sometimes. Praise God He forgives even monsters. If you're suffering today and also bitter at all those who are not suffering, then, before you can ever think of healing, you must deal with the sins of the heart. You must deal with your anger at God and other people. Now, to really make this hard, the Lord has another thing He wants you to do—that is, to pray for those who are doing well. Bless those whose lives are doing great and are filled with joy and laughter.

Wow, that's tough, is it not? But it is what we are called to do. It is a true sacrifice of righteousness. A dying to self and living unto Christ. Let's make that step today.

May 20 - I Know but I Can't

If ye know these things, happy are ye if ye do them. (John 13:17)

I remember way back when my first encounter with anxiety set in. I remember even more all the people who found out and tried to offer help. So many good friends, church members, and family offered all that they could. I was bombarded with devotional books, e-mails, notes of encouragement, counselors' phone numbers, CDs and tape series on anxiety. I had so many things to read, listen to, and watch that I am still listening to those materials today. People stopped by and prayed over me and with me. Some shared their stories and gave advice. They told me how God had me covered, and it would all be okay. One nice lady gave me a little wall plaque that said "life is good." I still have that one hanging somewhere.

The reason I bring all this up is to make this point: everything, for the most part, that people gave me was true and right. Their words were dead-on and true. The scriptures were wonderful, and the prayers cherished. It was all good, of that there was no doubt, but the problem was that I could not, for the life of me, apply them. They did no good; the devotionals did not help. I could read the Bible till I was blue in the face, but for the most part, I found no comfort. The question was, and is, this: why didn't I? Why didn't I get blessed through God's Word? Why didn't His words of comfort give me comfort? Why didn't the devotional books bring me healing and change? If anything, the CD series that I listened to actually made my anxiety worse as they went over all the symptoms; and if I didn't have them all, I did after listening to it. It didn't help that it wasn't even a Christian product.

Dear friend, please understand what I needed so much to understand: unless we apply what we hear and are taught, nothing will happen. It's one thing to read that Jesus will never leave us or forsake us; it's another thing to trust in that. It's one thing to read in Joshua 1:9 that we are to be strong and of good courage, but it's another thing to embrace it. I know, dear Lord, I know how hard this is. I know what it's like to feel so lousy, and all you want is to feel better. Words are words, and sometimes you just feel like screaming to everyone to just leave you alone. I know that, but I also know there must be a point in time when you start believing, even while you're in pain, that God is in control and is doing something good, that something good is coming, and to praise Him while you are waiting. It will take every fiber of your being, but it will be worth every bit of the effort you put into it. Believe Him. Trust Him. If, for any reason, do it because I was where you are, and I did it, and I made it through. You can too as I am no stronger than you are; in fact, I'm a worm of a person, a weak Christian with little faith, but I had enough faith to hold on.

May 21 - Endure Until Happy

Behold, we count them happy which endure. Ye have heard of the patience of Job, and have seen the end of the Lord; that the Lord is very pitiful, and of tender mercy. (James 5:11)

Dear friend, it's May 21, and you can almost smell the summer-cleansing rain. We are close to halfway through this year, and maybe you're halfway through your struggle. Maybe you're a quarter of the way through. Maybe it just hit you, or maybe it's the tail end, and clear skies are just ahead. Whatever the case may be, in your life, there is one truth that we must cling to. In order to make it, we must endure. I know how I hate that word since that word gives no signs of relief or comfort but only a picture of prolonged pain. If you have been reading this devotion since January, then one thing you would have noticed is this: endurance has been the key to most of the days of inspirational writing.

Dear friend, as I was writing this book, each day was based on prayer. Every single time I sat to write, I would picture you, the suffering child of God, and what you might be feeling. I would ask the Lord each day as I was writing to let the exact words you need to hear today be the words you heard. I also set out on a mission to write a blood-honest book, holding nothing back and telling you like it is. I didn't want this devotional to be filled with flowery, bombastic wording to impress you with my literary style yet leave you with empty words of cheerfulness that are simply lies. Today, as I write, this is no different than the other. Today I write, with inconvenient honesty, that sometimes the only thing we can do is endure one day more—enduring not simply for the sake of being a martyr, but enduring because you know, trust, and believe that Jesus will deliver you one day, believing that the Lord is very tender, filled with mercy, and that He hears all of our cries.

I say this all so when I tell you these truths, you will trust me. For if I am honest with you about the cold hard facts of this monster of blessing, you will also believe and trust me when I tell you the truth of your deliverance from it. I hold nothing back, and I pray I leave nothing out. Remember the Lord, for this is all about Him; every pain and trial is all about Him. It is for our growth and for our blessing. It is to point out our hidden sins and misplaced dependency.

Sometimes I might sound redundant, sometimes repetitive, but always in God's will, I hope. This is my prayer and my goal. Sure, I could tell you that just by blowing on a silver dollar and saying abracadabra four times that you would be healed. I could have promoted this book as the secret weapon against anxiety and depression. I could have said that just by reading it, all would be well. But like everything else I have told you, without applying what you have heard and believing what God's Word says, nothing will change. So today might just be another day where you just have to endure. No deliverance but just twenty-four hours of waiting a little while longer. Yet fear not. It is coming, and you can be new again.

May 22 - I'm Doing Nothing Wrong

But and if ye suffer for righteousness' sake, happy are ye: and be not afraid of their terror, neither be troubled. (1 Pet. 3:14)

Now, I know that none of us are sinless, nor can we ever be in this life. I know that if that was true, then Christ died in vain, for He died for a people who needed no salvation. So yes, we are all sinners, but what if you're a sinner saved by grace? A child of God through faith in Jesus Christ, a true Bible-believing Christian saved by faith alone and not of works. What if you're living holy and set apart, you give your proper tithe and serve wholeheartedly at your church? You share your faith and live a life fully sold out for Jesus Christ. You are as clean and pure as humanly possible in this sinful flesh. What if that is you and still you are T-boned by the surprise trial of anxiety and depression? All was going well and fine and then zap—you are taken right off your pure-white Stallion.

Sounds strange and odd, but it does happen, and Job, as we all know, is a perfect picture of that very scenario. So what's the deal? What's going on? What am I to do? There are no sins to confess at the moment, and no life change needed. Well, 1 Peter 3:14 gives us a little insight into this unusual dilemma. Let's read it together: "But and if ye suffer for righteousness's sake, happy are ye: and be not afraid of their terror, neither be troubled." So you are suffering, and it's not due to sin or a moral mistake. If it's not due to a trial by God or a lesson to be learned, then this scripture says this rather odd thing. This rather odd command: *be happy!* Besides the command to be happy, we are also commanded not to be afraid or even troubled. But why? Why not be upset or troubled? And why, dear Lord, should I be happy?

The answer lies in why we have fallen into this unusual trial: "you are suffering for righteousness' sake"—meaning that you are suffering simply because you are living right unto the Lord and that outside forces are attacking you because of who and what you believe in. This, my friend, is the dark demonic side of this spiritual battle we face. In case you didn't know it, the battle is very real, and living for Christ full-on is a dangerous road to travel. Simply by obeying God's commands, it can bring upon you Satan's attacks. Be it emotional, economical, physical, or whatever way he chooses—and God allows—Satan will go for your weakest link, and if it is fear or emotional instability, then watch out and keep that area well protected.

We don't go out in the sun if we are prone to sunburn, so we should take the same precautions when living righteously. We remember to put on our sunblock, and I'm not talking number 3 but more like number 100. In the meantime, and as odd as it is to say, be happy during this type of attack, for it is sure proof that you are living for the Lord. He is happy, and Satan is not. Just remember who wins the day.

May 23 - Rebuilding Day

Create in me a clean heart, O God; and renew a right spirit within me. (Ps. 51:10)

The word *create* is interesting. Though it is clearly part of the English language and many others also, it is still a word we don't use too often. Think about how many times you incorporate the word *create* in your daily life. Even when I'm building something in my backyard, it doesn't seem to be a creation as much as it is a project. I have built many a tree house having three boys, rebuilt some motor scooters, and restored some old cars and trucks, but I don't think I create things. To create is really to give yourself a big pat on the back, for to create is to start from scratch and make something that never was. I think the closest I came to that was building a pinewood derby car for my youngest son, Luke. We were given a block of wood, some wheels and axles, and a few directions. We kind of created a car, but did we really?

One place where we find the word *create* is in the Word of God. God is big on creating things, and He does it well. He does it so well that He has one up on us as mankind. He can create something from nothing. Right in the beginning, we see this in action. In the book of Genesis, God creates, but He goes even further. He creates without existing material. Sure, I can build a pinewood derby car, but can I create one out of nothing? Can I be placed in a locked room with only myself and my mind and create a wooden car? The answer is simple: I can't, not unless I have the elements and parts to assemble. In reality, what any of us does is really assemble things. Even car manufacturers don't really create in the true sense of creation. They might start from scratch, but even there, they still have metal, rubber, plastic, and iron. That's why God is so far above man and why man can never even come close to being like God.

It's also why I love scriptures like Psalm 51:10. It shows us what only God can do, which is to create in us a clean heart. It's taking that old nasty, mangled heart and making it new. Now you could stand up and say, "Hey, isn't God just reassembling old parts?" And you might be right, but in the case of man, He can't use all of the old parts. Those parts are corrupted and tainted. He has to add something that was not there before, which is the Holy Spirit.

When we come to know Christ as salvation, the Word says we become born from above. We are called a new creation; meaning, something not of this world is added to us. Something that only God Himself possesses. Why this is so exciting is because when it comes to our spiritual and emotional lives, God doesn't just rebuild us, He adds something new, something to overcome the fear and depression. He adds a spiritual check valve to our wild running mind. It is the Holy Spirit that steps in and does what we could never do. When fear oppresses us, the Holy Spirit will rescue us if we allow Him.

May 24 - Hide and Seek

And he said, "I heard Thy voice in the garden, and I was afraid, because I was naked; and I hid myself." (Gen. 3:10)

There are many reasons why we fall into certain hurts and pains. In the case of anxiety and depression, the reasons are even deeper and more complex. In some cases, it's a chemical imbalance brought on by environmental or occupational exposure. It can be hereditary or spiritual. There is situational depression as in—being down because you just lost your job. Or there is clinical depression where emotional functions begin to fail for no known reason. Behind them all, there is the Lord, working, allowing, causing, and training us to be more like Christ. The Lord does many strange things sometimes, at least in our eyes; yet no matter what He chooses to use or allow, it is good. God can only do good as we have discussed before. Depression seems like a horrible thing, but to the Lord, it can be a great tool.

It was depression that the Lord used to awaken me to ministry and to the emptiness of things. Regardless of what the Lord uses, He is always doing one thing, and that is getting our attention. When I was a child, a popular game was hide and seek. Today I don't know if children even play it anymore, but for me, it was part of growing up. We all know the rules: one person hides and another tries to find you. The thing is to not get caught, and when you do, you lose. Well, with God, we play that game in a way. We spend our whole lives running and hiding from Him. We might not think so, but we are.

Christian or not, we are always hiding or trying to hide from Him. It's a fruitless effort as you cannot hide from an omniscient God, the thrice Holy Creator of time and space. But like children, we think we can, and what we are trying to hide is really the issue at hand. Maybe it's a secret sin or a passion for something that is greater than our passion for Him. Maybe it's a lazy streak or a greedy tendency. Sometimes it's a lying heart, wandering eyes, a money-loving attitude, a false righteousness, or a judgmental attitude against other people. No matter what the vice, it is the one thing we wish God will not find out.

Well, our Lord in His ever-parent mode doesn't want to see His children not being all they were called to be. He desires greater things for us, wonderful places of ministry and usefulness. He knows that in our hiding place, we can't ever be what He has ordained us to be; so in His mercy, grace, and love, He flushes us out from hiding. What he chooses to use in doing so is up to His all-knowing mind. He knows best and knows what will turn us and get our attention. He may use a job loss, broken leg, death of a loved one, or even depression and anxiety. Fear is a great motivator, and until we fear the Lord alone, fear will always control us.

Dear friend, if God has chosen emotional pain as His tool of choice to pry open your soul to Him, save a lot of time and don't fight it. Let the depression do what it must, let the anxiety take you where He is leading you. When you arrive there, you will understand why He chose that particular pry bar.

May 25 - It's Fear

> *"Therefore fear thou not, O My servant Jacob," saith the lord; "neither be dismayed, O Israel: for, lo, I will save thee from afar, and thy seed from the land of their captivity; and Jacob shall return, and shall be in rest, and be quiet, and none shall make him afraid." (Jer. 30:10)*

We can spend years reading and studying the causes and effects of depression and anxiety. Maybe today you are tired of hearing them yourself, and you're ready to give up. Maybe you have heard it all, and in the end, you feel like nothing is going to remove this fear, so you must accept its reality and deal with it. Friend, I know how you feel, and I have been through every facet of the illness and sometimes sin. I say illness and sin because it can be both or neither. Read on in the companion book of the same name (sold separately) for a more detailed explanation of what I mean. But for us today, we must conclude for the most part that all of this, all of our pain, is really rooted in one word—*fear*. if there was one thing in my life that I could master, it would be fear. Wow, to never fear again. What a place to be as long as I am still able to fear God.

When I look over my years of being in and out of this battle, I always find fear at the core. Be it depression or anxiety, fear is the hub of the bike wheel around which all things rotate. Fear of everything—fear of losing a job, a loved one, your health, your money, fear of not having health insurance, fear of children dying, fear of loved ones getting cancer, fear of natural disaster, fear of the economy crashing and wars breaking out, even just the fear of a simple tooth that has to be filled.

It is fear that really ruins the day for us all. It's fear that displaces joy, and that's what hurts the most. My whole life has been one of fear and worry, the what-ifs of this or that happening. It has really brought me to the place where the rubber really meets the road, the place where we must put all of our cards on the table. Stand up and say, "Yes, I believe that God is in control of all things in my life, and so I have nothing to fear" or "I don't believe in God and never really did," because to live in fear and say I trust Him is an outright contradiction of terms.

Wow, that's scary to say, think, or even admit. Do I even really believe in God? Well, you know I do, and I trust Him with all that I am, and there is where we must go, to say today that God is real, as is His Word and His purpose for my life. He will do me only good and not evil. Friend, we *must* fall flat out on faith or simply fall down broken. God either is or His is not. I have seen the faith-life in Christ, and I have seen my life living the fear-life in Christ. One is pain; one is comfort. Sure, it's not easy, and there are times when the cares of this world do scare me and stir up anxiety in me. I do fall into slumps and bumps, but at the end of the day, God is on the throne and in control. Like Paul, I have decided to say *I am persuaded*. I am persuaded that God is alive and well, strong and mighty to save. Though He delays His moving, He still is all that He says He is. Trust, faith, affirmation are all weapons against fear. God's Word and His promises, they all are what we must hold on to if we are ever to fight this mighty foe of fear. We can, and we must!

May 26 - Not Now

If any man serve Me, let him follow Me; and where I am, there shall also My servant be: if any man serve Me, him will My Father honor. (John 12:26)

To serve God, it's what we are all called to do. Greatest in His kingdom is servant of all. Jesus had a servant's heart, and as we are to emulate Jesus, we should also have a servant's heart. When you're going through depression or anxiety, the furthest thing from your mind is thinking about serving others. When you're standing on a hot coal, you really don't care about your neighbor standing on a hot coal. It's a paradox of sorts that the Lord really places on our laps. Who do we really love more, ourselves, God, or others? Who is really the most important, and not just when things are going well for you, but even when they are not?

I remember having the Holy Spirit lay this conviction on me while going through depression. I would think to myself, *Come on, Lord, how can I possibly think about or even care about anyone else right now? Lord, you know what I'm going through and how much pain I'm in. I need to focus on me right now.* If you have ever been in that place, you know what I'm talking about. It really cuts us to the core and opens the door to the question, Is God possibly allowing my season of personal struggle just to see who I really care about the most? Ouch, that really hurts, and I care not to even think upon it. But still the Holy Spirit convinces me more. What about Jesus going through His time of great anguish and suffering? Did Jesus say, "Sorry, people. Sorry, world. I'm dealing with some real personal stuff right now, so you're going to have to wait until I work out My own issues"? Well, you can say, "I'm not Jesus Christ," and you would be right, but that doesn't change the fact that we are to model ourselves after Him. He is a picture of the suffering servant, is He not?

Notice in John 12:26 that Jesus doesn't have any escape clauses in there. He doesn't say, "Serve and follow Me, unless you're going through a hard time." No, He lays down the law, which is this: "If any man serve Me, let him follow Me; and where I am, there shall also My servant be: if any man serve Me, him will My Father honor." Funny how again we hone in on the last part, the "God will honor us" part. We like that part, and because of that, it's all we really care about. We miss all the prerequisites for that blessing, which are: "Honor, serve, and follow Me." Sure, it's hard, and the last thing we want to think about, but it is still God's Word.

So, dear friend, as hard as it might be today, think about a fellow person whom you know could use a call, a letter, an e-mail, a text. Pray for them and their problems. Think about a need in your church that needs to be filled. Think and pray about how you can serve God and even lead someone to

Christ—yes, even when you need to be held up to even walk. With all that you are, lift yourself out of your doldrums and gloom and say these mighty, bold words: Here I am, Lord, how can I serve you today?

May 27 - I Need a Quick Fix

Then Jesus said unto them, "Yet a little while is the light with you. Walk while ye have the light, lest darkness come upon you: for he that walketh in darkness knoweth not whither he goeth." (John 12:35)

Before I was a Christian, I lived like much of the world. During the late seventies and eighties, I was what you would call a sex, drugs, and rock-and-roll type of guy. I played drums in a heavy-metal band and had what they called, at the time, big hair. My life consisted of pleasing myself with sex, drugs, and rock and roll. When sadness came or the thought of another week of work, I would take care of my needs by any means that was closest. It was my *quick-fix* system, a system that our world today has mastered even more.

Today, in my counseling practice, I see many new and innovative ways of getting that quick fix, from cutting, drinking, online affairs to buying bigger and better toys. The quick fixes that are out there are actually too numerous. Yet one thing they all have in common is this: they are all filled with darkness. Friend, we can't feel God's healing light if we live in the world's darkness. We think we can, and we say, "But, Lord, I need this right now so at least I can feel good for a little bit."

I remember this one particular woman, whom I counseled, who had the worst depression and anxiety I had ever seen. When going through her very dark times, she would often text or e-mail me begging for permission to cut herself. Cutting is a phenomenon in itself today, which would require another book to cover, but it is a modern quick fix of darkness. Praise God she never gave in to that old habit, and today I'm happy to say she is living a new life in Christ. The reason why I speak of this quick fix of darkness is because it's a tempting place to run. The devil waves it in our painful eyes, and it does seem so appealing. A small reprieve is so appealing when you're facing twenty-four hours of pain, but we must never go there. It is a lie, a trap, and a pit of destruction. We run to it a little, and in time, we'll need a lot. The quick fix becomes a daily support. The enemy has you by the tail and is pulling you closer to him, only so you will be further away from the Lord. He is drawing us away from the light so we will live in darkness, and the longer we live in that darkness, the harder it will be to see our way out of it.

Friend, whatever you are running to for temporary joy, whether it be watching porn, drinking, or cutting, don't go there! Run from it and run to Jesus Christ. Stay away from those dark places, those dark Internet sites, those flirtatious games you are playing. They are all a lie, and there is no help or salvation in them. Run to the light of Jesus Christ.

May 28 - Free Delivery

"Be not afraid of the king of Babylon, of whom ye are afraid; be not afraid of him," saith the Lord: *"for I am with you to save you, and to deliver you from his hand." (Jer. 42:11)*

I never thought it would happen, but I have become a computer person. Not that I'm a computer geek, but that I depend on it. I remember years ago when I was a deacon; the question of purchasing a computer for the church was brought up for a vote. Out of the entire congregation, my father and I were the only no votes. It must be the Lord's irony since I use a computer every day in my office. I don't just use them for church either but for buying things online. It's been a dangerous mix for me and online stores. I like seeing that delivery truck coming around the bend with my package, and I like it even more if I purchased it with free delivery. It's becoming a popular thing now, and more and more, online stores are using free delivery as the bait to get you to buy, and they know that it works. Besides the *free* part, I like the delivery part, which means that someone else brings something to me so I don't have to go and get it.

When we go out to a restaurant, we like how people deliver the food to us, and we don't have to wait in line to get the food. It's sad that it has become an American thing, but be that as it may, it is nice. When it comes to the Lord, I find that He sticks to His word in this regard also. When He said that the greatest in His kingdom is servant of all, He lived by example. Now, don't get me wrong as many in the church do. God is not a slave to our whims and should never ever be looked at as a celestial servant. We must come to Him in fear and honor, of that there is no question. Yet what I do see in God's Word is that though He doesn't have to, He, as a good father, delivers on His promises.

In Jeremiah 42:11, and in many other scriptures, we hear of the Lord delivering into our hands many things. Our enemies are one, and victory is another. "'Be not afraid of the king of Babylon, of whom ye are afraid; be not afraid of him,' saith the LORD: 'for I am with you to save you, and to deliver you from his hand.'" Notice here the Lord's ever-working way with His creation. He commands us not to be afraid. He also tells us who not to be afraid of—those who seek to do us harm, whether they are actual people or emotional demons. He then tells us why we should not be afraid: "Because I am with you to save you." Then He closes His thought with a breathtaking, peace-giving, soul-comforting word of rest: "For I will deliver you from his hand."

Friend, it is God at the end of the day who delivers us. There is nothing of / or in our hearts that we could ever do to save us. In salvation, it is Jesus who delivers us from sin's curse. In daily living, it is God who delivers us from those who seek to destroy us. Again, be it man or emotion, God delivers. He always comes through—and even better than the mail service, He delivers in hurricane, war, and during the dangers of death itself. God delivers!

May 29 - Rest and at Ease

But fear not thou, O My servant Jacob, and be not dismayed, O Israel: for, behold, I will save thee from afar off, and thy seed from the land of their captivity; and Jacob shall return, and be in rest and at ease, and none shall make him afraid. (Jer. 46:27)

There are many unscrupulous people out there today who offer what they cannot deliver. It's sad to say that many of these people are right here in the church, and even worse, they are in the leadership of the church. I have never been a big fan of TV evangelists; not that they are all wrong, but most of them are less than honest. What's worse is what they are dishonest about. It seems to me that many of them are selling rest and ease of living just by sending in the right amount of money to their ministry. If that's the case, then the only ones who are resting and at ease are these ministers of lies. That might sound harsh, and maybe it is, but promising what you can't deliver is a serious offense. Worse is taking God's promises and twisting them to fit your agenda.

Dear friend, as we approach the wonderful month of June, I hope that it offers you all that June is. Now, I can't promise you that, but what I can do is tell you what the Lord promises you. And just as He promises new birth and summer sun in June, He also promises those who are His children a season of rest and ease. As we have done in the past, let's do the same here. Let's take a wonderful scripture like Jeremiah 46:27 and break it down, looking for God's truth to His people.

> *But fear not thou, O My servant Jacob, and be not dismayed, O Israel: for, behold, I will save thee from afar off, and thy seed from the land of their captivity; and Jacob shall return, and be in rest and at ease, and none shall make him afraid. (Jer. 46:27)*

This scripture might sound familiar, which is a good thing. See, the Lord often repeats His words of encouragement because He knows how quickly the hurts of this world can steal it away. "Fear not"—how many times does the Lord tell us not to be afraid? Many times, and we need to hear it again. "Oh My [*servant*] Jacob"—again, remember who we serve and what the benefits are in that service. Dear friend, make sure you are serving Him and Him alone. "I will [*save*] thee from afar off" is a future promise that is rock solid. You might be in great danger or under great oppression today, but the Lord will save you (future tense). God—next speaking to Jacob, who is Israel—promises His covenant people a time of future rest and being at ease. Not that it means they will be lying drunk at a beach party picnic, but that they will find refreshment to their souls one day.

Israel has had a rough journey in this world, but one day they will be back in their land in faith. The Lord closes this thought with this future promise. There will be a day when *nothing* will ever scare you again. Don't know about you, but that sure sounds sweet to my soul. To never be afraid again, I like that, and best of all, we can have that. Follow on, follow hard, and wait for the Lord. His promises are certain.

May 30 - Focus on Holiness Above All

> *Then the presidents and princes sought to find occasion against Daniel concerning the kingdom; but they could find none occasion nor fault; forasmuch as he was faithful, neither was there any error or fault found in him. (Dan. 6:4)*

If you have ever been to a car wash, you know what it's like. Watching your car go through that conveyor of cleaning is a fascinating thing. As a little boy, my father would often take me to the car wash, and back in those days, you could actually sit in the car as it went through. I would get so excited as the power brushes rolled around and over the car. My eyes were fixed on them, and nothing short of an ice-cream party could draw me away. As we go through our lives here on planet earth, there are many things that can draw our attention away from where it should be; depression and anxiety are some that have that effect. When we should be focusing on the things of God, those two monsters of blessing seem to have a tractor-beam pull on us. As we have discussed before, one of the hardest things to do while dealing with emotional trauma is to keep focused on God's will and work. It's a domino effect as keeping our hearts away from the Lord only doubles the effect of our emotional pain. The more pain we feel, the more we focus on ourselves and our problems. The more we focus on ourselves and our problems, the less we focus on the Lord, and so the less we can hear His Holy Spirit's direction and feel His comfort. It's a lose-lose situation with a big ditch waiting for us at the bottom.

Dear friend, as hard as it might be to do, one of the most important things we should be doing is focusing on holiness. Yes, focus on holiness as we are going through the fires of emotional hell. It is certainly the last thing on your mind, and the enemy knows it. Because of our misguided souls, he can misguide us even further into sin. Like the layers of a hornet's nest, sin becomes layers, which further separates us from the Lord. This now is where faith must step in, faith to trust in the Lord when it's the last thing on your mind.

In Daniel 6, we read about Daniel's squeaky clean armor of righteousness. It was this righteousness that the Lord honored and blessed Daniel for. Imagine being in such a bad situation, yet the world and the enemies of the Lord could find no fault in us. Imagine Satan's anger and the world's frustration. Yet even more, imagine the Lord's pleased eyes as He watches over our testimony of holiness to a world certain we would crumble under our dilemma, but we don't. That is faith, and that is pleasing to our Lord, and He can do nothing else but bless us and rescue us when it's time. Please the Lord at all times. Let His pleasure be our lifelong aim no matter how unpleasant our life may be for the moment.

May 31 - One Step Further

Brethren, if a man be overtaken in a fault, ye which are spiritual, restore such an one in the spirit of meekness; considering thyself, lest thou also be tempted. (Gal. 6:1)

The other night at church, we had a guest speaker from Egypt. He and his wife were followers of Islam before coming to Christ. When he spoke, he shared about the time he spent in jail for his newfound faith in Christ. He was raped and beaten many times. He was finally removed from prison but soon was back in. He explained how his faith was strong during his first trial, but this second time in prison truly pushed him to his limits. As he cried out to the Lord in sorrow and complained, the Lord placed in him a vision of the crucified Christ. Jesus reminded him of His constant abuse and constant rejection and hatred by the world. He quickly found new strength to stand for Christ again, and soon after his second release from jail and expulsion from Egypt, he was already praying for a way to get back in to that country to spread the gospel of Jesus Christ to the Muslim world.

His story and our May 30 devotion made me think on this: We might be asked to be holy through the hardest of times, but we may be also asked to do it again. Sometimes we will suffer a great loss or trial, and the Lord will deliver us mightily, and sometimes we might have to go through it again. If that's the case and trouble finds us again, we are still commanded to be holy. There is no clause that states, "Because you went through a hard time and stayed holy unto the Lord, the next time, you can coast." No, it's righteous and holy living every day through every trial, no matter how many times that trial may reappear.

Now, being a person who lives in the reality of today, I know what this life in Christ may ask of me, again not only once but many times, to endure but also to endure on an even higher level. What if you are facing a trial again and the pain is intense, and yet the Lord brings you a person who is suffering? Will you be able to minister to that person of the grace of God? Or will you pass him by simply because you have too much of your own pain going on right now? Ouch—again, it's one of those hypothetical situations that the Lord might place us in, and in those places of testing, He demands an answer to these questions: "Will you still serve Me by serving another in more pain than yourself?" All of these questions ran through my own mind as I heard that dear brother from Egypt speak. Can I dare complain of my pain when another is suffering a far greater pain? Can I dare turn down another person's need for help because my pain is all that I care about? Hard questions yet true questions.

As the Lord asked Abraham to go further and sacrifice his own son, so the Lord asks us again and again: "Will you still serve, minister, and fulfill My great commission even if it's during repeated trials?" We all know what the answer is, but will we answer that call of true faith waiting and watching for that sure promise of blessing yet to come?

June

June 1 - It Might Begin Today

And the lord said unto Joshua, "This day will I begin to magnify thee in the sight of all Israel, that they may know that, as I was with Moses, so I will be with thee." (Josh. 3:7)

June 1 and a new month begins. I love the word *begin*, at least when God says it. To begin means to start something new, to begin something that you maybe have never done before. From the world's point of view, the word *begin* can have a nasty taste to it—as in beginning a job or life when you really liked your old one. The word *begin* from the world's perspective always has a flavoring of fear in it, always a hint of negativism, yet never when God is beginning something new in us. True, when the Lord *began* His process of allowing depression to change me, it didn't seem so wonderful, but on this side of the Red Sea, it is wonderful. God cannot do anything that isn't intrinsically good. That's what God is, and so that's all that He can do. Even when God will judge the world, He will be doing good because sin needs to be judged.

Today, dear friend, is a day that the Lord is beginning something in you. I can say that because every day the Lord is beginning something new in us; that is, learning to be more like Him. Now, maybe today you don't feel like some new and wonderful beginnings are going to happen; maybe you're really struggling with fear, anxiety, or depression. Maybe it feels more like the beginning of sorrow than the beginning of joy, but not if you're a child of God.

In Joshua 3:7, as the Lord is raising Joshua in Moses's place, He uses the word *magnify*. From when I was a little boy, I always knew what that word meant; it meant to make something look bigger. Now, the item itself doesn't actually become bigger. No, the magnifying glass does that, and as long as you're looking through that glass, it is bigger. God began to magnify Joshua so that all of Israel would see what God sees. True, Joshua, to Israel, didn't seem big enough to replace Moses, but through God's spiritual magnifying glass, he was. What was even more exciting was that it began when God began it. So Joshua became magnified.

Dear friend, the hope of this message is one that we all can glean strength from. It is an exciting proposition to know that as God magnified Joshua, He desires to magnify you and me. No, not for ourselves but for Him So through Joshua, the people of Israel would see God, and through us, the people of our world would see Christ. Let the Lord begin a good work in you today. Let Him magnify you and lift you. Let Him do what we could never do on our own. Even in our deepest despair, the Lord can lift us higher than we ever imagined.

This is hope, this is truth, and this is waiting for all of us who truly desire to be servants of the Most High. Now, living only so you are lifted for self is a lie. Don't go there, but go to the cross and let the Lord lift you for Him. It is only there that the world can really begin to take notice and see what a magnificent creation we are. It begins today if you will only let Him, even if it means through depression or anxiety.

June 2 - To Begin, You Must Begin

For, lo, thou shalt conceive, and bear a son; and no razor shall come on his head: for the child shall be a Nazarite unto God from the womb: and he shall begin to deliver Israel out of the hand of the Philistines. (Judg. 13:5)

As with any illness, ailment, pain, or trauma, they all take time to heal. As with any treatment of these pains, spiritual or physical, they begin with the first step. If you had a hip replaced and were told that you needed physical therapy if you were ever to walk again, what would you have to do but begin therapy? Sitting at home and reading about the therapy wouldn't do anything, nor would even showing up at the therapist's office. I will go as far to say that even if you received your first treatment, it would not be enough. To learn to walk again, you must begin the retraining process of walking and training, which must continue. Take this example one step further. Each session of physical therapy is never the same. You start at stage one, and over weeks or months, it changes as you begin to walk more and more. What they had you do on your first visit is not what they would have you do on your tenth visit. So it is in matters of emotional and spiritual hurts and pains. There must be a beginning, but also a continued beginning.

So often in the struggles with depression and / or anxiety, we try for one day or even one hour, and we give up. We say we tried to begin, but beginning without continuing means nothing. The relief comes not simply from one day of trying but many days of trying. Sometimes we have some bad starts, but don't be discouraged. In my struggles with this blessed monster, I would get myself all set up for a new day. I would declare that today I was going to give it my all in overcoming it, yet sometimes I stumbled. But even in that frustrating stumble, I had to be committed to continued beginnings. I had to be fixated on trying again tomorrow and even the day after if I had to.

In Judges 13:5, the Lord set up Samson as one who would deliver Israel, yet did Samson deliver it in one day? Did he deliver it on the first day? No! Samson was simply one who would *begin* the process.

It says that "he shall [*begin*] to deliver Israel out of the hands of the Philistines." Samson first had to be born and then born again. He needed to be raised, tried, and tested. Did Samson fail and have some bad starts and setbacks? Sure did, and even worse, he had some sinful starts. Yet he did do what the Lord set him out to do. Maybe Samson wasn't the best judge of Israel, and maybe we might not be the best Christian in God's kingdom, yet we always get an E for effort.

Dear friend, if you are looking at a new day and saying, "I just don't have it in me today"—well, that's okay because maybe today you don't, but tomorrow you must. In attempting anything, there must be a desire of the heart, a *will* that wants healing, that wants new beginnings, and that's going to take persistence. So if you choose to *begin* your healing highway home, then start today but also continue on tomorrow.

June 3 - What Starts Must End

And the lord said to Samuel, "Behold, I will do a thing in Israel, at which both the ears of every one that heareth it shall tingle. In that day I will perform against Eli all things which I have spoken concerning his house: when I begin, I will also make an end." (1 Sam. 3:11–12)

I was thumbing through the scriptures one day and was reminded about the story of Eli again. I came upon 1 Samuel 3:11–12, and as I was reading it, a few things jumped out at me. Number 1 is that when the Lord begins to work in your life, you will know it. In Eli's case, it wasn't one that Eli would be happy with but God's work and move nonetheless. It also reminded me of beginnings and endings. Everything other than God Himself has a beginning and ending. I meditated on that thought for a moment, and only good things came to mind. I thought of the concept of beginnings and endings as a good thing, at least for a child of God. As believers, there can be no sad or hopeless ending. If the Lord chooses us to live longer on this planet, then we win. If He chooses us to go home to be with Him, we win. And if the rapture takes us all away, we still win. The end is not bad but good, and as our Lord is a God of beginnings and endings, doesn't that also mean that our depression and anxiety have an end? If it had a beginning, it will surely have an ending.

I don't know of many, if any, who are born depressed. It is something that develops over time. Depression is stirred by a trauma or brought to life by God Himself. Regardless of what brings the depression, we cannot deny that it has a start. The day it starts, the Lord presses His spiritual stopwatch, and when it has completed in us what He ordained it to do in our lives, He will press that button again, and it will end. In the meantime, while we wait for that second press of that button, there are things we can do. Things that the Lord is waiting for us to do. There is prayer and remaining steadfast in our faith. There is making sure our spiritual house is in order (one that Eli didn't work on). We can get our sinful life all confessed up. We can get back into God's Word, find a good Bible-believing Church, and even share our faith with the lost. These are all things that we can and should be doing. Maybe The Lord is not ending our trial of faith because we have never ended our life of sin and secularism. Whatever the case may be, we should at least be praying for the Lord to open our eyes to whatever area we are lacking in.

Let us not also forget and constantly remind ourselves about this beginning and ending thing and who is the beginning and the end. Jesus Christ is the Lord of time, and being the Lord over time, He controls time. Watch and see the salvation of the Lord. It's coming!

June 4 - Look Up!

And when these things begin to come to pass, then look up, and lift up your heads; for your redemption draweth nigh." (Luke 21:28)

Luke 21:7 through 28 doesn't seem like a great place to start a devotion for a person who is maybe struggling with depression or anxiety, but it sure is a good picture of what happens when it ends. Luke 21 finds Jesus explaining when the end will begin. The times of tribulations that this world will face one day and all the horrible events that will come with it. Yet as Jesus is explaining how horrible these things are, He ends the thought in an interesting way. In verses 28 of Luke chapter 21, Jesus says this: "And when these things begin to come to pass, then look up, and lift up your heads; for your redemption draweth nigh." Imagine going through such a horrible time and yet hearing Jesus telling us to look up. Look up for what, for whom? Look up because Jesus always comes in victory, and because of that, those who follow Him are always victorious too.

Now, of the end of the age and when that day might come is not our concern. What is our concern is living for Christ today as if He were coming today. If you are going through your own little tribulation time, your own time of great distress and emotional pain, the Lord's words are always the same—"Look up!" Lift your heads that hang down and your souls that are heavy. Remember that Jesus is the Lord of deliverance and hope. Today just might be the day that He removes or heals your pain. Today might just be the day that, as it came on you like a flick of a switch, it will turn off like the flick of a switch.

Dear friend, I know I have been saying this all through the year, that today might be the day. I know you are probably getting discouraged because maybe that day for you has not come yet. But dear friend, it will come as sure as we know that Jesus will come. If you are beginning to doubt this deliverance, remind yourself of the Lord's truth and faithfulness. Read Luke 21:7 through 28 and see how true the Word of God is. See how it is being fulfilled even in our world today. If the Lord can have our world today pegged so well and know of its certain end, can He not also know exactly when your pain and anguish will end? Look up, look toward the north. Remember where all good things really come from. Remember Christ's prophetic birth, His prophetic death and resurrection, and His soon-coming prophetic return. His words are sure, so we should also live in that surety. If dramatic, climatic events point to Christ's dramatic return and deliverance, then maybe our dramatic, painful promises that seem to be peaking only mean that they will soon be over sooner than later.

June 5 - Look Under the Bandage

For the time is come that judgment must begin at the house of God: and if it first begin at us, what shall the end be of them that obey not the gospel of God? (1 Pet. 4:17)

In ministry, one of the things you must get used to is being scrutinized. As a pastor, it's a common place to be and not always a comfortable one. People will scrutinize your sermons, your spending of money, your lifestyle and words.

My wife subscribes to a pastor's wives' forum on the web called "Life in a Fishbowl." It is something that those in ministry must get used to, and it can hurt when being scrutinized goes too far. Often our children will be judged a little harder than the rest of the children. Our marriage is placed under the microscope, and sitting on the boards of deacons and elders can even go deeper into scrutinizing your very core motives and objectives. It is the one thing they never teach you in seminary and the hardest part to get used to.

I don't think anyone likes having their life under a microscope, but in case you didn't know it, we are all under a microscope. It is the Lord's microscope of holiness that He holds over us as we are ambassadors for Him. That hot, focused ray from God can hurt sometimes, but only if we don't see the endgame and objective of the Lord. The Lord isn't trying to destroy us but make us better. He is trying to focus in on our areas of weaknesses so we can see them and change them.

Getting back to being a pastor, I remember seasons when I felt the elders and deacons were digging a little too deep, and I would become defensive and angry. Yet it wasn't until the Lord opened my eyes to the blessing of listening to correction that I was able to glean good from the worthy corrections and toss out the petty corrections. It takes a lot of soul-control and humility, but we all know how the Lord feels about humility. Friend, even while you are going through a time of deep pain, even while you are hurting enough already, keep in mind that the Lord might be using that hurt to also expose some dangerous soul cancer. It is during these times that we must be honest with ourselves and see if there is any sin or fault within us.

During my times in the pits of blessed depression, I discovered a lot about myself. I discerned my selfishness, my complaining heart, my lack of contentment, and my tendency to drift toward sin when in pain. I was also able to see so many of the blessings that I had I never seen before. Blessings like my physical health, wonderful wife and family, and my gracious Lord who dealt with a gentle hand even though I probably needed a heavy one. Today, even when you feel at your lowest, let the Lord examine your heart. Ask Him to visit every area of your mind and soul and expose any area that needs to be remolded. The sooner I was able to judge myself and find peace in being judged, the sooner my trouble of the heart passed.

June 6 - Sometimes a Mystery

But in the days of the voice of the seventh angel, when he shall begin to sound, the mystery of God should be finished, as He hath declared to His servants the prophets. (Rev. 10:7)

In all of my over thirty years of being a Christian, I must admit there were times and circumstances that God really confused me. Some things were just a mystery to me, and I simply had to trust in His sovereignty. He knows what He is doing, and that's all I need to know. Well, that's easy to say in this devotion but a little harder when facing a weeping family who just endured a great loss. In my years in ministry, two particular circumstances stand out where I really had no idea what the Lord was doing. One was over a long period of time when the Lord took home a mother, father, and brother by unusual deaths, leaving a young-adult daughter. When that young lady called in tears telling me that she found her brother dead in his bedroom, I quickly went into fear, wondering what I could possibly say to comfort her. All of those people were Christians, and till this day, I really don't know what the Lord was doing. Another situation was two deaths in the same family within a few weeks. Both were very young men, both leaving behind young children. I had to perform one funeral and, within a few weeks, another to the same people. Talk about confusion and chaos.

Yet, dear friend, it was not confusion to the Lord, nor was it chaos, as He cannot do anything that isn't perfect. Many times while going through my depression and anxieties, I would often scratch my head, wondering what the heck the Lord was doing. What was He trying to accomplish, and why now? I would find myself saying things like, "Lord, this is the worst time for me to be falling into this" or "I don't need this now. What are you trying to do to me?" Maybe today you are in that place of confusion, confused about this surprise attack that came upon you. Maybe you are angry at the Lord's timing and banging your head, trying to understand the possible good that can come from this. It is truly a great test of our faith during these times. To simply trust in the Lord's perfect will and wisdom takes all of the faith we have, which is already on short supply due to our current pain.

Friend, regardless of what you are going through, regardless of how bizarre the circumstances might be, regardless of the horrific pain you might be feeling, we must understand what cannot be understood, the mystery of God. Sometimes God is mysterious and beyond our realm of reason and understanding. Sometimes we just don't get it and maybe never will in this life, but it is still mandatory for us to trust Him when trusting Him seems like the most illogical thing to do. Trust the One who is mysterious because just as mysteriously the pain came, it just might mysteriously be gone.

June 7 - No Tears in Heaven

Turn again, and tell Hezekiah the captain of my people, Thus saith the lord, the God of David thy father, I have heard thy prayer, I have seen thy tears: behold, I will heal thee: on the third day thou shalt go up unto the house of the lord. (2 Kings 20:5)

There will be no tears in heaven, but on this planet floating in space, there will be plenty. That might be a sobering concept but true nonetheless. Today, as you search out for the Lord's leading and guidance, news about tears on earth doesn't sound too comforting, but it should be. I say this because of this: if we cry, it is certain that He hears. Friends, tears are not to be avoided but sought after. Show me a person who has broken down in tears, and I will show you a person who is ready for the supernatural. I have found in my life and encounters with people that until a Christian falls on his knees in tears, he can never be all that the Lord has planned for him. To be broken is to be ready to be repaired. To come unglued is to be made ready to be held tight. With depression and anxiety often come tears, and I have cried me a river of my own. Yet the tears were not for naught but for blessings.

In 2 Kings 20:5, we read about the tears of Hezekiah, but we also read about the Lord's response to them. The Lord declares plainly two things. First, He declares that He has seen his tears and second, that He has heard his prayers. The prayers came first, it seems, and then came the tears. I don't think we can have effective prayers without shedding some tears. Tears are one of the greatest shows of passion we can ever have. It is amazing how when one person in Church gives a testimony and then tears start to fall, all the other people listening begin to also cry. Politicians pick up on this quickly as a way of getting people to bend to their will by simply adding tears to a speech. Tears do motivate people to feel compassion, and the tears of God's children move God to act.

Continuing on in 2 Kings 20:5, we also notice that after King Hezekiah prayed and then cried, it was then that the Lord began to heal. As I have said before in this devotional, tears are a humiliating thing sometimes, even more so if you're a man, yet tears should never be suppressed or held back for they have purpose. Funny how with all the fuss about evolution and trying to prove that we are simply animals that evolved through the process of natural selection, we still can't figure out why people cry. It really has no purpose other than cleaning your eyes, but then why do they appear most when attached to sadness and sorrow? I know one thing, and that is after I have had a good cry through great pain, I do feel a little better. Maybe there is a release of some sort chemically that triggers this to happen. I don't know as I'm not a scientist or a doctor, but I do know this one thing, tears get the Lord's attention. Jesus wept, and soon after, a man was raised from the dead. If it's good enough for Jesus, then it's good enough for me.

June 8 - You're Not Losing Your Mind

I am weary with my groaning; all the night make I my bed to swim; I water my couch with my tears. (Ps. 6:6)

Have you ever had one of those days when you stand in front of the mirror and say to yourself, "What has happened to me? What happened to that person I used to be?" If you have, well you are not alone; and if you are like me, you might have had one of those days of completely falling apart and also saying to yourself, "I think I'm losing my mind." If you've been there, again, you are not alone. I remember in the depths of despair those moments when I truly felt like I can't move or function, thinking to myself, *I'm going to end up in a mental institution, rocking in some corner with drool running down my face.* I have truly felt that and was certain that was my future. In fact, I remember even wanting to go there as a place to run to or hide. Praise God that I had a wonderful friend / doctor who talked me out of it and assured me that, that was not what I needed.

It is funny how we run to things that are a lot like the womb. As I shared before, running back to our mother and father is not uncommon, and when that is not an option, we consider a hospital where "others" can take care of us and where we can just vegetate. Now, I am not saying that the hospital is never an option. I have recommended it to a few of the people I have counseled and most commonly in the case of suicidal leanings where their personal life and safety were in jeopardy. Also in the case when mediations need to be monitored or reevaluated. Other than that, a hospital stay will do nothing more but drain your pocket than offer any help.

Friend, unless you're battling with serious mental disorder apart from anxiety and depression, your best help is from friends, family, a loving church, a Christian counselor, and, if need be, a good doctor for medication. With regard to medication, for mild symptoms, any good general practitioner will do. If it is for deeper clinical depression and anxiety disorder, then a good, godly psychiatrist is what you should seek. Sure, they are hard to find, but even a secular one will do. I got most of my treatment from my family doctor. Were there times when he was not enough? Sure, but the Lord always knows what's best and how to lead us.

Now, let us get back to losing-our-mind issue. For the most part, those spells of breaking down and becoming bedridden are not the end of the line. They are not the call-the-ambulance time. I have been there and spent a few days in bed, yet I never lost my mind, whatever that means. A good friend and associate of mine who is a Christian therapist went through a worse time than myself and was bedridden for three months. He made it through and is happily serving God's people and even specializing in helping pastors who are in burnout mode.

So if you feel like you are losing your mind today, you are probably not; and even if you did, Jesus always knows where to find it. We must never forget who we are in Christ, a child of the Most High. We are His, and nothing can take us out of His wonderful watch / care. In the worst of times, rest and only believe.

June 9 - He Will

He will swallow up death in victory; and the Lord god will wipe away tears from off all faces; and the rebuke of His people shall He take away from off all the earth: for the lord hath spoken it. (Isa. 25:8)

He will lift you up! Praise God for those words, words of hope and help. The Lord promises to do many things, and as the Perfect Father, He comes through with them all. He will wipe away our tears. He will give us hope for a new tomorrow. He will be with us forever, and He will never leave us nor forsake us. Those are only some of the promises of the Lord, but what makes them even more special is that they are all true. As a young father, I made this promise to myself and to God, that I would never flippantly make a promise to any of my children if I didn't intend on making it happen. Sure, it was difficult at times, but it also kept me on guard for what came out of my mouth lest I make a promise that I couldn't keep. I am proud to say that as of today, I have only failed on a few, and I don't think my children ever caught on. The reason I was fixed on keeping my word was so my children would know what a promise keeper was and that the Lord is the best promise keeper.

I remember building a tree house that I had forgotten I had promised and kicking myself, but it had to be done to keep that trust. As with the Lord, He is the perfect dad, He is Abba Father, and One who is not prone to making impossible promises like we are as sinful men. God's Word is sure, and if He says He will wipe away your tears, He will.

Dear friend, as you go through this devotional day by day, you will hear a lot of my words, but my words without the Lord's words behind them will really do you no good. I am here writing this today because the Lord was faithful to me yesterday. He got me through, and so He will get you through. God is a god of victory. He does not lose or can lose. He doesn't just promise victory, He is victory to the tenth degree. He is hope, power, and love. Turn to Him and cry on His celestial shoulder. Remember His words and promises of old. Remember His promises for tomorrow and His words of great comfort, which are—He Will!

June 10 - Ah Comfort

And I will pray the Father, and He shall give you another Comforter, that
He may abide with you for ever. (John 14:16)

Ah comfort. We here in the USA seem to live for it, yet sad to say, our expectation of it has truly hurt us in understanding what suffering is really like. Make no mistake about it, suffering has its virtues, yet I will not lie to you and say I desire to suffer or that I don't enjoy comfort. In fact, I do enjoy comfort greatly.

One day I was shopping with my wife, Julie, at one of those buy-in-bulk superstores. As I was wandering about looking at tires, auto supplies, and electronics, I came upon this magical wonderful oh-so-comfortable object that seemed to be calling my name. It was one of those high-tech glider chairs with a floating footrest. No one was looking, so I sat down, and well, the rest is history. It was love-at-first sitting, yet buying it was another story. I left that chair thinking about the cost and if I really needed it. I circled around and came back and sat down on it again. So many thoughts ran through my mind—the wasted money, the people who are suffering and living on the streets—all as I mull over buying this silly chair. I knew if I just hinted to my wife, it wouldn't be long before we would be loading it into my SUV. I kept thinking back and forth between two thoughts: comfort versus need. I didn't need it, nor would I die without it. Heck, I have lived forty-nine years up to that point without one, and I was sure I could live another forty-nine. Of the cost, well, we really couldn't afford it, and as a pastor of a small church, I didn't want to look like I was a poor judge of money and only care about my personal comfort while people in the church were struggling.

Oh this battle within that Paul speaks about so passionately. Well, I am here to tell you that the wonder chair is sitting in my living room, and I do my best reading and studying on it. Foolish, maybe so, but the point I make is this: we desire comfort as humans, and the One who created us knows that so well. Not only does He know that our bodies need comfort but even more so our souls. When it comes to the pains of depression, soul comfort is what we need most of all. Buying a comfortable chair wouldn't have even been enough as all material objects lack in being able to comfort the soul. That is why I am so forever grateful to the Lord Jesus Christ that when He ascended, He also left us with the Comforter, the One who will guide, direct, help, and console our breaking, hurting hearts. It is God the Holy Spirit that indwells us and fills us with all we need to make it on this planet called earth.

Dear friend, if you are in need of comfort today, you could buy a new car with leather seats or you could be foolish like me and buy a comfortable chair. But what those things can never do is reach down to the core of who we are and gently comfort our pensive, empty hearts.

June 11 - Peace on Earth

And thou shalt go to thy fathers in peace; thou shalt be buried in a good old age. (Gen. 15:15)

Merry Christmas! Oops, it's June, not December. Well, Merry Christmas anyway because Christmas reminds me of one thing, peace on earth. I always thought it strange and confusing as a pre-Christian hearing about Jesus coming to bring peace on earth. I thought, *Well, if that's the case, He is not doing a very good job at it.* I would look at the world, especially the Middle East, and say, "No peace there." If you're a Christian today, or maybe you're not, please listen up, for I know there is one thing you seek. Actually, we all seek after it, and that is peace, not so much world peace—not that it isn't a noble quest—but for personal peace. We all want it, but sadly, we mostly don't understand where it is found. It makes me think of that old western country song "Looking for Love in All the Wrong Places." It is so true as we are a people so desperately in need for peace, so desperately desiring peace, and yet so not finding it.

Well, if you haven't found it yet, I will tell you where it is found and the secret mystery of that phrase *peace on earth*. See, Jesus did come to bring peace on earth, not collectively as in *world peace*, but personally as in personal peace. Peace with God, peace knowing that hell is not our destination, peace knowing that the Lord our God and Creator loves us, peace in knowing that we are right with Him. That is the peace Jesus came to bring, an inward peace so that outwardly, others would see it and want it too. At the end of the day, the world will feel God's peace, but only through seeing it in us first.

Also of peace, it is something that the Lord offers in that He will not force His peace on us. If Jesus came to bring peace on earth, then He would be making the world accept His peace and not allowing us the choice to choose His peace. Peace in our hearts is a choice, and the Lord will not force it upon us. The Lord could come down and stop all the wars, and one day He will, but for this dispensation in time, He will not. Not until we cry out for Him to do so. Not until we cry out and admit the agony we live in being separated from the One who made us.

Please, if you don't know Jesus as your Lord and Savior, then please make that decision today. Please repent and confess your sins and cry out to the Lord for a relationship with Him. Not for a life without problems, but a life that is right with God. Cry out for peace in your hearts knowing that you will spend all of eternity with Him. Not through our works of righteousness, but through His work on that cross. Peace is waiting for you, friend. The same peace He gives to the poor man in Haiti with nothing but the clothes on his back is the same peace He gives us here in the USA. A peace with God—start there and everything else will fall into place. Merry Christmas!

June 12 - I Can Do Nothing for You

And Joseph answered Pharaoh, saying, "It is not in me: God shall give Pharaoh an answer of peace." (Gen. 41:16)

If I haven't said it before, I will say it this time, "I can do nothing for you." That might sound like an odd thing to say coming from a Christian counselor, but what might sound even odder is that I say those exact words to every person who comes in for a consultation. It is true. When a new person comes in for counseling, once the paperwork is done and the information taken, I first begin in prayer, then I start the session by saying, "I can do nothing for you, but Jesus Christ can." People are sometimes taken back, but for the most part, as most are Christians, they understand that if anything good will happen, it will happen because Jesus Christ is good, not me.

It is really true with regard to all of us; healing comes only if the Lord allows it. You can have the best doctor and best counselor. You can try acupuncture or hire a psychiatrist, yet at the end of the day, it is Jesus who heals. As we will discuss during the chapter section of this book, even medication will not work unless the Lord is behind it. I remember way, way back when I first encountered my anxiety and depression. I would try anything to rid myself of this blessed monster. Yet notice the word I used—*rid myself*. I cannot rid myself of anything, nor can I cause anything to work unless the Lord allows. I don't know how many times I needed to learn that lesson. I would try this pill, that pill, this doctor, that doctor, herbs, massage therapy, diet change, and vitamins. "Why, oh Lord?" I would cry out. "Why won't any of these things work?"

In Genesis 41:16, Joseph brings this truth home when he tells Pharaoh where healing and answers really come from. Joseph also shows what character of man he is talking to. Friend, if anything is going to change in your life, it will be the Lord who does it. If anything is going to work in bringing about that healing, it will also be the Lord who allows it to work. Our focus must be solely on the Lord. Our faith must be solely in Him and His power. We must watch whom we give praise to and what glory we lay on people.

I remember being so excited about one thing working well in healing my anxiety, but as soon as I praised that person or thing, it would stop working. Funny how easy it is to praise people and medication and miracle powders yet how hard it is to say out loud, "The Lord God has made me well!" Praise Him always and make sure the world hears that praise coming from your lips and heading to their ears clearly about our Lord. Yes, He is listening!

June 13 - Don't Make a Move!

The lord shall fight for you, and ye shall hold your peace. (Exod. 14:14)

Before I was a pastor, I worked in the secular field. And as in many secular jobs, lunch is done around a table in an office building. As we would all sit around and read the paper and news, there always seemed to be one who would read the horoscopes. Funny thing about the horoscopes is they always say the same thing, it seems: "Today is not a good day for making important decisions." That is always a safe bet for anyone as making important decisions is—well, very important. In my life as a Christian, I have learned some valuable insight into this art form of choice—underload. What I have learned the most about it is this: don't make any choices while in a bad state of mind. I mean, don't make a life-changing decision when you are in great pain. I know this for a fact, for if I followed through with my harebrained ideas and choices during my dark days of depression and debilitating anxiety, I would have ended up far from where the Lord wanted me. Looking back, it is really amazing how wide and wild our imaginations can wander while in pain. Crazy ideas like moving, quitting my job, having an affair, taking up drinking, taking my life, and other such crazy things all crossed my mind.

Psalm 46:10 is a scripture that's dear to me and one I have hanging over my office door: "Be still and know that I am God." It is a great reminder of a few important life rules. First, God is the Lord, not me, so let Him make the important decisions for me. Second, shut up and don't move until the Lord tells you to. And third, know that God is in control and don't forget it. Over the years of counseling, I have also learned this to be true by what people have shared with me while in great distress. The most common crazy idea was quitting their job and moving away. "If I could just get away from the pressure and live in a quiet little town out west, then all would be well." Friends, I have some breaking news that will save you ten thousand dollars in moving fees. I moved from New York to California and back to New York. I moved to a little Mayberry-type town where the sun always shines and people are sweeter. The verdict is in, and it is all a lie. There is no nirvana-utopian place to live. Wherever you move, *you* come with yourself, and that means all your problems, fears, and traits come along for the ride. They cannot be left behind, so don't even go there.

As the scripture states, let us be content in whatever state we are in, both figuratively and geographically. Running and panicking are not where answers are found. Standing firm in Christ Jesus through life's trying times is the answer. So, in a nutshell, remember this word of advice from one who has been there. Don't make a move! Don't make a move while your life is in freefall and your wits about you have long left the barn. Stay calm. Wait it out in prayer—and no, it's not a good time to buy that sports car you always wanted.

June 14 - Get Help!

If thou shalt do this thing, and God command thee so, then thou shalt be able to endure, and all this people shall also go to their place in peace. (Exod. 18:23)

Moses was a man on the edge; right from the beginning of his ministry, he was reluctant to serve. When he was deep into his ministry, again, he was over his head. When he was trying to do it all and trying to minister to all of God's people, it was simply too much for him, and he was ready to implode. It is interesting to see in our scripture for today that Moses didn't see it. He was in it, but he didn't see it. He didn't see that he was sinking and slowly being overwhelmed into destruction. It wasn't until his father-in-law saw what was happening and stepped in with some great advice. He said, "Moses you can't do this alone."

In Exodus 18:17, we read these words, "And Moses's father-in-law said unto him, 'The thing that thou doest is not good.'" Moses, in all his great, well-meaning service to God, still got this reply toward his hard good labor: "This thing is not good." Could it be, friends, that we can be doing much good, much service, and yet still be in the wrong with God? Sad to say, we all fall into this place, and if we don't take the advice of people who care about us and see what we don't see, we will end up useless and of value to no one. In this age in which we live, we are under a lot of pressure, doing this and that, working, serving, and keeping our families together. Yet if we don't find the right place where the Lord wants us, we will end up being a broken vessel and, in turn, not being there for the people who really need us.

I remember a recent place I was where the pressure to serve was getting too heavy. It was a place where I took on much more than the Lord ever wanted me to. The pressure cooker was sounding its alarm, and I wasn't listening again! In this case, it was the Lord who spoke to me to get out and slow down. I was involved in way too much stuff, thinking I was doing good for the Lord, but in reality, I was not. I was involved in political positions with the town boards. I was sitting on all kinds of boards, chairing one, and way over my head. I felt all proud of myself about all I was doing except it wasn't anything that the Lord wanted me doing. Within one week, I dropped out and stepped down from 90 percent of my outside-the-church responsibilities. Even in the church, I stepped down from doing and volunteering so much. I simply just could not do it all, and it was downright prideful to think that I could.

So today if you are over your head, don't be afraid to listen to those who see it and get help from those who offer it. So many times we complain about having too much to do when the Lord is offering help, and we are simply not taking it. We are simply making the same mistake Moses made by thinking, *I can do it!* No, you can't, and neither could Moses. Get help before you need help.

June 15 - Be Under It

> *And He said, "I saw all Israel scattered upon the hills, as sheep that have not a shepherd: and the LORD said, 'These have no master: let them return every man to his house in peace.'" (1 Kings 22:17)*

One of the most frustrating things I hear as a pastor is this foolish logic: "As soon as I get my life in order, I am going to get back to church and service." It is frustrating, not because I want people in church, but more so that I want people under leadership. So many people who suffer with depression and anxiety make the same mistake and stay home, stay out of touch, stay away from where help is found. Church is not an option but a necessity, and also a place where you will hear what you need to hear. Many people who suffer with these emotional issues are also the same people who are so desirous to hear from the Lord, yet how do they expect to hear from Him? Many people will say such foolish things like, "Well, I do my church at home. I listen to brother so and so on TV, that's my church."

Friend, that is not church, nor can it ever be. In Hebrews, we learn about forsaking the assembling together. Simply put, make sure you are around a lot of Christians, and the best place to do that is in church. I can't emphasize enough the importance of being in church and sitting under a good Bible teacher / pastor. The Lord didn't assign the gifts of pastor and teacher for nothing. He gave out those gifts so the body of Christ could be lifted and trained.

In 1 Kings 22:17, we learn about the scattering sheep that have no shepherd. Sheep can't exist without a shepherd, and neither can we. We need their personal guidance and watch / care over our souls. The pastor isn't your God, this is true, and nor should he ever be looked upon as more than just an under shepherd, but he still should be sat under. Sad to say, today finding a good pastor / teacher is getting harder too. Many are becoming corrupt and worldly, and this is not by chance. Satan knows the church is crumbling, and the best way to knock it over completely is to go after the leadership. Once they lose credibility, then no one will seek out their advice.

What is one to do when the pickings are slim? Easy. Keep looking and praying till you find one.

It seems strange to me that many people will put all of their soul into finding a good car, job, or doctor, but little effort into finding a good church. God has a church for you out there somewhere. Maybe you might have to travel a bit, but isn't it worth it as it might just be the place where your answers may be found? With all the other things we must do in finding help for our affliction of the mind, let us not forget the spiritual side. Not just Christian counseling either but weekly Christian training. Remember, church is not just a place for you to find answers but a place that you can also serve. Counseling is great, but it alone can make us very *self*-focused and not God-focused. Find a church, find a good pastor, and get under his teaching ASAP.

June 16 - Their Peace Too

And the fruit of righteousness is sown in peace of them that make peace. (James 3:18)

Of all the negatives that come with depression and anxiety, the worst of them is one that you might not consider. That is the way of selfishness that permeates the soul while in the grasp of this emotional pain. Selfishness, at least in my life, always ruled my heart when going through that dark place. Selfishness also takes on many different faces. Selfishness is also laziness, pleasure-seeking, indifference, apathy, and the worst is the lack of concern for God's work in the hearts of fellowmen.

Dear friend, when we get to the place where we no longer care about the great commission of bringing the good news of Jesus Christ to the lost, we can no longer be in God's will. I know that's a bold statement, especially when fighting the battles of depression, but it is still truth. There is never an escape clause when it comes to the work of the cross. It never says, "Go tell the world about Jesus Christ unless you're depressed." I know this to be true for two reasons. Number 1 because the Bible never gives me that escape clause, and number 2 because I have lived it out. I have been in the deep, dark depths of anxiety and depression, and yet I still led people to the Lord and ministered to hurting people's needs. Did I want to? Was it easy? Was I struggling while doing it? You bet I was, and I would go a step further and say it was the hardest thing to do.

I remember one particular situation where a young mother was watching her husband die in a hospital bed. The couple was in their very early thirties and had two young children; one child was about five years old. I was called to go minister to them at the hospital, all the while I was battling a heavy bout of anxiety. I could barely function, but the Lord convinced me to go, and so I did. I sat with that wife and mother and held her hand. I prayed over that dying young man as he listened to a phone message from his five-year-old daughter telling him she loves him. I then had to comfort that wife and ended up leading her to the Lord in prayer. I know there were a lot of *I*'s in that statement, but believe me there was no *I* doing this but the great *I Am*. The Lord truly carried me through that and held my hand as I held hers. A few weeks later, I had to perform the funeral service for that young man, and I was still no better emotionally. Why do I say all of this today and lay this heavy burden of service on you? Easy, because the Lord laid it on me and also gave me the strength to do it.

Friend, if we are ever to find peace through this mess, we must be bringers of peace. We can only bring peace to others if we care as much for them and Jesus Christ as we do about ourselves. I could have stayed curled up in a ball in bed during those days—and trust me, I wanted to—but the Lord had more important things for me to consider than my own pains. If our pain is to be overcome, we must first be more concerned about God's peace. If you know someone who is hurting today, go to them and tell them about Christ. Yes, even while you are hurting too.

June 17 - Simple As Knowing

Grace and peace be multiplied unto you through the knowledge of God, and of Jesus our Lord. (2 Pet. 1:2)

Grace and peace, who doesn't want those two wrapped in a bow and set at your table? As a person who has suffered with depression and anxiety, I would have sold my right arm and leg for them. Interestingly enough, they are found in the most unlikely place "through the knowledge of God." What does that exactly mean, and could it be that simple once we understand it? What's even more amazing is that it doesn't just offer us grace and peace through this knowledge of God, but grace and peace *multiplied*. That's a pretty bold statement, and one worth looking into. Today let's dig a little and see if there is something that we are missing in our quest for peace. It says *through* the knowledge of God and, might I add, of Jesus our Lord also. To go through something is to use it as a vessel, a bridge, a passageway, simply meaning that it's the path we must follow, and that path leads us to knowing about God and Jesus Christ. Okay, so let's say we are even able to somewhat know God and Jesus our Lord, what can that do for us?

The answer is simple in that *through* deep Bible study and meditation, we get to know more about God. We learn more about His character, power, mercy, grace, watch / care, and so many other things. Now, when we learn more and more about Jesus Christ each day, our minds and hearts are filled less and less with the knowledge of ourselves. There is simply more room for Him and less for us. In case you haven't been there, well, let's just say it's a peaceful place to be.

The Bible even says, "to be filled with the Holy Spirit" and to not be filled with wine or things that we try to replace God with. This is also an act of continuance. It is not that we top off our tank and run; no, it's a trickle fill of God each day. It is each day (being filled more) with more of Him. Can we ever know God completely in this life? No. It won't be until we enter eternity with Him that we will truly see Him as He is. But for now, we need to seek Him and know Him as much as humanly possible. When we do, we will begin to feel that grace and peace of God because we will understand God's grace and peace. Is it easy to achieve? No, but it is mandatory that we attempt it daily. Know all about the Lord. Learn through personal Bible study and devotions. Learn through attending a good Bible-believing church. Sit under a good anointed pastor / teacher and ask a lot of questions. Be that annoying pebble in the shoe that won't rest until all that can be known is known. When you do, again, you will find grace and peace, and both of them multiplied—how cool is that?

June 18 - What Will He Find

Wherefore, beloved, seeing that ye look for such things, be diligent that ye may be found of him in peace, without spot, and blameless. (2 Pet. 3:14)

When I was in my late teens to early twenties, I was still living at home. I was unsaved and living as any young adult from that era would. When my mother and father would go away for a week to visit my sister in California, it meant one thing to me, and one thing only—party time! I would notify all my friends ahead of time and get it all ready. I would prepare the beer, potato chips, and sadly, the drugs. The girls were invited too and so was the band. The stereo was cranked up real loud, and the party would start the minute my parents left and continue until they came home. Now, the reason why I bring up this common story of teenage angst is because of the concern that always haunted my mind in those days; that is, what would they find when they came home? What if my parents found remnants of drugs, alcohol, or even worse, a broken vase that my mother cherished? I would also worry about them coming home early and catching us right in the act, which did happen once or twice. My point here is the great concern I had in being caught doing evil when my parents hoped they would catch me doing good. They were just my parents. Can we imagine what should be our concern about God finding us with our hand in the cookie jar, or worse?

Friend, though we struggle with emotional issues, that does not exclude us from righteous living. How we live our lives counts just as much to God in our dark times as how we live it in our happy times. God doesn't give us a free ride because we are sick or hurting. Holiness is a given in the Lord's economy. I remember a gentleman I knew who had a very hard life and was going through a very difficult divorce. He was in great despair yet felt that because of that great despair, he had freedom to sin a little more than he did before. Church attendance dropped way off, and he began dabbling with women even before he was officially divorced. His justification was always, "Well, my wife is sticking it to me, and so I'm going to stick it back a little also." He concluded that all's fair in love and war.

Dear child of God, that is so far from the truth. And if you are suffering today and using that mindset to dabble a little in sin to ease your pains, well, my advice is—don't do it! God is watching our lives, and He doesn't have to have a surprise inspection as He inspects our lives every day. The question we must ask ourselves as we wonder why our healing has never come is, What will He find in our lives when He comes? Or worse, what has He already found? If you have dirt under your rugs, lift it and clean it out (1 John 1:9).

June 19 - Beware the Peace Takers

And there went out another horse that was red: and power was given to him that sat thereon to take peace from the earth, and that they should kill one another: and there was given unto him a great sword. (Rev. 6:4)

During the future tribulation that the bible speaks about, there will be one who comes not to bless but to curse. Not to give personal peace like Jesus did but to take peace away. He will come under the pretense of love and peace but will be a deceiver, and many will follow his lies. In our lives today, there are those people and things that attempt to do the same thing in our lives. There are things that promise peace but only take it away, ways that promise peace and joy but only leave us empty and depressed. Following are a few examples of things in my life that seemed so wonderful with promises of joy and peace that ended up being peace takers when I forgot where my true joy and peace really come from.

Once in my old secular employment, I felt very happy and at peace because the president of my company was a good friend and liked me. I felt so at ease and protected in that arrangement until he had to step down and another whom I didn't know took over. Suddenly my peace giver became my peace taker. I was in a panic because that in which I trusted changed. The lesson here that the Lord taught me was, "Trust in Me, and I will never change. Trust in men, and they will." Another of my many lessons in this area was that of wanting a Jeep again. As I have told you before, I am a big Jeep lover and have built a few and have had a few. Going through my midlife crisis, I began to get depressed and sad. I thought, *I need a Jeep again to lift my spirits.* Well, that whole episode in my life is a pathetic picture of lust for a material object gone wild. I became obsessed with buying another Jeep to restore and concluded that I deserved this due to my many years of painful ministry and emotional anguish. So I pushed and hounded even against my wife's will and purchased one online with money I didn't have borrowed from a friend. Forty-five hundred dollars were lost in one day through an online scam that caught me hook, line, and sinker. I still had to pay the money back to my friend and had no Jeep. With my tail between my legs, I was horribly humbled and embarrassed of how an intelligent person can be so easily led astray through a possessed heart fixed on a peace stealer.

The Jeep that never came gave me no peace but instead it took peace. I had less joy and peace than before, and on top of that, I was out all that money. It took me a year of being down and beating myself up to get over it. Yet praise be to our Lord who, through supernatural means, ended up giving me a Jeep a few years later. I had to repent, acknowledge my error, and wait on Him. Friend, beware of the things that depression and anxiety can use to drive us in an attempt to find temporary peace and joy. What is a peace stealer in your life that you believe is a peace giver?

June 20 - How to Be Happy When Depressed

Behold, we count them happy which endure. Ye have heard of the patience of Job, and have seen the end of the Lord; that the Lord is very pitiful, and of tender mercy. (James 5:11)

People today seem to have very little patience when it comes to being happy. From childhood and waiting for Christmas to bring us toys, it was simply too long of a wait. Our impatience turned into anger and bitterness, and even on to adulthood, it has transferred over. We now have speed passes, quick passes, and microwave ovens. I even have this new coffeemaker that can make a cup of coffee in about one minute flat. Of waiting for anything, it is simply not in our DNA anymore. We want it now, and we will not wait a minute longer. It's a serious problem that has really affected all areas of our lives. Even our walk as Christians is hurt as we no longer understand the fine art of being patient and being content in whatever state we are in. This weakness also carries over into our emotional and spiritual life.

In dealing with depression and anxiety, we have no desire at all to wait it out. We have no will to even see it linger on even one more hour. Of all my complaints to everyone I spoke to, this one would ring loudest: How much longer will this go on? I wanted the splinter removed now. I wanted the pain in my arm to be removed now. Of enduring such things, it was just too much to ask from a feeble human like me. To endure, we have spoken of this before, is never well taken. As a world, a nation, a people, and even a church, we have no stomach for endurance.

So when I came across James 5:11, it really knocked me over that one of the keys to being happy is enduring. Wow, what a conundrum, what a paradox of the heart and mind. It is like holding a scorpion in one hand and a slice of apple pie in the other. In order to get the apple pie, the scorpion must be allowed to sting you. It's a tough call indeed, and one we can't seem to be at peace with.

When I was going through my many phases of depression and anxiety, be it my average situational depression or my full-blown clinical depression, I was lucky if I could muster up the energy to brush my teeth, let alone let a scorpion sting me. See, I didn't want to do one more thing, no matter what happiness it promised, and that was to endure one minute longer. "No, no, no," I would say. "I will not endure anymore. I want out. I want deliverance, and I want it now." Sad to say that no matter what I determined to be the way things should play out, God's Word said the complete opposite: "Behold, we count them happy which endure. Ye have heard of the patience of Job, and have seen the end of the Lord; that the Lord is very pitiful, and of tender mercy" (James 5:11).

I didn't like reading that scripture, and I didn't want to hear anymore about Job; but at the end of the day, the facts were the facts, and if I was going to live, survive this, and be happy again, I was going to have to endure it a little while longer. Friends, I am happy again, so it is true.

June 21 - Who Is Like You

Happy art thou, O Israel: who is like unto thee, O people saved by the lord, the shield of thy help, and who is the sword of thy excellency! and thine enemies shall be found liars unto thee; and thou shalt tread upon their high places. (Deut. 33:29)

Yeah, I know it sounds corny to say, "Who is like you?" Sounds like something some motivational speaker would tell you to get you all pumped up and positive. True, there is no one like you, but that can be looked at from two different vantage points. We can say there is no one like you, and that could mean that no one is as lost, broken, foolish, dumb, and ignorant like you. No one is so hopeless like you, and no one is so far from ever being healed. That's what we even think of ourselves sometimes, but it is not what God's Word says. When God speaks of Israel, David, or John, the apostle whom Jesus loved, He is not speaking in general terms but in distinctive facts. We are unique from one another and not by chance either, but by design and purpose. There is no mistake about us and nothing that could ever make us hopeless. Such a case would be to say that God can't save you because you are too far gone.

When I discovered that my weaknesses were not accidents of destruction but tools in the Master's hands, then I began to understand life a bit more. I was able to see clearer before I was in complete darkness in my riverside pity party. All through the scriptures, we read how we are wonderfully and fearfully made. We read about Christ's great love for us, so much that He would lay down His life for us, about God's great love for us that He would send His own Son to die for us. The more I read the scriptures, the more I was able to see how wonderful and unique I really am.

In Deuteronomy 33:29, we see how the Lord felt about His chosen people, Israel, how He lifts them as so special to Him.

> *Happy art thou, O Israel: who is like unto thee, O people saved by the lord, the shield of thy help, and who is the sword of thy excellency! and thine enemies shall be found liars unto thee; and thou shalt tread upon their high places. (Deut. 33:29)*

If you want a confidence builder, then meditate on all that says. If you want to really feel good about who you are as a child of God, then read about Christ's love for His bride. We are the bride of Christ, and any groom, I know, sure thinks the world of his bride. He didn't just pick any old gal to marry but one that is to his liking.

Dear friend, God loves you so much that He offers you a special place in the His economy and His Kingdom. Today stop looking at yourself as some lost, malformed, and underdeveloped perversion and begin to see yourself through the eyes of the One who made and created you. He loves us, so we must be lovable. I know many Christians focus on us being dirty rags as sinners, and we are. We are truly lost in our sins, and there is not one of us who is righteous in His sight, but we must have something of worth as the Lord loved us enough to send His son. God would be a fool to die for dirt. He died for us in the form of Christ because He sees what a regenerate work of wonder we can be. If God sees that, then why don't we?

June 22 - Acting on Hearing

Happy are thy men, happy are these thy servants, which stand continually before thee, and that hear thy wisdom. (1 Kings 10:8)

Many of us who have been Christians long enough know the routine. We go to church on Sunday, we tithe our monies, and we read our Bibles. Some of us take it further and even have a little fish plastered on our rear bumper. We know the hymns and also most of the words to our favorite praise-and-worship songs. We know the pastor and his wife; we have seen a few Christian concerts and have been to a few Christian seminars. If we could, we would wear Christian underwear. We know the entire lingo and when to say amen, yet with all of our knowing and all of our wisdom of tradition and dogma, we lack one very important thing: we don't live according to God's wisdom. Even if we do it one day, we certainly don't do it every day. It's like evangelism. It is something we are called to do, to be fishers of men, to preach the gospel of peace to everyone we meet, but do we do it daily? I use evangelism simply as an example as I know the realities and limitations that are out there in its regard, but I also use it to make a point.

Friends, in order to ever be where we need to be, we must be *in Christ* daily. We must not simply listen to God's Word on Sunday morning or simply read it in our daily devotions, but we must hear it. To hear God's Word is to take it and then use it. It would be like trying to put together a gas BBQ grill but only reading the assembly directions and not pay attention to them. To read them but not do what they say. I have put together a gas BBQ grill or two, and it's no picnic. You simply just can't read those instructions; you must follow every single step.

In our lives as Christians, and even more as Christians who are suffering from depression and anxiety, we must heed every single one of God's words if we are to ever make it, when it is easy and convenient and when it is hard and very inconvenient. It will be tough, and it will seem fruitless at times, but we must be persistent. If we are to truly show our love for our Lord, we must also show our love for His Word. Faith begins with loving that Word and loving it enough to follow it even through the valleys of the shadows of death. Let us today make a commitment not just to listen to God's Word but also to begin to hear it.

June 23 - Too Much Sleep

And she made him sleep upon her knees; and she called for a man, and she caused him to shave off the seven locks of his head; and she began to afflict him, and his strength went from him. (Judg. 16:19)

Oh, for night to come so sleep can follow. That used to be my philosophy of existence when anxiety and depression ruled the day. Living and longing for the evening hour so I could close my eyes to all of this pain and drift off to another place. Sleeping is something that God created for our very existence, and so it is good, and even more, it is totally necessary to live. In a recent study that I read, it stated that if sleep was kept from you long enough, you could actually die from lack of it. Though it's never been proven, it would make sense that a body that doesn't rest at the least won't work the way it was designed. As with all good things that God has made, they can also be abused and corrupted as in music, sex, and joy. Music can be used to draw you to the Lord or used to turn you away from the Lord. Sex can be used for its designed purpose of showing the deepest expression of love between and a husband and a wife, yet sex can be perverted and become dirty and an abomination to the Lord. Even the pursuit of joy can be turned upside down when joy becomes the target and Christ as only an obstacle to joy. Simply put, joy apart from God is no joy at all but a lie and a god unto itself.

This all brings us back to sleep—oh, blessed wonderful sleep. Oh, to have a restful night sleep, to pillow your head under those cool, dry sheets and comfy quilt in winter. It is good, but it can become a dirty, nasty place where only dark thoughts of desperation are grown. When I was going through those few months of that bedridden stage, my bed became a snare to me. I would sneak into it, run to it, and hide in it. Soon those clean sheets became dirty sheets, and I was not out of the bed long enough to even make the bed. It became a picture of my life—undone, messy, dirty, self-absorbed, and hopeless. Instead of looking forward to getting up and serving the Lord, it became a place I didn't want to leave. The more I stayed in bed, the less good sleep I also achieved. So what was once a haven for rest became a place of torment filled with restlessness.

Friends, if that's where you are right now, I pray that you would get up and out of that place. If you don't have an accountability partner as in a spouse or family member to keep an eye on you, then please get one. In these places, we must be monitored, or we will waste away. As we read in our scriptures for today, we see that Samson found his place of sleep where all his strength was taken. In his perverted slumber-rest, peace and strength were stolen from him, but did he not also have a part in letting that happen?

Too much sleep is not a healer to those who suffer but can be a place where it actually has the reverse effects. Get up, get out there, and fight to live. Our sleep can only be sweet when the Lord Himself endorses it. Any other sleep is lazy and selfish, and the Lord will have no part in it, nor can He even bless it.

June 24 - Less Is Better Than More

There is a sore evil which I have seen under the sun, namely, riches kept for the owners thereof to their hurt. (Eccles. 5:13)

All my life I have been a person who loved things. As a youth, I played drums in a few local rock bands. My drum set became my god, and I spent great sums of money there. When cars entered my life, I spent much money there having them look just as I wanted. I collected folding knives, and at one time, I had over one hundred knives, some very expensive. I was always a *things* person, and I always wanted more things. Bigger, better, faster, and cooler was my life song. When I had an opportunity to advance in my career, it was the same thing: Move up the ladder and become bigger. Make more money. Know more important people. I was forever in a state of collecting things and positions.

Even as a pastor, I was always trying to be more than I really was, wanting to be recognized by being a part of local politics and such. One would think I would have learned after all the empty joy those fleeting positions gave me, yet being sinful at heart, I kept pursuing more and more. I was never happy with a small church, always wanting a bigger one. Never being happy with who I was or what I have done simply stole all the joy out of living. Friend, if you believe that more is always better, that more is where you will finally find peace, well, I hate to disappoint you, but it's a lie. It's all a lie, and we can take it from one who knows, King Solomon. He had it all and more, and yet with all he had and all the fame and wisdom he possessed, he ended up writing the book of Ecclesiastes. In doing so, he gave us a picture of a life with everything. In his own words, he said this, "It's all vanity and vexation of spirit."

In our society today, this idea of getting more to get happy is forced on our face from commercials to Hollywood. Even many TV evangelists sell this notion, and the people just run to it like bees to honey. At the end of the day, the results are always the same: empty, bitter, and lonely lives. Unless the Lord is our all, nothing will bring us joy. I have had a lot of things like I said, and at one time, I earned a lot of money too. Yet it meant nothing, and in fact it was at the height of my achievements and wealth that I fell into depression. Oh the irony of it all. To have all I ever wanted or could ever have imagined and being so empty and even ready to take my life at the same time. So many might wonder at that, and some did as they questioned my pensive state, "How could you be so depressed when you have so much?" In their hidden thoughts, they even thought, *Let him walk a mile in my shoes, and he will see something to be depressed about.*

When I look back on those days, I am happy that the Lord allowed them to fall upon me. I'm happy that I learned at a relatively young age the pettiness of things. They surely mean little; they grow wings and fly away. They do even less for us. If you search for anything in this life, search for Christ and His righteousness, and as the book says, "and all these things shall be added unto you."

June 25 - You Will Dance Again

A time to weep, and a time to laugh; a time to mourn, and a time to dance. (Eccles. 3:4)

I'm a big superhero guy. Guess I never really grew up because I still enjoy a lot of the new movies coming out. To be able to be something that we are not able to be, I think appeals to all of us, especially men. There was a spoof superhero movie that came out a few years back, and one of the villains says this line to his sidekick, "Don't worry, you will dance again." He was talking about getting back to their old evil crime world again, but in the Bible, the Lord speaks about *dancing again* through King Solomon. In Ecclesiastes 3:4, we hear these famous words spoken.

In life there will always be "a time to weep, and a time to laugh; a time to mourn, and a time to dance."

Kind of interesting that all four of the flavors of life are listed, and also interesting is that we will all most likely experience them all. Sure, some of us more or less than others, but they are still the constants of life.

As I read them, I see myself there in each and every one. I can picture in my mind all the times I was in each place of those emotions. I have wept, and I have laughed. I have mourned over a loss, and I have also danced in the joy of sweet victory in the Lord. All of them are unique, and in a way, all of them are necessary to experience the other. I cannot truly dance for joy unless I have known the depths of weeping. I cannot truly laugh unless I know the pains of mourning. One always makes the other sweeter and more intense.

When God's people, Israel, crossed over the Red Sea, I do not believe they truly understood true dancing in victory until they were first trapped up against the Red Sea. Did they not dance on the other side like they never danced before? When you are going through difficult times in life, dancing is the last thing on your mind. Sometimes we think about when we danced in the past, and it makes us sad as we ponder if we will ever dance again. We assume that even if we were to dance again (spiritually), it would surely not be as wonderful as it once was.

Dear friend and fellow sufferer, to make that conclusion is to take away the wonder that is the Lord our God, to limit Him to only past victories and past joys. It's to say that where we are now is too far gone for even the Creator of time and space. It is assuming that the Lord's massive power has been all but depleted, and there is not much left worth having. Well, I am here to tell you that you will dance again. You will laugh again. Crying and mourning can only go on for so long, and as night must turn into day, surely sorrow must turn into laughter. Please don't let your current situation discourage you as I have seen people weep with millions of dollars and others laugh in a wheelchair. It is not our circumstances that give us joy but where we are in Christ. Get out those dancing shoes and keep them in plain sight, and no, it's not wishful thinking but a fact. God says we will dance, and so we will, whether here or in the new Jerusalem.

June 26 - The Rock Flower

Then shall the lame man leap as an hart, and the tongue of the dumb sing: for in the wilderness shall waters break out, and streams in the desert. (Isa. 35:6)

On a recent men's retreat, we were blessed to be able to go up to the mountains of upstate New York. Yes, they do have mountains and wilderness in New York; it's not all city. I say this because when I lived in California for a while, everyone whom I told I came from New York always assumed that New York was New York City. All city all the time and that I went to high school in the Empire State Building. So for all of you non-New Yorkers out there, a tree does grow, but only in the mountains of New York, which are amazingly wild. While on our first hike of the men's retreat, we came across this massive natural stone wall. Above it was an incredible waterfall that just set the day on a high note. Yet what really caught my eye on this wilderness mountain trail was the absence of flowers and color, at least until the appearance of a lone yellow flower jumped out at me.

It was a lone flower growing right out of a stone wall. We took a picture of it simply because it was so amazing. I then added it to my devotion time when we read the Word of God. In that impromptu devotion / Bible study, I spoke of how hopeful that rock—flower really is. It spoke to me of the life in the dark, of the power of God to bring forth living things where there is only darkness. In the prophetic words of the prophet Isaiah, we see the same imagery. Though it's hard and difficult today, tomorrow it will not be. The lame shall leap like a deer; the tongues of the mutes shall sing. The water shall be flowing where today there is a dry and dusty desert. That is a promise of God, not of me. That is the truth for a future that is certain for those who trust in Jesus Christ as Lord.

Friend, the Lord our Maker is not bound by rock walls and dry desert lands. He does not see a barren land and conclude, "Only death here, better move on to greener pastures." No, He sees only what His power can do, and that is *anything*. He is not limited by impossible situations, nor is He discouraged by troubling times. He cares not about our limitations because He only sees possibilities. He doesn't look at the blind man and conclude, "This man will never see." No, He sees a blind man and declares, "This man will I use for My glory."

Today, as you struggle with impossible problems, paralyzing anxiety, or overwhelming depression, remember this: God doesn't see them as issues but as possibilities for greatness, as a place to flex His holy might and do amazing things. He always sees us not as we are but as we will be. Cry out to Him today and ask Him to turn your dry, barren land into rivers of flowing waters. He can, and He will if we are but strong enough to believe.

June 27 - Misunderstanding God

And when the disciples saw Him walking on the sea, they were troubled, saying, "It is a spirit;" and they cried out for fear. (Matt 14:26)

I don't know about you, but I don't like change. I don't like surprises either, and as a person who struggles with anxiety, the sudden shock of the unknown can set me off, whether it's a problem phone call from work, an unexpected health issue, or body pain. They can scare you if you don't understand what they really mean. Most people can attest to the uneasy feeling of waiting for test results from the doctor. The many times in our lives when something happens that we do not expect can really get us off balance like a drunken sailor on rough seas (spiritually speaking). Many times the root of fear and anxiety in a Christian's life is simply misunderstanding what God is doing.

When a loved one unexpectedly ends up in the ER, we often begin to question God's purpose in such a tragedy. Life can be like that—a place filled with potholes that blow out brand-new tires or falls that break a leg while on your well-needed vacation. In my own life, I would often question God when it came to going away. I seem to get sick often when I go away. A few times I got food poisoning. If you ever had food poisoning, you know it's no walk in the park. One year I went away for a well-needed family rest, and after the first two days, we received a call that my father had died. We had to pack up and come back home from Virginia to New York. The year after that, while coming home from vacation, my father-in-law passed away. The year after that was the year I got food poisoning.

We can scratch our heads and try to draw a conclusion. *Maybe God is telling me not to go away anymore* surely was a thought. Because of this cycle of issues, I became filled with anxiety about ever going away again. Was it logical or wise to draw this conclusion? Of course not, but as humans, that's what we do. One of the lessons the Lord has taught me through these odd and unusual circumstances is this: Don't try to figure out what you can never know. Instead, simply trust the Lord whom you know and the past faithfulness He has always shown you.

It's easy to become afraid when we don't understand as it was with the disciples of Jesus when they saw Him walking on the water. It says they were troubled; they even cried out in fear. Sure, maybe they truly didn't know it was Jesus, but they still should have known what Jesus always taught them: "Don't fear if I am with you." Though Jesus wasn't with them in the flesh at that moment, was He not with them in word? Today we even have it better because the Lord has given us the Holy Spirit to permanently indwell us. So when we see things we don't understand, we don't have to be afraid because even though we can't see Him, He is with us. Of depression and anxiety and the things that go bump in the night that make us jump, we might not understand why they happen, yet we only need to know who is in control of all things. Even those scary things have purpose, and even my vacations from hell had purpose. Hey, I wouldn't have them to share with you today if I didn't live through them, amen?

June 28 - Meeting God Can Be Scary Sometimes

And the angel said unto her, "Fear not, Mary: for thou hast found favour with God." (Luke 1:30)

One of the things we all want to do is meet the Lord. We often think to ourselves, *If I could only meet the Lord face to face, I would feel better.* Well, that might be true, at least until we read about what the Lord is like. He is a consuming fire, a righteous judge, and yes, filled with love for His creation. We might assume coming in contact with Him would be easy and laid back simply because we know of His loving side, but think about meeting the president or king of another country. Before you can actually sit down and talk, you have a lot of secret-service people with black suits on. The point I am trying to make is this: though we all want to have an encounter with the Lord, we don't understand what we ask.

Jacob left his encounter with God with a hip out of joint for life. Moses's countenance was changed, and that was only after seeing a quick glimpse of God's glory as it passed by. Meeting God is necessary to really be what God wants us to be. We must have that road-to-Damascus experience. Speaking of which, think of Saul who met the Lord that day and became Paul. All of these people were never the same again, so why should we think any less of our encounters with God today? Now, you might be thinking to yourself, *Encounter with God? I thought they didn't happen anymore.* Dear friend, they happen all the time; it's just that we don't see or understand when it does happen. Of myself, my encounters with the Lord, which forever changed me, happened during my times of blessed depression. When paralyzed with anxiety—again, another encounter with the Almighty. Spurgeon dealt with depression, and it was there that he had a close encounter with the Almighty. All great people of God must encounter the Lord, and in that encounter, they must be willing to walk away broken, bent, and never the same.

Meeting God is not like meeting a friend for coffee. You don't skip along after that encounter as if you just had a haircut. No, this is a meeting with the Maker of time and space, the very One who holds matter and atoms together. He is the Star Breather and Planet Maker. He affects you when you meet Him. We hear of people who meet movie stars and walk away starstruck. Well, would there be any less of a reaction after meeting the thrice Holy God? When Mary, the mother of Jesus's humanity, had her heavenly encounter, her first reaction was fear. She only met an angel, yet it was so overwhelming that she concluded it was a scary thing. Yet what did the angel say to Mary? "Fear not, Mary, for you have found favor with God."

Dear friend, what if our encounters with deep depression and anxiety were actually the results of an encounter with the Lord? What if He is also telling us the same thing? "Fear not, my child, for you have found favor with Me." Certainly not all depression and anxiety seasons are encounters with the Lord, but maybe some are. I know mine were, and I have never been the same since. If you are not sure, cry out and say to the Lord, "Dear Father, was that You that day?"

June 29 - Meeting God Can Be Scary Sometimes (Part 2)

And there came a fear on all: and they glorified God, saying, "That a great prophet is risen up among us; and, That God hath visited His people." (Luke 7:16)

It is interesting when we study the Bible to see some common threads that run through it. In the case of fear, it appears to always accompany those who have been near or have witnessed a work of the Lord. We must be careful, friends, that we do not take our Christianity too lightly. It is not a little thing to be the bride of Christ and to have your very lives atoned for by the living sacrifice of another. Too often we look at our redemption and newfound faith as nothing more than joining a new club or gym. We look at the *benefit package* and the *perks* and say, "Sure, I'll join." Dear friend, woe unto us if we ever look at our new life in Christ that way. Woe unto us if we don't understand what cost was paid for us to be called a *friend* of God. To be adopted into God's family is much more than a mere paperwork trail. We do not see God's glory in its fullness right now, and that is our problem. We conclude—because we do not see God's glory as Moses did—that it is not that glorious. What do the scriptures say about this topic? Well, they say that "the heavens declare the glory of God." Point being is—though we aren't standing facing the burning bush does not mean that we cannot see or experience a bit of God's glory. Like I said yesterday about being in the presence of God through our very struggles and pain, so too can we catch a picture of God's glory through the things He has created.

I cannot emphasize enough the need to get out into creation. Go to the water, mountains, even out on a quiet, starlit night. Get out and ponder its majesty and wonder. A young couple in church just had their first child. To me, it is always a place where the fear of God is found. I look at that little child and the two parents and say, "How could they create this?" Well, they cannot; only God can. Childbirth, even procreation itself, is a wonder to behold and to contemplate. That is what is missing today, our wonder and awestruck response to what God has done, is doing, and will do. We do not stand in awe because we take it all for granted.

Every Saturday night as I walk back from my office, I look up at the sky and think about what is going on. I am standing on a giant ball being hurdled through space. There are billions of stars that surround me and gravitational forces that hold me. How can I observe this and not stand in fear and wonder of such a God? I could just walk by it and not think on it, but that's what everyone does, and so everyone sees nothing but chance and randomness. Friend, let the fear of the Lord fall upon you as you mull over what we are as humans and even more as Christians. It should send chills down your spine in awestruck wonder even simply at the mention of His name. If you are not at that place of this fear and wonder, then you really haven't arrived yet at truly knowing the Lord. Ask the Lord to turn you on to His glory and majesty. Be prepared because He will.

June 30 - Meeting God Can Be Scary Sometimes (Part 3)

Men's hearts failing them for fear, and for looking after those things which are coming on the earth: for the powers of heaven shall be shaken. (Luke 21:26)

As we finish out another month, we are presented with another gift of a new month. Our Lord is continuing to offer us new beginnings and new starts. He places failures behind us and offers us new chances ahead of us. He is in some respects *renewable energy* that keeps on giving and giving. I remember one particular phase of my emotional struggles when I abused God's wonderful grace and second-chance character. I just kept on sinning over and over again, continually running to this one sin to feel good and escape the pain of the anxiety and depression. It was my conclusion that I could just surf on home riding God's grace and forgiveness. I also concluded that if the Lord knew the pain I faced, that He would allow me to indulge myself a bit. How could He judge or punish me for a little sin here and there when He knows how much I am hurting? I was soon to learn a new lesson in my spiritual growth as He clearly said, "Oh no, you don't."

Pain is no excuse for sin. After a little while of playing with fire, the Lord cleared the air and let me know that righteousness is still our goal. Even in pain, we are called to live for Him. The Lord led me to think of a scenario to better understand how He sees things. If my child had broken his arm and had to wear a cast all summer vacation, would that give him the right to curse at me and live a lawless life all summer? When I saw it that way, I understood and was able to share that lesson with others. Seems that this is a common misunderstanding among people, and I have the counseling records to prove it. More than one time I have heard from the mouths of Christians this silly and childish concept. If my marriage is a painful place and I am not having my needs met, why then would God hold it against me to have a little fling on the side? To have my sexual needs met so I could feel good? Hey, wouldn't God want me to be happy? I kid you not about these flawed understandings, and to really shock you, these two particular cases were not men but women. I thought them odd to think in such a way, but like I said, the Lord put my nose into my own sin so I too could see the error in it.

Today I say this all to bring home a very important point, and one that I am sure you do not want to hear. The Lord is coming back to judge this world. There is no free ride, and no matter how rough life on earth is, God does not or cannot look past unatoned sin. Friend, in your life of suffering, do not make the mistake that I did by running to sin as a temporary fix to your pain and think that God won't care. He cares, and He cares a lot, so much so that He sent His Son to die for those sins. Today, even in your pain, you must still live for Him. Turn from sin and turn to Him in fear and honor. Sin is no joke, never was, and can never be. Turn loose those things that so tightly bind you to them.

July

July 1 - Help I Need Somebody

And the lord God said, "It is not good that the man should be alone; I will make him an help meet for him." (Gen. 2:18)

They say behind every great man is a great woman. I guess that's not politically correct to say or maybe even wrong, but I know in my life it is all too true. No, I'm not a great man, but my wife is truly a great woman. I bring this up to make this point: it is very hard to make it through depression and anxiety alone. Not that it's impossible, but it sure helps. If you're a man or a woman, single or married, it doesn't matter; we need help, and I mean personal, hands-on help. It doesn't matter from whom it comes, whether it be from a caring mom or dad, friend, or thoughtful coworker. We simply need someone to keep an eye on us as we go through these dark spells. If you have no one, well, then the Lord will use His Holy Spirit to be that watcher because being alone in this is very hard.

As I look over the scriptures, it is rare that we find people alone all the time and forever. People always seem to be around people. Some good, some not so good, but regardless, we need others—family, those who love us. When I went through my dark days, it was my wife who made me get out of bed, made me fight on. It was God working through her that made me read my Bible, and she wouldn't let up until I was healed. She was instrumental in my deliverance, and at times, she had to get downright hard and angry.

If you have ever been to a gym or lifted weights, maybe even gymnastics or martial arts, one thing that you will always find alongside that training is a trainer. A spotter to watch, motivate, and to make sure you don't lift or do too much, one who pushes you. In the spiritual world, we need the same type of person, yet many people choose to go through these emotional issues alone, and the reason is mostly pride. Pride in the fact that they don't want anyone to know what struggle they are facing. Friend, this is not of God, and as the scriptures state, "Pride goes before a fall." We must humble ourselves and pray for that right person to whom we can reveal what we are going through. Even if it is a person who lives three thousand miles away, it's still a person who can call and check on us. This is so vital in our healing process, and if we don't reveal ourselves to someone we trust, we simply won't make it. I know that's a hard thing to say, but I say it to motivate you to find that person with whom share. Choose them wisely as we don't want to share too much with the wrong person.

Again, if you're alone in this, you can rest assured that God will fill that role; but if it is simply due to pride, then you can only blame yourself. If you don't have someone today, then cry out to the Lord and say those famous words, "Help, I need somebody." The Lord is faithful and will provide the help you need in whatever form He deems best. Also remember this last point: this person isn't to be your god but simply your helpmate and nothing more. If we are to depend on anyone, it should only be the Lord. The people He sends are just those serving their Master and ours.

July 2 - Oh to Only Believe

And straightway the father of the child cried out, and said with tears, "Lord, I believe; help thou mine unbelief." (Mark 9:24)

Oh to believe. It might sound like an odd thing for a Christian to be asking, but if we are honest with ourselves, we know this is true. Friends, we do fall in and out of belief. To say we never do is a lie, for if we are always in true belief, then we should never have a single worry or care. Is it not true that if we are in belief, we believe every single word of God? So if we claim to believe every single word of God *all the time*, then we would believe it when Jesus says, "Fear not." Well, the facts are in, and if you are like me, there have been times when you have questioned what God was doing and why. For me, there were times when things were so bad that I just began to question God's very existence. Blasphemy, you might say—well, then I have blasphemed against God. I'm in good company because many great men and women of God have been in that place.

David Wilkerson, from World Challenge, in his devotional book, wrote about *when all means fail*. He spoke about the times when things are so over, so done, so bleak, that Satan will place in our minds the question of God's very existence. It happens, friends, and it's nothing to be ashamed of. What it shows is that we are human, and faith is not a natural attribute to sinful man. Faith takes trust and wisdom of God's Word. It takes all that we are to take that next step in the dark.

Just today, as I pen this devotion for July 2, it is actually July 4, and I received a text message from one of the people I counsel. Being a holiday, I screen my calls to see if it is an emergency—well, it was, and the text said, "Pastor Scott, I'm in great depression, please call me." So I called back right away and heard this broken voice of a broken child of God. This lady has struggled with depression and anxiety for a long time, and this past year was a bad one. She was at the end of her rope, and her faith was fiber-optic thin. She couldn't receive words of encouragement from the Lord because it meant nothing to her in this very dark day. I simply spoke loving words and shared with her how I know what she is feeling and that I know it will pass. I know this because I have come through it. Even though she couldn't even pray, I could pray, and I told her that I loved her in Christ and that though this is her darkest day, one day she will smile again. Her lot didn't change. Her faith or lack of it didn't change. But her heart was lifted just enough to make it one more day.

Dear friend in Christ, there will be days when we can't even pray for a healing because we are simply praying that our faith is restored. Our Lord is big, He is strong, and He knows our frail human hearts. He knows that our faith can become razor thin, and He has made provision for it. Remember that even before we loved Him, He loved us. Even when we don't believe in Him, He still exists and keeps working in our lives. So for those days when you are not sure what you believe anymore, God has you covered. It is those days when the prayers of others carry us where our prayers can't.

July 3 - You Want Me to Do What?

And a vision appeared to Paul in the night; There stood a man of Macedonia, and prayed him, saying, "Come over into Macedonia, and help us." (Acts 16:9)

I know I have shared this thought before in this devotional, and I will share it again. Friend, even in the very center of our trials, the Lord might be calling us to minister to another. I liken it to being in a hospital bed, diagnosed with bone cancer, in pain and barely alive, and then hearing the Lord say to you, "That person in the next bed needs you. Please help and minister to them." Say what, Lord? You want me to do what? Being a pastor and Christian counselor, it is part of my job to receive calls in all hours of the night, twenty-four seven, seven days a week. Most of the calls are for help, help during a sickness, accident, or personal struggle. No matter what the hour or time, I must speak to these hurting people or sometimes visit them ASAP. Well, that's a pastor's job, but it is also our job as children of God through faith in Jesus Christ. We are always on call, friends, and there is never a time or place where we can ignore a person's cry for help.

Sadly I have dropped the ball on some as I just didn't have it in me, but the resulting conviction of the Holy Spirit was worse than the 3:00 a.m. phone call. We have to go, friends. We have to minister where and to whom the Lord sends us. It might be on the checkout line when you are in a rush to get home and cook dinner. It may be on vacation when you just want to relax. But the facts is this: if a person is crying out to Christ for salvation or guidance, and we are the ones that the Lord summons for the call, we must obey it. It is kind of like being a superhero, as funny as that might sound. Sometimes I feel like I have a cape and tights under my clothes that I must change into whenever the emergency beacon light flashes my way. In a way, it's exciting and a blessing to be the one that the Lord calls on. No, I'm not a superhero, not even close, but I am an ambassador for Jesus Christ, called just like you to preach the good news to the world.

Why I bring this up again today is because of the timing that the Lord deems best. Yes, even in depression and anxiety I have been dispatched, and no, I wasn't happy about it, at least not until after when the blessing of the Lord came upon me. Yes, there are rewards, blessings, and perks to this sacred mission of hope for the hurting. There are those wonderful pats on the back that the Lord gives out once in a while. They are so worth it, but just make sure it's not you patting yourself on the back. You can always tell because my pats never last more than a minute or two. No, the Lord's thumbs up are clear and definitive. So today, be a blessing even when you feel like you need a blessing. Watch what happens when you take that step of faith and place another's needs above your own. Hey, isn't that what Jesus Christ did for us on the cross? In the end, we can't go wrong by emulating Christ's love even through our pain.

July 4 - What People See

That the communication of thy faith may become effectual by the acknowledging of every good thing which is in you in Christ Jesus. (Philem. 1:6)

I don't want to sound redundant, but I guess the Lord leaves me no choice. Today will be a slight repeat of yesterday in the fact that what people see in us is just as important as you and I being healed. Yesterday we spoke about being asked to minister to others while in the depths of pain and suffering. Today we will build on that and add a deeper dynamic. Today we will speak about the *burden of bearing the light*. In case you haven't figured it out, there is a burden in this Christian life, and it is this: always being *on*. What I mean by that can best be explained by sharing a pastor's life. When my wife and I entertain people or go out to the movies or dinner, we don't leave our ministry hats at home. No, we have to always be *on* for Christ. What we say, do, and watch and where we go are always being observed. I never realized how true this was until one year on vacation, we were close to a thousand miles away from home, and behind us at the gas station filling up was another Christian from our church. That really made me think, and I couldn't help but imagine, *What if my wife and I were fighting or listening to an improper song or doing anything that a Christian shouldn't do?* Here I think I am so far away from ministry and being a pastor, yet I'm really not.

In Philemon chapter 1 verse 6, we hear of this burden of bearing the light. That we are to make sure we communicate by how we live all the things that are of Christ. That people would always see in us the light of Jesus Christ our Lord. That would include situations and things like smashing my finger with a hammer at a church-work party and not screaming out expletives, cruising in my Jeep with my top down and making sure my radio is not blasting worldly music, or worse, being at the beach and checking out girls in bikinis. We are to not just have the light of Christ in us but also bear that light with honor. Almost like being held responsible for transporting a million-dollar car from one state to the next, you would want to make sure you care for it with the deepest regard.

During our vacation Bible school camp, our children would often play a game where they would have to race against another team by carrying a raw egg on a spoon. You know you have to get the job done quickly, but you sure don't want that egg to be dropped. In the case of depression and anxiety, I realized how this translated into my responsibility as a Christian. Sure, I wanted to scream out and complain to everyone I came in contact with, but I must first think about God's greater purpose and make sure I carried His "egg," so to speak, with honor and care. What would the saved and unsaved world see in me? What representation of Christ would they get? Wow, it's hard, but nonetheless, it's our responsibility as a child of God, one being given the gift of salvation and not wanting to tarnish that gift.

July 5 - Look for the Good

Many, O lord my God, are Thy wonderful works which Thou hast done, and Thy thoughts which are to us-ward: they cannot be reckoned up in order unto Thee: if I would declare and speak of them, they are more than can be numbered. (Ps. 40:5)

Well, it is about ninety degrees today here in New York. Funny how we just had a very nasty winter about five months ago and yet we are already complaining about the heat. I remember speaking to my wife close to the end of that long winter and saying, "I can't wait for the heat of summer." We are a strange bunch of people, aren't we? We always want what we can't have, and when we receive it, we don't want it. People with curly hair want straight hair and believe those with straight hair are having all the fun. Then there are those straight-haired people who want curly hair.

As a young man, I was very underweight, so much that I would be picked on for being skin and bones. As a teen, it really bothered me, and I tried everything I could to gain weight. I dreamed of one day gaining those pounds, and when I became a Christian, I actually added to my prayer list the specific weight that I longed to be. You guessed it, I am over fifty now, and guess what I'm trying to do? Now I am a tad overweight and can't seem to drop the few pounds I need. Imagine our dear Lord listening to my rants and saying, "Can't you ever be happy? What is it that you want to be, heavy or thin?" Well, the Lord knows what I want, and that is perfection: the perfect weight, the perfect life, the prefect church, and the perfect family. As I grow in Christ, I often think about my childlike attitude and wonder if the Lord feels about me the same way I feel about my children's selfish, unthankful attitudes.

Friends, we have so much, and yet we find that we focus on what we don't have most of the time instead of what we do. In my struggles with depression and anxiety, though it has all but passed, I still complain to the Lord that my anxiety has not been removed 100 percent. I don't just want it under control, I want it gone, eradicated, finished, over, done with, and history. It is amazing that as I am feeling so well right now, I still find things to complain about. I so quickly forget where I was and how desperate I was. Will there ever be a time when I simply praise the Lord for all He has done, will do, and is doing in my life? Surely I can find plenty of things to be thankful for, yet I find it hard to do so.

In Psalm 40:5, we hear of all that the Lord has done for us and how we should be celebrating these blessings. Problem is I only compare my life to my life. I don't compare my life to people in other parts of the world who are struggling and thankful even for a morsel of bread and a beaten-up Bible that they can read. There are so many things we should and can be thankful for, yet in depression and anxiety, they are the furthest thoughts from our mind. We say things to ourselves like, "When I am feeling better, I will praise Him." No, friend, we must praise Him now right in the thick of the mire. He is waiting for that praise in the fire before He will ever put His water of life over and on it.

July 6 - Just Music?

Let the word of Christ dwell in you richly in all wisdom; teaching and admonishing one another in psalms and hymns and spiritual songs, singing with grace in your hearts to the Lord. (Col. 3:16)

So it is still summer, and winter is a long, distant memory. Today you are facing things that make you feel like it is winter. It's amazing how emotions control us so much that even the nicest day, a brand-new car, or even a big raise can't overcome the depression within us. Depression is just that, a place where all that you were have been compressed into a simple living and breathing body and not much else. People can dance and laugh around you all they want, and joy just can't be found. Today I received another text from another person asking for prayer. They asked me to pray for their sister who is having chemotherapy; her husband just hung himself, and a relative just passed away. What can I do for that person but pray, for they are in a state of emotional and situational depression?

Nothing short of Jesus stepping down from heaven and scooping her up in His arms could deliver her. It is during these times, friends, where a simple, often-missed tool of God needs to be introduced: the blessing of music. It might sound like too little, too late, but I tell you, the Lord speaks through anointed music. Songs, hymns, and spiritual songs played and / or sung can lift a heart maybe just high enough to hear the Lord's Word of encouragement. No, it's not the cure-all, but a tool of God, which—when used in conjunction with everything else we have spoken about or will speak about—can raise us from the ashes of disaster.

In my deep days of depression, I would slip away on my Walkman (yeah, I was dating myself), pop in a cassette tape of Christian music, get on my bike, and just ride until I couldn't ride anymore. Sure I had to fight and push to do it, but I was often able to hear the Lord speaking to me those words I so desperately needed to hear. At other times, I would get on my treadmill and watch a live clip of a worship band singing praises to the Lord.

Now, I know there are times when we simply don't want to, nor are we up to being that physical. I know it because I have lived it, but as we begin to heal, music can be the catalyst that moves us speedily up the ladder of deliverance. If you're a hymn person, then just open up a hymnal and simply read the words. The words of some of those old hymns can really move mountains. If you are up to it, sing as you read, as the Lord loves a singing heart of praise even if it is a heart that is hurting at the time. If you're a big praise-and-worship person, then tune in to that Christian radio channel or pop in your latest gadget and go about your day.

Again, friends, imagine the testimony to a lost and dying world when they see you singing out to the Lord who seems to be allowing you to suffer. The world will scratch their heads and wonder why we trust a Lord that at times allows us to struggle. It is truly a sweet savor unto Him, and He will surely bless you for that walk of faith.

July 7 - Help Will Come—It Must

Having therefore obtained help of God, I continue unto this day, witnessing both to small and great, saying none other things than those which the prophets and Moses did say should come. (Acts 26:22)

Sometimes it is really hard to understand that the Lord will help us when that help seems so absent from our lives. It's like during a storm and the power goes out. You call the electric company, and they tell you they are working on it when you know there is also ten thousand other people who need power too. You know that though they say they're coming to fix it, in your heart, you feel it's just a lie or a ploy to push you off. Help is what you need now, not later or next week. You have meat in the freezer that will go bad, and you need power to run your heater if you are in the cold of winter. This scenario is all too familiar to us here in the east cost of the USA. This past spring, a massive, record-breaking hurricane came through and knocked out power for weeks in some areas. After a while, we just stopped calling the electrical company because it seemed fruitless.

The Bible warns us about calling out for help from the world, from mankind. In Psalm 118:8, we are instructed to only trust in God and not in man. Yes, we need people sometimes, and the Lord will work through people to help us, but we should never depend on people but only on the Lord.

In Acts 26:22, Paul speaks in the past tense about the Lord's help. He says that he *has* obtained help from God. I like the word *obtained* in the KJV Bible. It means we have apprehended God's help. It is in our hands, and no one can take that help away. It is our possession. Just as a child who is born into a family has obtained a part in that family, and that place cannot be taken away, so is it impossible for us to not get help from the Lord. A parent will always, or should I say, *should always* take care of their children. That child doesn't have to wonder if they will be fed or clothed because as part of that family, it is a given.

Friend, if you're in that place today where you have waited and waited for the Lord's help, you have waited and waited for the help of friends and family, and you have waited so long that you are tired, well, here is a word from the Lord—He will help you because you are His child. And if He didn't help you, then He wouldn't be a very good father, would He? As for friends, they may come and go. They may be there for a while then all of a sudden they are gone. But of the Lord, His love and trustworthiness is a guarantee. If you're waiting, then wait longer still, for He will not delay His aid one moment longer than He should. If it still has not come after that waiting, then maybe the Lord is providing help, and you just don't see it. Maybe the Lord wants you to get up and pull yourself up and stand in His strength by stepping out in faith. Maybe the Lord's help is found in you trusting Him.

July 8 - Other Ways

Drink no longer water, but use a little wine for thy stomach's sake and thine often infirmities. (1 Tim. 5:23)

When I was a professional mechanic years ago, I learned one lesson: there is more than one way to skin a cat. If there is a problem with getting an engine part or component off, we must then be creative in doing so. One of the drawers in my tool chest was labeled "custom wrenches / tools." It was the drawer that looked like Dr. Frankenstein got a hold of and made these unique and odd-looking tools. I would often come upon a situation where I just couldn't get a part removed unless the wrench or tool had a special bend or modification done to it. I would actually take a wrench or tool, cut it, grind it, bend it, and sometimes weld another tool to it to make it work. In some cases, it was a tool that could only be used for that one specific application and nothing else.

In the matter of emotional issues like depression and anxiety, sometimes we come to a place where a specialty tool is needed. Sometimes an unorthodox method is needed to get you passed that hump. Now, I won't go into this in detail here as I will spend an entire chapter on this in the book part of this devotional, but sometimes, medication might be needed. Many people don't realize it, but Timothy might have suffered from a mild form of anxiety. It seems that he was a nervous one, and often Paul had to encourage him with the Word of God.

In 1 Timothy 5:23, Paul recommends a much-debated solution. Some believe that in this scripture, Paul is suggesting that Timothy drink a type of stomach-acid-reducing aid, a very diluted mixture of alcohol. Now, this doesn't mean to go out and start drinking, nor does it mean to start taking tranquilizers, but it might mean that there are other ways to get you out of that hole and unto healing in Christ. Sure I am being a little gray here as I don't want to delve into this very sensitive subject unless I can do it deeply.

In the meantime, until we can discuss this further, it might behoove you in your current distress to see your family doctor. Yes, even your general practitioner can guide you into other possibilities. Maybe some blood tests need to be taken. Maybe your sugar needs to be checked. Maybe exercise is needed or hormone levels evaluated. Vitamins and herbal remedies can be tried, also changing your diet as in reducing caffeine or your sugar intake. Some artificial sweeteners can cause depression, or at least will not help ease it. I have even heard of people using acupuncture or acupressure and foot reflexology to ease anxiety. Again, check with your doctor first and have a good physical examination.

Dear friend, the Lord will never leave us or forsake us. And in the matter of health, whether it be physical or emotional, He has an answer for that too. Seek Him, keeping all options that He may bring to the table as viable ones. Make sure they are safe and legal, and then go ahead and trust that when He leads you to water, it will be the right water for your ailment and / or for your soul.

July 9 - Opening My Eyes

For we brought nothing into this world, and it is certain we can carry nothing out. (1 Tim 6:7)

During the ups and downs of living this Christian life, the Lord has taught me many things. Of all the things I was taught that did truly edify me was this: nothing is worthy of our passion except for the things that point us and others to the cross. No matter what we do and say, live and possess, if it is not worthy of pointing others to the cross, it is of no value. I say this with no reservation or hesitation. Be it my family, wife, children, or all of my possessions, if I cannot put the cross first, then the cross must be second to them all, and that can never be Christ's will. In Luke 14:26, we read one of the most shocking statements ever made by Jesus Christ; at least to me, it is.

To read them is like taking an axe to everything we hold most dear—"If any man come to Me, and hate not his father, and mother, and wife, and children, and brethren, and sisters, yea, and his own life also, he cannot be My disciple."

Friends, I never understood that scripture and the divine essence of it until I faced the soul-tearing forces of glorious depression. It was through deep, dark, soul-wrenching depression that the Lord opened my eyes and made me glance into His. It was not until depression lay hold of me that

I truly understood what He was trying to say. For those of you who have been there or may be there right now, don't waste that moment until you squeeze every bit of glory out of it. I believe for some of us, it is only through soul-crushing depression that we can truly see the pettiness of things and the glory of Christ, the vanity of life apart from Christ, and flat-out love for Him. It was in my depression that I realized how worthless everything is and how much wasted passion I placed into them—my money, possessions, career, and all the things that I held so dear, even my wife, children, and extended family. Without Christ ruling my heart first and foremost, by default, they would rule my heart; and no matter how much we claim to love Christ above all else, until we can love everything less, we can never see into the eyes of the Lord. We can never see what the Lord is trying to show us. He must be first, and the best way to ever reach that place is to take away all the worth of everything else.

In my dark days, I was able to reach that place. Not that I didn't love my children, family, and church, but I was able to finally love them less. I know it's a very deep concept to embrace, and one that, for some, might take a lifetime; but, dear friend, without arriving at that place, you can arrive nowhere. Depression took me to that precipice and threw me off, and as I tried to grab hold of all that I loved and held dear, they all slipped through my fingers like fine beach sand. Until I reached out only for the mind and heart of Christ did I understand the mystery of life in Him. Don't run from your depression; instead, try running deeper into it until you find that golden chalice that is Christ.

July 10 - Opening My Eyes Even Further

And whosoever doth not bear his cross, and come after Me, cannot be My disciple. (Luke 14:27)

Wow, July 9 was a tough one, was it not? I apologize for taking you so close to the glory of God, but, dear friend, is that not where the victory lies? Oh these deep things of Christ. I never even intended to go so deep in my walk with Christ. I was truly satisfied with my lukewarm pew-warming Sunday existence. I simply wanted a nice life, family, good job, some toys, and maybe a nice vacation now, and then maybe some real good healthy years and a lot of fun in the sun to go along with it. What's interesting is that I was given all of those things right off the bat in my young Christian walk. It was all so nice and easy and just as I had hoped—*Christ in a bottle*, I figured in my mind. Like a genie in a lamp, just rub it the right way, and all your dreams would come true. Oh did I miss the mark, and praise the Lord that He quickly shook spiritual sense into my foolish, ignorant soul.

Dear friend, if you have that picture of being a Christian, then you have been taught very wrong. This life in Christ was never about this present life but about eternal life, and to make it about this life now is to cheapen all that Christ did on that glorious cross. Oh how I walked cocky in that corrupted (another gospel) lie. We need to see, and then when we think we see it, we need to see even further. Just when your eyes are squinting at the light of Jesus Christ, then we need to ask for even more light. In Luke 14:27, the continuing scripture from yesterday's devotion, we see the picture even clearer. Jesus says this: "And whosoever doth not bear his cross, and come after Me, cannot be My disciple."

Again the Lord hits us with a one-two punch and leaves us wobbly on the floor. "To bear My cross," what does that mean? Heck, I don't like bearing anything, let alone a cross. And didn't Christ do all the cross-bearing for us? I think as we look deeper into this, we see not only Christ bearing our sins on His cross, but also a picture of how our life would be lived on this earth. We must also bear the cross that we have been given as examples to the world of where our joy truly comes from. What did Christ do on that cross but lay down His joy and comfort and carry our pain instead? He carried our burdens and sins so we would not have to. People look at Christ and can see that He only did that which pleased the Father. He did that which was always the Father's will. So as we live this life here, we should be that same living example.

With regard to our depression or anxiety, we might have to bear that at the same time we serve Christ. We may have to prove to the world by example that our joy is not in our pleasure but in the Lord's. Friends, good fortune is not what draws people to a life for Christ, but a person who forsakes all of their comfort and glory for Christ. When people see that, they take notice, and soon they will be asking you, "What makes you serve this God that leaves depression in you?" It is then we can say—"Because my joy is not found in my happiness, but it is found in His."

July 11 - Even God Has a Limit

He shall deliver thee in six troubles: yea, in seven there shall no evil touch thee. (Job 5:19)

When I first became a parent, I truly thought I understood what love really was. Sure I loved my wife, and before her, I loved other girls (don't tell her). As a child, I loved my mother and father and always will. I even love my dog, Buddy, and all the pets that I have had over the years. I have loved many things, and I do mean things. I have loved cars, trucks, rock bands, movie stars, and things I would collect and place on bookshelves. I loved hanging out with my friends, and I loved going to the beach. All of these things were a picture of love to one degree or another, and when I fell in love with my wife, Julie, I thought I had reached the mountaintop of that feeling. Well, as the Lord would always seem to have it, there is always more to the story. As I stated earlier, I thought I knew what love was until the day my wife and I had our first child. To see that newborn child, part of me and part of my wife knit together by the very hand of God, I tell you, my walk with Christ jumped ten levels. And as each day of parenting went by, a new understanding of love came forth. As the years went by, and we went from babies to toddlers to preteens to young adults, my understanding of love was magnified even more.

I learned about a deeper love, may I say, God's love. When I compared my love for my wife to my love for my children, there was no match. Loving my children blew the love for my wife out of the water. Not that I loved her less but that I loved her differently. I truly understand now also why the Lord has us call Him Father, and we are to be referred to as His children. It is only in that relationship dynamic that we can understand how much God loves us. Friend, He loves us so much that compared to my love for my children—which, like I said, is through the roof—His love is one million times greater. What is the same though is the type of love. It's a nurturing love, a protective, guiding love, a love that can be driven to punish a disobedient child and a love that would place you in front of a train for that child. It is the closest thing we have in this side of heaven to God's love.

Now, I lay this long foundation out to bring you to this all important place of hope and healing. If the Lord love us so and sees us in such pain, would there not be a time when He would say, "Enough, you may hurt my child no more"—a place where in God's sovereign rule, He will stop the tides of time and Satan himself and say, "No more will my child suffer. No more will this world and its evil persecute my redeemed creation." Our Lord does love us that much, and though we are pounded on every side and pummeled to despair, there will come a day when the Lord will end it. It will end, and of that I am certain. And even more like Paul, may I say, "I am persuaded that God will do just that." Find peace, dear friend, in being a child of the greatest Parent one could have.

July 12 - The Carpenter's Tool Belt

Every moving thing that liveth shall be meat for you; even as the green herb have I given you all things. (Gen 9:3)

Of the many trades that I dabbled in, one was that of a house framer, another an electrician. The one thing they both had in common was that old tool belt I had to wear. I often wondered if Jesus, as a carpenter, had one. I am not sure, but I know He has one as God. Now, it says in Genesis that we are made in the image of God, and if I may ask for pastoral license here, may I also suggest that we have a tool belt also? Friends, as ill-equipped as you feel to deal with today's problems, rest assured it's a lie. If we are soldiers of the cross, then would we not be given spiritual weapons? If we are servants of the Most High, then wouldn't we be given the tools to serve? The Bible speaks about equipping the saints, and we all know about the full armor of God and how we are to put it on every morning. With that being said, let us then also conclude that our Lord has given us all things. The food we need to eat is all over planet earth. The water we need to drink and even the medicine we use to keep us alive, all of it comes in one way or another from things found on this planet.

Our Lord truly supplies us well, and that being the case, He has given us all we need to face depression and anxiety today. In the spiritual realm, we have a tool belt filled with resources. We have faith, mercy, power, hope, and a can-do command from our General. That's just in the first compartment of our spiritual tool belt. We haven't even gotten to the second compartment. In there, we have prayer, grace, forgiveness, and can we forget the indwelling Holy Spirit of God Himself? If we think about it, it's almost like overkill, but not so much when you think about the battle. See, the enemy has his war chest of weapons too. He has deception, temptation, fear, and confusion. Add on top of that doubt and a feeling of helplessness. Put these all together and we can easily be taken down. Each day we must consider these tools, those of God and those of the enemy, those that we are given and those that we still need to attain.

Dear friend, our Lord doesn't take His children and just throw them into a dark, evil city and say, "Okay, now survive." No, He trains us and guides us and prepares us for what lies ahead. Our problem seems to be only that we don't know what tools we are carrying. We don't know because we don't study God's Word. We don't desire to know the One who sustains us. We focus more on what we don't possess and what the enemy does, so we fall into fear and anxiety. When that happens, our tool belt only becomes excess luggage to us and a hindrance instead of a help. That is not God's fault but ours.

Today, as you face a new one, remember our dear Lord. Remember His equipping of us. Remember that He has called pastors and teachers to show you the equipping, and if we are not under a good pastor or serving in a good church, then how can we ever know what's really in our spiritual tool belt? Today let's make it the day when we start learning about all the Lord has done and will do for us. That's our responsibility and no one else's.

July 13 - But You Don't Know Me

And Abraham was old, and well stricken in age: and the lord had blessed Abraham in all things. (Gen. 24:1)

How many of us go through life comparing ourselves to others? It seems to be the nature of the depressed and anxious. My life as a child, though I wasn't depressed and had, for the most part, a happy childhood, was still one filled with insecurities. I never felt I was smart, good-looking, or good at anything. In sports, I was one spastic young man, so much that a bully who haunted me all through junior high called me by that word whenever he ran into me or, should I say, whenever his fist ran into me. My stomach was another issue, always upset, always had me running to the bathroom. That weakness would follow me until this day, though it has gotten a little better.

If the Lord would have told me way back when that I was ever going to be anything in this world, I would have hidden deeper behind the last row of chairs at school. I remember being called up to the blackboard to do a math or spelling problem—I would simply be mortified, and did I mention my bad stutter that still follows me? It's under control today, or else I couldn't be a pastor, but it is still there and does reappear every now and then to keep me humble.

Dear friend, I expose myself to you today so you understand how unimportant our weaknesses are to the Lord. If anything, the Lord sees our weaknesses as golden opportunities to do mighty things for Him. Think about it. If the Lord only used the mighty to do His work, then the world would always assume that our mighty deeds were through our own power. Yet when the Lord takes a broken, frail vessel like me, the world must declare that some other power is behind that person because Scott, the Scott they know, could never do anything like that on his own.

Dear friend, as you read your Bible, and I trust that you do, notice all the misfits and weaklings the Lord has called into great ministry. Look at Moses and his fear and excuse of not being a good speaker. Look at Timothy with his nervous-Nelly persona. Think of the prophet Jeremiah, sometimes called the weeping prophet, or Jonah, who ran the other way when the Lord called him into duty. There are many more, and the one virtue they had in common was that they were wet clay. I say wet clay because God can't use hardened clay—you just can't mold it anymore, but soft, pliable clay like you and me can be. Though it might not look like much in its present form, it can still be formed, and that's what the Lord cares most about. So all of our excuses why we will never amount to anything, all of our excuses why depression and anxiety will never leave us, to that the Lord says *nonsense*. Can the clay tell the potter what he is or is not?

Friend, if I might step out even a bit further, might I add that you have a better chance of being something really important to the Lord than anyone else? The Lord has truly chosen the foolish things of the world to confound the wisdom of the wise. I am a foolish vessel, but I am great in the Master's hand—you can be too!

July 14 - Not All Things, Lord

So Aaron and his sons did all things which the lord commanded by the hand of Moses. (Lev. 8:36)

I once knew this Christian man who was having an affair. He was married, and his wife never knew about it. He was happy in his little private, self-approved world, but soon the conviction of the Lord would fall upon him, and he let that other woman go—well, should I say at least he tried to let her go. See, to him, as long as there was no sex, no contact, no dates, and no actual relationship, it was somehow still okay to keep this sinful relationship going if only by a thread. I would see him and see his darkened spirit and ask him if he cut off all ties with that woman. He would say, "Yes and no." I asked him, "What do you mean yes and no?" Well, he said, "I just e-mail her when something important happens in my life and nothing more." I quickly told him he is again playing with fire, to which he replied, "But I can't let go of that one last thing. God surely doesn't mind just some e-mails back and forth."

Well, you know what my answer was, and it brings home this point for today. Friends, we can't just cut out a little of the cancer that is sin in our lives, and we can't even cut out most of the cancer that is sin in our lives. No, we must cut out all of the cancer in our lives no matter how small or insignificant it might appear to us. Sin is a dangerous thing to play with. It is like poison in a glass of water; it doesn't matter if you only have an eyedropper of it dropped into a glass of water or a full glass of poison, no one is going to want to drink that water. As to our lives in Christ, the Lord feels the same way. We can't call ourselves holy unto the Lord and yet dabble in the things of the flesh. Not even a little sin should be overlooked.

In my life of struggling, the Lord also used depression, anxiety, and many other trials to purge me of sin. Not that I am sinless, which would be an impossibility, but I am at least certain that even my small sins will block and hinder any healing that I can ever pray for. If I want the Lord to rule in my life, then sin must not rule in my life. If I think I can still hold on to a few "little sins" and still get away with it, I am sadly mistaken. Dear friends, if sin wasn't the major issue of our time, then God certainly went overboard with sending Jesus to the cross for it. God cannot do wrong, and so in placing Jesus on that cross to atone for our sins, it is clear that sin is everything and the first issue we must deal with if we are ever able to move forward or ever find healing. Today let go of it all, clean out the closets, and let the moths fly away. Let's do it before the little silly moths leave us filled with ragged, damaged garments. Instead let us place on the garment of righteousness and be blessed.

July 15 - Pray About All Things

For what nation is there so great, who hath God so nigh unto them, as the lord our God is in all things that we call upon Him for? (Deut. 4:7)

Ever feel like you are just a burden to the Lord? I have at times, especially when my daily prayer list begins to be so trivial that it's downright embarrassing. It used to bother me, of my trivial prayer life and as a newer believer, that I had no tolerance for people who would bring such requests to prayer meetings—things like prayers for their pets and such. I had no tolerance of my own little silly prayers, and I had no tolerance for anyone else's. In that season of only praying *big*, as in for big important things, I learned a few things. Number 1 was, who was I to tell God what was big and important and what was not? Was a child's prayer for their lost stuffed bear any less important than my prayer for a loved one with cancer? So I began to do an experiment and began logging my prayers and keeping track of when they were asked and when they were answered. I also threw in some insignificant ones just to test the waters. Well, to my surprise, the Lord was right on it, and not only were my big prayers answered, but even my little baby ones. I also found out that the less specific I was in my prayer request, the less specific God was in answering them. On the flip side, the more specific I was with my prayer request, the more specific was the answer. This last point became a very true revelation and one that I still follow to this day.

Dear friend, pray about anything and everything. Pray in detail with the expectation of getting it answered. When I really began to see the results, I then began to pass on my new find to friends, who, in some cases, thought I was going overboard. One friend I knew in the Lord was single for all of his life and was in his early forties. One day while sitting in his kitchen, I said, "Brother, have you ever prayed to meet a wife?" He said, "Well, yes and no, I guess." Well, I said, "That's not praying. Right now I want you to make a detailed list of what your heart's desire would be in a Christian wife. Pray it and wait on Him, believing He will answer." Well, almost a year from that date, I was at his wedding watching him walk down the aisle. Of the details in his list, they were all met as far as I know. His big smile couldn't hide that fact.

Today, as you ponder what your future holds, as you wonder what to pray, and as you stagnate on simply praying for healing from anxiety, why not take it a step further and write down a list of requests that you would like to see in your life? Be insanely detailed in that list. Pray it according to God's will and only for His Glory and don't forget to log in the date and the hour. Then move ahead in faith praying for the needs of others first. Also, let us never forget to pray for the salvation of friends and family, also for the peace of Jerusalem. Close it in Jesus's name and wait in confidence for what the Lord can do in your life with just a fragment of faith driving it. Pray, dear friend, for all the little things in your life, for nothing is little to our Lord.

July 16 - Even Depression?

The lord hath made all things for Himself: yea, even the wicked for the day of evil. (Prov. 16:4)

Proverbs 16:4 and scriptures like it, as in Isaiah 45:7, certainly cause a lot of tension in the realm of theologians and such. Certainly God has made all things, we can all agree on that, and maybe we can agree on Him making all things for Himself as in Revelation 4:11. But can we also agree on that He also made pain, evil, and suffering for Himself? Would a God, whom we dearly serve, also make (as in *allow*) such things as depression and anxiety for good? I guess the question really is—does God create evil and bad? That has been a question for the ages, yet I feel the answer is simple and sure. God is good, and in being intrinsically good, it would be impossible for Him to create anything that is evil. But let's go one step further and say that God made all things for Himself, a concept that the *prosperity gospel* finds hard to accept. Well, the scriptures are clear no matter what I or any televangelist or theologian proclaim. God ultimately made *all* things for Himself; of that, let there be no mistake. Next, of evil, it is impossible, yet God did make man with the freedom to choose good or evil. In taking that risk, which is not really a risk since He knows it all beforehand, He made man, and man chose evil. Of what the Lord does with those who choose evil—well, if they don't turn to Christ, He then uses them in their evil state to bring about the affairs that must come to be, things like the end times and tribulation. He knows all things, but still cannot cause evil but simply use it for good.

Scratching your head at this point? Sure it's a tough one, and better debaters than me can hash it out in eternity, but the seemingly bad things in this world, they too can be used by God for amazing good. Ergo, I give you depression as one of them. Did God create it? Or does He simply use the results of a fallen world and make lemonade out of lemons? Depression, anxiety, cancer, whatever your lot in life may be, and no matter what the cause, God, in His masterful way, still can take that blessed monster and make it a blessing. As I have shared with you before, depression and anxiety were the springboard that made me what I am in Christ today. Without them, I would not be writing this book, nor would I be a pastor, Christian counselor, or even have written my first book. I would go as far as to say that without those emotional land mines that took me by surprise, I would not even be a very good Christian at all. I can be very prideful, full of myself, and selfish. Of compassion, it was on a sliding scale in my life, yet the Lord had to break all of that in me. He had to cut me down to size lest I lift myself higher than I should. Like Paul, my thorn in the flesh has kept me better in check than having no thorn in the flesh. So call depression evil if you choose, but first, wait and see what a Holy God can do with even the worst of things.

July 17 - Hate Never Heals

And it came to pass, as the ark of the covenant of the lord came to the city of David, that Michal the daughter of Saul looking out at a window saw king David dancing and playing: and she despised him in her heart. (1 Chron. 15:29)

Michal, the daughter of Saul, while looking out her window, saw David dancing and having a good time. She didn't think too highly of his joy, and even more, she despised him in her heart for it. How can this happen, one might wonder? How can one human being see another human being happy, and instead of it making you happy, it makes you angry? Well, Michal might have had some reasons, but we all know there is never a reason to hate another. In my struggles with anxiety and depression, I have had my seasons of hate. Not so much hate maybe, but an anger at all the people who were laughing and enjoying life while I had to live in this tomb of terror. I guess it's more envy, but we all know that at the root of most sin is anger. When we covet, we do it in anger. When we complain, it's in anger. Name the sin, and anger is somewhere buried with it.

Friends, it's a very hard thing to see the world around you laughing and thinking you never will again. That is why holidays are very hard for us who struggle. This brings us back to watching others celebrate. We must resign ourselves to the fact that, for a while, we might have to struggle through some of those holidays. Like when someone loses a loved one, the first (everything) without them is very hard: the first birthday, anniversary, thanksgiving, and so on. They will be hard, but not forever, amen! In the meantime, we must be careful not to be angry at those who are enjoying life. As hard as it might seem, we must try to be happy for another's joy. Even the scriptures, when speaking about the church, challenge us to weep with those who weep and rejoice with those who rejoice. If one is hurting, we all hurt; and if one is being blessed, let's be happy for them. If it becomes a difficult issue for you while you are healing, then make a point to stay away from birthday parties and the like. It is not a sin to let your heart heal by resting spiritually for a season. Just make sure you don't stay too long in that resting place. We must come back to the land of the living just as a person with a broken leg must eventually take off that cast and begin walking again. One day that person must also dance again on that healed leg. Sure, it will be a little scary at first, but if done gradually, it can be accomplished.

I would often tell those whom I counsel, when dealing with anxiety, that when they get back into the social aspect of life, to take it easy and try to drive themselves to events and engagements. Never go with a group of people too quick as you might still have that trapped feeling that can bring on anxiety. Go alone, meet your friends there, and know that you can leave whenever you feel overwhelmed. That's not being paranoid; that's being wise and letting yourself heal gradually. In time, when you are back with your friends and going to parties, the hatred won't be there anymore because you'll be smiling with them. Hey, my friend, that day will come; it is for certain.

July 18 - Go Out and Splurge

Behold that which I have seen: it is good and comely for one to eat and to drink, and to enjoy the good of all his labor that he taketh under the sun all the days of his life, which God giveth him: for it is his portion. (Eccles. 5:18)

Today is one of those lessons we love to learn, those instructions of God that we have no trouble obeying. Well, that's unless you struggle with depression and anxiety. One of the first signs of falling into depression is a lack of desire to do what you used to do. Namely, things you enjoyed, as in hobbies, sports, going to the beach, and even shopping for you ladies out there. Well, I should clarify that since I am a pretty good shopper myself, and when I say *good*, I mean I know how to spend money, not save it. As I have shared with you in the past, one of my passions was working on my old army Jeep. I have had a few Jeeps that I have rebuilt, but that army one I spent years and a little money on. I would love to come home after work and go into my garage and tinker with it. When I had no money for parts, I would just sand and scrape off the old paint and bang out the dents; some nights I would be out there till 3:00 a.m. I found great joy and release there, but not always. My wife knew I was struggling when I would come home, look at that old green pile, walk back in the house, and lay in bed. Sometimes I would just lay there and cry. That's a sad story, but it's not the end of the story because the Lord lifted my heart again, and before long, I was there banging away.

Friends, though some might disagree with me, life is very short. Most of us serve the Lord in some degree or another, and with that serving, it's also okay to have some fun. Fun and resting, though not the same, do share some qualities, one being taking our mind off things. Friend, if you have worked hard and your bills are paid and the family and church are in order financially, then go an splurge. I'm not saying to go out and buy a $150,000 sports car (unless you truly can afford one), but for most of us, yes, you worked hard, you've been through a dark season, and you need to have some fun. Maybe right now you are not there yet, and that desire to go back to your passions is not there. But that doesn't mean it won't come back, so while you may be in that season, think about when you will be feeling better and start planning that project or vacation. If you're barely getting by and you might never have enough to do those things, well, the Lord makes provision there too. Sometimes enjoying life costs nothing but strolling on the beach or rocking in your favorite chair and reading a good book like you used to enjoy. Those times will come again, and when we daydream about them, we are actually showing the Lord that we have faith that He will get us out of this valley. So plan for the happy things you long for, and even though you are not up to it now, tell yourself, "Because of Jesus Christ, one day again, I will."

July 19 - Mind Control

For God hath not given us the spirit of fear; but of power, and of love, and of a sound mind. (2 Tim. 1:7)

If you have been keeping track, you would have noticed that I have not been using typical, popular scriptures to build these devotions on. I feel that some scriptures are used so often that they lose their significance and then become ineffective. Scriptures like Romans 8:28 have been beaten to death and overused so much that their true power is never felt. Today I am going to break my trend and use a popular scripture but nonetheless very powerful. I might even use it more than once, so be on the lookout for it. Second Timothy 1:7—this scripture has a great many psychological aspects to it. One we see is that of the mind's cognitive choices. We also see one of the spirit, one of love, one of power, and one of what we desire the most: a sound mind.

Friends, we can and must learn from this scripture what the Lord is trying to say. Many different emotions make up who we are, and if we don't get those emotions and thoughts in proper order, we will end up with cognitive dissonance. That might sound like an overly technical term, but it is what we are. See, in the state of anxiety, for example, many things are going on at once, which leads to confusion. We have our survival fears, which are placed there by God, but then we have our anxieties, our irrational fears, which we place there. As Christians, we have the Holy Spirit in there also. Love is there too, but we have not the wherewithal to harness it. The only thing we don't have in this cornucopia of emotions and feelings is power—God's Power.

Now, that you are completely confused, let's break it down into what we can understand and apply. Let's say today is a day that you feel anxiety. Who is causing it? Is it God, yourself, or an outside stimulus? These are things we must organize and think about. The next question for ourselves refers to God: Is He really with us, or is He something we think we believe in but really don't? Then we need to take those two opposing ideas and see which one is true. My fear—is it true? In most cases, anxiety is based on nothing but the fear of fear. That being said, there is no fear but the one I imagine in my head. Next, God—is He real or something I made up? God is real, and because He is real, then anxiety cannot control me because God needs to control me. When I get these truths and lies in order, then I can start feeling the power. The Power that God gives to those who let Him rule over their lives.

This morning, and every morning, go through the truths and lies about how you are feeling. What is the worst-case scenario? Friend, of all the days you have spent being afraid, has any of those fears really come to fruition? What of God? Has He ever not gotten your through the worst of the worst? Did you ever explode in fear? Or did you make it through the day and wondered how you made it? Friend, anxiety is an overwhelming emotion and also a tricky one. Every morning, we wake up and make the mistake of asking ourselves, Am I anxious today? How do I feel today? If we drill ourselves every morning on how we feel, we will most likely create anxiety through apprehension when instead we need to develop peace through faith. Meditate on these today.

July 20 - Letting God Rule

And let the peace of God rule in your hearts, to the which also ye are called in one body; and be ye thankful. (Col. 3:15)

I was born with a defect; it's called the syndrome of "I can do it." I like to do things, which is not a bad thing, until you want to do everything. Normally what happens next is you are doing so many things that you get tired, angry, and bitter at everyone else who is not doing anything. For me, it's a circular dilemma with no end in sight but frustration. Let me further explain this problem and the point we need to understand this day. Ever since I was part of a church, I have been a volunteer. If a list goes up on the bulletin board, my name is on it. When I became a deacon, it was a perfect fit because there were plenty of things to do. I just loved serving and working around the church. That was fine for then, but it became an issue when I became a pastor. It was so hard for me to see things that needed to be done around the church and have to wait for others to do them. So I would do them all, get overwhelmed, and then get angry that no one else was doing them. But then when people wanted to help, I became agitated because they never did it the way I wanted it done. I went back to doing everything, became bitter and tired, and left myself angry at the people again.

It was very hard to do, but it was a lesson I needed to learn. I ended up making a note to myself and sticking it on my desk; it said "not my problem." When a bulb was out or a door was broken, I would make myself not fix it. The note was a novel idea but didn't really work because I have OCD, and leaving things in disrepair is very hard for me. But one day, I will be able to just let others do it, which brings me to our title for today (let God do it) "Letting God Rule." It is such a wonderful concept but oh so hard to live out. Even more than a wonderful concept, it's also key to our sanity.

In Colossians 3:15, we are told by Paul to *let* the peace of God rule in our hearts. Notice that it is something that we have to do. We can't let God rule our hearts if we are fixed on ruling instead. Like my obsessive issue, I can't let others do what needs to be done around the church unless I let them do it. Sure they might not do things the way I want. Maybe I would have done it another way, but that's all part of submission. When it comes to the things of God, it's the same thing. We all have issues, and we would love for the Lord to deal with them, but in reality, we don't want Him to because we might not like how He accomplishes them. We want things in our life done our way, and God doesn't always do things our way. Today let's try together to let God rule in our lives so we can get the peace we desire so badly. Let's give Him the reins to our lives and turn us where we need to be turned. If we don't, we will end up frustrated, irritable, and anxious. Sometimes it is as simple as saying, "I cannot do it all, and that's that. Lord, please take control of what I never had control over anyway."

July 21 - Fighting in God's Name

And whatsoever ye do in word or deed, do all in the name of the Lord Jesus, giving thanks to God and the Father by Him. (Col. 3:17)

It's amazing how we can easily apply scriptures to all kinds of situations in our lives but not to issues of the mind. As we have shared before, and as we will talk deeply about in the companion book (sold separately), for some reason, mental and emotional issues seem to be a taboo in Christian circles. God's Word is for everything except for those unspeakable things. Funny, I received an e-mail from one of our missionaries the other day. She asked for prayer as she had a personal issue she was getting help with. I knew right away what it was, and sure enough, I was right. She was suffering with anxiety, yet what bothered me so was how we all are so secretive when it comes to these taboo issues. If she was suffering in the hospital with a heart problem, she would have said it, but because it was an emotional issue, it's the unspoken taboo.

I pray this book breaks that silly concept as if God made a mistake and never thought that Christians would have emotional issues. That being said, I want to start that breaking of the taboo chain links by starting with this one in Colossians 3:17. It speaks about this: "In whatever we do let's do it in the name of the Lord Jesus, giving thanks to God and the Father by Him." Well, can't that include fighting the struggles of depression and anxiety? Can't we today get up and state, "Lord, today I am fighting a battle. It's one of my mind and heart. I will fight this battle in Your name and do it for Your glory."

Dear friend, I don't just think we can, I know we can, and we should. Today and every day, we need to take this battle out of the closet and put it out on the kitchen table for all to see. We need to look at our emotional struggles as we would look at any other struggle. If I was fighting for my wayward child, would I not pray for that child and do it in the name of Jesus Christ? If I was starting a new ministry, starting a new job, or leading a person to Christ, would I not there also do it in His name and for His glory? We must stop placing struggles and desires on a sliding scale. We must stop deciding what needs God's intervention and what does not. Everything needs God's intervention, and until we start understanding that, until we start bringing everything to Him in prayer, we are micromanaging what is not ours to manage. Let's fight this battle as we would any other, and when the battle is won, let's be sure to stand up in church and proclaim God's victory.

Imagine the hope you would give to that quiet person in church who hears you stand up and proclaim, "I was struggling for years with depression and anxiety, and through the many workings of our Lord, I have been given victory." That quiet soul sitting in the pew will never forget that testimony, and I'm sure they will be looking to talk with you after church. Pride goes before a fall; of that, there is no doubt. Let's stop being so prideful about our struggle and realize that all along maybe it was our pride about this issue that kept us from ever being healed. Give God the glory in all that you do—in everything!

July 22 - And Do It with All Your Heart–For Him

And whatsoever ye do, [do it heartily], as to the Lord, and not unto men. (Col. 3:23)

Continuing on with our thought from yesterday, we come to Colossians 3:23, which takes the purpose of fighting one step further. In our struggles with emotional issues, there will come a time when we are not even sure we want to live anymore. Sometimes it seems just too hard, and the reasons to keep moving forward don't seem compelling enough. Fighting depression and anxiety for a few months is one thing; fighting it for a few years is another. Fighting it for a lifetime is almost too much to ask. I know people who have struggled for a very long time, and I myself have struggled on and off over the years. But regardless what your struggle is like, sometimes one hour more seems like too much. I know because I have been there, yet in being there, I know something else. Sometimes it's not about how you are feeling but how others are. Sometimes it's about how your world would be radically changed if you weren't around anymore. It's about your children, wife, husband, parents, friends, coworkers, and church family.

Depression has a way of making us only think about ourselves. It has a way of focusing on our hand in the fire more than your loved one's. It can be all-consuming and self-centered at times. During times when you feel like that, it can be very easy to simply want to give up, run away to a distant place, and just curl up in a ball and weep. Sometimes it is so bad that even running isn't enough, and ending your life starts to look appealing. I've been there too, but, dear friend, listen to me as I plead with you in this one area.

If we are going to make it, we have to go even further than fighting to live, further than striving to keep going, further than doing it for the people in your lives. We must take it to the next level, and that level is staying alive because that's what the Lord wants, holding on for another day because that's the Lord's will.

Dear friend, it is never the Lord's will for you to give up or give in, and it's certainly never to end your life. I say this today because sometimes even family and children aren't going to be enough to keep us moving. Sometimes money and health aren't enough to make us hold on. If there is anything we must look to when fighting in those pits, it's to look to the Lord. If we are to do anything in this battle, we are to do it for the Lord. It is to go even further and do it for the Lord and, in doing it, giving it all you have. It's calling every fiber of your being to attention to keep going as you keep looking unto Him. We can make it. We will make it. But we might not make it if the Lord isn't the driving force in our making it. Children and family are great motivations to keep fighting as I mentioned, but what if your pain is greater than the sorrow of leaving them? That is why we must do it always unto the Lord. For He is the one we must please at the end of the day. And let me be perfectly clear, it is He whom we will have to face if we make the wrong choice. He hears, He loves, and He knows our pain. You will be okay if your eyes are set on the Risen Son, and if we set our eyes on the One who has risen, then won't we also rise?

July 23 - With You—Always

> *Teaching them to observe all things whatsoever I have commanded you: and, lo, I am with you always, even unto the end of the world. Amen. (Matt 28:20)*

As a young teen growing up, my greatest fear was that of being alone. It wasn't so bad when I was in grade school, but when the teen years hit and people started dating all of a sudden, I became lonely. I was not what you would call a girl magnet, and attaining a girlfriend seemed like only a dream. What made it worse was watching all my friends with their dates. The holidays and Valentine's Day when I never had anyone to share with also was quite painful. I wish I could say it really never bothered me, but it did; and as I lay alone in my room, I would often have nightmares of being old and alone. I would think to myself, *What if I never find a girl, and I never get married?* I would often picture myself as some lonesome street person pushing a shopping cart, wearing rags, and having a long beard. My feelings were not unusual as many feel this way in life, yet as a Christian, this no longer has to be the case.

In Christ, we are promised many things, and one of them is never being alone. Some may say, "But I am alone." Well, maybe you are in a physical sense but not in a spiritual sense. I have heard people describe to me feeling alone on New Year's Eve in Times Square, New York. That might sound odd when you are standing in crowds of thousands, but it can feel that way in life. On the other hand, I have heard many more people describe feeling great comfort and fellowship with God locked in a prison cell or alone on the mission field in a cold dark hut or room.

Dear friend, in these struggles of the mind and soul, we will have times when the enemy tries to convince us that God has left us and we are all alone. It is a lie and one right from the pit itself. Jesus reminds us over and over again about Him always being with us; though not physically, He is with us through the Holy Spirit. All through the Old Testament, we read of saints of old who felt alone, yet the Lord was with them. Think of Elijah all down and out and feeling like he wished he was dead. What happened but the Lord came and was with him? I don't know where you are today, but maybe you're a part of a large family with a spouse and many caring friends, or maybe you are on your own and have nothing but the clothes on your back and this book in your hands. It doesn't really matter to the Lord because He knows what you need and who you need. If you need company, He will bring it. If you need something else, He will bring that too.

Many times when counseling single people, I find that their greatest prayer is for the Lord to bring them a love to hold and snuggle. They feel that if they had that, all would be well. Maybe so, but I have a mate and a snuggle partner, and I still fell into depression and anxiety. Friends, at the end of the day, the Lord wants us to know one thing—Do you want Him? Do you need Him? If you do, He will manifest Himself in some means or another and will be with you always. If you need something else in your dark time, He will bring that also. In all of this, remember that He will be with us even until the end of the age. Now that's a great companion.

July 24 - Happy and Working

For thou shalt eat the labor of thine hands: happy shalt thou be, and it shall be well with thee. (Ps. 128:2)

Sometimes life can be a downright back-breaking drag. If you happen to be one who is working real hard and yet hate your job, then you understand this. It seems it's quite common today to see people so miserable in their employment that they conclude it is their job that's making them feel so down and out. Each day, they drag themselves out of bed to the shop or office. While working, they daydream about breaking away and finding blissful joy somewhere else. "If only I had a better job or a better boss, if only I had that dream job I desire so much, I would be at peace." We conclude that the Lord knows our pain, and if He wants us happy, then that must mean finding us a new employment.

Friend, in our quest to find joy and peace, there is one thing that stands true, and that is—if you don't find peace where you are, you will never find it somewhere else. So many people, myself included, have left careers and geographic locations in hopes of finding that nirvana on earth. It just can't be found because where you go, unfortunately, you come with yourself. If anything, the Lord is trying to show us this: Be happy just with Me wherever you are, and then we can talk about moving on later. See, with the Lord, it's always about being at peace with Him no matter what because to His mind, looking for happiness anywhere else means that He is not your joy and peace.

When I took over my first church in California, I had to work full-time in carpentry, much of which was on my knees doing cleanup work for a boss who was half my age. I was yelled at and demeaned all day, and then I had to go home and be a pastor of a tiny church, which had a million problems to deal with. Again I would fall into the trap of thinking, *It's this place, it's this church, it's this job, it's this state.* I even started to think, *It's this wife and family that are ruining my life. If I just had everything new, all would be well.* Oh foolish, foolish me. I praise the Lord for unanswered prayers.

Friend, if you have a job, and even if you hate it, keep going. If you have a life, a family, and a situation that is not what you imagined, still keep going. Ask the Lord not for something new, but to simply find peace where you are. Try with all you are to be thankful for what you have because if you don't, you are in reality telling God He has given you garbage. Find peace in the little He has given you, and then He will give you bigger things to do for Him. Work where you are, as if everything depended on it. Be the best poop-scooper (if you happen to be one) that you can be. We are to be content wherever we are, even if that's in the worst place in the world. That, my friend, is true faith—not demanding that the Lord bends to our wishes but trusting and being at peace in His current plan for you today. Stand there a little longer and be thankful and happy for what it brings you. Also remember it's not about you being happy, but Him. When God is happy, everyone is happy.

July 25 - It Doesn't Have to Be This Way

And among these nations shalt thou find no ease, neither shall the sole of thy foot have rest: but the lord shall give thee there a trembling heart, and failing of eyes, and sorrow of mind. (Deut. 28:65)

The Lord is clear in His workings in the lives of His chosen people, Israel, and He is clear with His workings with us. Without the Lord, bad will happen, and with the Lord, only good. Fear will reign in our lives when God is not reigning there, and yet joy can reign if we allow Him to reign there. The world today is a frightening picture of what happens when God is removed. It is a picture of just how exact and perfect God's Word is. If God said it, then it will happen. If God said that the world will crumble without His blessings, then it will crumble.

In Deuteronomy 28:65, we see a graphic illustration of a world and people without Christ. It's never the Lord's will to leave us in such a place as it is our choice to live in it. Pigs choose to live in filth because they like it. Take him out of that pit, and he will run back in. Take a sinner ruled by his sin, and no matter how far away you drag him from that sin, he will run back to it. When I was an early teen, there used to be horse stables where you could rent horses in groups and go out for a trail ride. It was fun and easy because the horses knew the routine so well that you just basically sat there, and the horses did the rest. One thing the horses did best was getting back to the stable because they knew that was where the food, water, and the rest were. You really couldn't stop them from that appointed return, and so the trail rides became uneventful.

Sometimes we are like that as God's children. We are so used to a certain sin and way of living that we can't stop repeating our past mistakes. Listen. If there is ever going to be real change in our lives, there must be real change. If every time I do A, then B happens, then that's always how it's going to end up. It amazes me how often we make the same mistakes and are surprised by the same results. Why am I so filled with anxiety all the time? Maybe it's because I do the same thing, play with the same sin, and yet expect a new outcome. Friend, I am not judging you but pointing out my own experiences. Many of my anxieties are from living the same way over and over again. I know the Lord wants this and that to be changed in my life, but I keep doing the same this and that over and over again. I'm always shocked when the results never change, and I even say to myself, "Next time I am going to be different."

I truly believe that things don't have to be the way they are sometimes. Sometimes they are because we refuse to handle them differently. If I trust in the Lord and follow His will, then things will go according to His will. If that is the case, then that must be good, good for God and for me. Yet I don't because I do what I do best, which is doing what I always did in the past. Today let's stop doing the same old thing. Let's do the hard things that have to be done regardless of how afraid we are. Let us truly be new creations in Christ and not just say we are.

July 26 - Leave Me Alone!

And all his sons and all his daughters rose up to comfort him; but he refused to be comforted; and he said, "For I will go down into the grave unto my son mourning." Thus his father wept for him. (Gen. 37:35)

Ever have one of those leave-me-alone days? I have had plenty of them. You know, those days when people are e-mailing you scriptures and sending you CD seminars to listen to. They all mean well, and you know they care, but sometimes you have had enough. Sometimes there is nothing anyone can do for you but leave you to the Lord. It might sound mean or heartless, but sometimes that's what we need. Sometimes in raising my children, I have learned that lesson also. With my middle son, it's been a hard road for me and my wife doing all we can to guide and help him to where the Lord wants him to be in life. But there came a time when we couldn't coddle him any longer with kind words or even financial help. He needed to be placed in the Lord's hands and left there. It takes a lot of faith, mind you, and it's not easy, but it is what works best.

We see it all over our society today; we are the helping-everyone-into-poverty society. We are helping people so much that they never learn how to depend on the Lord. Sure there is a time to help the homeless and the downtrodden, but there is also a time to leave them with the Lord. Maybe today you are in that place where everyone wants to help you, but it isn't working. Maybe you secretly want their help because you are afraid of truly trusting in the Lord. Maybe you are getting tons of help from friends and family, but it scares you as you know that you're still in pain. All of these places are not good places to be. They are face-the-music places in life's struggles, times when you know the calvary isn't coming, and all you have left is your Bible and the Lord Jesus Christ. Humbling, I know, but it is also sometimes where things really start to happen. Sometimes it's the place where the rubber meets the road, and true healing begins.

Dear friend, in our life on earth as followers of Christ, we all must come to that place in our journey where we ask ourselves, is Christ truly enough for me? We never really know until we are faced with just having Christ and nothing else. So badly we wish that this pill or that pill would work, that this vacation or job change would lighten our load. We reason that going back to drinking will ease the pain and help us along. Please hear my words today. Hear my life song crying out to yours: Christ is our only hope, and Christ will fulfill that hope. He is, and will be, all we need. He will guide, comfort, and correct that which needs correction and guidance. Listen for His still, quiet voice, His calm, directing hand. Wait alone if you must because it is hard to hear Him in a crowd of helpers. Let the Lord be your comfort and trust Him in His promised mission of comfort.

July 27 - The Closer You Get

And He said, "I will make all My goodness pass before thee." (Exod. 33:19)

I love the story of Moses wanting to see God's glory. I love how getting that close to God is a risky thing in some regards. God's glory is an awesome thing to be near to, and it has its good points and bad points. Getting close to God should be all of our goals, but sometimes we shy away from getting too close because we don't want the Lord to see all we really are—as if He doesn't already know. But in our little minds, we do believe that getting too close is too risky. I have known many Christians who like to keep the Lord at arm's length. Just far enough away to live my life the way I want and close enough to cry out to Him for help if I need Him. It is truly a two-edged sword to live that way, and we quickly find that we end up cut and bloody more than not.

There's an old saying that goes, if you want to get in the water, you have to jump in with two feet. Just go all the way or don't go at all. I'm one of those tippy-toe people who take so much time getting in the water that by the time I am in, it's time to go home. People don't like waiting for us, so they grow tired and give up on us. With our Lord, it's the same thing—as we read in Revelation 3:16, Jesus speaks of His hatred of Christians being lukewarm. If you think of it from a relationship standpoint, it makes sense. Say you are dating a person but you decide to only get involved halfway, or they only want to get involved with you halfway. I don't think that relationship is going anywhere.

Dear friend, in our struggles with depression and anxiety, we can't be afraid to get too close to the Lord, nor can we make the mistake of staying too far away. We need to dive in all the way or don't dive in at all. Sure getting real close to God seems to have drawbacks as in living full-on for Christ all the time, but look at the perks. Moses was never the same after just getting a little close to God's glory, and so it will be the same for us. People will see the change; people will notice His glory through us. Most of all—the closer we get to God, the better it will be to hear what He has to say about us. We will know Him better and understand Him more. His words will become our words, and His will, will become our will. When we fall, He will be right there, and when we are hurting, we won't have to go far to crawl under His wing of righteousness. We will know what He likes and doesn't like, and we will be quick to learn the lessons of life we need.

Sure some people won't like your new zealousness and enthusiasm, but who cares? As long as the Lord is happy with us, isn't that all that matters? Friend, if God is good, and He is, then wouldn't that goodness rub off on our hurting soul if we are up close and personal with Him? Get close to the Lord today, closer than you ever thought possible. Don't let anything or anyone stop you in your pursuit of that fellowship. Fellowship with the Lord, isn't that what we all want anyway?

July 28 - I Will Show Them

> *When I say, "My bed shall comfort me, my couch shall ease my complaint;" Then Thou scarest me with dreams, and terrifiest me through visions: So that my soul chooseth strangling, and death rather than my life. I loathe it; I would not live alway: let me alone; for my days are vanity. What is man, that Thou shouldest magnify him? and that Thou shouldest set thine heart upon him? And that thou shouldest visit him every morning, and try him every moment? How long wilt Thou not depart from me, nor let me alone till I swallow down my spittle? I have sinned; what shall I do unto Thee, O thou preserver of men? Why hast thou set me as a mark against Thee, so that I am a burden to myself? And why dost Thou not pardon my transgression, and take away mine iniquity? For now shall I sleep in the dust; and Thou shalt seek me in the morning, but I shall not be. (Job 7:13–21)*

Poor Job, a man in so much pain and also so much anger. As I read the book of Job, especially Job 7:13–21, I can't help but be brought back to my place of agony. I remember my anger at the Lord, the confusion and—the I'll-show-them attitude. I was bitter and angry, and I wanted the world to know it. I wanted God to know it. What did I do to deserve this? *Okay, I am a sinner, I'm sorry. Kill me now, or what does it even matter anyway? I get up only to go back to bed. Nothing gives me comfort, and nothing ever will. I'm picked on, and it's not fair. I don't understand any of this.*

Dear friend, if you are at that very dark place today, I ask you to remember one thing: the words and thoughts that you are saying and thinking are just words and thoughts. One day you will be saying you are sorry to the Lord for ever thinking such things or performing such actions. Praise be to our Lord who knows and understands our frail hearts and bodies. He will forgive us, and we will be ashamed for ever getting so nasty.

So let it all out if you have to. Get all of your anger and nastiness out of your system, but don't let out so much that you can never take it back, that you will hurt the ones you love in ways that cannot be reversed. Get it out of your system quick, but also confess it just as quick. The Lord knows what He is doing, and one day, it will all make sense. Right now it's a rotten, nasty place you are, but it won't be forever, and one day you will sing mighty praises to His name. Trust me, you really will praise Him again and like never before.

July 29 - After the Darkness Comes the Dawn

Thou shalt increase my greatness, and comfort me on every side. I will also praise Thee with the psaltery, even Thy truth, O my God: unto Thee will I sing with the harp, O Thou Holy One of Israel. My lips shall greatly rejoice when I sing unto Thee; and my soul, which Thou hast redeemed. (Ps. 71:21–23)

Don't you hate played-out, fluffy phrases? "After the darkness comes the dawn"—come on, can't we come up with something better than that? Well, they still haven't made a better mousetrap or a better way to sew than with needle and thread. Sometimes the old standbys are the best. It's true; when the sun goes down, it rises again. When the winter is over, then comes the spring. I remember buying another one of my old Jeep projects. This one that I purchased was probably a bad call on my part. I should have known better as it had bad rust and was a beach runner. Anyone who knows about buying Jeeps on the East Coast knows that you should never buy one that has been on the beach and lapped with saltwater. Well, I bought it anyway even after changing my mind many times. As I suspected, it was rotted. Rotted break lines and rotted plating. But what was worse was that I found a completely rotted section of frame. You could see right through it—how could I have been so blind? My heart sunk as I just wasted all my money on something that was garbage.

Sometimes we feel like that about ourselves. We only see our weaknesses, failures, flaws, and complete uselessness to anyone, let alone God. Depression and anxiety make us see that more about ourselves, and it only drives us down deeper into these emotions. Well, I didn't tell you the end of the rotted-junk Jeep story. See, I had a body-shop friend come over to look at it. He said, "No problem, let me have it for a while and let's see what we can do." We towed it over to his shop, and after a few weeks, it was like new. Then I got it back and finished the restoration, and now many look at it like a prized show vehicle.

Dear friend, that is the same with us. We see a hopeless cause, but God says, "No worries, I can fix that. Let me have it for a while." He cuts, grinds, chops, and hammers, and before you know it, you're a new creation in Christ. Even we ourselves can't believe what the Lord has done in our lives. We stand in awe at this once great mess that is now a great success. I often look at myself and say, "Lord, I don't know how you took a mess like me and turned me into something that I would have never dreamed." It's almost like a dream, and I have to pinch myself.

The Bible says that man looks at the outward appearance, but God looks at the heart. We see what we are, yet the Lord sees what we will be through His amazing creative powers. We see rust and rot, but He sees an opportunity to blow people away. When that day comes, we will be able to rejoice and praise the Lord for the mighty new day He has begun in us. In the meantime, get used to praising Him now.

July 30 - I'm Just So Tired

Thy right hand, O lord, is become glorious in power: Thy right hand, O lord, hath dashed in pieces the enemy. (Exod. 15:6)

Another new day and I hope that where you are the weather is wonderful. Here in New York, it's another rainy, overcast summer day. It is hard to plan outdoor events in New York as our sunny days are few. What's worse is, the cloudy, overcast humid summer days tend to make even the highest in spirits very tired. It kind of breeds laziness, and the oppressive humidity feels like walking around with ten bags of cement tossed over your shoulder. Add to the weather the pensive emotions of the melancholy, and you begin to feel powerless. Your motivation to fight seems so low that you wonder if you will ever have it back again.

Having no power just drains you, and it even makes it hard to go after more if it could be found. Like running out of gas, it doesn't matter if the gas station is right around the corner; you still have to push that car to get it there. Even more so if you don't know that gas station is right around the corner; it might as well be a million miles away. You look at your heavy car and that long road up ahead and determine, "Even if it was one mile up ahead, I just couldn't go on." What you really need is for someone to pull over with gasoline, someone who will even put it in your car for you. See, in the place of utter weakness and despair, we don't even have the power to put the gas in our car if we had it. We are just like a slug lying slumped over on the backseat unable to even see beyond our steering wheel.

Dear friend, that is when the Lord pulls up to us (supernaturally) and not only has a can full of gas, but also a legion of angels with their service-duty clothes on. The Lord not only brings us the gas (power), but also puts it in, washes our windows so we can see again, sits us back up in our front seat, and puts on our safety belt. We need to simply turn the key and start driving again. Power is so often what we need, and in a way, we know it, but we think it's our power that is missing. We look in our tank of power and realize we have none to give and we become even more powerless and more depressed. That's the problem: looking for power in all the wrong places when we need to be looking for power from one place only—Jesus Christ. God is glorious in power with enough to spare. Not just power for our needs but power to fight off the enemy, who also wants to kick us when we are down.

Always also keep in mind that the Lord's power is limitless, always filled to the brim, and always more than enough to get the job done. All we have to do is pray and trust in His delivery time. We might be looking down at our gas gauge right now, which seems to be bouncing off (E), but no worries, He is right there and ready to fill us when it's time. Stop looking for that gas station or tow truck, but look for and trust in Jesus Christ alone. He delivers.

July 31 - Yes and No

We are troubled on every side, yet not distressed; we are perplexed, but not in despair; Persecuted, but not forsaken; cast down, but not destroyed. (2 Cor. 4:8–9)

Paul, how did he do it? I can read 2 Corinthians 4:8–9 and say yes to all that Paul is feeling, yet I can also read those verses and say no. No, Paul, I don't know how you did it. Yes, I am troubled on every side, but *I am* distressed by it. Yes, I am perplexed, but *I am* in despair. Sometimes I am persecuted, but *I do* feel forsaken in that persecution. I feel cast down too, but *I do* feel destroyed. What's your secret, Paul? How did you remain so calm saying these things even when sometimes you were in prison? Paul was truly an amazing man of God, but let's not forget he was also a sinner, not a supersaint. He was not perfect and had his times of doubt and despair, I'm sure, but even in that, the Lord made sure it didn't linger too long. Paul needed to be up and encouraging because many people and the early church depended on his words.

Second Corinthians 4:17–18 has a little glimpse of this power of Christ working in Him:

> For our light affliction, which is but for a moment, worketh for us a far more exceeding and eternal weight of glory; While we look not at the things which are seen, but at the things which are not seen: for the things which are seen are temporal; but the things which are not seen are eternal.

As we read these scriptures, let's notice Paul's attitude and where he finds his peace. Notice that it is not in having his situation changed but in changing how he looks at his situation. Notice how he does this by looking ahead and not looking at what is. Paul, through the power of the Holy Spirit and through a good knowledge of the Word of God, is able to see what's really going on. He remembers the past mercies of the Lord upon him and also the past mercies of the Lord on others. He knows that this life is temporal, which means the pains of it are temporal. Paul also keeps his heart in an *up* mode by thinking about all the glories that will be waiting for him in eternity, all of the promises of God—some for now and some for later. It is almost like being in an accident and having your right arm badly wounded, and as you are going to the hospital in the ambulance, instead of staring at the wound, you drift off and think about the future baseball and tennis games you will be playing. You focus on what will be and not what is. You do what the Lord always tells us to do, which is look to His sure promises even in our present calamities.

Sounds too simplistic, I know, and sure, if your arm is in throbbing pain, how can you think about playing tennis? Well, the fact is you can't, but in fellowship with God and through the power of the indwelling Holy Spirit, you can. That's the secret; it's using what God has given us, which we often forget we have. It's learning how to use God's power and then taking that power and looking at all that we are going through—through His eyes and not ours.

August

August 1 - Just Think Positive Thoughts

Neither filthiness, nor foolish talking, nor jesting, which are not convenient: but rather giving of thanks. (Eph. 5:4)

Well, it is August 1, and the summer rolls on. One thing about the summer on the East Coast is great beaches and those little airplanes that fly over pulling silly banners advertising some silly product. What's amazing is even though no one takes the ads seriously, everyone still reads them. It is like driving past a horrible accident on the highway. You know it's bad, but you just have to look. Today in the Christian world, as well as the secular world, there seems to be a lot of foolish things floating by that catch our eyes. I speak of the "power of positive-thinking people." You know who they are. They are usually on TV a lot, and they sell a lot of books. They usually have a real happy smile on their book covers, and they always seem to have a clever saying to go along with their clever titles. Now, that wouldn't be so bad if they were selling comic books, but people are making millions of dollars off our desire to hear a clever life sentence, which we somehow believe will make everything better.

Today I want to share some of these silly POPT (power of positive thinking) gibberishes with you. We might laugh, but we really should be crying. Friends, these are the words of men, which mean they have no power, and yet we believe them. I will follow the power-of-positive-thinking blast with the truth of the Word of God. Let us compare and see to which we should really be listening: 1) I am capable of accomplishing anything that I want. 2) Right now, as I think this thought, circumstances are shifting to flood every aspect of my life with happiness. 3) I release my fear of failure. I am motivated by love, always. 4) Happiness is everywhere I choose to see it, in the wag of a dog's tail, in the laugh of a child, in the bloom of a flower. (My comment: What about in a person's death, in abuse, in poverty, in war, in hatred, in suffering? Um—really?) 5) I accept that there will be challenges when pursuing my goals. I have the knowledge and ability to overcome anything in my path. 6) I choose to be proud of myself. 7) I release all my negativity and hold joy in my heart. 8) I fully accept myself and know that I am worthy of great things in life. 9) I choose to be happy. 10) I already have the experience and understanding I need to perform my absolute best.

Friends, I could go on and on. Maybe you think these little cute sayings are good to hold on to—well, what if they are all lies? If someone throws you a pink brick to hold on to while your ship is sinking, does it matter how it makes you feel or if it can really save you? Dear friend, be careful of these lies that bring false hopes with no legs to stand on. Do you want truth? Well, how about these? "The Lord is the strength of my life" (Ps. 27:1), "Greater is He that is in me than he that is in the world" (1 John 4:4), "God always causes me to triumph in Christ Jesus" (2 Cor. 2:14). I could add about five hundred more, and they are all truth. Forget the power of positive thinking and let us focus on the power of Christ.

August 2 - Humility Is Key

And Moses and Aaron came in unto Pharaoh, and said unto him, "Thus saith the lord God of the Hebrews, 'How long wilt thou refuse to humble thyself before me? Let my people go, that they may serve me.'" (Exod. 10:3)

Sometimes we can look at a problem and assume that to repair it would take great power and wisdom. As a young mechanic, I was taught one thing by a seasoned mechanic, which had been always stuck in my mind and saved me a lot of time and effort. It was to go for the easy stuff first; meaning, if an engine doesn't start, do not assume it needs a new engine. Don't start rebuilding the engine. First, go for the silliest and most ridiculous stuff. Maybe it has no fuel. Maybe you have a burned-out ignition fuse, which would take minutes to change and pennies to replace. Now, that could simply be a wishful way of troubleshooting if it wasn't so true. For the most part, every machine and mechanical thing that I have ever worked on that seemed broken was a simple, silly fix.

One day my wife called me and told me that we had big problems. She said she was at a shopping center, and her minivan key wouldn't turn. She said it was jammed, and the steering wheel wouldn't move either. She told me I better call a tow truck. Well, it ended up being her wheel was turned too far when she shut off the engine, and pressure was pushing against the key-lock mechanism. She was not too happy when I left work, showed up, simply turned the wheel a half-inch to the left, and started the engine. In life, I have found this also to be true, as well as in spiritual matters. Take, for example, the simplest yet most prayer-blocking emotion, pride.

If we have pride and refuse to humble ourselves, then the Lord will not answer our prayers. Proverbs 29:23 says, "A man's pride shall bring him low: but honour shall uphold the humble in spirit," and 1 Peter 5:6 says, "Humble yourselves therefore under the mighty hand of God, that He may exalt you in due time." When you have time go through your Bible and look up all the scriptures on pride versus humility, see how humility opens the floodgates of God's blessings and pride keeps them closed. Now, you might wonder how pride can play a role in depression and anxiety. Well, it can play many roles, and as we have shared before, admitting you have an anxiety issue is a good place to start. It seems like admitting we have high-blood pressure is acceptable, but admitting we have an issue with depression is not. Why is that? Why are we so prone to make up a story of why we haven't been in church for a few weeks when it is due to depression? Where I see the lack of humility in full swing is certainly with regard to medication and mental issues.

We will deal with this in the chapter part of this project, but for today, chew on this: if you have any issues with pride and lack of humility with regard to your struggle, you must let them go and confess them to the Lord. The Lord is a stickler about pride, and it should not surprise us, for isn't it pride alone that keeps us from coming to Christ in the first place? Pride must go, and humility must reign in our hearts. When it does, the Lord will reign in our hearts, and that can only mean one thing—peace.

August 3 - Who Are You Hanging Out With?

Mark the perfect man, and behold the upright: for the end of that man is peace. (Ps. 37:37)

In life, there is at least one thing that is for certain—people will be a part of your life. Unless you live in a remote desert isle somewhere with no human contact, you will have to choose who to spend your time with. This might sound like a no-brainer, and you might be wondering what it has to do with depression and anxiety. Well, it has a lot to do with it. Who we spend time with truly does define who we are. Friends can truly make or break us like in the case of Job's friends, who really did more harm than good. As to friends, they are the few people in life whom we can choose. Coworkers, neighbors, and in-laws we can't choose, but friends we can; and in choosing them, we must choose wisely.

In my counseling practice and also as a pastor of a small church, the greatest deterrent to spiritual growth is the refusal to let go of bad friends. I was counseling one young man who was highly addicted to painkillers. He came from a well-to-do, wonderful home. He was a clean-cut young man with so much to look forward to, yet one thing would always destroy the progress he made. He would go away to rehab for months, get clean, then come home. It would only take one night of hanging with his old friends, and it was all back again.

For young people today, as well as young married couples, if they do not change who they fellowship with to a 95 to 5 percent Christian-friends ratio, then they will always fall back into despair. Unless you are super strong-willed and one who leads the crowd instead of following it, you will always be drawn backward by your acquaintances. For one thing, the world cannot give you the right advice from God's Word. They may mean well, but in the end, they are just friends of the world, and they can only advise you based on what the world tells them. Not that everything they say is wrong and won't help, but for the most part, we need praying, church-going, and rock-solid Christians to lead us on to victory. Just having a solid friend who understands the Lord and understands you can be such a blessing. One who is also not close-minded and judgmental too.

I made a choice years ago in my early Christian walk to try to always stay close to those who were more spiritual to me than less. Those who were less spiritual to me tended to ease me into backsliding and further away from the things of the Lord. Those who were more spiritual tended to draw me closer to the things of God and His will for my life. In church and in life, keep your eyes open for those who have that peace of God about them. Watch for those who have that true Spirit of Christ all the time, every time. Not just those who want to appear to be holy, but those who actually are. Sure, they might be hard to find, but that doesn't mean we shouldn't keep looking and praying for them. Don't get too attached, but stay close enough so some of their grace and Christian virtue rub off on you. Having that one friend whom you can call at 3:00 a.m. is sure a wonderful blessing to have. Also remember to be a blessing to them and not just a drain.

August 4 - Worship as the Ship Is Sinking

God is a Spirit: and they that worship Him must worship Him in spirit and in truth. (John 4:24)

Today in the modern Christian church, there is a big to-do about worship. People, when looking for a new church, will often be more concerned about the worship team than what the pastor is teaching and what the church believes. I know this to be a fact because in my little church in New York, we have lost many people who wanted something bigger and better. They wanted something more cutting edge with regard to our worship "experience." This whole idea of the worship experience has left a lot of people confused about what worship really is. To most, it is overly produced music that gets you so worked up that you forget your problems and simply enjoy the show. That may be well and true, but that doesn't mean it is biblical. Worship and music are not synonymous with each other; meaning, good music isn't necessarily what we need for good worship.

Take, for example, a romantic evening with your soon-to-be spouse, the night when the big question is to be popped: is it where you go or what words are said? Do you really care if a band is playing, or do you care that this is the night that your two lives will be forever changed? Sad to say that even in that case, people still like the big show over the small words, but I think you get my drift.

Friends, to worship God is something that we know little about yet talk much of. Worship is to take what is everything to you and place it on the floor with the dirt and the dust. It is to be willing to take your prized possessions and toss away all ownership in exchange for getting closer to God. It is loving God more than you love life itself and anything life can offer. It is not only saying that you will but proving that you would. It is sharing the gospel with a coworker even with the risk of losing your job in the process. It is bowing your head at a busy restaurant to pray over your food and not caring who is watching. It is being completely honest on your tax returns no matter what it costs you because it is only God that you aim to please. It is losing your home in a horrible storm and saying like Job, "The

Lord gave and the Lord has taken away, blessed be His name anyway." It is doing what the writer of the famous hymn did after he lost his children in a shipwreck and penned those famous words, "It is well with my soul." And yes, it is being in the depths of despair and anxiety and also saying, "Lord my God, if this be my lot today, even so, it is well with my soul."

That, dear friend, is true worship; that is, exercising faith in a way that the Lord truly honors. And I don't care what your worship leader says or how big the band plays. I don't care how many hands are raised in praise or how moving the "experience" is. Worship is worshiping God by not worshiping anything else. Not the music, not the feeling, but the One who made all things. Yes, I have trouble with this one too, and to worship the Lord when my heart is hurting so is truly as difficult as lifting a school bus with one hand. Dear fellow sufferer, I can't lift a school bus with one hand, but in Christ, I can do all things—even worship my God while weeping in pain. Do it and see what happens.

August 5 - Success!

Then shall He give the rain of thy seed, that thou shalt sow the ground withal; and bread of the increase of the earth, and it shall be fat and plenteous: in that day shall thy cattle feed in large pastures. (Isa. 30:23)

Of all the many judgments that the Bible speaks about, it also speaks about blessings. Of all the promises of God's dealing with evil, there is God's promise of success for the righteous. I'm so excited about all those promises of blessings and success, and not because I think God owes me anything or that living life properly in Christ means there is a mansion with my name on it, at least not in this world. Sure, I could own a mansion, but if I am depressed and suffering with anxiety, what good would it do me? Success and blessings spoken of in the Bible and those spoken of by many pastors today aren't always on the same page. Success, as well as blessings, is promised, but sometimes not in the forms we assume.

Dear friend, the rains will come, and the sun will shine. Sometimes there will seem to be longer seasons of rain than last year, but regardless, the sun will shine again. I might have had a bad week or month of struggling, but there will also be a week or month of joy. A loved one might have passed on to be with the Lord, but we will be with them again one day. I know these successes are not what you had in mind. We want success that go on and on and that are filled with unspeakable bliss. We want healing that starts right now and never goes away.

Friend, sometimes in my struggles with emotional pain, success was getting through a hard day and smiling at its close. Sometimes success was having to do a difficult project and completing it without any anxiety. See, sometimes successes in this life are short-lived ones, yet are they not still successes? As I sit here on my computer and write this August devotion, I sit back and wonder, *Lord I can't even believe I ever had to deal with depression and anxiety, and to the extent that I would write a book about it. It is not what I expected and surely never what I thought I would suffer from, yet there is success, Lord. Success for You and me because this book is being written, and if it could only have been done by me going through these struggles, then I guess it's a grand success.*

Life is never what I expected it to be as I'm sure it is not what you expected either. We all kind of pictured each year a little closer to the golden goose. A little easier and a little more blessings. Our health would be perfect, and all of our children would turn out just right. Our friends would never let us down, and our employment would never falter. Sundays would be sunny, and picnics would never have rain. I think the first time I skinned my knee, I knew something was up, but it's life, is it not? Of success, what is it really but accomplishing what the Lord has in store for us to accomplish—for Him! If we leave this world with those things even half-completed, I believe the Lord looks at us as great successes. Life is good, friends, even though some days don't feel like it. Life is never what we planned or dreamed, but it is what the Lord has ordained, and of that, we should have great joy.

August 6 - I Don't Want to Read Another Word

The entrance of thy words giveth light; it giveth understanding unto the simple. (Ps.119:130)

If you are like me, you probably have a house full of devotionals. As a pastor, besides my home collection of devotionals, I have my office filled with more books on more issues than you can imagine. As a Christian counselor, I have even more books and studies on all sorts of issues, from depression, anxiety, and cutting to teen suicide. I have all the great study guides and pamphlets too, and did I mention my CD and DVD collection filled with all the greatest Bible teachers and preachers? I have attended seminars and taught seminars. I have traveled from the West Coast to the East Coast listening to the best of the best Christian leaders. I receive newsletters and magazines on the latest Christian counseling techniques and how to evangelize better. I have them all, friends, and I would be lying to you if I told you I read them all.

After a while, we are just so inundated with information that the information overload itself can give us anxiety. Sometimes my head feels like it will simply explode if I have to absorb one more bit of information, not to mention the sermons and Bible studies I have to prepare each week. Now, one would think that I would be so filled with the Lord that worry and doubt wouldn't be able to find a place in my mind. Well, the bad news is this, friend: with myself, as I am sure with yourself also, these things provide very little lasting, life-changing insight—one of the reasons of the imbalance we all have with regard to the Lord's Word. Maybe it's the most masterful ploy that Satan has ever put over us, but I truly feel that with all of these (other) things I read, I seem to read less of God's Word instead.

Take my wife and me for example. Each morning we try to read one or two devotionals plus one, two, or even three at night. We pray in the morning, and we pray at night, yet out of all those "godly" writings that we read, a very small portion of it is actually the Bible. Now, you would think that, as a pastor, I read the Bible a lot—well, yes and no. Yes, in fact, I read it and study it to put together my sermons and such, but that's not really meditating on God's Word; it is reading it for the sake of finding something that *other* people need to hear. Did you catch that? Finding something for other people to hear. How many of us do the same thing when we find a good devotional or nice quote from a famous pastor and say to ourselves, "This would be great for so and so to hear"?

Dear friend, though I am writing a devotional—and sure it would be great if millions of people read it—at the end of the day, without reading the Bible, we really have nothing. So please today, add to your daily readings the Word of our Creator and King—Jesus Christ. When all is said and done, well, it better be His words that we remember more than mine or anyone else's. Read the Bible, for it is there alone that we will ever find life-changing faith.

August 7 - I Just Can't Do It Anymore

I am not able to bear all this people alone, because it is too heavy for me. And if thou deal thus with me, kill me, I pray thee, out of hand, if I have found favour in thy sight; and let me not see my wretchedness. (Num. 11:14–15)

Moses, Moses, poor dear Moses, a man of like passions and weaknesses. It is interesting how we look to the people of the Bible as if they were supermen and women. As if one day they were mere mortals, and like superheroes, they somehow fell in a vat of toxic poison and became superhuman. I don't remember anyone in the Bible wearing a cape, maybe some long robes here and there, but no capes. Often when I read this account about Moses, it reminds me of myself. Not that I am a Moses but that people are too much for me to bear alone sometimes.

Being a pastor and Christian counselor is a double whammy, and there came a time when I couldn't do both. There were times when I was inches away from quitting it all and hanging up the cape (I didn't own). Sometimes I wish I had a cape so maybe I could fly away, but reality is what reality is, and I was stuck in the situation where the Lord placed me. Life is hard, people can be mean, and problems can overwhelm us. There have been many days when I had to go on my knees in prayer and tell the Lord, "I don't think I can do this anymore. I think maybe you called the wrong guy." Look at Moses. He was even thinking about taking his own life under the strain of leading and living.

One might ask why Moses wasn't able to carry the load if the Lord truly called Moses. God did call him to lead His people from Egypt, but did God make a mistake? Did God not figure out the human limitations of Moses and his character flaws? Yes, God figures all these things into the equations. Heck, He created us, so He knows what we are—and as the Word says, "Men at their best state are all together vanity." Friends, there are going to be days when you feel like giving up, when nothing is going right. Even when you are taking all the right meds, still you can't come out of the hole.

Friends, a little note that we will talk about later, medications can do a lot, but they cannot cure sin or the results of it, nor can they change life and its problems. Pressures of all sorts will be placed on us; some so great that we feel our very souls will be destroyed. In those times, there is no medication that can change those situations but only faith in a God who can. When we feel like we can't go on anymore, when we feel like we have had enough—well, maybe we can't—through God, we can. I have been in the worst situations where everything spelled destruction, yet somehow, someway, the Lord pulled a rabbit out of His hat and saved the day. Why does He wait so long? I really don't know; all I do know is that He knows what He is doing. Sometimes we just have to trust in that one thing alone.

August 8 - Healing Through Pain?

But He was wounded for our transgressions, He was bruised for our iniquities: the chastisement of our peace was upon Him; and with His stripes we are healed. (Isa. 53:5)

Ever wish things weren't as they were? Like needing rain so the grass can grow? I like my grass green, but I don't like the rain, especially when it falls on the church picnic. On our church property in New York, we have a lot of trees, which give great shade in the heat of summer, but they are a pain in the fall when the leaves all come down. Clouds are great when you are laboring out on a hot summer day, but not so great when you want to sit out on the beach. Yeah, things in this life sometimes seem to be set up just to make us miserable, or maybe not. Maybe things are as they are because of the fall of man, but even in the fallen world, we can still find God's purpose in them. Take the charred ground after a crop fire. Farmers long ago learned that burning a field actually made the soil better for the future harvest.

The other day, this idea of good coming from bad was again brought home to me. A family in church had a wonderful Christian daughter who lived her life squeaky clean up until the summer after her graduation between high school and college. The family was deeply hurt when their daughter got caught up with a bad crowd from school, which led her to a few months of drinking and crazy parties. Their daughter did all of this behind their backs and ended up with a smashed car, which opened up the can of worms to what was really going on. The parents wept deeply as did the young woman. I met with them as they all wept and spoke of their broken hearts. The father was so distraught that he wanted to step down from ministry. The mother was on the verge of a nervous breakdown, and the daughter wept for the pain she caused her parents and how she felt she would carry this scar for all eternity. I tried to calm their hearts, but for a long time, they would not be comforted. Well, she went off to a Christian college that September and lived a wonderful life for the Lord. She never touched that dark lifestyle again only because she saw its ugliness. In the end, that pain gave way to purpose, and good came from bad.

True, these situations never look so wonderful while we are going through them, but if we could only see what the Lord sees down the line, they would make a whole lot more sense. I have seen children drown in backyard pools only to lead a parent to the Lord through that death. A dear brother in Christ broke his neck at nineteen while riding his motorcycle to live as a paraplegic until the age of sixty, and yet in those years in that wheelchair, he led more people to the Lord and touched more lives than he ever would have had he never broken his neck.

We might ask why the Lord works in such a way and why He can't just make good happen from good. Well, the answer is simple: things are not good, so the Lord takes the broken, fallen world and uses the pain as a springboard to blessings. As the Lord used the death of His son to bring healing to millions of souls, so He can take our depression and anxiety and also use it to bring good and blessings.

August 9 - Getting There from Here

And an highway shall be there, and a way, and it shall be called The way of holiness; the unclean shall not pass over it; but it shall be for those: the wayfaring men, though fools, shall not err therein. (Isa. 35:8)

I remember an old movie where one fellow asking for directions asks another fellow, who replies to him these funny words: "You can't get there from here." As funny as that sounds, it is also how true it feels sometimes. Yeah, sometimes it feels like we can't get to new and wonderful things in our life if we are starting from a place of emotional and mental struggles. We think to ourselves, *How could I ever be of any use to anyone if I am such a mess to even begin with? How can I be anything when I am nothing? How can I become anything for Christ when He has to start with a pile of nerves and sin?*

I hope as you are reading those words, you are also noting how faithless they are. How unsupernatural they are. We are totally discounting the power of God, prayer, and the impossible. Yes, the mission might seem impossible, but we are working with the God of the impossible. He doesn't need musclemen to lift heavy loads; He just needs people of faith to trust Him to do the lifting. When God called Samson to do mighty deeds of strength, and you read about it the first time, how many of us pictured Samson as a massive body-building beach showman? Take a read of the story of Samson in Judges one more time and see if God says he was a big dude anywhere. We assume he was because we always think in the natural realm. For example, big acts of lifting require big muscles.

Dear friend, the Lord doesn't look for big, strong, tough, bold people to do His work, but in fact, He looks for the complete opposite. He looks for the little and despised of the world. He looks for people like you and me. Of getting to there from here, we only need to remember this one thing: the way to God and the way to accomplishing great things is not found in us but in holiness. So often we strive to rid ourselves of this emotional baggage by human reasoning and tactics—and sometimes the Lord just might use some human resources—but at the end of the day, what the Lord requires from us is holiness. The fighting and straining can help out, but most of the time, if done in our own strengths, it will come to nothing.

Friends, we are not called to be great or powerful or to go door to door selling something for Christ. No, first and foremost, we are called to be holy. I cannot tell you how many times I spent so much effort trying to figure out how to get rid of this burden of anxiety and such and, at the same time, forget all about the call to be holy. It is as if we think that doesn't really matter or somehow the Lord gives us a pass on obeying Him and His words because we are so weak and oppressed.

Holiness is our call, and we must obey it above everything else. We cannot complain to the Lord for unanswered prayers if we haven't done everything in our power to live holy lives unto Him. Even in pain, even in sorrow, our call to live as billboards for Christ must continue. So yes, we can get to healing from sickness, but we must be faithful first in doing our duties as children of God.

August 10 - Does God Know You?

And the sheep hear his voice: and he calleth his own sheep by name, and leadeth them out. (John 10:3)

It might sound like an odd way to start a devotion, but sometimes we need to crack an egg open before we can cook and eat it. Dear friend, if you are reading this devotional book, you are probably reading it for a number of reasons: 1) you're suffering from depression and anxiety; 2) someone who cares about you suggested you read it; and 3) you are at the end of your rope and will desperately try anything, even God. I say *even God* because if you haven't noticed, this is a Christ-centered book. It is not a book about emotional issues with some religion thrown in, but it is about Jesus Christ the Lord with some emotional issues thrown in. Just as we cannot make our car move without an engine, so we cannot get to the place of healing if we don't have Christ.

To many different people, this idea of "having" Christ might mean different things. To some, it is being a religious person, maybe belonging to some denomination or church. Maybe to you it simply means just being a spiritually-minded person who likes a bit of God with your coffee. Maybe you believe a little God can't hurt, but you will focus mostly on the emotional side of the book. Today, August 10, might be the most important day of your life because today I want to explain what this "Jesus" thing really means. Today I want you to place your pains on the shelf and focus on the Carpenter of that shelf.

Friend, your religion won't save you, nor can your spirituality or good deeds save you. Being in tune with cosmic forces won't save you either. None of those things mean anything, and so this book will do you no good if you don't first *have Christ as your Lord and King*. Jesus is calling all of us and has been since before time began. Even in our sins and troubles, He still calls out and desires all to be saved; no, not from your pains here on earth but from your separation from God the Father for all eternity. Hell, death, sin—they are all very real and very much a problem that we cannot fix. No, we cannot fix any of those things, but Jesus Christ can by His atoning death on the cross.

We have a problem, friends, and it is sin. No matter how big or how small, we just can never be good enough to be close to the Father. The Ten Commandments are not so much a code to live by, but a ruler to show us how far off the mark we are. Sin is the issue, and as long as we have unconfessed and unatoned sin, we are forever lost. What we need is to acknowledge what we are and trust in Christ's death on the cross for our sins. Once there, then we can call Him Lord and Savior and King. We must confess Him as Lord over our lives with nothing else between us. It is not so much "Do we know God?" but "Does the Lord 'know' us as children, His children by faith alone?"

If we are His, then we will hear His voice when He leads and guides us. If you are not hearing God's call and direction, that may mean you are not even a child of God; and if so, then this devotional will do nothing for you. Please, today, call out to the Lord and confess your sins and ask Him into your heart as Lord and Sovereign King. Then we can start making some eggs.

August 11 - Sometimes All Alone

And the lord said unto him, "Surely I will be with thee, and thou shalt smite the Midianites as one man." (Judg. 6:16)

God promised Gideon, "Surely I will be with you, and you shall defeat the Midianites as one man" (Judg. 6:16). God assured him, "I have sent you—therefore, I will be with you." Many times we will have friends and families to help in our days of desperate needs. We have spoken before throughout this book how important those colaborers and prayer partners are, but that does not mean we will not have days of having to go through it alone. *All alone*, what a scary thought to many of us. I remember in the very dark places of my anxiety, this fear of being alone. As I have shared with you, my wife would be pivotal in my healing, but even in that, the Lord didn't like my overdependency on her and would soon test my riding skills without my training wheels. They were very hard times as my wife would go away often to visit her mom in California. Sometimes I would crash completely without her, but in time, I had to learn to cope without her.

Many times the Lord does give us that crutch or cane to help us hobble along, but sooner or later, we need to walk on our own two feet. There were many times I would have to make myself go away on trips alone just so I could make sure I was trusting in Him alone. Like I said, some days weren't good, but they needed to happen. I didn't die nor self-destruct. I just had to deal with some crazy panic attacks. In fact, the worst of my times, for the most part, were due to doctors playing with too many meds trying to set me right when in reality they overmedicated, and I became an emotional disaster. Even in those times I still had to stand up and fight, and even with my wife with me, I still stood alone because there was not much she could do but watch me bake in a state of overmedicated confusion. (Side note: Though general practitioners can do a good job of prescribing medications, there is nothing better than a *good* godly psychiatrist.)

Be that as it may, this being-alone part is a difficult dynamic yet one very necessary in your healing curve. Like riding our bikes without training wheels, it is hard and scary, but we *must* get to that place sooner or later— alone without help from anyone, alone with only Christ to hold our hands.

Dear friend, if the Lord calls us to that place of emotional battle and He calls us there alone, then would He not make a way for us to make it? Step out, get right, let go, and begin to walk even with shaky knees and a pumping heart. We must get there if our faith is truly in Him. In time it will become easier and easier to go through it alone, but don't rush yourself— baby steps always.

August 12 - But What If I Fall?

Now unto him that is able to keep you from falling, and to present you faultless before the presence of his glory with exceeding joy. (Jude 1:24)

Leaving off from where we were yesterday, let's talk some more about this training-wheel scenario. If you ever rode with training wheels, you quickly found out how truly scary they were. They were not as wonderful as you had hoped, and you certainly couldn't keep up with the other kids without them. You were trapped in your first paradox—to use them and ride yet not keep up with the other kids, or to not use them and fall down and still not keep up with everyone. As they say, it is not the long fall off a building that kills you but the sudden stop, and so too with training wheels. We need them, or we will fall, and that sudden stop might draw some blood from those new knees. Isn't it funny that, as a child, falling always seems to be a major issue? Not so much when we grow up, at least not until we are senior citizens.

As a child, the solution would simply be to not fall any more, but besides training wheels, what are we to do? Well, there is the parent factor. Mom or Dad running next to you as you peddle and wobble all over. It is good because you are riding, and it is good because you are not using training wheels, but it is still not what you really want with regard to the "cool" factor as your parents are still running beside you. Reminds me of being an adult Christian and knowing I need God to make it, but people seeing me need God is embarrassing. Some people use drugs and other things to be their training wheels, and that might look more "cool," but then again, they still can't keep up with life in that drug-induced training-wheel dilemma. Well, it is back to God again, and the choice is again back to us: ride through life without falling but ride with that parent following you around in case you fall. Hey, the older I get, the better option two sounds. Maybe it is not so bad to have another following you around in case you fall. Maybe it is only my pride that keeps me from living life in that assurance of God going everywhere with me.

Dear friend, we have to make choices as we grow, and pride has a lot to do with them. In many ways, when we choose Christ, we have to swallow our pride. But just as driving around with one of those emergency little spare tires is embarrassing, it still gets you where you need to be. Maybe how we look at things is the problem. Maybe it is looking at that silly little emergency spare tire as adult training wheels, and maybe it is being thankful that we have one instead of being embarrassed that we need one. To come to Christ, we must die to self. We must be able to say, "Yes, I have some issues, and without this spiritual training wheel, I can't get around. But you know what? That's okay." It is okay that I need Jesus, and it is even more okay that He is there for me to help me up when I fall down. I don't know anyone who walks around with only one leg and doesn't need help. Friends, we are born broken in one way or another, and unless we run to Jesus Christ, we will have to walk around broken all of our lives. I choose to walk with Christ even if the world mocks me. I know one thing: I am walking, and at the end of the day, isn't that what we want anyway?

August 13 - More Fears or Less?

He shall cover thee with his feathers, and under his wings shalt thou trust: his truth shall be thy shield and buckler. Thou shalt not be afraid for the terror by night; nor for the arrow that flieth by day; Nor for the pestilence that walketh in darkness; nor for the destruction that wasteth at noonday. (Ps. 91:4–6)

I'm a big news guy; well, at least I was for a very long time. If you watch the news a lot, it has a very bad side effect: it induces fear. If you didn't have anxiety or things to worry about, you will after you watch it. Isn't it interesting that almost all news is bad news? Why doesn't the good news make it into the papers? Imagine reading, "No one was killed today, and Mrs. Joan had a great day at the beach." I remember early on when reading my Bible how surprised I was of all the bad news there. Wars, sickness, earthquakes, and rape. I would think, *Well, at least I'm not living back then*, but then as the news in our age began to get bad, I started to think, *Hey, this is worse now than during Bible times.*

Is the world today giving me more fears or less? It doesn't really matter. What matters is how we deal with them, and the best way to learn that is to see what people in the Bible did. Did they take medications? Maybe they would have if they could. Did they go to counseling and see a psychologist? Maybe in a way they did as they sought out soothsayers and counselors of their own. But for the most part, it seems that through all the wars, devastation, drought, and death, God's people always did the same things: a) panic then b) prayed and then c) always ended up seeking comfort under God's wing.

Let's go through Psalms 91:4–6 and see what they did and what God offered them.

> *He shall cover thee with his feathers, and under his wings shalt thou trust: his truth shall be thy shield and buckler. Thou shalt not be afraid for the terror by night; nor for the arrow that flieth by day; Nor for the pestilence that walketh in darkness; nor for the destruction that wasteth at noonday.*

Some things don't change, do they? 1) It is God who does the covering and protecting. 2) It is in God whom we should trust. 3) It is trust in God's truth that really made it all come together. 4) The result is always the same: "We should not be afraid of the terror by night or by the arrow that fly's during the day." Notice one thing here. Does God stop the scary things or the arrows that fly? No, he doesn't, and all He really does is comfort you while they fly. He gives shelter, not a home but a temporary shelter in this life, for our home is only in the future life. Sickness and destruction seem to always be flooding over our world, and people always seem to be running from them in fear and panic. We really haven't changed much as a people, and of our fears, they seem to be the same. So if our fears will always be there, we must make a choice: a) let them destroy us, or b) run to God for safety as they run rampant in this present age of destruction.

Dear friend, wars, sickness, and problems are simply here to stay, and all we can do is do what God has always told us to do, which is run to Him; and in running to Him, truly believe and trust that He can keep what He has promised.

August 14 - Never Forget This One Thing

To the chief Musician upon Gittith, A Psalm of David. O lord our Lord, how excellent is thy name in all the earth! who hast set thy glory above the heavens. (Ps. 8:1)

If there is one thing we must hammer into our heads day and night, it is this: Our God is good! Of this, there can be no wavering or vacillating. God is good, 100 percent good and has no possibility of ever not being good. He cannot be angered into acting anything but good. Nothing we can do can change His goodness to us. This is hard for us to ever understand due to the simple fact that apart from Christ we are not good. We are so used to not being good and meeting people who are not good that it is hard for us to comprehend an intrinsically good being. This is not hard to understand in our world today as we live in a world with far less examples of goodness. There was a time when we trusted people and politicians, a time when we left doors unlocked and keys in our car ignitions. If you think about it, the mere fact that we need locks on everything shows us how *not good* we are as a people.

Today, does anyone really trust our national leaders no matter what party you belong to? With all this evil running rampant, it will naturally be harder for us to believe that even God is good. We think, *How can He be good when there is so much bad?* Dear friend, our Lord doesn't just act good or do good things, He is the essence of what good is. Simply put, He is *good* in every aspect of the word. His very being defines goodness in all its forms. As the Lord doesn't just give or show love but is Love, so is God good. He is good all the time, in every place, and in every way. Why is this so important to those of us who suffer with depression and anxiety? It is simply because it will help convince us that good can only come from it. It is impossible for our present suffering to be anything but good for our near future.

When we look up at the heavens on a clear night and see the stars and the moon so pristine and glorious, we know that it is good. When we think of our planet hurling through space yet not being flung out into space, we know that it is good. When we see a newborn child suckling at its mother's breast, we know that it is good, and that good is God since He is the only Good One. Now, some might say, "Well, you see good in the newborn child, what about a newborn child that is deformed? Where is God's goodness there?" Dear friend, God is good even there, and for me, to truly understand it, I would have to be God. I am not, so I don't know where the good is in that situation, but I still know that God is good.

See, that's what keeps our faith strong and us moving ahead in our struggles. It is looking at a bad situation and saying to ourselves, "Yeah, it sure stinks right now, but my God is good." We must embrace this or we will have to assume that God is evil, wicked, and not in control. If that is true, then there is no God. And what does that do for our depression? God is real. He is good, and that's the end of the story. I believe it, know it, and trust in it even when life sure makes me feel like throwing in the towel. God is good, and we must live in that knowledge.

August 15 - The Worst Fear

The fear of man bringeth a snare: but whoso putteth his trust in the lord shall be safe. (Prov. 29:25)

I was recently dealing with a church issue, one between people. Silly, isn't it, to even say that because 99 percent of our problems are people. Within a three-month space of time, I had to deal with three different people with three different problems. These particular problems were compounded because these three particular people were—smart, bold, outspoken, had a good understanding of the Bible, and for the most part, a little legalistic. As if it was not enough to deal with one person, I had to deal with three like this over an extended amount of time. Well, my anxiety started to kick in, and I wondered why and what made this situation so anxious and frightening. The answer came clear as I was reading my daily devotional.

Proverbs 29:25 was what the Lord hit me over the head with: "The fear of man brings a snare." What does that actually mean? When we fear people more than we fear God, we place ourselves in a trap with soapy sides. We become so intimidated by people's opinions and loud voices that we tend to cave in on our own voices. When it comes to the Word of God, this can be devastating, and many pastors do cave in, especially when the people whom they fear happen to be big givers or influential in the church. The fear of man can cause us to make choices that we would never make otherwise. When we fear man, we really fear and respect their words more than God's.

The fear of man is like playing baseball and deciding against your own better judgment to not use a mitt when you are playing catcher. You know it's wrong, and you know it will hurt, but this very important person on the team told you not to use a mitt, and you are too afraid to ignore him. You choose the pain instead of what's right. You go home each night holding your hand in a bowl of ice, wondering why you keep doing this to yourself, but then you do it again. In time, it is not just the ball hitting your hand that hurts, but just seeing that person. Their very voice brings chills down your spine and anxiety to your soul. It is a circular sickness that will never end until you start listening to whom you are supposed to—Jesus Christ.

It's amazing how little honor we give the King of kings and how much honor we give people who are kings in their own minds. Much of this is from how we are wired. Some of us are born bold; some born chickens. Yet that doesn't mean that's how we have to stay. I was born a chicken, and people have been beating me up since I was a child. I caved and followed the crowd and paid the price. But the good news is we don't have to. We can be bold as a lion when we live through the Lion of Judah. I have been learning this hard lesson with my heels dug in, and slowly I am learning how to lead and not fear what people say. Yet sometimes, when my armor isn't on, the enemy uses that naked stance and hits me with a 1-2-3 punch. If we are not ready, old fears can come back. Dear friend, today let us cry out to the Lord and proclaim, "Lord, forgive me for honoring anyone but You. If I fear people's opinions and don't fear Your commands, then who can I blame but myself?"

August 16 - Trust

Trust in the lord with all thine heart; and lean not unto thine own understanding. Proverbs 3:5

Proverbs 3:5–10 are some very important scriptures that we simply can't leave out. Sure they are overused and tossed around a bit too much, but they still are the words of God, and words that really lay out a step-by-step approach to change, healing, and deliverance. Today we will go over verse 5, and each of the next few days, we will go to the next verse all the way up to verse 10. We will break them down in simple form and say it like it is, as there is no mystery to these scriptures but pure, honest, real truth. Let us begin with Proverbs 3:5 and the lead word, which is *trust*.

Friends, we really don't know what trust is, and it is probably why we suffer so much in this life. Oftentimes we confuse *trust* and *believing*, as if they were the same, and that's where the problems begin. Friends, I can believe in many things yet not trust in them for what they do. I believe in high wires that circus people walk on, but I don't trust high wires. I believe people can stick their fingers in an electrical outlet and live, but I don't trust that story to try it myself. To trust is to step out on. Next, we have "with all thine heart." I can maybe trust the high wire if I have spotters and a safety net, but I still might not trust in it with *all my heart*. The reason why I might not trust in it though it has been explained to me is because I still am using *my own understanding* (i.e., I know from past experiences that even when I walked on a curb as a child, I fell off, so why would I walk on a high wire?)

Proverbs 3:5 lays out the foundation for our *building of faith* to sit upon, and without understanding the total dynamics of it, we can never go to verse 6, 7, 8, 9, and 10. We simply cannot graduate to second grade unless we pass first grade. For many of us, we are forever left back and live as children when we should be living as adults. If we take a visual look at that, we can see how silly it looks. Imagine sitting in a first-grade class when you are twenty-five years old. It does tend to make one feel foolish and wonder where everyone else went. Much of our fears of living are because we still have that childlike fear of everything around us. We cannot do adult things because we are still children. We do not strive to be adults or leave that class because, in a way, we like being cared for like a child and never want to really grow up. Being taken care of is addicting and hard to break free from. It is simply easier to accept the lie that we are not able to grow, and so we except our permanent state of immaturity and actually enjoy it. Like the proverbial college student who stays in school for ten years under the excuse that they cannot decide what to do with their life yet really never want to grow up because it is simply too scary out there, and as long as they can use that excuse they can prolong youth forever.

At the end of the day, it all brings us back to trusting God. Without true trust, we will never leave the safety of the first grade. How do we learn to trust God and take the next step? Find out tomorrow.

August 17 - Acknowledge

In all thy ways acknowledge Him, and He shall direct thy paths. (Prov. 3:6)

Verse 6 of Proverbs 3 seems doable, yet when we investigate it further, we quickly realize it's a major step. Sure, I can maybe turn that page of trusting in the Lord, but can I do it in all areas of my life? A perfect example of this is one that most Christians have no problem with, which is eternal life. I have no issues at all trusting Christ's work on the cross for my eternal destiny. I know that when I die, I will forever be with the Lord. It is easy and a done deal, and I can boast that I do truly trust the Lord, but—and here is the stickler—do I trust God (that same way) in everything I do? In verse 6, it says to "acknowledge Him in all our ways," which means to give credit and trust God in every single thing I do while living my life on planet earth.

It means being bold about Jesus Christ in every situation. It means in my taxes, in my conversations, in my private time on the computer, in my shopping, no matter what it is, I am still putting God way out front for all to see. It is to live, breathe, sleep, talk, and be a child of light directing everyone I meet to Jesus Christ. It is making sure my language is clean, my TV habits are pure, and all of my interactions with people are always with the intent of promoting Jesus Christ as Lord. It is buying a new car and placing Christ at the top of the list: "Does He want me to have a new car? Should I do this? Can I afford it? Will it hinder my giving to the church?" It is planning a vacation and at the same time thinking, *Hmm, there is that family in church who has no money and food. I wonder if the Lord would like me to forfeit my vacation or cut it back a bit so I can give them a (secret) love offering to help them out.*

See, it isn't as easy as we think, and even when we think we are trusting the Lord with all that we are and possess, maybe we are not. We love the second part of verse 6, yet we never reach it because we never get past the first part: 6b) "and He shall direct thy paths." Oh how we all love that second part and oh how we would love for the Lord to truly direct our steps. Sometimes we think, *He never directs my steps*, and we wonder why when the answer is simply because we never *acknowledged* Him in all our ways. If you are like me, you are thinking to yourself, *Hey, this is impossible. No one lives like that*. Well, I wouldn't be too sure about that. Sure, I would agree that most don't, but to say none is a stretch. I know a few who do, like some of our missionaries, like some people who choose to live in near-poverty conditions so the gospel can go forth.

Look back in history at some of those famous evangelists and martyrs for Christ. They are there if we look hard enough, and as to us living that way, well, maybe we can't to its extreme, but we could sure do better than what we are doing. I know I can do a lot better in this area, and if I truly wanted to go all out, I could sell some of my prized possessions and give it to missions. Did not Jesus tell His followers to sell all and follow Him? Ouch, that really hurts, and well, it should. Yet how much do I really want healing from this depression and anxiety? Sometimes, maybe not that much.

August 18 - Depart

Be not wise in thine own eyes: fear the lord, and depart from evil. (Prov. 3:7)

Okay, this is not getting easier but actually harder. We might even be asking ourselves, "Is it even worth this effort?" All of a sudden, our depression and anxiety really isn't that bad. Maybe I can live with it if I have to as long as I don't have to follow these steps. Or maybe it's time we started following these steps and stop calling ourselves followers of Christ when all we really are, are just fans of Christ. "Jesus is great and all, but I still have to live, and if living for Christ means living that way, then what's the point of living?"

The problem, friend, is this, and it's the same problem most of us have: we do not know what Christ really offers, and if we don't know what He offers, then maybe we have never tasted it, and so how can we say it is not worth it? This makes me think of the woman at the well. Jesus said to her, "Woman, that water that you drink will leave you thirsting again, but the water that I offer you, well, let's just say it's water that is out of this world (my rendition)." If we don't know what we are missing, we just may never desire to pursue it. What if our depression and anxiety are simply controlling us because we are not letting God control us? What if we think we have this Christian life down, think we have tasted it, found it so-so, and because of that, we never seek to go any deeper in Christ?

In Proverbs 3:7, we start to see why these questions are so important. God says in verse 7 "to not be wise in thine own eyes." What can that mean but to not think you have it all figured out? To not conclude that you've learned all there is to learn about God, the Bible, and this life and you have found it lacking? "To not be wise" does not seem like proper English, but in its literal rendering, it says it very clear: live as if you know nothing but the goodness of God. Don't try to figure things out or try to understand God's plan for your life. Don't question Him or dare tell people what God should do for them or you. Just simply be. Just simply exist as if you were a bird or an animal who knows nothing more than the knowledge imparted to them at creation.

Animals, if you think about it, can live in relative ease of mind simply because they only concern themselves with what God made them do: fly, crawl, display beauty, and declare the glory of God. The Bible even declares that creation itself is really in existence to do what God commanded while glorifying the One who made it. Again, Proverbs 3:7 says, "Be not wise in thine own eyes: fear the LORD, and depart from evil." Read it again and again. Do you see it? a) Admit you know anything. b) Honor and reverence the Lord. c) Stay away from evil; in fact, run from it because it's all around you. Come to this place, friend, and you're ready for the next step.

August 19 - It Shall Be

It shall be health to thy navel, and marrow to thy bones. (Prov. 3:8)

Now, we come to the good stuff, the rewards and the results of all that obedience. Sure, the hill can look high as you pedal your bike up, but oh what a view when you arrive. Cutting grass all day in the summer heat is no fun, but when it is all trimmed and finished, what a pretty picture it is. Isn't it funny that it is human nature to stop and look at what you just accomplished after a long and tiresome project? When the carpenter finishes that chair, and the wood has been all buffed, does he not pause for a moment to observe it, or even more, does he not take a seat and feel its solid beauty and a deep sense of pride?

In my struggles through life, there has been no greater joy than to look back and see God's hand in my mess. To look back to the darkest, sin-filled, and sometimes painful times and still see God's goodness. I often wonder why the Lord spent and continues to spend so much time on me. I am so frail and fall so often. I'm not very smart by the world's standard, and I have made a lot of mistakes. I have trampled on His grace and abused His mercy. I have said one thing and done another. I have preached one thing and then took part in what I preached against. Sometimes I wonder why the Lord doesn't just snatch me off this planet and take me home. God is truly good and truly amazing, and His grace is certainly enough for me.

Friend, if you think the effort is not worth the result, then you haven't really been watching what the Lord is doing around you. God is doing so many things through us it simply boggles the mind. Think of your own life. No matter how little or how much you have achieved, isn't it a miracle that you're still alive, breathing and loved by God? He could have taken you home, struck you down, pushed you aside, and yet He still is pushing you onward. It is worth it all, and if you haven't arrived at that place of seeing it yet, you will. Read Proverbs 3:8 and ponder why it's so worth the effort, why it's so important to push and climb through the daily struggles, always keeping your eyes fixed on Jesus. It is worth it, and I will say it again, it is all worth it.

"It shall be health to thy navel, and marrow to thy bones." The navel here, I believe, speaks about the center of who and what we are. As a child in the womb, it is where the lifeline to our mother comes through. Would we not want a healthy lifeline to the Lord? As to the marrow in our bones, well, I am not a doctor, but I know that the marrow is where life-sustaining blood is formed. Blood is spoken of often in the Bible, and without it, we cannot live.

Dear friend, if we can truly trust the Lord as He truly desires, then what He has waiting for us in this life and the life to come will well be worth the pain to arrive there. Our lifeline to God is Jesus Christ, and if we are to hear from the Father and gain direction, should not Jesus Christ be allowed to thrive and envelope all that we are so that His life becomes our lifeline? It shall be!

August 20 - Honor

Honour the lord with thy substance, and with the firstfruits of all thine increase. (Prov. 3:9)

As we read and meditate on the Lord's Word each day during this short series, in Proverbs 3, notice one thing: the spiritual sacrifice asked is getting greater. Okay, so maybe I can trust and follow and lay all that is important to me down for God, but what's this I hear today? To honor the Lord with my money? To honor the Lord with my very being? And every time I get more, attain more, and achieve more, I have to give a portion of it back to Him? It sounds like it is a place where we need to draw the line. *Hey, I work hard for what I have, and no one handed it to me.* Isn't that what most of us are thinking right now? *Hey, Lord, I'm struggling with depression and anxiety. My life is falling apart, and what little I have left, I have to give to You?*

Now, why would the Lord want this from us? Why would He continually ask more of us? If you remember the story of Abraham and Isaac, you know how far the Lord could push. It seemed like a person whom God was going to bless with so much, He also asked for so much. First, Abraham was given this great promise and then nothing. He had to wait years and years. Then when he thought it was coming together, it all fell apart when he had a child with Hagar. Then when Sarah finally had this "child of promise," the next thing he knew was he had to kill him. Now, stop for a moment. Did the Lord actually tell him to kill Isaac, or did He ask him if he would sacrifice him? It did not matter much to Abraham because as far as he was concerned, he was going to have to kill Isaac.

That brings us to another point. Why does the Lord ask us to do and go through such confusing things? Is the Lord having fun playing with our heads, or is He looking for something much deeper and bigger? Maybe He is simply looking for unconditional love. It really makes us sit back and reexamine why the Lord made us and all of creation in the first place. Could it be that all the Lord wants is to be loved back for His great love toward us? Could it be that all we go through, besides being partly the result of the fall, may also be partly due to the Lord's desire to see if we really, truly, honestly love Him simply because He is God and for no other reason? Loving Him not simply so we can get blessings in return but loving Him because we love

Him. After all, He did make everything for Himself; check out Revelations 4:11.

Dear suffering friend, honor the Lord with all that you are. Get used to questioning yourself about your motivations. Every time you obey a command or lead a person to Him, ask yourself this question, "Did I just do that so I would get a blessing or because I love Jesus Christ above everything else in my life, even more than the desire for me to be happy?"

August 21 - Filled

So shall thy barns be filled with plenty, and thy presses shall burst out with new wine. (Prov. 3:10)

Well, it is the last day of our short study in Proverbs 3:5–10. Isn't it amazing how just a bit of God's Word can go such a long way? How He can say so much life-changing words in so few sentences? If we look back over our entire lives and all that we have said, have we ever said as much in five sentences as the Lord has said in these? Let's do a recap of what we have learned so far, how it applies to our struggles with emotional issues such as depression and anxiety, and where it leads us at the end of the day: a) trust, b) acknowledge, c) depart, d) (it shall be) and e) honor.

Sure, it appears that the Lord requires much from us, but does He really, compared to what He gives in return? As we said yesterday, above all, He desires our absolute love for Him, but He also requires that, that love is real, pure, and freely given—meaning that He wants our love for Him to have no strings attached, no selfish motives. When we *trust* Him, He wants it to be real, full-on, and intense. When we *acknowledge* Him, He wants it to be in everything we do and say. When He says to *depart* from things, He means all things that are not of Him, for Him, by Him, and all things that do not bring Him glory.

Notice so far the give and take. Not that He owes us anything, but knowing that we are but sinful beings, He understands how important it is to us to feel comfort from Him. Notice also how after we accomplish a, b, and c, how d is the blessing for us. Notice also that it must always end up back with Him as in (e)—*honor* Him. Never forget to honor Him, for without Him, there is nothingness, darkness, cold, fear, and confusion. Notice also the everlasting and nonexhaustive grace again that follows that obedience. This brings us to f, which is verse 10 of Proverbs 3. To be *filled* is the inevitable end to being right with God: "So shall thy barns be filled with plenty, and thy presses shall burst out with new wine."

Dear friend, never forget the ever-present indwelling of God, the Holy Spirit. Being filled is not something we must wait for but something we must acknowledge. The point being, we are always indwelt by God the Holy Spirit, which happens at salvation. The problem is that we don't realize we are indwelt with His presence, so we never feel the filling. He is there, but through our sin, disobedience, and selfishness, we are constantly snuffing out that candle of God's light. Ever notice how every once in a while you feel that *joy of the Lord*, yet most of the time, you don't? It is due to us walking and living in the flesh more than living and walking in the Spirit. We simply choose sin more often than we choose obedience. Yet when we do choose to walk and talk in His power and light; verse 10 reveals what that all means. So shall our *storehouses* be filled, and not just filled, but filled with plenty; meaning, it will be just what we need. Just enough of God's grace, wisdom, and power.

When it uses the word *presses*, I feel it's more of a verb than a noun. The word *presses* in Hebrew means "to excavate." That the Lord will dig out all that was hidden and buried by disobedience and hall it out so all can see. And at the end of this process, we will be filled. Maybe not always healed 100 percent, at least not in this life, but filled with all we need to serve our Lord better while we live this life. Yes, at the end of the day, it is about Him. Grasp that truth, and it will all begin to make sense.

August 22 - But Are We Listening?

Then the lord answered Job out of the whirlwind, and said. (Job 38:1)

Whoever really takes advice and is satisfied with it? It seems like all through my life, people have been giving me advice. My father, my mother, friends, family, coworkers, and even strangers all give me advice. Do you ever go shopping and have a complete stranger see you looking at something and say, "Don't buy that thing, I have one at home, and it's garbage." Interestingly, that seems to be the only advice we are prone to take, advice from strangers about things not to buy. My dad gave me plenty of advice, which ended up being true, yet I never heeded his wisdom and had to learn the lesson myself. I guess that's the circle of life as they say: parents give advice to their kids, their kids don't take it, and when they get to be parents, they give their kids the same advice only for their kids not to take it.

One day, my middle son, the rock star, was at a music store trying out another guitar. Some business-type guy comes up to him and flashes some fancy business card and tells him, "Wow, I've been watching you play. You're amazing. My company is looking for new acts, and I would like to get a demo of your music." Next thing I know I get a phone call from my son explaining what just happened. Of course he is all excited thinking that he was just discovered and will soon be a star. He never applied for the job at the music store; the real reason he was there was because he assumed his life was now set. As a dad, I knew what I had to do, and I knew how it would be taken. I would share how that type of thing happened to me at his age by some unscrupulous record producer, how it was a big lie, and yes, my son would reply in anger, calling me a dream-crusher. Well, that was just how it all went down, and after some time had passed, I asked him in sincerity, "Did you ever hear back from that record producer?" We all know what the answer was, but more than that, we need to learn what the lesson was.

Friend, no matter what you are going through, there will be many people with advice at the ready. They will tell you all kinds of things about your depression and anxiety. They will tell you don't do this or don't do that. Take this, but don't take that. They will recommend *their* special doctor, coach, witch-doctor friend. What will be hard during these times is being able to discern what's really the right thing to do. What do I do? Where do I go? Who do I listen to? Even my advice in this book might confuse you, and it might not be the right thing for you, but never forget this. Somewhere in all the voices, there is one that is the *voice of truth*. Did you just hear what I said? There is a voice of truth; there is the way you should go. The problem is with all the other voices, we tend to block out the one voice we need to hear the most. The voice of the Lord, our Maker. The voice of truth.

Notice after Job goes through his fits of rage and valleys of ignorance how the Lord waits quietly. Notice how the Lord won't force His will on any of us especially if we are not listening. No, He waits until the dust settles and there is nothing left to say. It is at that time that the Lord's still small voice loudly speaks logic and sense into our souls. It might take time. It might be a while until we get what He is trying to tell us, but one thing is certain: He is speaking and simply waiting for us to listen. Psalm 118:8 says,

"It is better to trust in the Lord than to put confidence in princes." Check out that scripture and plaster it on your bathroom mirror.

August 23 - Lions and Bears

And David said unto Saul, "Thy servant kept his father's sheep, and there came a lion, and a bear, and took a lamb out of the flock." (1 Sam. 17:34)

Ever hear the phrase *what if?* What if everything that is happening, has happened, and will happen to you has a divine purpose? During my thirty years of being a Christian, I have seen a lot of troubles come my way in the form of scary obstacles. They never came, for the most part, in the form of cute little pink sheep, not that they can't; but they were always in the form of monsters: mean people, bad news at work or from the doctor, a car accident, a financial disaster, or a tumble with temptation and sin, sometimes even a great challenge that seemed so far above my pay grade and skill level. It seems the Lord was always hitting me with things that He knew were way above what I could ever handle.

When David, as a young boy, encountered a lion and a bear, I'm sure he wasn't thrilled. I'm sure David's first response was not joy but hesitation, until he remembered the Lord was with him and through the Lord's power, he could defeat anything or one. The one thing I know David didn't ever think about at that moment was that the Lord was going to use his success over these two beasts as a way to boost his faith later on in fighting Goliath. Isn't it interesting how the Lord strengthened David by having him face a monster of a problem, a problem that would be far above the pay grade of a shepherd boy? I mean how could a shepherd boy kill a lion and a bear? Isn't that impossible? As I look at my youngest son, Luke, now at age eleven, I just can't see him taking down a full grown bear and lion. I can't in human reasoning, but God could, and He did see that in David when He allowed these beasts to enter his life. Hmm, I wonder where those beasts came from. Did God send them or Satan? It doesn't matter because God allowed it and used it for good as He uses all monster invasions for good.

Dear friend and fellow sufferer, sometimes God is going to allow monsters to enter your life. Be it in the form of sickness, debt, calamity, or simply problem people. Whatever the way, the reason will always be the same, not to destroy you but to enlarge you. Ever wonder how David felt after defeating those beasts? I bet he was one cocky young man for a while, feeling like he could take on anything or anyone. Sure, David knew that it was God's strength that ultimately gave him the victory, but remember, people in the Bible are not sinless, and neither was David. In all of his holiness, he was still a young man, and we know how young men get about beating things up. Yeah, David, can I say, had to have had at least a tad of pride over that battle.

If you are facing bears and lions today, and you feel they are way out of your league, well, remember David and the millions of other Christians who have to face and fight monsters every day. Remember that they have a purpose, and though Satan might send them to destroy you, God uses them to make you stronger. And mind you, not stronger to sit and look at your muscles in the mirror, but stronger to fight again. And when you do fight again, you can bet the battle will be bigger and the monsters stronger. All you have to remember is who is really fighting those battles and know who always wins. One way or another, dear friend, we win if Christ is with us.

August 24 - He Is Sending Help

And it came to pass, as Aaron spake unto the whole congregation of the children of Israel, that they looked toward the wilderness, and, behold, the glory of the lord appeared in the cloud. (Exod. 16:10)

During my first battle with depression and anxiety, I remember this one feeling that would follow me through my second and longest bout. It was the feeling that help was never coming. Yeah, people told me it would pass, and that helped me beyond measure; but during my second bout with this wonderful monster of blessing, the delay in healing was much longer. Soon the promise of healing and reprieve didn't seem like enough. Soon faith-filled patience became faithless annoyance, which turned into destructive, hopeless despondency. It is one thing to hear that help is on its way; it is another thing to actually see it so you can rest in it. When your home is burning due to great fire, the words from neighbors that the fire department is on their way mean very little as all that you own is being destroyed. Even when you hear the sirens in the distance, it still offers little hope as the fire still rages on unquenched. No, it is not until the trucks are there, set up, and water is actually putting the flames out that any type of joy is found. Sometimes problems and trials like those we suffer burn so intensely that any promise of the fire going out seems foolish. Each day that it lingers feels like an eternity, and each day in that eternity only reminds us of how much is being lost.

In my most recent and longest battle with anxiety and depression, all I could focus on was the loss. I would ruminate in my brain all that was tossed in the fire as this pain burned on. All my work, my family, my ministry, the souls whom I led to the Lord, all of it was for nothing, and ruin was all that I saw. I could only focus on me, so all I saw or cared about was me, my legacy, my achievements, and my testimony. I remember talking to the Lord during a violent prayer session. I remember telling the Lord how all of this loss and ruin were on His shoulders as He was the one who was going to look bad when I finally crumble and fall. Interestingly, it was my own words that spoke wisdom back at me, yet this time, with divine propulsion. The Lord spoke back at me and said, "You're right, it is My neck on the line if you fall, so why are you worrying so much about it?" It took me a while to understand how to take what the Lord had said, but in time, it began to make sense. As David said himself as he spoke in prayer to the Lord, "If I go down to the grave, who will give you praise?" Suddenly the burden was lifted off me and placed where it should have been placed long ago, on the Lord.

Dear friend, barring sin in our lives, which the Lord will have to correct us for, our trial of faith is not always so much about us but about how people will see the Lord in us and, in turn, turn to Him. When we are in pain and suffering, the Lord is very concerned about how we will handle it and what image it will leave behind. Not so much an image of us but an image of Him. If the Lord doesn't send help, then the Lord will be affected negatively. He will send help, be it in a cloud or in a song, but He will send it, and when we are delivered, many will be drawn to Him by His workings in us. At the end of the day, it is His testimony that is on the line; and as long as we are being faithful and trusting Him through this furnace of fire, it will be His responsibility to deliver us, as He delivered His ancient people Israel time and time again. For if He never delivered them, who would be following Him today?

August 25 - Time to Lie Low

Get thee hence, and turn thee eastward, and hide thyself by the brook Cherith, that is before Jordan. (1 Kings 17:3)

Elijah is an amazing biblical character, and one worth looking into, from megahighs to megalows. If he went to see a psychiatrist today, they probably would have labeled him bipolar. Certainly he was not bipolar, but he did know what it was like to be so right with God, so on fire for Him and then in a short time be so distant, broken, and far. Elijah's story is a dynamic one of great theological significance, yet with all the *Bible stuff* aside, we should not dare forget what the Lord did to him when he was at his lowest. The Lord told Elijah to run, lie low, hide himself, but not just anywhere, but a place where He would be able to work on him and rebuild him for ministry again. What's interesting also is that the Lord sent him off alone. The Lord wanted Elijah alone, alone from the hustle and bustle of life. Alone from the people and the noise of living. Alone and away from ministry and confusion.

In our life and struggles, sometimes the Lord wants us to be set aside and apart. Sometimes simply just to hear Him better and sometimes to keep us away from the enemy while we spiritually recharge. Now what it means to get away for a while can be manifest in many forms, meaning that it doesn't always mean going to some retreat to live like a monk. Too many people feel that great spiritual growth is only found on top of a remote mountain, which can be true to some degree but still not always necessary or even logistically possible. Let's face it. We live in an age where we all have to work one or even two jobs just to get by. We have kids to drive all over and raise, and many of us have families and homes that are in great need. Life is crazy busy, and going away to some wooded glen, though very appealing, isn't always possible. Unless you are very well-to-do and can afford the time and travel, for the most part, we are stuck with our limitations in that area.

In ministry, when I feel like I am burning out, the advice I get from my pastor friends is a sabbatical for a few months. I always chuckle inside as maybe their big congregations or denominations can afford to send their pastor away and keep their church running at the same time. But here in real Ville, being the only pastor of a small nondenominational church makes that almost impossible. So I, like you, can only dream about long walks and meditation by a crystal stream in the Netherlands. No, we need to still get away, but maybe only in the virtual sense. This can be anything from going down to the ocean for a walk or maybe just going into your car outside your apartment and just getting alone. The key here is not the place but the alone part. This means that all cell phones, radios, and electronic devices off and Bible open. It also means no family, kids, or people around. Like I said, this is not impossible even in a big city. The key part is to get alone with the Lord, confess your sins, and open up your heart. Oh, don't forget to open your ears too. We often spend so much time talking to God and asking for things that we never have a chance to hear what He has to say. Be still and listen!

August 26 - Slain but Established

As unknown, and yet well known; as dying, and, behold, we live; as chastened, and not killed. (2 Cor. 6:9)

If there is one thing that always amazes me as a Christian, it is this: to see a life so beaten up and broken and yet still see the Lord bring good. As a pastor, one would think that my faith is rock solid and super big, but in reality, I walk many times in little faith. There have been so many times I had to deal with families and people whose lives were such a mess that I didn't think God could fix them. I look at a situation, and I weigh all of the difficulties on my little faithless scale, and to me, it seems hopeless. I know it doesn't sound good for a pastor to be hopeless sometimes, but I am just being honest with you.

I remember one such person, a young girl whom I was counseling for many years. Her family were church members, and this girl gave me a run for my money. From drugs, sleeping around, problems with the law, it seemed to never end. She only grew worse as she got older, and it was not uncommon for me to have to stand with her and her family in court. She tried to take her life so many times I lost count. I would just pray for her, and in my heart, I felt she was going to end up pregnant, dead, or in jail. We sent her to all kinds of rehabs and homes, Christian retreats, and what have you, but it was always worse. I never wanted to tell her family, but in my mind, she was over. Well, you guessed it; the Lord did a work and turned her around. I want to say that I hate it when He does that, but that would be horrible.

The truth is I would love to be proven wrong every day. Where my faith ends, the Lord's mercy and power begins. What seems over and done to us is simply the Lord just getting started. What seems hopeless to our little minds is only a better opportunity for the Lord to work a miracle. What's even more amazing is the worse the situation, the more incredible the deliverance. I would have to say I am proven wrong more times than proven right, and I am glad. I should know better as my own life is a shining testimony of the unending grace, mercy, and power of the Lord. It is a power so incredible that absolutely nothing is out of reach for Him. As we read through the Word of God, we see this formula completed many times over. From the depths of despondency to the heights of new life in Christ. It just never ends, and God's new creations never stop being new creations.

Dear friend, if you are in that place today and you are thinking to yourself, *Yeah, but you don't know how messed up my life is. God could never fix this*, well, think again because nothing, and I mean nothing, is impossible with Him. Maybe that's why the Lord allows us to fall so far sometimes simply so we can compare horror stories and the victories that came out of them. So many times I will get a call, an e-mail, or a text from a person who will say, "Pastor Scott, I have really messed up big time, and my sin is so bad that I'm ashamed to tell you." My reply to them is always the same: "I bet I can top you, because you don't know how far I have gone, what I have done, and I'm still kicking." God's grace certainly is enough, and I can't stop saying it. God's grace is enough and even more. So if you feel like you've fallen too far, well, you don't know then how much grace God laid in store for you when Jesus died for you on that cross.

August 27 - Our Hope Is Different

Who against hope believed in hope, that he might become the father of many nations, according to that which was spoken, So shall thy seed be. (Rom. 4:18)

I think there are more things written about hope than anything else. Well, maybe love is written about more, but hope comes in a close second. We hear a lot about hope these days, and I would go as far as to say that hope is on a rise in public usage yet ironically believed in less. It is kind of like the boy who cried wolf. You can only promise hope so much until the people start not to believe you anymore. Today our politicians have even joined the bandwagon and stolen another word that really only belongs to God. We hear of hope for a better future, a better economy, and a brighter day for our children. There is hope for new cures for cancer and AIDS, and yet they seem to be only words.

I remember this past New Year's Eve watching the people on the news at Times Square in New York City. The TV crews were going around and asking the people in the vast crowd how they felt about the new year, and amazingly, everyone they spoke to said that this new year was going to be good. They just felt it in their bones that things were going to start turning around. All the people admittedly confessed that this last year was a bad one, with horrific storms, a crashing economy, and political unrest throughout the world. Their logic was this: things could only get better, so this new year must be a good one. Well, as I am penning this devotion, it is actually July 23, a mere seven months since that new year's hope, and as far as I see, it has only gotten worse. One might ask then, "Why are things getting worse? And why aren't we turning a corner to better and brighter days?" The hope is all in place, and the optimism was on ten at January, yet still no move on the actual better life scale.

Dear friend, the answer is simple, and it is found in our word of the day—*hope*. Where do we really place our hope? See, hope is not a force that stands on its own and is self-fulfilling; no, hope only works based upon the resource where it is built upon. If I hope in potato chips for a new day, then it is pretty obvious that nothing is going to change. See, it is really about where the sustaining force of that hope originated from. Today people are simply hoping in things to change the affairs of men but basing the outcome on hopeless men to fix it. We are hoping in politicians, who are mere mortals, to repair what only a supernatural being can repair. Hope, it's really a hopeless word when we see it for what it is. I can hope I don't get cancer, but what can that word do of itself? I can hope my bills get paid this month, but if there is nothing behind that hope, what good is it?

Dear friend, the hope of man is just that—wishful thinking. We might as well be rubbing a rabbit's foot. The word *hope*, by its very nature, holds no hope at all. It is chance, a roll of the dice, a good hand in a card game. No, we have something better than that as children of God through faith in Jesus Christ. We have God's hope, which means this: we have a positive expectation that what God has promised will come to be. Suddenly hope takes on new life because now it has power behind it. When God tells us to hope in Him, He is actually saying that this thing will happen, not because we say we have hope, but because the Lord our God ignites that hope and then makes it happen. Hope in God, and you will never be hopeless.

August 28 - No One Like You

There are, it may be, so many kinds of voices in the world, and none of them is without signification. (1 Cor. 14:10)

Okay, so it sounds kind of corny, but it's very true that there is no one like you on planet earth. I will go further and say that there has never been another you. You are unique, and so much so that God made sure there would be no copies. Okay, for you sci-fi people, maybe one day they will clone you, and maybe the body can be duplicated, but a soul cannot. That twin or clone or look-alike—they are not the same soul, mind, or will. But back to our uniqueness, well, we are, and that makes you and me very special to God, so special that He specifically designed us to walk, talk, act, and be as we are. He chose your hair and IQ. The only thing he didn't do was make you do what He wants. For that, He imparted us with free will. A will to choose good from evil, right from wrong. To live in sorrow or to live in victory even in our times of weakness.

Dear friend, we are significant, and being significant, we have a purpose for that significance. No matter what that significance might be, be it in a deformity or a handicap, you are still uniquely made. Friend, no one puts the effort into tooling a new tool or item without a purpose for that item, like the person born blind or in the case of Fanny Crosby, the famous blind hymn writer. She was not an accident without a divine purpose. Look at all she did for the gospel's sake. Or like my dear friend who was a quadriplegic yet a mighty witness for Christ. Friend, we can lose an arm in a horrible accident and make a choice where we go from there. We can (a) be angry, bitter, and never leave our house again, or (b) learn how to live with one arm. I say that with all due respect as I don't know how hard that is, but I know people do it.

I have even seen a tripod canine. A three-legged dog. It's amazing that after losing that limb, animals don't go into depression; they learn how to walk on three legs. I must admit I find myself a bit jealous of that ability, and sometimes I try to emulate them by trying to live with depression and / or anxiety. Wow, it's not easy, but that doesn't mean it cannot be accomplished. Sure, there is pain, suffering, and defeat as we struggle along, but what choice do we have? Like I have shared before, if I didn't make a choice to go on even before I was better, I would be dead. Sure, it took every fiber of my being and the power of Jesus Christ to just get up, get dressed, and face the day, but I had no other choice. If you are at that place today when you just don't want to fight anymore, where you just can't seem to find a good reason to get up, well, I leave you with these words: There is no one else like you, and that being fact, then there must be a reason for you. Not to move on and upward is to tell the Lord He designed a product with no purpose. A product maybe with a bent this or a turned-down that, but a creation of God nonetheless. Learn how to be you. Learn how to live in the body and mind He created you with. You just might be amazed what you can do with one arm in Christ, and to Him certainly will go the glory.

August 29 - I Know I Can, I Think I Can

He staggered not at the promise of God through unbelief; but was strong in faith, giving glory to God. (Rom. 4:20)

Roller coasters are fun; well, they used to be when I was a younger man. I don't know why our tastes change, but I don't like going up and down real fast anymore. Speaking of going up and down, it sounds like the story of my faith quest. I don't know about you, but my life of faith is on par with the Israelites. One day I am on fire for Jesus Christ and ready to take on the world for Him, and the next day—well, you know how it goes. It is just so frustrating because I know I could live in faith if I really, really tried, but it just seems like sometimes I am just too lazy. It sounds funny, but I get faith lazy. I get myself into a place where things are going south; I think for a moment of God's promises, but that's it. I quickly shut off that thought simply because it would take too much mental effort to keep that faith tank filled. It is almost like driving my big gas guzzler around. I know if I drove it slower and took some extra effort, I could save a lot of gas, but it's just so hard, and I don't have time to drive slowly. The results are always the same: an empty tank that never seems to be full.

See, the problem you and I both have is that we stagger at the promises of God. We read them, know them, heard about them, and even seen some people experience them, but we don't think they would or could work in our life. Sometimes we even question if we are really Christians, if we really have the spiritual power that other people have. We even get jealous at those who are prayer warriors and wonder why we can't have such blessing and success. We even, in our bitterness, find reasons to put those people down and mark them as too Christian and kooky with their faith: "They're always going to church, always praying, and praising the Lord. Always have some new bumper sticker about Jesus." Yeah, it is easy to ridicule those who have what we want yet can't seem to acquire. Faith is one thing we feel we don't and won't ever have simply because we always see ourselves as just another person lost in a sea of faces. Today, dear friend, I have something to say about that bad attitude. If the great people of God had that attitude, where would we be today?

In Romans 4:20, it says, "He staggered not at the promise of God through unbelief; but was strong in faith, giving glory to God." What that means is, He kept on going even when things didn't seem to be going. I don't think we really understand how long people kept going in the Bible, how long they waited and wondered. For many great people of God, they endured for years waiting for the promises of God to happen. Yet the key was not in the fact that those miracles did eventually happen, but in what those people did while they were waiting for them. They staggered not! They trusted in a God who is good and held on to that. They didn't just wish, but they knew and were confident that God would never fail them. Did they have times of doubt? I'm sure they did, but they didn't stagger or miss a step on that long road of faith. And like I recently heard, what if the answer from the Lord for you is just around the next bend? What if you gave up and in just a day too soon? What a sad waste of years that would be. Don't think you can, know you can!

August 30 - But Is God Really Big Enough?

And being fully persuaded that, what He had promised, He was able also to perform. (Rom. 4:21)

Picture this—your septic tank is full, and raw sewage is flooding your basement or bathroom. So you call a service that you found in the yellow pages or online. You keep looking out the window as you wait for this company to come, and you are feeling better because their AD was very impressive. You are expecting a crew of men in white overalls with high-tech pumps, equipment, big trucks, and flashing lights. Imagine how you would feel then to see a man show up on a bicycle wearing a cut-off T-shirt, ripped-up jeans, and holding an old dirty toilet plunger. Your heart and hopes would just drop, and you can envision the tears forming in your eyes. Certainly this person is not up to the task, and if you have seen him before you called him, you never would have called him in the first place. Any hope or excitement that you had of your sewage flood being fixed just flew out the window.

In our struggles with depression and anxiety, we are often looking for that big fancy truck with all the bells and whistles. We read ads online about new-fangled cures, and the more impressive the webpage, the more excited we get, and the more hope we have. Sadly, many, if not most of those gimmicks, are just that—gimmicks. For if they really worked, there would be no one suffering.

Dear friend we must understand this: the more we understand the Lord—know Him, seek Him, embrace His Holiness—the more faith we will have in Him to be big enough to fix us. In Romans 4:21, we see that healing and victory are attained through big faith. And not just faith in something happening one day, but being persuaded that it will. Paul liked that word *persuaded*, and well, he should because it's a word that we must also learn to love and understand. We must be fully persuaded, as it says—which means there is not one shred of doubt in our hearts. It is climbing down a mountainside for the first time, and the climbing trainer handing you the climbing rope. If you are not fully persuaded that the rope can hold you, you will not step off the edge.

In reality, it's a wise way to live. We all too often trust in things that look strong enough but are only lies or false hopes. Yet when it comes to the Lord, that's when all doubt and fear should fade away. Are you ready to trust Him? Are you fully persuaded that what He has promised—He meaning *God*—will be able to perform it? I think some of our problems in this area can be likened to our septic-flood analogy. Sometimes we want God to look like the big fancy clean-up crew when He only appears as a man on a cross. We look at that cross and think that He certainly cannot be enough to fix my mess. This Jesus reminds me of that man with the plunger. What is ironic is—that's why the Jews didn't acknowledge Jesus as their promised messiah because they too were expecting a royal fancy king to save their day. Friend, Jesus is big enough, and remember that He is no longer on that cross. He defeated sin, death, and the grave, so He can certainly defeat our depression and anxiety. Yes, He is big enough, big enough to hold the very galaxies beyond the galaxies in the palms of His hands.

August 31 - That's Only for Them

But for us also, to whom it shall be imputed, if we believe on him that raised up Jesus our Lord from the dead. (Rom. 4:24)

If I don't mention it somewhere else in this book, or you don't pick up on my references to it, I will tell you now—I'm a big Titanic buff. I don't know why or when it started, but show me a documentary or book about the Titanic and its sinking, and I'm spellbound. Maybe it's the bizarre chain of events that took place that almost seem too organized to be by chance. The maiden voyage, the captain's last trip as a captain before he retired, the ship being called unsinkable, the lookouts who didn't have binoculars, the speed they were traveling, the ship that could have come to save some people but shut off their wireless system and went to sleep. I could go on and on as the list of things that went wrong couldn't have been worse.

Sometimes our life appears like that—a list of circumstances that fall into place that are so crazy that we even say to our friends, "You can't make this stuff up." I don't believe anything is by chance as that notion is completely absent from Gods Word. God, being sovereign Lord, knows everything, and nothing is just a roll of the dice. As to our Titanic story, another part of the lesson is the class system that was allowed in those days. Many of the people who were saved were from the first class. The horror of the scene of the third-class people was the real tragedy: people locked behind gates, trapped in their third-class section of the great ship while the first- and second-class people were reached out for first. Even before the ship sank, the class system was obvious to all. The third class knew that some things, or should I say a lot of things, were off-limits to them. They would often be made aware of this by signs and crew who would point to the fact that "this is not for you," which really means, "That's only for them." Imagine how that made those third- and second-class people feel. Is there not a lifeboat also for us?

Dear friends, many times in my life, even before I dealt with depression and anxiety, I would often think to myself, *The good things of life, the blessings of God, they are not for me but only for them.* When depression and anxiety hit, and the deliverance was delayed, I really began to think on this notion: "I guess God's blessings will never reach my life. I guess I'm locked out of joy and peace and trapped in this body of darkness." Today I want to shake that lie from your brain cells. Today I want you to understand that God's blessings and new life are not just for "them," but for any who call upon Him in faith.

In Romans 4:24, this truth is made crystal clear: "But for us also, to whom it shall be imputed, if we believe on him that raised up Jesus our Lord from the dead." I'm here to tell you today that you are the "us also." The promises to Abraham and Moses and all of God's children are promises to *us also.* Sure, there are some that are unique to Israel and to the church, but for the most part, God's promises to all of His creation are ours. Ours if only we step out in faith and believe.

September

September 1 - There's That Faith Thing Again

Therefore being justified by faith, we have peace with God through our Lord Jesus Christ. (Rom. 5:1)

Faith, sometimes I just hate it when people tell me I need to have more. I don't outwardly say I hate it, but inwardly, I find that little monster of pride poking out. Like when you are driving and someone tells you to slow down. Or when your spouse, friend, or even child says, "Hey, watch out for that car!" You are glad they told you, yet you hate being corrected. Normally our response is, "Yeah, I saw it." Faith, or the lack of it, is a lot like that. We know as Christians we should have it. We know it's pivotal in our walk with Christ, yet we are embarrassed to admit we really don't know how to get it. We see people who seem to have faith. We read of great missionaries who live and walk by it, yet we really don't know how to possess this "true" faith.

We pray for it; that's the one thing I believe we mostly do. We ask the Lord to increase our faith, and we might even ask other people to pray for our lack of faith. It is really a frustrating thing as everything in the Bible is based on faith. All the promises of God are based on faith. It even says that if we just had a tiny bit of true faith, well, the sky would be the limit. In the book of Hebrews, we read a lot about faith in chapter 11, which is commonly called the faith chapter. We see all the things that people did through this faith, and yet it seems to aggravate us even more. Jesus speaks of the faith of a child, which really confuses us as we think of children as too trusting, which could lead them into danger.

Dear friend, today I want to share the wonder of faith with you and the only place where it can be found. Faith only comes by reading and hearing God's Word. You can pray for it, but you do need it to grow within you. Romans 10:17 clearly states that "faith" comes by hearing the Word of God, be it through daily reading, devotionals, Bible studies, or a Sunday morning sermon. The more we saturate ourselves with God's Word, the more our faith muscle begins to grow. Now, one would think that it sounds too easy, and it really is if it weren't for the enemy's master plan; that is, to keep you from the Word of God. See, he (Satan) has come up with an incredible plan; it's called distractions, things like life, TV, radio, music, movies, magazines, hobbies, fun times, self, etc. All of those things, though not bad in themselves, have one common denominator, which is—*keeping us away from God's Word.*

We don't go to church as much as we should nor read the Bible. If we are honest with ourselves, we really hear God's Word about 15 percent of the day, and that's if we are being gracious, which would mean that 85 percent of the time, our minds are being filled with empty calories, things that fill us but leave us empty. So we have no faith because of no knowledge of God's Word. What's really sad is that even after reading today's devotional, most of us won't change a thing about our "God" intake. We simply love the things of this world more than the Word of God. There is no other answer, and it's the main cause of so little growth and progress in our walk with Christ. How far, friend, do we have to fall to really want God's Word and, with it, possess that healing faith?

September 2 - But I Hate This!

And not only so, but we glory in tribulations also: knowing that tribulation worketh patience;
And patience, experience; and experience, hope. (Rom. 5:3–4)

If you were to ask the opinion of the typical teenager who has to wear braces, their response would mostly likely be, "I hate them!" No one likes to have to carry or wear something that makes us stand out. If you have ever broken an arm, you know the discomfort and nuisance it is to have that heavy cast to drag around all day. I remember, when I was a child, a woman neighbor who broke both her legs. My mom volunteered to help her and didn't know what she was getting into. A person with one broken leg is a bit of work, but a person with two broken legs is a friendship breaker or maker. I don't have to go into the details, but using the bathroom comes to mind. I think situations like that are the line in the sand where we say, "I don't know if I can help you that much."

Now, if that's our side of the story in viewing the details of a friend with two broken legs, imagine the person who has the two broken legs. There is no love or joy in their heart for their current situation, that is for sure. Like anything that limits or changes what we are used to doing but no longer can, it can get old real fast, and trying to find God's peace and a reason to praise Him can be very hard to do. What makes this even more frustrating is the fact that it's exactly what the Word of God tells us to do. We are told to "glory in tribulations." Well, what's a tribulation but a trial of your faith? A faith test of sorts, and we already know how low our faith level is to begin with. Now, I'm not taking sides here, but some things are easier to "glory" than others. A broken arm, okay, maybe I could, unless it happened just as I was to start my new job that required two arms, which was to pay the bills on which I was already behind.

But when it comes to depression and anxiety, here is where I show some favoritism as they are already the results of any trial, which is normal simply because you are not happy about the situation. But deep, emotional depression and debilitating anxiety are not a broken leg or a lost job; they are a state of mind. To "glory" in that place has been the hardest thing I have ever had to do. To be praising the Lord while I feel like ending my life, well, it's a tough one. If you are reading this book, then you know what I am talking about. People who don't understand just don't know, and they could never know, how we would rather be dying of cancer than face depression.

Dear friend, I hope I made my point and you understand that I know what it's like, but that being said, it still doesn't change the fact what Romans 5:3–4 commands us to do: "But we glory in tribulations also: knowing that tribulation worketh patience; And patience, experience; and experience, hope." I'm not saying that I can always do it, but I am saying that we must! It is God's greatest test of our love and trust in Him. When it's over and we have made it to the other side, we will have gained great insight into the deeper things of God. Even if it is a little baby praise—still praise Him in that storm.

September 3 - Even Thinking Those Thoughts

For scarcely for a righteous man will one die: yet peradventure for a good man some would even dare to die. But God commendeth his love toward us, in that, while we were yet sinners, Christ died for us. (Rom. 5:7–8)

Unconditional love is a very popular phrase these days. We all want it and proclaim that we give it. Whenever I give marriage counseling, it's the most desired thing. The husband wants it and feels he gives it, and the wife wants it too and feels that she gives it. That is why marriage counseling is my least favorite counseling. Be that as it may, unconditional love is a real thing, but sadly, it's only real when it comes from God. Humans, as much as we claim to have it, really don't. We can come close, especially when it comes to our children, but as those children get older, that unconditional love meets up with some heavy testing. As people, it is one thing to talk about giving unconditional love, but it is another thing to know it's real when receiving it. Even when it comes to the Lord, we question if His love is truly and always unconditional. I know this to be true simply because I have sat with many Christians who have questioned if God could still love them after what they have done.

One nineteen-year-old girl sat in my office in tears after being involved in some questionable activities. She agreed that God could forgive her but wondered why He would forgive her. I know that feeling, especially after dealing with depression and anxiety. Those of you who have really been in the darkest, deepest places, you know the thoughts and actions it can bring you. I have thought the worst things that I have ever thought while in the grips of depression. The worst would be wanting to take my life, but also cursing God and even asking the devil to come and destroy me. Yes, I hate to admit it, but I have cried out to Satan and said these horrible words: "Okay, you win, I'm finished and beaten, so bring me to the depths of sin, and I will jump into whatever you place in front of me." I have had thoughts of doing unspeakable sins while in that dark place and even came close to its door. I thought nothing of my family or friends and became completely enveloped in myself. I have even crossed the line and cried out to God that I no longer believed He even existed and, as most of us have at times, questioned if I was even saved. I have called Him a liar and hated my wasted life and blamed Him for all my pain. Though all of these episodes didn't last more than a day, or sometimes even just moments—and though there were very few times when I ever fell that far—I still remember how quickly I wanted God back and how frightened I was that He could never forgive me.

Dear friend, I'm here and alive to tell you that He still loves you and could never stop loving you. Confess your sins as quickly as you can. Cry out to Him in true repentance, change your ways, and accept His true, unconditional love. Second Timothy 2:13 says, "If we believe not, yet He abideth faithful: He cannot deny himself."

September 4 - Rather Hug than Hit

Much more then, being now justified by His blood, we shall be saved from wrath through Him. (Rom. 5:9)

If there is one thing we all need to learn more about, it is the character of God. What is He like? What does He desire, and what really pleases Him? Is He one who can't wait for us to fall so He can spank us? Is He a god that laughs at our trials and testing? Does He like to see us suffer while He waits for our soon demise? Is He unfair, selfish, cruel, and vengeful? As horrible as all of those characteristics are, it's sad to know how many times we think they are a picture of Him. The world, in unbelief, has no problem accusing God of all those things and worse. Famous devout atheists have been known to say wicked, horrible things about the god whom they don't even believe in. That's not surprising coming from spiritually dead sinners, but coming from spiritually alive sinners like us, it's a horrible shame.

Dear fellow sufferer, I challenge you to take some time and study God's Word with the one intent of discovering what He is really like, just as if you were choosing a mate for your son or daughter and the background checks you would love to make if you could. Well, God's book is an open book, no pun intended. He is always asking us to seek Him and search for Him. To come and know Him. When you do, and you honestly read and study His Word, what you will walk away with is one thing you never expect—peace to your soul. Yes, even with all the judgments He pronounced on certain peoples and places, you will walk away knowing that God is very fair, slow to anger, greatly patient, and greatly compassionate. Yes, when disobedience appears, it is dealt with, and often it is dealt with harshly, so we can see how we should desire His grace through His Son and live under His law.

Remember, the law is simply a schoolmaster to show us how imperfect we are, and the cross is to show us what great lengths the Lord went to, to reconcile us back to Him. No, the Lord does not want to hit us, as nether any good parent desires to correct their children. No, a good parent, of which God is a picture, corrects only because they love. God never takes pleasure in that correction but only has remorse for it. He desires to love us because that is what God is—love. Yes, He is just, and He will exercise that justice one day after this life is over upon those who never accepted His forgiveness while they were alive.

Please, dear friend, learn of God's love and grace, grace so deep and wide that if it were an ocean, we would all drown in it. Grace is what God is, and it's not words that you say before you eat dinner. No, grace, God's grace, is favor upon a person who deserves punishment. It is the favor of God that He desires to bestow upon all of us, yet sadly, a gift that many won't receive because of their own choice. If I can ask for scriptural license here, may I say that God is a hugger, not a hitter. He will hit if He must, but He would surely rather hug. To know Him is to love Him in every sense of the word. And when we do know Him, we won't be so worried about things simply because we see how much He truly wants what is best for us.

September 5 - Perpetual Deliverance?

> *And when he came to the den, he cried with a lamentable voice unto Daniel: and the king spake and said to Daniel, "O Daniel, servant of the living God, is thy God, whom thou servest continually, able to deliver thee from the lions?" (Dan. 6:20)*

In the world of energy, finding the perfect fuel has been the quest of many. In the engineering world the quest has been to find the perfect machine. In both areas of science, the quest for the perfect fuel and machine has come pretty close, but as we all know, close only counts in horse shoes. In engineering, the idea of a machine that once in motion will stay in motion of its own power is a dream. Those who have tried to accomplish it knew that if it were possible, they would be very rich men. Imagine a fuel that could run our automobiles and provide us with power, all at the same time creating no pollution yet being plentiful and low-cost. Well, we can keep hoping, but apart from God, there is no such thing. And speaking about God, well, He is the Perpetual One. He keeps our hearts beating from the womb to the grave. Of the planets' and the Earth's daily cycles, well, I don't think too many people worry about the earth stopping its rotation. See, the only true perpetual motion and energy is the Lord as He truly does keep everything moving; and as far as I know, I haven't gotten a bill from the Earth's rotation company yet, so it must be free.

Now, why I bring this up is to give us all the peace that we need when it comes to our healing. If we see the Lord as weak and His power exhaustible, then we might think there can come a time when God can no longer help, a time when God would say, "Sorry, but you have depleted all my resources due to your constant depression and anxiety, and I am going to have to drop you." It would be as if the Lord was our insurance company, and due to our many liabilities to Him, He could no longer carry us. As silly as that might seem, sometimes we think that way. Friend, our Lord's power is inexhaustible and eternal. The Bible says that our God is a consuming fire, the first and the last, the beginning and the end—the Living God. We are not talking about a lawnmower engine here, but a power source of a magnitude not even describable in human terms or reason.

Dear friend, no matter how many times we call upon the Lord, He is and will always be able to deliver us. His power is everlasting, and His truth endures. He is from everlasting to everlasting, and I don't know anything that man has ever made that can hold that promise. Trust in God, never in man, and see Him deliver you again and again. And if need be, again and again to the tenth power.

September 6 - No Hurt Will Come Upon You

My God hath sent His angel, and hath shut the lions' mouths, that they have not hurt me: forasmuch as before Him innocence was found in me; and also before thee, O king, have I done no hurt. (Dan. 6:22)

In my struggles with depression and anxiety, one of my fears was that the damage done to me would be everlasting. I was sure that I would be forever affected in a negative way. They say stress is a killer, and during my dark struggles, my blood pressure was getting high, and my sleep patterns were completely off, as well as my eating habits. During my second and worst bout, I lost over thirty pounds. I lived on bananas and water. I just could not keep anything down. I would look at myself in the mirror and see the shell of the man I used to be. I would lie in sweat, truly watering my pillow. I could no longer play with my children, nor did I have the strength to simply walk up steps. My stomach was an issue, as also were heartburn and cramps. My stomach was in such a bad state that blood was all that would pass through me.

Now, I paint you this bleak picture not to disgust you, but to make you understand that even in this sickly state, the Lord never had intentions of harming me. Some might find that hard to believe, but I am here to tell you that it's true. At the time, I didn't see it, but I do now; and physically, I am feeling great, and if anything, I need to lose a few pounds. As we have shared before, in order to make it through God's testing and grooming process, we must never forget His love for us. He never wants to destroy but only to make us better.

As the Lord allowed Daniel to go through great testing, keep in mind that the Lord only had good planned. The lions never ate Daniel, but he still had to go into that den. Notice that it was God who shut the lions' mouths so that evil plan would be used for good, God's good, Daniel's good, and of us all who would read this account for ages to come. Notice also that Daniel points out why He didn't have to fear any retribution because he knew there was no evil found in him.

Like I have said before, the first thing we all need to do is to see if there is any sin within us. As women do self-breast exams, so should we all do self-sin exams. Confess whatever you find suspect and then rest in knowing that no matter how deep a pit the Lord allows you to fall into, no damage will come to you. There might be a few grey hairs added to your head and wrinkles to your skin, but if anything, there will be a Christlike glow about you. Just like when Moses came down from the presence of the Lord. Moses never looked the same again as the face of eternal mind had shown upon him. Depression and anxiety can take a lot out of you temporarily, but they can never take out of you the new wisdom and light that God has placed in you.

September 7 - Do This Well and Be Blessed

His lord said unto him, "Well done, thou good and faithful servant: thou hast been faithful over a few things, I will make thee ruler over many things: enter thou into the joy of thy lord." (Matt 25:21)

I have had a lot of crummy jobs in my youth and even some while in a bivocational ministry. I have washed dishes, cleaned toilets, worked on cars and trucks, framed houses and played lumberjack for a while. I know what menial, manual labor can be like, and for two years, I even worked as a landscaper in the sweltering heat of summer. Through all of the places of employment, it was hard to find purpose and pride in doing that work. I remember the real bottom of the barrel for me when I worked at a lamp factory wrapping lamp parts in newspaper and packing them in boxes to ship out. To be honest with you, I never took pride in that job and could care less about it. Now you might agree with my twenty-year-old attitude, but I was wrong, and I didn't know it or understand it until I became a Christian only a few years later at twenty-three. It was not an easy lesson to learn, but as the Lord moved me up the ladder to better employment, He also taught me about doing everything you do as if God is watching and grading you.

No matter who is not around, always remember that God is around, watching, waiting, and seeing what kind of person you really are. I learned more than once the benefits of working with integrity and honor even while doing some not-so-fun things. It was at those times that, through the providence of God, the right people saw me and my work ethic, and before you knew it, I was moved way up the ladder making more money than I ever believed. At my peak in the secular world, I had a private parking space by the front door with my name on it. I thought about who I was, and there were some lessons to learn there too. But the point is this: even while you are going through a difficult time, and working unto the Lord isn't your top priority, do it anyway. Do it anyway because He is always watching. He is watching to see where He will move you next because in these heavy places of testing, the Lord sees truly what kind of person you are. If you are to be raised to higher things, what better test to see if you would serve the Lord in little things?

Here are some examples to strive for as you go through suffering times in your life: 1) Always keep evangelism at the top of your list. What better true sacrifice is there than leading a person to Christ while you feel like taking a jump off a bridge? 2) Keep working at your employment, and do the best job you can possibly do. Work hard each and every day, never giving in to the temptation to quit. It's amazing what the Holy Spirit can carry you through even while living in darkness. I was teaching four classes at a vocational school to a class full of students while in the grips of massive anxiety. Somehow the Lord allowed me to come alive for the hour or two and, at the same time, stand in front of a blackboard and teach. Because

I was faithful in that, He later moved me higher than I could have ever imagined—ministry.

September 8 - I'm Falling, But....

When I said, "my foot slippeth"; thy mercy, O lord, held me up. (Ps. 94:18)

He said, she said—that seems to be the core of most marriage problems. Even in any disputes, there always seems to be two sides that never appear the same. In auto accidents, the two sides can seem to be from different planets, and yet somewhere, the truth remains hidden. As I have said in the past, of all the counseling I have done over the years, marriage counseling is the hardest. I cannot tell you how many times I would meet with the husband and then the wife, hear their story, and then scratch my head in wonder. It's simply amazing how two stories about the same situation can be so varied and different. What's even harder is to determine which is really closer to the truth, if there is any truth in it to begin with. I would often listen to the wife first; I would sit for an hour, taking notes and listening to her side. It would always sound very compelling, and I would find myself siding with her and even starting to have compassion for her. What's even worse is I would start not to like the husband and judge him in my mind. Yes, you guessed it—when I would meet with the husband, the same thing would happen in reverse, and I would feel so bad for that poor man living with such a horrible wife.

Well, that's what *used* to happen, but as I grew as a counselor, I began to see that truth is a very hard thing to find, and the best place to find it would be having them sit together and tell their stories. That seemed to help, but then again, no one wants to expose all their dirty laundry, so many important details would often remain forever lost behind walls of pride. I say this all today to make a point about different *points of view* and how things appear to our inner person. Many times we see failure and pain. We see a hopeless situation that can only get worse, at least from our perspective.

In my own life, I would look at how far I have fallen, and I would set out all the troubles metaphorically on a table in front of me and draw a skewed conclusion. I would say to myself, "My depression is getting worse. Nothing is working. Therapy isn't doing anything. Bible-reading, praying, elders laying hands on me, even medications are not working. Life as I know it will soon crumble into dust, and there is no one to help me—oh, woe is me." If you have ever been there, then you know what I am talking about, but...I love the word *but*. Even more, I love how the Lord uses it so many times in the Bible.

Like in Romans 6:23, which says, "For the wages of sin is death [*but*] the gift of God is eternal life through Jesus Christ our Lord." That *but* makes a whole lot of difference, and it should also make a whole lot of difference in how we look at our current situation. Yes, my foot might be slipping, and yes, it might look bleak but..."thy mercy oh Lord will hold me up." Notice this scripture in Psalm 94:18—I hope you noticed that I changed it because what it is really saying is even better. See, the writer is conveying a past truth to a present situation. He writes *when* as in past tense. When my foot *slipped*—meaning, in the past—thy Mercy, oh Lord, held me up. This is not a wishful thought but a proven promise. The Lord held me up when I fell or when I thought I was falling, and so He will hold me up again. Dear friend, the Lord, through His mercy, will hold you up.

September 9 - Fret Not Thyself

A Psalm of David. Fret not thyself. (Ps. 37:1)

In Psalm 37:1, I would like to focus in on three words in particular: *fret not thyself*, such a nice grouping of words and such a simple command. In modern-day English, we would simply say, "Don't worry about it" or even "Why are you getting so upset? Don't let yourself get all worked up." No matter how you say it, the command makes so much sense but is still always so hard to do. People would often say that to me while I was going through my dark, glorious days: "Just stop worrying so much. It's all going to be okay, just have faith and relax. Just let it go, just chill out, just take a deep breath. You'll be fine." I have to tell you, I am not a violent person, but after months of hearing those words, I felt like punching someone in the nose. I think what made me most upset was the frustration in knowing that most people had no idea what I was going through.

Dear friend, if you get anything out of this devotional book, I hope that it is this: *someone understands what you are going through.* You are not alone in this mystery sickness that no one seems to understand. I know what it is like, and until you walk a day in our shoes, no one has a right to tell us how to deal with it. Depression and anxiety are not switches that we can throw on and off. They are not a broken arm with a clear problem, which a doctor can set, and in time, it will all be well again. Our problem is hidden deep inside, and even the best psychiatrists, unless they have been there, don't even know.

See, when a doctor trains in bone setting, he can see the broken bone and be taught how to fix it, but with emotional problems, it's miles apart. The greatest psychiatrist in the world has no idea what our pain is. They can only read about it in textbooks written by people who have never been through it either. They might have patients who tell them how they feel, but without feeling it, how can you ever know what to say or do?

Well, our Lord God took things one step further, and when He became a man through the incarnation of Jesus Christ, He made Himself so that He would feel everything there is to feel in being human. God, through Jesus Christ, would be a man in every aspect of being a man but without sin. I believe Jesus felt a lot more than we read about. We know He wept, was hungry, lost a friend, and was betrayed, but I believe He also got splinters being a carpenter. I believe this because I know our Lord's character, that He would make sure Jesus would feel everything, so when He would tell us to *fear not*, He would say it with experience behind Him. Did Jesus feel depression? Maybe, I don't know, but I wouldn't be surprised if He did. One thing I know is that He probably had the worst panic attack in history when He shed drops of blood in the garden.

Dear friend, I can tell you today to fear not because God told me to fear not. I trusted Him because I knew He wouldn't tell me to feel something if He didn't know everything I was feeling at that time. He knows our pain better than we do. And He has not stopped saying these words—*fret not thyself*. God will come at the appointed time and grant us peace. Trust Him!

September 10 - It's Dark Down There

For Thou wilt light my candle: the lord my God will enlighten my darkness. (Ps. 18:28)

For those of you who grew up watching cartoons on Saturday mornings, you might remember a classic one where a certain rabbit says to a certain gun-toting, hat-wearing, mustache-growing cowpoke, "Don't go down there, it's dark down there!" I remember it well, and it still makes me laugh. Yet of the darkness, it is no joking matter; it's one of the places where the secular mental healthcare providers and the Christian-based ones part ways. We will discuss this hopefully in the chapter part of the book, time permitting, but be that as it may, darkness is a very real thing no matter what the secular professionals tell you.

Dear friend, this is why finding good, godly counsel is so important, and in a perfect world, adding a Christian psychiatrist would be the icing on the cake if medications were needed. See, the problem is this: if one doesn't understand the spiritual warfare we face and how real it is, they will never take it into account and so leave us only partly healed. There is darkness. Satan is very real, and he is part of our problems quite often. But to tell your doctor you believe this might have him send you off for deeper evaluation and place you on antipsychotic medications. It's truly a sad place that we have to fall into, but it is what it is, and sometimes, keeping our dark beliefs to ourselves and shared only with Christian counselors might be the best bet.

In my life as a Christian, this reality of a true spiritual battle didn't come to realization until many years later. I had no idea how real the darkness was and how powerful its pull could be. I needed to understand the forces that were out to destroy me and my testimony in Christ. I needed to understand that this battle was much bigger than me, and no medication on planet earth could beat it alone.

Dear friend, never underestimate the powers of darkness and never ever play with them. It's temping to dabble even as a Christian when Satan waves the carrot of temptation before us while our desire to escape our present pain keeps our eyes and ears dangerously open to his suggestions. Depression is truly a place of darkness, and the darker you go, the less light you see. True darkness needs to be dealt with through the Holy Spirit's power as we see when the disciples tried to cast out a demon and could not. Jesus's words to them were that this type only came out through prayer and fasting. This points to the depth that darkness can reach.

If you remember one thing today, remember this: darkness can only be removed by light. Not just any light but God's light of truth. Reading the Word of God, prayer, and fasting, they are all crucial. Having a team of prayer warriors also doesn't hurt, holding you up daily in this struggle, even an accountability partner to keep an eye on your journey. I'm not saying to stop taking medications or the therapy you might be under but to simply keep in mind the spiritual darkness that often comes with depression and emotional issues. Remember Satan's greatest desire is to have you take your life. In my struggles, that voice was a common one and verbal as well. It is no joke, and should never be taken as such. Darkness is real and so is God's light. His light will expel our darkness; of that, there is no doubt.

September 11 - Waiting and Watching

I will stand upon my watch, and set me upon the tower, and will watch to see what he will say unto me, and what I shall answer when I am reproved. (Hab. 2:1)

If there is any great test of faith, it's to be in a place of deep emotional pain, crying out to the Lord, and yet getting no reply. It does happen, and sometimes more than we would like. It is at those moments when our faith is stretched so far we would expect it to break under the load. If you have never been there, trust me, you will, and know that the Lord saves this trial for His very special ones. If there is to be a great working in your life, then there is to be great waiting. As we study the Bible, we see that many, if not most, of God's greatest leaders and followers had to wait through long seasons of silence. This is not a torture test from the Lord, but a muscle-building test. It causes us to truly stretch our faith necks way out over the chopping block; it's a place where pure faith is grown and defined. There are many people with faith but few people with great faith. As great wine only comes through long seasons of sitting silent, so does great faith come from long seasons of waiting silent.

Now here, dear friend, is the key to this very difficult process and how to endure it. It is not so much found in the waiting part but in how we wait. See, waiting takes on many forms. Watch people in traffic on a hot day in a big city. Not all wait with the same mindset. Some wait patiently knowing that the traffic will move again, but some wait growing angry and thinking that the traffic will never move again. Improper waiting always leads to impatience, and impatience always leads to anger. Find a person who follows the Lord but cannot wait, and you will find a person who gets angry at the Lord in that waiting. Again the key is in how we wait, and the answer is found in watching. To watch for the Lord while we are waiting is the method that pleases Him the most. It's a soul that has very large ears and very big eyes. A soul that holds its head upward and never lets it slump downward. It's a heart that is excited as it waits knowing that today might be the day.

I think the best example of this waiting is found in watching a dog wait for a snack. My pet Beagle is a great waiter. He sits patiently watching me eat and never gives up hope that one day I will throw him a treat, and it will be great. He never knows when that will be, but he knows through his past experiences that I always eventually give him that treat. Sometimes I don't give it to him, but he doesn't care because he knows and is persuaded that one day I will again.

Now, I know that might sound simplistic and not very helpful for a person in deep emotional pain today, yet if we truly love our Lord, we will find that it is the best thing to do as we really have no other choice. So today, let us wait for the Lord, and in waiting for Him, let's watch for Him also. To watch is to be optimistic that our Lord will come to the rescue just in time. It's to know that though deliverance may not come today, it will come tomorrow.

September 12 - When Nothing Makes Any Sense

Jesus answered and said unto him, "What I do thou knowest not now; but thou shalt know hereafter." (John 13:7)

If you have ever watched any type of craftsman, you will always see them do something that makes no sense. I remember when my middle son, Aaron, started playing guitar. He really got into it, and soon he was buying better and better guitars. I remember when he was taking lessons and learning how to tune his guitar. I was shocked when the guitar tech at the guitar shop put on new strings, tuned them all up, and then with his whole hand, grabbed each string and pulled it as hard as he could off the guitar body. I cringed as I watched him do that and asked him with a bit of tone in my voice, "Why did you do that?" After he calmed me down, he told me that pulling the strings stretches them so then on the second tuning, it will stay in tune. They simply needed to be pulled beyond their natural state to end up in their best state. I knew he was telling the truth when he retuned and played that guitar. It was sweet, beautiful music to my ears, and I would never forget that lesson.

Life in Christ can be like that sometimes. I might even say it can be like that a lot of the time. There just seems to be so many circumstances where the Lord does the most unusual things, sometimes things so bizarre that we wonder how any good could come from it. Our first reaction is always faithless as deep inside we get kind of angry at the Lord. Words like, "Why now, Lord?" and "This can't be good." Questioning seems to be our first reaction when strange things happen, and we know right well who it is that we are questioning. That quick response says a lot about what we think of the Lord. We are basically screaming out that He better let go of those new strings before He breaks our guitar.

Friend and fellow sufferer, I know it's hard, but I have learned not to question so much anymore. This life of depression and anxiety and all the emotions in between, it can be a roller coaster of a ride. I will go through years of feeling great then, out of nowhere, a bout with the monster appears. I will suffer for a week or two and then it's gone, and I am back to normal, all the while saying to myself, "What was that all about?" Well, if God is in control, and He is, then it was about something. I know in my life it's a great attention-getter. Whenever I drift too far from the Lord, or when a certain sin grabs my flesh, there is nothing like a shot of anxiety or depression to get my focus back on Christ. I have had times of great ministry blessings where I was able to minister to many and handle great stress with ease, then there were times when a very small problem would bring my anxiety back.

Dear friend, when all is said and done, it is best to remember these words of Christ: "What I do thou knowest not now; but thou shalt know hereafter." It doesn't mean it will go away sometimes, but that we will, at the least, understand why. Sometimes knowing why is just what we need anyway.

September 13 - A Little Strife Goes a Long Way

Awake, O north wind; and come, thou south; blow upon my garden, that the spices thereof may flow out. (Song of Sol. 4:16)

I don't think there are any of us who desire strife, trouble, and an upsetting of the applecart. For the most part, we are a people who like things to stay the same. We like to be in our comfort zone where there are no surprises. It's funny that as people we do enjoy surprises but not when they come from the Lord. We always seem to feel that a surprise from the Lord would be something not good or detrimental to our welfare, but if we know the Lord, we also must know that, that would be impossible.

Dear friend, sometimes the worst thing in our lives is lack of movement. If you are going through years of *living in Christ*, and it's as quiet as a church mouse around your life, then something is wrong. The Lord likes to shake things up, and shake things up He does. I often chuckle at people who claim that living the Christian life is a boring one. Well, they haven't lived my life, and add on top of that being in ministry, and *boring* is the last word in my mouth. I would have to say that the day I came to Christ till this very day, it has been a rocking and rolling roller coaster of a ride. I have moved clear across the country two times, was almost killed in a horrific car accident, have been pastor of two churches, one in California and one in New York. I've been through church splits, board-meeting fights, spiritual-wickedness battles in high places, and was suicidal, as well as extremely happy. From radio-show host to newspaper columns, the Lord has brought me to places I never dreamed possible, attending fiery town-hall meetings to becoming chaplain at a racetrack.

This last week, a film crew came to our little old church to film a documentary. Wow, what a crazy wonderful ride it's been. Yet with all the good and the exciting always came the bad and the painful. Getting food poising on vacation was fun, and being accused of all sorts of things by disgruntled church members and leaders wasn't so fun. Throw in some depression, anxiety, and thoughts of giving it all up, and you have a life set on fire by heaven itself. When I say *fire*, I mean good fire, cleansing fire of judgment, and lessons learned. After great trials in my life always came great victories. My first bout of depression was what moved me to become a pastor and write my first book. Strife and turmoil can be good if they are from the Master's hand.

Dear friend, if the Lord is taking you through a fire of affliction, scream out these words to Him, "Don't stop!" Don't stop the Lord when He is on a roll. Don't fight back if the Lord is trying to show you something. Let Him lead you as that's what He does best. He leads, guides, and comforts, and sometimes He does the best work through strife and trouble. If you have no trouble in life, then there will be no growth. I remember when the Lord actually started to rock my world. It was the day I prayed, "Lord, do whatever it takes to make me into the man of God you want me to be." I had no idea the permission I was giving the Lord. Well, let's just say He rolled up His sleeves and said, "Let's get busy then."

September 14 - Promises Are Great Things to Know About

Whereby are given unto us exceeding great and precious promises. (2 Pet. 1:4)

If you have been living long enough on this great big blue marble, then you know the truth about promises. Number one being this—*most of them never come true.* We learned that very fast when our parents, out of the goodness of their hearts, made promises that they never fulfilled. From there, we learned from friends in school who promised us things or promised to be at a certain place at a certain time. Then you have sayings like, "All is fair in love and war." Then there were the people whom you loved and promised you the world only to leave you for another. That first hurt was of great pain, and it is one that you will not soon forget. As we grew older, we learned about broken promises from employers who promised us the world, promotions, more money, and yet they were all just words. When we got even older and started to purchase items like cars and houses, we also learned the lessons of false promises. "I promise to throw in a year's worth of lawn care if you buy this house" never happened. "This car was driven by a little old lady only on Sundays. Trust me, this car will never let you down."

What's sad is that it takes time to learn about these false promises, and for a while, we tend to take people at their word. It is truly a sad day when we learn that even the best of people, even Christian people, can let you down. I would even go further and say you haven't been let down and had a promise broken till you have had it broken by a brother or sister in Christ. That hurt seems to be the worst kind of hurt and one that I still have a hard time with. I have been promised so many things by so many church people that never came true that I just don't accept promises anymore. When it comes to money, well, let's just say this—if you lend someone money, just expect to never get it back. That way you won't have to bear the agony of chasing them down for fifteen years.

Okay, so now that I have totally discouraged you, let me bring you to the point I am trying to make. Promises of men are just that—promises of men, and we know what the Bible says about them. See Psalm 118:8. But I want to talk to you about the promises of God. They are rock solid and unbreakable, promises of hope, new life, eternal life, redemption, comfort, guidance, help, encouragement, blessings, direction, protection, and sometimes even healing. These are the promises we need to build our life upon. True, it's difficult because we've had so many promises broken in the past, so it will take time to regain our confidence in them. Yet when we start to learn more about the Lord, we will start to see that His Word is sure; it is steadfast and certain. It never changes nor can be compromised. If the Lord says it, shall He not do it? Remember the Lord is not a man, so how can He lie? He cannot—which means that every promise to you is a promise that is on its way. Trust it and get used to trusting it. He is faithful, and His Word is truth itself. Now that's a promise worth waiting for.

September 15 - Only Broken Things Can Be Fixed

By reason of breakings they purify themselves. (Job 41:25)

I know, but I can't help it. I am an object-lesson-type person. I have worked a lot of different careers from blue-collar to white. I have been a tradesman and sat behind a desk in education. I would never change those years, even in those hard laboring jobs because through them, I have gotten the greatest object lessons and learned the greatest life lessons. For today, I'm going to go back to my mechanic days, when I had to troubleshoot large heavy equipment. Sometimes when something wasn't working right, the fix was simple and easy, but in those rare instances, it was time to tear that monster apart. Some of the hardest problems to find is when an engine, in a car or truck, shows a very slight symptom, one that is not major but can become major. They are very hard to find as sometimes their quirks are intermittent. Sometimes they are so subtle that you are not really sure if there is a problem at all. It was in those cases that an engine would simply have to be taken apart, disassembled, and, as we would say in the field, torn down.

Sometimes things need to be broken and disassembled to their lowest form. In the case of the engine that would not stop burning oil, every piston had to be removed and laid out on the work bench, all the nuts and bolts made into little piles. Oil and grease were all over, and engine parts scattered. It surely looked like a mess, but it had to be if each part could be closely observed and tested. Every bearing had to be placed under special gauges and meters to measure for wear. Oil was sent out to a lab to check for contamination, which would help pinpoint the problem. It was ugly and intimidating, especially if you were the one who had to put it all back together again.

Dear friends, in my life as a Christian, I have seen the Lord do more through broken vessels than through any other means. Sometimes, in order for the Lord to make us into what He really desires us to be, He must break us apart into tiny pieces. It can be frightening at times as all that we once were would no longer be recognizable. In that place of disassembling, we can look useless, like so many parts scattered about with a hopeless air about them, just a mess with no chance of ever being reassembled again. True, that's how it might look through our eyes and even through the eyes of onlookers, but not through the eyes of the Lord. No, He sees potential ready to be reassembled. A person who was once barely living in that past state but now under the Master's scalpel being prepared for supernatural missions.

Dear friend, if you feel like you are having some sort of a breakdown, then maybe you are; and instead of fighting it, let the Lord break you, break you so much that everything that was wrong and malfunctioning can be made new and improved. Maybe our healing is always delayed because we are always rebelling the breaking. If the Lord deems best to break us in order to make us, then why stop Him? Let His hammer and chisel chip and tear down what He must, for the sooner we are torn down, the sooner we can be rebuilt.

September 16 - Dwell Under, Not Over

They that dwell under His shadow shall return; they shall revive as the corn, and grow as the vine: the scent thereof shall be as the wine of Lebanon. (Hosea 14:7)

One of the hardest things about getting people to come to a saving knowledge of Jesus Christ is getting them to understand that there is someone above them. I'm talking about the atheists and agnostics of the world. It seems to be very difficult to get to the nuts and bolts of salvation when the person doesn't even think they need it. If a person believes themselves to be fully in charge of all that they say and do and have become, then it becomes very difficult to bring them to Christ. Let's face it. Most of us, even Christians, have a hard time submitting to authority in one form or another. Wives and husbands, when coming for marriage counseling, simply refuse to submit to each other's place as ordained by the Lord.

In our world today, we all seem to be brainwashed into a mindset of supremacy. We long to simply be supreme and above all. We don't want to work for the boss; we want to be the boss. Today, respect for the authority, even of local law enforcement officials, is so lacking simply because we don't want to be under anyone's control. It's pride, selfishness, arrogance, and downright attitude of thumbing our noses at the Lord. Sometimes we truly feel that we know what's best for ourselves. We will not listen to any advice or follow any counsel. When it comes to emotional issues, we can become so hardheaded and prideful that we let so much time go by, and we only slip deeper into the darkness without even knowing it.

In this battle over depression and anxiety, timing is critical. If we catch the symptoms soon enough, we can avoid much pain later. Sad to say, that's rarely the case as so many, if not most people, who are nearing that place of burning out or breaking down just won't listen to others who see it; instead, they continue on refusing to admit they have any issues and then it's too late. I have a dear friend whom I feel will eventually fall into anxiety and depression if they don't watch out; but if I were to even suggest that I see some danger signs, they would go ballistic on me in utter denial that anything is wrong with them. Pride is the tool that Satan seems to use to his advantage when it comes to keeping us from getting help.

Dear friend, the answer is to *dwell under His Wings* now! In Hosea 14:7, we see the benefits of *dwelling under* the Lord's care and guidance, not after the mess is made, but before. Sure, we can always run under the Lord's wisdom after, but that just means He has that much more repairing to do. The key is right now, while you are just teetering on feeling a little overwhelmed, to cry out to the Lord and say, "Lord, am I doing too much? Am I crossing that line to burn out and break down? If so, Lord, I call out to you today in total humility and ask for the counsel and guidance I need." Sounds too easy, but it is that easy. The only problem is most of us will never cry out before it happens because our pride has convinced us it could never happen.

September 17 - Remote Control Only Works If You Let It

So he fed them according to the integrity of his heart; and guided them by the skillfulness of his hands. (Ps. 78:72)

If you have ever been to a carnival or even an arcade, you have seen those games where you control a crane's claw in hopes of picking up a toy or stuffed animal and dropping it in the receiving box for your excited removal. I hope you know what I'm talking about as I have surely wasted hundreds of dollars over the years either trying to win myself or helping my children win. It is a frustrating machine and designed so you rarely win. The claw has no teeth, the items are stuffed tightly in the gravel, and the motions through the remote control joystick are too jerky. A smooth, gentle touch is what's needed, but due to our excitement of possibly winning, we always blow it. Remote-control operations are something that has really taken off in our modern world. Just about anything can be purchased with some type of remote controller, from our TV, DVD, and game systems to our garage-door remote openers. Wherever you go, there will be a remote-control something, but they don't always work. Batteries die, buttons fail to make contact, and our first response is frustration. Now, if we get frustrated when our little systems and worlds aren't working properly, can we imagine how the Lord feels?

Dear friend, in case you don't know, our Lord God has a dear plan for our lives. From the day we were born, He has been trying to get our attention and point us to the right direction. Like any good parent, He desires only the best for us, and it frustrates Him to see us going left when His wills for us that day is right. Now, don't get me wrong. The Lord is not a puppet master, and we are not His puppets. If that were the case, we would always do what the Lord wants all the time. Certainly that's not the case, but He is a good Father who has a plan. He has a road for us to follow and a path for us to take. At the end of that road is His perfect will for our lives. Whether we make it there or not is not up to Him but up to us.

Look at it this way—remember that arcade game we discussed earlier? Well, the Lord is the one working the joystick, and we are the claw that is responding to His direction. His will is that toy being picked up by the claw. Now, if that claw doesn't pick up that toy, it's not the master behind the joystick but the proper signal not making it to the claw. The Lord our God sees the dilemma that we are in. He sees the depression and anxiety that we have fallen into. He has a plan to get us out of it, a system to bring us through, and yet He doesn't discount our free will to not respond to His remote control. Every day He tries to direct us to the right help we need, the right counselor, maybe even the right medication. He speaks to us through His written Word and through His anointed preachers and pastors. What's lacking is our response to His skillful hand. If you feel Him pushing you south, then go south. If you feel Him pushing you west, then go west. The concept here is learning to understand the Lord's signals, and the more we learn of His Word, the more we will learn to understand His signals. Read His Word, know the Creator, know what He wants you to do.

September 18 - To Laugh, You Must First Hunger

Blessed are ye that hunger now: for ye shall be filled. Blessed are ye that weep now: for ye shall laugh. (Luke 6:21)

I love my children and have been blessed to have them. Three boys and no girls. I don't know why we never had any girls, but I'm sure the Lord knew what He was doing because these three boys have been enough to handle just in themselves. Not that they were, or are, bad boys; in fact, they are all wonderful children, and being a pastor's kid hasn't made it easy for them. From my oldest to my youngest, they have all given me many object lessons and sermon fodder. My middle son, Aaron, has been the most interesting so far. His love for the Lord Jesus Christ has been a blessing, but his irrational life skills have been challenging. When I say irrational life skills, I mean in relation to what we as adults see as rational. By all respects, his irrational life skills are no different than any other nineteen-year-old's. He simply wants the cart before the horse. He wants the wages before the labor. He is a great young man, but recently, the realities of life have hit him hard between the eyes. Hard work and patience are needed before blessings and prosperity. He wants the money, wife, and American dream at nineteen when that won't come for many years and, in some cases, might not come at all. It is called being content with where you are in life even if it's not your *dream* job or situation.

In the Bible, we see this concept clearly, and in Luke 6:21, Jesus Himself leaves us with no doubt. We must hunger before we can be filled, and we must weep before we can laugh. If I could, I would like to add my own rendering to this verse: "We must weep now to better appreciate the laughter that will come later."

Dear friend, in our quest for healing from depression and anxiety, we must understand this: laughter shall come but only after we have learned what we need to learn through our crying. Jesus even adds to this thought by saying that those who understand this will have a blessing and that we become the blessed who can weep now knowing that we will laugh later. This rule is so important today as it's so deficient. We are a *now* society, meaning that we want everything now. When I was in high school, no one had new cars, but instead, we all had clunkers. This made us appreciate what we had and strive for bigger and better things later. Today our children are given new cars as their first car, and we expect them to grow with a sense of gratitude. But how can they if there is nowhere to go from up?

Dear friend, Abraham needed to wonder and wait on the Lord before he could receive the promise. Moses also had to wait in the wilderness. Most all peoples in the Lord's economy had to crawl before they could walk, so what makes us think that we can have anything sooner than the Lord has ordained? If you are going through that season of waiting and pain, then remember that after that season comes the season of receiving and relief. If it were not, so then the Lord would have told us so. Dear friend, relief is on its way; of that, there can be no doubt. But to have the relief before the pain would only make us never appreciate the relief because we never knew pain.

September 19 - Daddy, It's All Broken

He said, "Bring them hither to Me." (Matt 14:18)

We all know the scenario. A child's toy just fell apart, and they are devastated. They come to the parent with a pile of broken parts. Daddy or, in some cases, Mommy are asked to fix it. I love the faith of children and, even more, so did Jesus. We often wonder what Jesus meant by His often mentioning about little children and the kingdom of God, about little children and faith. Well, it's really not that hard to figure out. Children have a very noncritical faith. If we tell them the sky will be green on Wednesday, they say, "Okay!" If we tell them that on Friday lollipops will fall from the heavens, they will believe that too. That is why we must be careful of what we do tell children as Jesus warns those who would offend a new believer who have that childlike faith. Just think about how our children believe in the fairytales. We tell them about Santa Claus, the tooth fairy, and all the fictional characters who supposedly wander our homes in the dead of the night in silly outfits. Sounds more scary to me than anything else, but the point is this—they believe us.

Friends, we need that kind of faith, and that is why Jesus points out that type of blind, trusting faith. If He says the Red Sea will part, then we should believe Him. If He says the rains will fall or not fall on a certain day, then we should believe Him there also. If He says that He will return for His bride one day, we should believe that too, and I think that most of us do—but. Why is it that we have trouble believing Him in regard to us being okay with our mental states?

When the bread and fish seemed not enough to feed the masses, what did Jesus say? In Matthew 14:18, He said, "Bring them to Me. [Give Me your trial and trouble and let Me hold it in my hands. Your hands are too weak and frail, but My hands are the hands of God.]" If we are struggling with fear today, we need to bring that fear into the hand of the Lord with true faith that He is able to make them go away. If you are struggling with a certain sin, bring that to the Lord and lay it at His feet. The way and attitude with which we bring them will determine what results we have. If we come doubting that He can change anything, then He probably won't. No, it's the faith of that child that the Lord so longs for that will make the mountains move.

It might sound silly, but in my family, when there is a major prayer need, I often bring it to my youngest child, Luke, who is eleven years old, and I tell him to pray for me as I know the Lord loves the faith of children. I know also that when Luke prays, He really believes that God will answer, when sometimes I get wishy-washy. I tell you, his prayers are powerful, but only because He truly believes against all odds. Now, maybe when he turns twelve, that might change, but for now, he is my last little prayer. Anyway, back to our devotion, let us all bring to Jesus (in belief) all our sins, worries, fears, angers, doubts, and reasoning. Let's leave them by faith in the capable hands of Jesus Christ.

September 20 - A Truth Never Spoken

And blessed is he, whosoever shall not be offended in Me. (Luke 7:23)

Through the year, so far we have spoken about many things in relation to depression and anxiety. We have gone through many scriptures, trying to learn how to cope and overcome this blessed monster of emotional pain. But the one fact we must not forsake is this: we want it gone. We can talk about the causes, the chemical imbalances, and the way the Lord is using this pain to make us better, but between you and me, I simply want it gone. I want it taken off me, wrapped in a big metal box, and tossed into the deepest parts of the sea. I don't want to learn anything more or go another day; I just want to be myself and laugh and enjoy the things that everyone else seems to be enjoying. There is even a secret part of me that hates this pain so much that I might even try voodoo if it would work—well, not really, but you know what I mean.

Desperate times call for desperate measures. I know that you, like myself, are ready to roll up your sleeves and sign on the dotted line of healing. Promise me an ironclad cure, and I will put my house for sale to pay for it. Up to now, you are probably going, "Okay, okay, I agree with you, but where are you going with this?" Dear friend in pain, where I am going with this is here: Jesus Christ can't be taken out of the loop. The day we gave our hearts to Him in faith, we became sealed unto the day of redemption. We are Christians and adopted into God's family. No matter where we run or hide, He is there with us, and being ever with us leaves us with this all important fact—we can't do anything apart from His will, and that means if we truly love Him, we must live for Him. I say this because any healing or blessing or miracle cannot happen without us being sold out and on fire for Him. We all so often wear the Christian shirt on Sunday yet really don't care to be known as one of His on Monday. Oh, we do when it's not awkward, but you know how many times you and I both deny who we are and who we really believe in.

The point today is this: if any blessings can ever come into our lives, we must first never, ever be ashamed of the One who died on Calvary for us. That means in all places, at all times, in all situations, Christ must be outfront and foremost in our lives. We cannot wear Him loosely but hold onto

Him tightly. We must clutch onto His Word and will at any cost and for any amount of time He calls us to wait. We are Christians! Before we are women or men, rich or poor, intelligent or ignorant, we are first Christians. We are followers of Christ, and the world must know it. Even in our depression and anxiety, we must never be ashamed to admit it. We must never be concerned if our emotional pain is a poor testimony for Christ. No, in fact, the Lord would love for us to proclaim our pain as Christians so they would see that we follow Him not for joy but simply because He is *God*. Once we put Christ way out-front even in our pain, then Christ will even be more prone to heal us. This might not be what your heart wanted to hear this day, but it is certainly what is true.

September 21 - Not All That Glitters Is Gold

And if any man obey not our word by this epistle, note that man, and have no company with him, that he may be ashamed. (2 Thess. 3:14)

If you are struggling still today, and your patience in your pain is growing thin, then you might just fall into the category of being prone to drink the pretty pink poison water. Pain is a tricky thing; it can lead you to take desperate measures. Have a toothache long enough and tying that string around your tooth and to the nearest doorknob doesn't seem too far-fetched. I speak of this today because time drags on sometimes, and seasons flow into other seasons. Fighting depression and anxiety can get old real fast, and to feel good again can seem further and further away each day. In my struggles over the years with this particular pain, I have toyed around with many odd and even evil thoughts of ridding myself of it. Just dabble a bit on the Internet under cures for anxiety and depression, and the sky is the limit, from powders to herbs and oils to electronic gizmos. Someone is always selling something for what ails you.

I knew one young lady whom I counseled who only found comfort in cutting (self-mutilation). This is a common direction people take, especially young females. Others find temporary relief in self-satisfaction, and one man I know became so consumed in his quest to find momentary relief that he would masturbate nonstop until he was bleeding. Others turned to street drugs; some to prescription drugs, which sadly many doctors are all but too happy to prescribe to you. Some turn to drinking; some to having affairs.

A very young lady whom I counseled in her midtwenties used sex to rid herself temporarily from her tormenting anxiety. She basically sold herself sexually to any man or woman who would have her. She ended up in a very bad place by the time I was able to reach her. Let us not forget the end-all in our minds—suicide. It has crossed many a mind, but for some, it has crossed over the line to where it was planned and, in some cases, executed. It is sad to say that in this evil world today, we will not have a shortage of even so-called friends who give you all kinds of wicked advice. Not to mention Satan who is the ring leader in the quest to end our very existence.

Dear friend, I add this very dark devotion today to warn you of the tricks of the trade. Not all that glitters is gold, and not every treatment you read or hear about is genuine. In our scripture for today, we are warned to have no company with anyone who does not follow what our Lord has proclaimed. That might sound easy to filter out, yet I have met some very odd Christians in some very odd churches doing some very odd things and proclaiming it is all of God. Please try the spirits to see if they really are of the Lord. Make sure that what you do and take is something that your family and pastor know about. Don't play lone ranger and look for pain relief in the darkness; you might just find it. In a multitude of counselors, there is safety. Consult with many trusted godly friends and family before you enter any waters that just might not be that holy. Prayer, confession, and repentance will always help in making sure you are able to see the light through the darkness.

September 22 - What if It's Not About the Pain?

> *For because thou hast done this thing, and hast not withheld thy son, thine only son: That in blessing I will bless thee... And in thy seed shall all the nations of the earth be blessed; because thou hast obeyed My voice. (Gen. 22:16–18)*

There are some Bible stories that we have heard so many times, they lose their relevance. We have heard of Moses parting the Red Sea so many times, it just seems to lose its thunder. We hear about the cross so often that every Easter sermon just rolls into the next. I have made it a point in my Christian life to take that which is old and worn-out and, through the Holy Spirit, add new life into it. My Easter sermons are not like most as I try to make the truth fresh and alive. It's the same with well-known scriptures and Bible stories. I hope you have noticed that I have tried very hard not to use typical scriptures to make my points in this book. But then again, sometimes old stories of biblical truth just can't be passed by.

In today's devotion, I want to bring you Abraham again. What was it really all about? Was it about his son being offered as a sacrifice? Was it about the faith test of Abraham? Or the picture of Christ through the offering caught in the thicket? Sure, it has many parts and many points, but to me, I see one point that stands out far above the rest: obeying God at any cost. Sure, Abraham felt emotional pain and torment beyond what any of us could ever imagine. Sure, going through those motions of preparing his son for death must have been gut-wrenching, and sure, the faith needed to get to that place was far beyond any faith I have yet to achieve. But again, what about the obedience?

Dear friend, I believe in our struggles with depression and anxiety, we often fail to see the forest through the trees (whatever that means—I really don't know). I believe we think it's all about the pain, the surprise turn our life has taken that we never envisioned from a child. We think only on how we can rid ourselves of this ugly, hideous mess. We are so bent on finding its cure that we never stop and sit to ponder why. Why, Lord, why has this been laid upon me? Is it divine punishment, a curse? Is it due to sin or simply a chance occurrence due to heredity and/or genetic mutation? Well, it could be any and all of those, or it could be simply for the Lord to see if we can truly obey Him.

See, I can obey Him when He says to go to church on Sunday (funny how many can't these days). I can obey Him in tithing my monies, watching my language, keeping an eye on my lusting, trying to love my neighbor, reading my Bible and my prayer life, but can I obey Him in living with this if this is His will? What if this is my cross to bear, my cross to hang on, the thorn in my flesh? Do I suddenly say, "Well, that's it, Lord, this is where I draw the line in following You"? Do I say, "Enough is enough, Lord. I struggle with money, marriage, my kids, and just living a normal life, but adding this emotional baggage just broke the camel's back. I am done and out of here"? Dear friend, I truly mean this for you to really contemplate: what if the only reason the Lord has allowed this to be a part of your life is to see if you will obey Him still? Will you?

September 23 - Stuff Happens

Be not afraid of sudden fear, neither of the desolation of the wicked, when it cometh. (Prov. 3:25)

When I look back over my life and try to pinpoint what made me so susceptible to anxiety, which led to depression, I would have to say one thing: perfectionism.

Obsessive-compulsive disorder, otherwise known as OCD, is what many of us have. We can spot it early on if we look carefully enough. It's found in how we play with our toys and friends. It is needing everything to line up, be in order, go the way we want, stacking crayons by height and books in alphabetical order. I never knew I had this because things, for the most part, as a child, went pretty well; my parents made sure of that. It was later on when I was married, had children, and worked full-time in a high-pressure job. When responsibilities became heavy and things didn't always turn out as I planned. Suddenly little things began to eat at me: the rattle in the car when I drove it, the grass not being cut just right. The more life happened, the more I realized things didn't always go according to plan. Babies cry all night even though you had plans of sleeping all night. People disappoint you, and hopes get crushed. Life just happens, and there is nothing we can do about it. It's a fallen world, and the unexpected needs to be expected.

I must say I can remember the first shot of anxiety that hit me, yet I didn't know what it was at the time. I was washing my car, and it wasn't coming out just so. I became obsessed with cleaning it so much that I couldn't stop rubbing the tires because they didn't look black enough. It was there that I said, "What is wrong with me?" My point today is this: if we don't prepare ourselves for life's unexpected stumbles, we will be forever tripped up by them. I have had to train myself over the years to let things be—which is not easy when you have full-blown OCD, to let things be a little messy, not always lined up, and left crooked on purpose.

In Proverbs 3:25, we see a warning not to be afraid of sudden fear, those things that pop up all day yet are not really that big of a deal as we make them. Flat tires happen, fender benders happen, the washing machine breaks and leaks water all over the basement floor. Children hit balls into your car and leave a dent. Stuff happens, and the sooner we are able to just let-live, the sooner we can just live. Sometimes it takes talking to ourselves in logical formulations: "Okay, so person A at work is spreading rumors about me, and it's eating me up—so what? God knows the truth." "My vacation plans had to be changed due to a sickness, okay, better being sick at home than away." "Today when I get up and face this day, things might happen, problems may arise, and that's okay because my God has it all worked out." It might sound silly to talk like this to ourselves, but from my own experience, it has changed a lot about me and my anxiety. Nothing is really that important, and the only thing I should really be concerned about is where I will spend eternity. Of that, I'm okay because I am in Christ, and He is mine, so I can let that one go.

September 24 - When Bigger Stuff Happens

And fear not them which kill the body, but are not able to kill the soul: but rather fear Him which is able to destroy both soul and body in hell. (Matt. 10:28)

Okay, let's be fair here—sometimes things happen that are big, things that really rock your world. Are we not to be afraid then? Are we not to get upset and be filled with anxiety? Dear friend, I have had to deal with the full gamut of life issues. From the death of a loved one, major money issues, being laid off from my job, sickness and unexpected hospital seasons. Those things are very real, as are the phone calls at 3:00 a.m. when one of your teens has been in an auto accident. I have lost all healthcare benefits and had to stop taking my prescription cholesterol medication simply because we couldn't afford it. Major problems do arise, and never when we think they would, and always at the worst time.

Only after my first few months at my second church, a week before I would preach my first Easter sermon there, I was involved in a major accident where my car rolled over four times. I was not in sin. There was no neglect, but it just happened. All of these things are part of life just as the smaller issues are. With regard to these things, we have only two choices: let them destroy us and wait each day for them to happen, or simply plan on them happening, and if they don't, then celebrate. Dear friend, in order for anxiety not to control us, and for our fears not to rule us, we must put every thought and tragedy in its place. I know it sounds odd, but it is so true. What I had to do was this: to understand that today I can lose my wife to cancer, tomorrow my little guy can get hit by a car, next week my home can burn down, and that's just the way it is. Now, what would that change in the big scheme of things? Sure, a lot of things would change, but some things can never change. Heaven stays the same, God stays the same, and my relationship and rewards stay the same.

I often preach this tidbit to my congregation: as Christians, we cannot lose. If death takes us, we win as we end up with our Lord. If the rapture comes and snatches us all away, we also win in a glorious way. And if the Lord chooses for us to live another year on planet earth, then we also win there as we have another year to spread His good news and another year to serve and praise Him. Yeah, it does get hard, and the big unexpected problems can really rock our world, but, dear friend, we must remember this: it never rocks His world. He knows about every problem that so easily besets us, and He is aware of our limitations in dealing with them. Sometimes we simply have to say to Satan, "Bring it on, for my God is bigger and stronger than you, and nothing can take me out of His loving arms." Of our salvation, it is the one thing that neither man nor Satan can take from us. Our place in God's family and His love for us are rock solid and sure. Anything else is just passing pains that, in one hundred years from now, no one will care about or remember.

September 25 - There Will Be a Day of Rest

And it shall come to pass in the day that the lord shall give thee rest from thy sorrow, and from thy fear, and from the hard bondage wherein thou wast made to serve. (Isa. 14:3)

If you have never traveled by car from California to New York and back again with a deadline to meet in the dead of winter and with a cat and three little children, then you don't know about the need to rest. In my call to ministry, that's exactly what I had to do—blizzards and all. On the way to California, it was potty breaks and finding hotels that would take our cat— we actually snuck him into a few—until my eldest son, Jacob, convicted us of being deceitful Christians. He was right, and on the way back, we only stopped at hotels that really allowed cats. Now, I know that driving across the country isn't the same as living a life of pain and suffering, but it is to some degree a picture of the rewards that are always waiting for us on the other side.

Dear friend, there are some things that are guaranteed in this life, and even the world jokes about them: taxes and death, but I would like to add another, which is rest. There will be rest from our sorrows, and not just because I say it, but because God's Word says it. Our God is a God of time, which means He is a God of beginnings and endings. Just read the book of Ecclesiastes, and you will learn about that. As sure as we all were born in a moment of time is as certain that we will die in a moment in time. Neither doctors nor millions of dollars can delay what God has already planned. But like I said before—on top of this being born and dying, there is also rest. Jesus speaks about it in the New Testament, as well as we read about it in the Old Testament. Because God is also our Creator, He also knows how we are made and what we need. Even God Himself rested after He created time and space. We are bodies and souls that need food, water, exercise, and yes, rest. When we get sick, the first thing we are told to do is rest. We are told this because even secular science knows that the body heals itself when it rests. If the world can figure that out, then certainly our Lord can. And as we go through the worst of trials, whether they be depression or anxiety or anything in between, He knows that we need rest, and so He will make sure we get it. For those of you who have suffered with anxiety, you know the crash that comes after an attack and how your body desires to sleep.

When I traveled on that coast-to-coast trip, we were kept motivated by fixing our hearts on a few things, that sooner or later we would get there, and that sooner or later a rest stop was coming. See, we needed to look forward to two types of rest. One was the little pit stops that kept us pushing each day, the ones where we could stretch our feet, the kids could run around, and we could use the potty. Yet we also kept our hearts fixed on the big rest, the destination, the goal that we set out for to find. That was getting to where the Lord wanted us to be when the journey was over. Both types of rest are needed on a long trip, and both types are needed in a long life. Dear friend, both types of rest are coming. I know this because the Bible tells me so. But after that rest, it's back to work; and even in heaven, I believe there won't be much cloud-floating time but ministry there too. The ministry of worship and ruling—I can't wait.

September 26 - He Does Not Change—and That Is good

Rejoice in the lord, ye righteous; and give thanks at the remembrance of His holiness. (Ps. 97:12)

One of the wonderful gifts the Lord has given us is that of remembering. I am always amazed at how far back I can remember, and with detail. The world talks about their supercomputers and their growing memory capacity, but they can't shake a stick at what we can retain in these pineapple-shaped spheres we call our brains. Sometimes remembering can be a bad thing, like when a traumatic experience has taken place, and we try to forget that pain. But sometimes God doesn't want us to forget some things, even bad ones, so maybe we should be careful with what we try to erase. Speaking of remembering, there is one thing we must make sure our minds never forget. We must never forget the holiness of the Lord. This is important is because when we are facing very difficult times, like what you may be facing today, instead of focusing on the situation so much, we should focus on God.

I love how David in the Psalms would *encourage himself* in the Lord. We need to do that, to remind ourselves of the unfailing love and rock-solid integrity of the Lord, to remember things like His power, forgiveness, grace, mercy, love, patience, and long suffering—also His ability to heal, make new, and create something from nothing, to look past our sins and see what we will be, not so much what we are right now. To remember the cross, the pain He bore for us, the blood He shed for us, His everlasting love toward us even when we were in our sins. To remember His ability to know all things, be at all places, and work all things together for good. Let us not forget the people whom He saved, the weaklings He made strong, the chickens He made lions, the blind He made see. All of these things must be remembered if we are ever to be what the Lord wants us to be.

In my life, a great tool in dire times has been to remember past mercies. To remember the worst of times when all odds were against me and the Lord pulled me through. In order to never forget these great miracles in my life, I actually started keeping a diary of all my prayers, when they were asked and when they were answered. I recorded them in journals and still have them till this day. Then when computers came around, I just started a file. I have been keeping records of God's amazing mercies for so long now that when I doubt, I can just take a peek back at some horrible times, read my own words of desperation, and then see how often the Lord acted mighty on my behalf. It's a simple aid that helps me remember His holiness and power. Today let's stop focusing so much on our current trouble and focus more on God's past mercies. He has never let us down, and He never will. Remember this!

September 27 - One Thing Troubles Can't Do

And ye now therefore have sorrow: but I will see you again, and your heart shall rejoice, and your joy no man taketh from you. (John 16:22)

I remember seeing a memo going around on a popular social-media site on the computer. It read, "All the things cancer can't do." I thought it looked interesting, so I began reading it. Cancer can't take away your salvation, your God, your place in His Kingdom, your capacity to love, to forgive, to bring a soul to Christ, to pray, to worship. The list went on and on, and the last thing that jumped out at me was the most profound, it was this: cancer can't take away your joy. Well, some might disagree, but with the children of God, myself included, I never saw anything but joy in the Lord.

As I have shared before, the greatest example was a dear young lady, with three very young children, who recently went home to the Lord. She was dying quickly of lung cancer that went into her bones. The last time I saw her, we prayed for healing but also for something more: we prayed for her family, children, and husband, that they would never hate God or blame Him, that her family would grow to know Jesus Christ. This lady had some incredible faith, and she had joy in the Lord. She had peace knowing that if the Lord chose not to heal her, she would be with Him for all eternity, and her pain would be no more. People would come to visit her and stand in awe of how they were the ones being sad and ended up being encouraged by this woman's light of Christ dwelling in her.

Dear friends, the world and its troubles can take a lot from us. They can take our money, our homes, and, in some countries, even our families. We can lose friends, jobs, health, and mobility. There is no question about what troubles can take away, but again, the one thing they can't take away, unless we let them, is our joy in the Lord. Satan has been trying for eons to take that away from us. In reality, when he is allowed to get at us and take many things away, it's not the things lost that he tries to get us to focus on, but that we would get angry at God and no longer have joy in Him. See, Satan wants us to curse God and cry out about His wickedness. That is Satan's goal: not to destroy us per se, but that somehow we would get to hate God.

Little tip here that I learned actually from one of my counselees is this—no matter how bad the pain or the trouble, the best thing we can do is praise God. That is the one thing that makes Satan shrink and shrivel. You can almost hear him cry out those famous words from that famous old movie, "I'm shrinking, help me." At the name of Jesus, demons flee, and through the praise of God, Satan is crushed. Today let us not let Satan take away the one thing he despises so much about us Christians, and that is our joy in the Lord. Rejoice, dear friend, because though we cry today, if we also praise today, tomorrow we will rejoice.

September 28 - What's So Great About Being Me?

The meek will He guide in judgment: and the meek will He teach His way.
(Ps. 25:9)

Seems all my life I have never been happy about being me. As a young teen in junior high school, this really became evident. Not that I felt it on my own, but others put the thoughts in there, and once they took root, I owned them. Before I knew it, I believed everything I heard about myself. I was told I was too skinny, not good at sports, ugly, my nose was too big, I stuttered when I spoke, I was dumb. By the time I entered high school, that's exactly what I became. It was then that I really hated being me. I was afraid of everything, had no self-confidence, and wanted to crawl in a hole. I was laughed at and picked on, which only enforced my inadequacies. I was meek in nature and was told that my meekness was a sign of weakness. My peers told me this, so I believed it. As they say, you become what you believe yourself to be by what others tell you. I didn't know Christ at that time, so there was no other opposing viewpoint telling me what I was *in Christ*. I didn't know that I could do anything in Christ Jesus. I didn't know that the Lord has chosen the base things of the world and the things despised by the world to confuse the wise of this world. I didn't know that, so I became the complete opposite.

Dear friend, if you are like me back then, you know how hard it is to like yourself if you appear to be so much less than the others. When I got older and depression and anxiety came in, I really hated myself even more. When my mother would tell me how special I was and that one day things would be different, I would simply say to myself, "Yeah, but what's so great about being me?" Dear friend, the word *meek* has been hijacked by the world and transformed into a liability. What's sad is that the Lord sees it a whole different way.

In the Beatitudes, we see Jesus's completely different take on meekness as He holds it up as the greatest virtue to possess. The best explanation I ever heard on spiritual meekness is this one: A horse is a very strong animal. Pound for pound, it can crush us without batting an eye. It is a walking mass of muscles and power. Standing still, unharnessed, it's just strength being wasted. Stand next to a horse or ride one, and you'll know how inferior you'll feel next to them. They are magnificent creatures from the Lord, yet the one other thing they possess is one we don't expect. Horses are very meek animals. They are not out to kill and destroy. They do not want to eat you or crush you but, if anything, to serve and carry you. With such a great mass of power, it is amazing how a little bridle and rein can control such a beast with the simple tug of the rope. They are truly *strength under control*. That is what meekness really is—not weakness, but strength, a force that appears weak but can do great things if just led properly.

Dear friends, we are spiritual horses, and the Lord is our rider and guide. By ourselves, we don't have much bravery, but with just one tug from our Master's hand, we can move mountains. I am glad I was made meek because the meek are easily led by their masters; the arrogant and bold-in-self are not. They are of no use to God, but we can be, if we so choose. Blessed are the meek, amen.

September 29 - It's Good to Crawl Under a Rock

Thou art my hiding place; Thou shalt preserve me from trouble; Thou shalt compass me about with songs of deliverance. Selah. (Ps. 32:7)

One thing we tend to do when anxiety and depression take hold is to want to hide. We want to run and keep running. We dream of having a secret place where we can go to like a certain superhero has in his fortress of solitude. I once counseled a lady who actually had a fictional place that she would run to. She called it her *Alaska*. She would often tell me, when times were tough, that she was going to Alaska. Obviously, she never went to Alaska, but she sure wished she could. My question to her was this: Why need an Alaska anyway? What would you find there that would give you peace? Her answer made sense to some degree. It was a place where all her troubles were not allowed to enter, a place where no one knew her or her past, so she could be a different person. It was a place that she could find rest and safety, a place of comfort and hope. A place that only she could go to and that no one else from this life could follow.

Honestly, it didn't sound too bad, but reality is what reality is, and that was just an impossible dream. I hate it when that happens, when reality comes along and spoils our plans. In our minds, it all just works out so perfectly, and we can't understand why it wouldn't work. Like my dreams of becoming a rock star and traveling the world and playing my drums. It would be so great, but it is just not reality. As to hiding, well, even some of those dreams are a type of hiding, hiding from reality and its pains. Now, not to take all the wind out of our hopeful sails today, but there is something to this hiding-place mentality. The Lord Himself speaks about a *hiding place*, a place where many of the virtues of that fictional *Alaska* are actually found.

Dear friend, when you are in a place of trouble, pain, and worry, when the rain is falling so hard that even your new umbrella can't stay off the drops, it is at that time when the Lord does provide for us a true hiding place, a place where many things are found, a place where we are preserved from trouble, a place where the Lord circles around us and where all we hear is the good news of deliverance from the Lord Himself. So it's okay, run and hide under Jesus Christ. Crawl under that Rock that is Christ, through which nothing can penetrate.

Now, note one difference about this hiding place of Jesus Christ. It is not a place to run and hide to escape life's problems but a place where we can take momentary shelter and then jump back in the fight. All other hiding places are places of defeat and denial. My wanting to be a rock star is only my running away from life's realities. Running to Jesus and hiding in Him is much more; it is acknowledging that life is hard but also acknowledging that God is good. We run, hide, get powered up, and then jump right back in. And if need be, when the powers of darkness chase us down again, we need to simply dash back under that Rock. Besides, even when we are not under the Rock, we are always standing on the Rock through salvation. Jesus Christ, the Rock, is never really too far away from us at all. In fact, He dwells within us and will never forsake us. So let's hide today if we have to, but let us hide only so we can get back out again and

do the Lord's work.

September 30 - Not Now!

He that giveth unto the poor shall not lack: but he that hideth his eyes shall have many a curse. (Prov. 28:27)

Ever been looking through the Bible for a scripture to lift you out of your current trouble only to find one that adds more trouble? That happened to me when I was searching the scriptures for help for myself. It seems, now that I think of it, I am always looking through the scriptures for things for me, my blessings, my good fortune, my health, my fears, my burdens. If I am truly honest with myself, I find that over the years, I have spent much more time looking for answers for myself and praying for myself that I just might come off as a bit selfish. Well, that can't be since I'm a God-loving Christian, one who reads the Bible and prays. I go to church on Sundays and even have a fish emblem on the back of my car. How can I be selfish? Well, the Holy Spirit is knocking on my heart right now even as I type out these words. I am selfish many a time, if not most of the time. I care more for me (secretly) than anyone else. Sure, I put on a great, caring show, but the Lord knows what's really on the inside.

It is like when I come across a scripture like Proverbs 28:37. The first thing that comes to my mind as I read it is this: *Not now! Lord, I don't have time for that now! I don't have time to help the poor or lead another person to Christ. I did that last year when I was feeling better, but today I am a mess, and it is time to focus on me.* Hum, that sounds logical, but is it scriptural? Is there ever a time when our present pain and suffering is an excuse not to care about another's pain and suffering? Well, if the Lord says it's time to sit back and recharge, that's one thing, as He did with Elijah. But unless we're 100 percent sure that God is telling us that, we have no excuse not to serve.

As Proverbs 28:27 says, "He that giveth unto the poor shall not lack: but he that hideth his eyes shall have many a curse." This means that it doesn't matter how we are feeling when it comes to doing the Lord's work. We can say, "Lord, *not now* with this person at work who is looking for answers. I'm too caught up in dealing with my depression." Think how that really sounds, dear friends, and take it to the next logical level. Say you're a fireman and a house is on fire and people are burning inside, but when you get there with your truck, you look at the house and say, "I would love to help them, but I just don't feel up to it. I'm tired, weak, and dealing with my own issues." I don't think anyone in the news would let you slide with that excuse. Imagine the headlines: "Fireman lets family die in fire sitting in his firetruck, says he was too tired and dealing with a lot of issues at home." No, there wouldn't be too many sympathy cards for that man.

Dear friend, the enemy, Satan, has one goal in mind, and that is to get us off our game, to get us so into fixing ourselves that we have no time for others. He does a good job at it as we are very easily persuaded that our needs are more important than anyone else's. Sure, we can convince ourselves that no one knows our pain. But that's not true as Jesus knows our pain and yet still instructs us to reach the lost. I'm pretty sure Jesus was having a pretty bad day when He was going to the cross. And I'm pretty sure He didn't say, "Not now, Lord, I have too much trouble that I am dealing with. Let the world pay for their own sins." Yes, I know this is a harsh lesson, but it's one that I, as well as you, must accept.

October

October 1 - Just and True

And they sing the song of Moses the servant of God, and the song of the Lamb, saying, great and marvelous are thy works, Lord God Almighty; just and true are thy ways, thou King of saints. (Rev. 15:3)

Today, as we start a new month, can we truly say and believe that *just* and *true* are the ways of God? It is a tough question to ask when things are not going well and an easy question to answer when they are. Dear friend, I want you to start this new month looking for healing, hope, and heavenly help. It might have been a rough summer for you. Summer is a very hard time to be depressed and struggling. We see so many people laughing and living life, and when we are not feeling just right, it can bring us down. Well, summer is over, and the fall is on its way. Sure, many say that fall is not a good time to be depressed or suffering with anxiety. Well, maybe so, maybe not, but I don't think there is ever a good time for pain. It stinks in whatever season you are in, but I will say this, God is not bound by seasons. I have felt my best on a cold November day, watching the leaves fall, and my worst on a sunny August day at the beach. Forget the idea that you need a sunny location or a better season. It is God who makes one happy and filled with peace. It does not matter what month it is or what place you live. I have moved from California to New York and back, thinking that sun was my answer. It is simply not true. Now, I am not discounting vitamin D deficiency and how important the sun is to our mental well-being. And I never suggest coming off medication in the fall but in the spring.

All of these things are true but not written in stone when it comes to the Lord God. Our Lord is bigger than moods and methods, and if He deems that your season of healing is October, then October it will be. This month, I don't want you to get all melancholy about the return to school or the end of the summer. No, I want you to get excited about the Lord of the seasons. You might have had a rough go, but this month could be your salvation and turning point. As our scripture for today says, we can trust the

Lord because "He is just and true." He is, friend, and because He is *just*, we know that He will always do what's right. Because He is *true*, His promises in His Word will come to pass. These are great words of hope for all of us.

Even right now as I am typing this devotion, I am struggling a bit with anxiety. It comes and goes in my life, and yet I have learned that the Lord knows what He is doing, and this will pass. I will always be okay again because the Lord does not lie. Also in our scripture for today, we see the words *great* and *marvelous*. God, in everything He does, is great and marvelous. So even though today I am struggling a bit, and maybe it might take a few weeks to get out of this cycle, God is still great and marvelous. My hope and prayer for all of you who are reading this devotion book, especially today, is that you will be excited for what our great, just, true, and marvelous God will do. He wants to start today.

October 2 - The Good and Bad of It

O lord, thou hast searched me, and known me. (Ps. 139:1)

Sometimes we live our lives as if they are a secret. We truly believe that no one knows our darkest thoughts and intentions. We go through life fooling so many around us, so much so that many who know us best are shocked that we suffer with depression and anxiety at all. Even in my counseling practice, I have had people come from my own church to talk, only to find out they are suffering and have been for years. It still surprises me how good we are at hiding our pain. In this modern day of the church, it is no small thing that a large portion of the people sitting in the pews right next to you are on some type of medication for emotional issues. That's just in the church, what of the world?

Dear friend, this should not frighten us but open our eyes to knowing that something is truly going on and in epidemic proportions. There is a mass moving of emotional darkness flowing through the world and yet a great denial of its existence. The reason for this is due to man's pride and misunderstanding of emotional issues. Because of the stigma of being on medications or struggling with emotional concerns, we develop this stealth persona. This cloak of everything-is-all-right-with-me illusion. Just as alcoholics are often good at hiding their demon, we become proficient at it too. And just as alcoholics become *functioning* alcoholics, if there can be such a thing, we too become functioning emotional time bombs. I find it so sad that we must hide and struggle all alone while together and through Christ we can find hope and healing.

In our scripture for today in Psalm 139:1, we learn two things that might give us fear or might give us joy. It should give us joy, but due to our nature, it tends to promote fear instead of the comfort it was meant to bring. See, God knows us, everything about us. He has searched us and is searching us daily. It also states that He *has* known me, which is in the past perfect tense, which means He has *always* known me. He *knew* even before I was born how I would be. This is not a thing of chance, friends. Our state is not one of surprise but expectation. God expected us to turn out just as we are because He knew we would. Now, that can anger you or scare you, but it should give you great reason to celebrate.

Dear suffering friend, if He knows all things and knew all things about us, then He also knows why we are as we are. He has made provision for us, and it is up to us to search out for that provision, waiting for us to be victorious even in our state of pain. So yes, we might not like knowing that God knows every thought, but I'm glad He does when dark thoughts of suicide come over me, thoughts so dark that I would dare not share them with another. Yet He knows, and there is no scheme of man that can dwarf God's will. Let us rejoice today that He is searching yours and my mind daily. He feels every pain and thought. Being able to do this means He is also able to know what's best to do to bring us through. No doctor can have that kind of inside information, yet God does; and because He does, He can plan out the best course of treatment for our long-awaited victory. Let Him in your mind, as well as in your heart. He is there anyway, but our pride of denying it keeps Him from working in us.

October 3 - When It's the Pressure

O lord, thou knowest: remember me, and visit me, and revenge me of my persecutors; take me not away in thy longsuffering: know that for thy sake I have suffered rebuke. (Jer. 15:15)

As we have seen through our daily devotions here, and through the chapter part of this book (sold separately), we know that emotional trauma comes in many forms and for many reasons. Sometimes, it truly is a chemical imbalance. Sometimes it is clinical. Sometimes it is simple melancholy. The factors that trigger our emotional pitfalls are as far and wide as the oceans themselves, yet sometimes it is just plain old stress that brings it on. Sometimes it is just life handed to you too fast and too heavy and for too long. It can be money problems, business issues, health issues, family issues, church issues, and relational issues. They can all pile on and on until we simply just cannot carry them any longer. Add to that the real problems of enemies that seem out to destroy all that we are, and it's the straw that breaks the camel's back. If you are struggling with that type of emotional turmoil today, then God has something to say about that too. If I can use a vernacular of the day, "He's got your back."

Dear friend, I really believe that we fail to understand what's really at stake each day that we wake up and face the world. It is not just doing our "own" thing, and that's that. No, if we are children of God by faith in Jesus Christ, then we leave our homes with a target on our backs. The more you serve the Lord and love His will, the bigger that target becomes. All of the pressures and time clocks we have to deal with, they are all part of the master plan of Satan to knock us down, trip us up, and get us so off target so we become useless to the Lord. If he must do it through personal stress and life issues, then he will. Make no mistake, this pressure cooker called life is nothing new, and dare we not ever think that we have it harder than any before us. Look to the World War II generation and what they faced daily. They faced death, loss, famine, poverty, and uncertainty. The great depression was something that we have never seen the likes of, and yet we feel overtaxed today. I do understand how this can happen because I too was born in the pampered age of the 1960s and lived only knowing good times and Christmas joy. My parents were of a different lot as were probably yours, and yet today we seem to be falling apart over the simple strain of just coping with daily living. Well, history aside and all of the whys left for others to debate, we are where we are today. Overladen with care, worry, and fear, and we don't even know why.

Dear friend, if we are to make it, we must peal off the fear of loss and ruin and place on us the fear of not pleasing our Lord. That is what is missing, our true fear and honor of God. If I'm depressed today, it is only because I am living for what the Lord never promised. If I'm suffering with anxiety today, it is because I am worrying about what the Lord already has taken care of. For the most part, our daily depression and anxieties are manufactured cartoon monsters that don't really exist but in our minds. Let them go and look to Christ. He offers peace, and He offers it abundantly.

October 4 - When Sin Sets In

But thou art a God ready to pardon, gracious and merciful, slow to anger, and of great kindness, and forsookest them not. (Neh. 9:17)

We have to be honest with ourselves. Sometimes there is no other reason for our present state of turmoil other than our own personal sin. This would happen to me often. I would fall into depression or anxiety then be so angry at the world that I felt it my right to dabble with sin or enter into sin, full knowing what I was doing. I would call it my premeditated sin or my willful sin. Sometimes maybe even crossing over into spiteful sin. Spiting who, you might ask—well, God of course! Foolish, yes, I know, but foolish is what we do best when we let our present pain block out rational thinking. It's amazing how we are so childish sometimes and ready to duke it out with the Lord as if He were a playground friend. What's worse is when we are doing fine, feeling great, and for no known reason, we decide it's time to sin. We jump in thinking, *Well, it's been so long, a little toe in the water can't hurt.* We do it, embrace it, and if you're truly saved, what comes next destroys all the progress we have made in feeling good again.

With me, when I sin, it seems to be an instant jolt of anxiety that hits me. Great sorrow for sinning against the Lord floods into my soul and also great fear of what will happen next. Anxiety begins to build, disgust at myself starts to foam around me, and depression becomes the cherry on top of my silly stroll down sin lane. I become so angry at myself for allowing this to happen again, for being so weak and willing to play with the forces of darkness, which I know are a lie. It is at these times when the enemy loves to really jump on us and our feelings by adding ones, things like, "You're a disgrace as a Christian, look at you going to Church and living a lie. What a phony you are, you're probably not even saved." Then next come the fears of riding these self-loathing emotions like a surfer rides a good wave. We begin to contemplate going to hell because we are not even sure if we are saved. It is a spiral that gets faster as we go deeper. We stop reading God's Word and even stop praying, assuming that it doesn't matter anymore.

Regarding going to church, we convince ourselves by saying, "What's the use as I'm such a hypocrite anyway?" We then begin to believe we are too far gone even for God's grace and mercy. We stop asking for forgiveness because we don't see how God could or even would want to forgive us. It is at those very times when those thoughts of taking your life start to fester again. Dear friend, listen to me! If there is one thing you need to listen to in this devotional, it is this: all the things I just read to you about how we are too far gone, they are all lies from Satan himself.

Listen—1 John 1:9 tells us that we can confess our sins at any time, no matter how bad they are, and God *will* forgive us. There is no sin or place that you could fall into that is beyond the Lord's reach. Please stop believing your own lies and the lies of Satan. If those lies were true, then Christ's death on the cross would be a weak one with only limited power. It is a power that would work only on some people, but not on someone as evil as you. Please, you know that's not true, and if you don't, well, I'm telling you today. Christ died for us all, and His blood covers all our sins. His blood covers past, present, and future. There is nothing, and I mean nothing, that is beyond His forgiveness and mercy. Please, today cry out to Him in repentance, and He will forgive you, and His love will forever be with you.

October 5 - He Will Be!

The lord also will be a refuge for the oppressed, a refuge in times of trouble. (Ps. 9:9)

So many times when counseling families going through a divorce, one of the saddest things to see is what the young children must endure. All they want is for Mom and Dad to be back the way they used to be. They want to know things *will be* good again. But instead of feeling the confidence and safety that a child should feel within a family, they have to settle for questions and doubts. I call it the will-be syndrome. When once they knew Dad was coming home, when once they knew Mom would always be there, it now becomes this haunting thought in their minds, *Will be?* Will Dad be back? Will Mom still care for me? What will be? What will become of me? What *will be* my new future, my new life? Will there ever be security in my life again? These dear children can only cling tighter and tighter to their little stuffed animals for so long. Soon they grow up, and there is nothing to snuggle with any longer to give them that security. The question of what will be is now forever a part of their psychology. I pray that you are not in that place, and if you are, please stay with your husband or wife, for the Lord will hold us all accountable for our children's emotional stability. If you can't, then make darn sure they never have to worry about what will be.

Now, in relation to us and our Lord God, when we are going through depression or anxiety, we also have that will-be syndrome to some extent. We wonder if God will be there for us when the times are hard. We wonder if God will be able to repair us when we feel the damage is too great. We wonder if God will be near enough to grab hold of when there is no one else to hold on to.

Dear friend, Psalm 9:9 gives us all the assurance we need when it comes to the will-be syndrome. He will be there for us forever and beyond. Psalm 9:9 says, "The LORD also will be a refuge for the oppressed, a refuge in times of trouble." Notice the "will be" part of the scripture. The Lord also will be a refuge, that spiritual teddy bear for those of us who are oppressed by pain, fear, depression, and enemies. The Lord will be a place to run to in times of trouble. I like the "will be" parts of the Lord's Word. In fact, we never read of a "might be" in His word when it comes to His faithfulness. Please, today forget about the might-be fears that invade our minds and souls at times. Never give them credence in the slightest. Remember our Lord as the God of *will be*. He will be there for us even though the mountains shake, though the world turns its back on us, though our minds are covered in darkest fear—He *will be* there for you and me. Of this, we can be most certain.

October 6 - Do We Really Know God?

And they that know thy name will put their trust in thee: for thou, lord, hast not forsaken them that seek thee. (Ps. 9:10)

The word *effort* is one of those words that always conjures up sweat and labor in my mind. It means I have to do something even when I am lying back in my easy chair with a cup of coffee. I don't know about you, but doing things sometimes is not fun. Getting up and going to work can be a drag. Doing what is right can even be harder. If you are going through depression and / or anxiety, doing things, anything, can take every bit of effort you can muster. As I have mentioned before, sleep is often a companion to depression and anxiety. In some situations, it becomes like a drug or one that we escape to. It is very dangerous to get caught up in this lazy state of apathy. Today that is why I want to speak about what needs to be done even though we feel like we don't have the get-up-and-go to do it. That is, we must strive to know the Lord.

Dear friend, this is not an option or a suggestion or even a good idea; no, this is God's command. We must strive with all that we are to know God's Word and, in knowing God's Word, end up knowing God. That is the end-all; that is the goal and focus of our existence. Once we know the Lord and learn His ways, power, and grace, we will begin to feel more secure in following and trusting Him. It is like getting into a boat that looks pretty shabby. It has rot and holes and cracks all up and down its hull. You have no confidence in it, so you won't be prone to trust it to take you across the canal. So many times we see God as not being big or strong or sound enough to carry us over to the other side. We see Him only through religion's eyes, and religion has a way of making God looking less than perfect. No, we are to look for God as He is, not as men tell us. We need to seek Him while He can be found, and in seeking Him, we are to also know Him.

As an example, take your favorite movie star. If you were a big fan that followed him or her around, you could be known as one who is "seeking" that movie star, but would you really be one who actually *knew* that movie star? Chasing God all day is not finding Him, nor is it knowing Him. In fact, it can be even worse as the seeking without finding can leave us tired, exhausted, and discouraged. In time, we will just give up and conclude that God can't be known. Dear friend, God can be known and wants to be known. He wants to see the effort we put into knowing Him and the zeal we exercise in that process. We will never have enough trust in God to get us to where He wants us to go if we never know Him. But those who have sought Him and found Him, God says this to them: "He has not forsaken you." God has not and will not forsake those who seek Him. Seek the Lord today. Let it be a greater quest in your life than even seeking to feel better. If you do this, you will find Him; and in finding Him, you will find peace.

October 7 - But He Is Doing Nothing but Hurting Me!

Sing praises to the lord, which dwelleth in Zion: declare among the people His doings. (Ps. 9:11)

Ever have to babysit a friend or neighbor's child and they are a terror? What do you say when they come to pick them up but "Oh, Johnny was an angel"? We see this all the time, like when our friends ask about the new dress, pants, haircut, or whatever they have purchased. We always find it hard to find a reason to praise them if we really can't stand it. I remember this group of three elderly men in church. They wanted desperately to perform a few songs for the church, yet I knew how lacking in talent they were. I decided they were so bad that I couldn't have them face the embarrassment of a morning service, so I created a special night for music and song. They played and were very happy, but when they asked me all a glow about how they sounded, what could I do but say, "It sounded good guys"? I knew I lied, and what's worse was how painful it was to come up with that praise. It was actually a traumatic thing for me as I love music but can't stand it performed badly. Well, that was beyond bad, and to this day, even the slightest bit of praise still eludes me.

Another area where I find this hard is with automobiles as I am a lover of cars and trucks and anything that has an engine in it. When a person buys a new car and asks me all excited about what I think, well, what if I think it's the ugliest car to hit the market? Oh well, but it reminds me of going through painful times in life and knowing that the Lord also wants praise for it. Over and over again, we are told to praise the Lord for everything, which is fine when I just had a great day and all is right with the world. What's hard is when pain, torment, and grief are overflowing my soul, and I am still called to sing praises. Notice it is not just to give praises but to sing praises. Ouch! It's one thing to say, "Thanks, Lord, for this season of depression," but it's another thing altogether to have to sing about it: "Oh, Lord, how I love this day of tears and pain, sorrow and grief, la la la." Now, though I am being sarcastic about it, does not mean we can pass on this command of God. No, we are to praise Him through the storm, and not just by mouthing some words, but in sincerity and truth; meaning, we must really feel it and believe it. Some might say to that thought, "Well, how can I really be happy and praise the Lord if I'm so miserable? How can I do it without faking it?"

Dear friend, here is the point we so often miss. If we truly love the Lord with all of our mind, heart, soul, and strength, then it won't be hard. It won't be hard because we know that God is doing what's best all the time, even when it hurts. An example would be to need surgery, and when the doctor says he has to put you under, cut open your gut, and when you are done, it will be weeks of pain and healing—then thank your doctor for that surgery. Well, funny thing is, we do thank our doctors, but why? We trust them because we know they know what they are doing, so even if they have to cut us with a knife, we can still praise them. Friend, if we had as much faith in God as we do in our doctors, then we would be praising Him all day long, even when we are going through painful life surgery. Praise Him because it's the greatest sign of our trust in Him you can show.

October 8 - It's as Clear as Day

He forgetteth not the cry of the humble. (Ps. 9:12)

Well, I have been a Christian for a long time, and in those early years, I did question a lot of things. As new believers, we do have our moments of wondering what is real and what is not. I know I must have asked Jesus into my heart a half-dozen times before I felt for certain that He was really in there. As new believers in Christ, we are very similar to children. We have a lot to learn, and sometimes, it does take that burnt finger to really understand that fire burns. In my case, the lesson that really sunk into to me was that of pride versus humility. It took a while, but when it sunk in, it stayed sunk in and has never left.

Dear friend, if there is one thing that is always a constant and ever-present truth in God's Word, it is that God truly does bring down the proud. I have never been so amazed in my Christian walk as when I would test this truth. It never failed and, like clockwork, was always right in my face. Whenever I would boast about who or what I did or what I made or had achieved, like a shot of lightning across the sky, I would be humbled. It never failed, and to this day, it never fails. I have to say it is the greatest proof I ever needed to see that God is very real. On the flip side, it was just as evident. When I would truly humble myself and do things quietly for no one to see but the Lord, again that shot of lightning would hit me, but this time to lift me up.

I remember at one particular place of employment this truth was ever working. I would let others take credit for what I did, and somehow the boss would find out the truth, and I would get the raise or promotion. Yet when I would boast about my new plan or idea, it would fall flat on its face, and I would be left empty. Humility is truly an attribute of God that we should all seek, one that is so rarely seen today for that matter. A truly humble person, let alone a Christian, is almost nonexistent. We have become a people of boasters and braggarts. We have fallen so deep in love with ourselves that our love for the Lord is nowhere to be found. If you don't believe this, then ask yourself how many times you mention the Lord's name in a day as compared to how many times you mention yours—as in "I did this" or "I did that" or "I'm going here" or "I bought that." Just look at the social-media sites on the Internet and see where the focus is. I'm just amazed how so many people feel the need to tell the world that they are having a cup of coffee now, or they are brushing their teeth now. The reason why I bring this point up is because—the Lord only raises up the humble, and if we are not humble, we can forget about ever being healed.

Dear friend, if you are struggling with depression or anxiety, then let people know. Don't be all prideful because of what people might think of you. What we need to focus on instead is caring more about what God thinks of us. Today let's all put our best foot forward and come clean about who we really are. To say, "Dear Lord, I am lost, broken, a sinner, and afraid." To say that and mean it might just be the greatest step you could make in becoming the new creation that Christ called you to be. Remember in Psalm 9:12: "God forgets not the cry of the humble." The flip side of that then would be—He will not hear the cry of the proud. It is something to think about.

October 9 - When I Can't Lift Myself Up

Have mercy upon me, O lord; consider my trouble which I suffer of them that hate me, thou that liftest me up from the gates of death. (Ps. 9:13)

In the day in which we now live, a lot of things have changed. Our morals, ethics, and what makes us tick are all bent and distorted. It is sad to say, but a lot of what we struggle with today is due in part by what our society has created. We have, for the most part, become a cradle society, meaning that we haven't gotten far past the womb in self-sufficiency. We have been coddled so much from childhood to adulthood that we still need to run to our parents for help. A recent study that I read said that as of 2013, 36 percent of young adults in their thirties are still living at home.

According to how things look, there doesn't seem to be any signs of that changing. I began to notice this forever-young syndrome while my middle son, Aaron, was playing soccer. At the end of the season when they gave out trophies and awards for best player and things like that, they also made sure that everyone got a trophy. When I asked why, they said, "So everyone feels good about themselves." Basically, so no one feels sad.

Dear friends, that is completely against the Word of God because it clearly says, "There is a time to laugh and a time to cry." Crying and losing are part of life, and if we are trained to think otherwise, guess what happens? Depression and a long list of other emotional issues enter. I have to admit what really made this clear to me was when my son said, "Dad this trophy doesn't mean anything because everyone got one". He was right and that is what is so wrong with us today. Now that's the bad news and it is just how it is. I don't think we can ever turn back the tide of what we allowed to happen. We will continue to be a world filled with sad, disappointed, unthankful, depressed, and scared people. Yet the good news is this, God always has a way or a provision to combat our failings.

In Psalm 9:13 we find the peace we so desperately need today. It is knowing that the Lord has considered our trouble and has adjusted the comfort we need for the occasion. He knows we are a mess down here, and He knows just what we need. It is not really anything new; it is what we all always needed. We need God to lift us because we can't or never really could lift ourselves up. Today it is just more obvious than ever before. Dear friend, if you are hurting this day and thinking that your situation is so unique and difficult that even God can't figure it out, well, think again. Our Lord has considered our trouble from every perspective and direction and knows just what to do. All we have to do is believe that He knows all these things and has made a way to lift us up out of the pit of despair we may be in. He knows, and that's all we need to know sometimes.

October 10 - Looking for That Calm

And He saith unto them, "Why are ye fearful, O ye of little faith?" Then He arose, and rebuked the winds and the sea; and there was a great calm. (Matt. 8:26)

Today I want to focus on anxiety. Though depression and anxiety are often companion problems, each one of them deserves its own dissection. I have often asked myself what I thought was the worst thing I had to endure, depression or anxiety. It is really a tough one because they are both so overwhelming in their own ways. What I will say is the anxiety, when dialed in at ten on the intensity scale, sure comes close to beating out everything else.

I remember one season in my life when, through the mistake of my doctor who was just a general practitioner and probably shouldn't have been giving out such medications in such an extreme case as mine, I was given meds that increased my anxiety instead of controlling it. He was treating me for what he thought was depression, but really was rooted in anxiety. Well, it was like pouring gasoline on a raging fire. My anxiety was so out of control that I felt as if I would crawl out of my skin. I couldn't sleep, rest, work, or do anything. All I could do was find a dark corner and rock back and forth, clutching my knees to my chest. What was so horrific about this was the lack of relief. There was simply no place to go, nothing to take or do. It was like being on fire but having no water around to put it out. I would spend hours weeping uncontrollably, crying out to God and sometimes pacing all night long begging with all of my heart to have one single moment of peace. It was hell, and now that I remember those days, I guess it was worse than depression as in depression, at least I could crawl under my blanket and sleep. This was torture; there is just no other way to describe it. No prayer or person or scripture could comfort me. What I needed was (1) to get off this medication, (2) find a doctor who knew what he was doing, and (3) find the great calm of God that only He could offer.

Dear friend, Jesus is the great physician and offers the greatest sedative known to man. It is the comfort and peace of God Himself. Now, I am not saying that at times certain sedatives are not needed, as I surely wish I could have found one during those days, but that God is ultimately what we need to find to have true lasting calm. Today if you're struggling with anxiety from mild to wild, well, the answer is always the same. We need to call on the Lord and seek His direction and wisdom. Sometimes He will give it directly or sometimes He will give calm by directing us to where and whom we need to see to get us the help we need. We must never forget that the Lord uses men and their wisdom many times to heal our wounds. They come in the form of godly counselors, therapists, or even psychiatrists. These things are not against God but can be used by God just as God has offered the cures to so many sicknesses through the science of man. But again, it all starts with finding that calm that only comes from Christ, a calm that either leads us to help or a calm of God that is the help.

October 11 - Abounding in Hope

> *Now the God of hope fill you with all joy and peace in believing, that ye may abound in hope, through the power of the Holy Ghost. (Rom. 15:13)*

For most of us, following God and calling ourselves a Christian isn't that big of a deal. Most people that you meet in fact will say they follow God and / or belong to some church or organized religion. The question we really need to ask ourselves is this: If believing in God or being part of some denomination is the key to peace in our hearts, then why are there so many miserable people? Sometimes I get in trouble for asking these types of questions, but I say if they are out there, we should ask them. So what is going on? Why is there so much depression, pain, fear, and sorrow? Why aren't Christians walking around with smiles on their faces and a skip in their step? Well, first off, I don't even think the apostles were walking around laughing and dancing. No, life is a grave and serious place, and if we are laughing all day long, then we might have a problem there too. Life is filled with trouble and trials, and the very nature of those ingredients only fosters a wise and careful demeanor. Sure, we can smile and enjoy the blessings of the Lord, but some things need deep introspection as we ponder life, death, and living for Christ. So like I tell all my counselees, in living this life, don't strive for a ten-level day and don't settle for a one-level day. What's realistic and what the Lord only promises in this life is a level five-day. That's a day somewhere in the middle between happy and sad. Now that being said, how do we at least acquire that level in life? The answer, as always, is found in scripture.

In Romans 15:13, we see some of the keys to finding that *abundant hope* to sustain that level five through the best and worst of times. Romans 15:13 says, "Now the God of hope fill you with all joy and peace in believing, that ye may abound in hope, through the power of the Holy Ghost." Not to go into a deep Bible study, but there is much truth and intricate detail here: A) the God of hope, do you know Him? B) He is the One who needs to fill you, not the world or its ways. C) What does He fill you with but all *joy* and *peace*. D) How is this achieved but by believing, which means much more than going to church but devouring all that is of God? E) And if we come to know the Lord in such a deep way, the results are abounding in hope, so much so that no situation or storm can upset its control. F) And lastly, to keep all of this working as God intended, it must be through the power of the Holy Spirit, meaning that of our own strength, we cannot ever achieve it.

So, dear friend, this *abundant hope* is not so much a place of ecstasy but a place of sustainability. It is abounding enough to hold a level five through the worst of times. It is holding at DEFCON 5 through the greatest and the worst days of living. I think that's the best we can and should hope for on planet earth—for ecstasy only happens in Heaven.

October 12 - Our Core Desires

> *Better is the sight of the eyes than the wandering of the desire: this is also vanity and vexation of spirit. (Eccles. 6:9)*

There is a lot of talk these days about core beliefs. We hear this term a lot in political circles. What are we really all about? What are our core desires and goals at the end of the day? It is a scary question to ask, and one I don't think most of us want to be asked. Sure, we like to ask other people what they are really about, but we don't like it asked of ourselves, especially by God. Imagine if you will this scenario: the Lord Himself asks you to write a paper describing what you really are and what you really stand for. Now, you know that He already knows the truth, so lying is out of the question, yet somehow you think if you word it just right, you can trick Him. I'm glad I don't have to write that paper because, like I said, the Lord already knows the answer. The question really is, do we know the answer?

Dear friend, I want you to truly think about this today. What you decide in this area really will define what and who you are. It will also define and maybe explain why healing is not coming so speedily. No, we are not talking about perfection but about direction. What direction is your life ultimately pointed? Is it due north or due south? Are we forever on a quest for holiness or for happiness? Wow, those words truly send shivers down my spine. What am I truly living for, holiness or happiness? God wants to know. Heaven wants to know. Everything that we are and do is based on that answer. Are we here to have a good time, laugh, play, retire, and die, or is there something more, something bigger? I tell you if we are here to be happy, then we can't be here to be holy. And if that is the case, then we really care nothing about Jesus Christ or His will. Our goal then is selfish and evil and has nothing to do with the Lord; but if we are here to be holy as unto the Lord, then we will end up happy. Quite a conundrum, I know, but one that we must come to grips with.

Ecclesiastes 6:9 says, "Better is the sight of the eyes than the wandering of the desire: this is also vanity and vexation of spirit." This scripture is a perplexing one open to different people's understanding, but there can only be one interpretation. Friend, desire and sight are as far apart as holiness versus happiness. It is better to focus our lives on seeing the truth and running to it than to use our eyes to see what we desire and running to that. If that is the case, then we can't be desiring God if we are desiring everything else instead. Again, in our quest for healing and deliverance, we must ask why. Why would God want to deliver us from our pain when, as soon as we are delivered, we will run back to our desires? But if He knows that what I desire is only holiness, then He would quickly deliver us when our crucible recreation is complete. Who we are means much to the Lord; what we really desire means everything.

October 13 - Even if That Happens

> *God is our refuge and strength, a very present help in trouble.*
> *Therefore will not we fear, though the earth be removed, and though*
> *the mountains be carried into the midst of the sea. (Ps. 46:1–2)*

The other day I met a young lady who came for counseling. Now, I have been counseling for a very long time and have come across people in the worst of the worst situations. I have even said to myself in the past that this truly is the worst set of circumstances that I have ever come across. Well, this young lady just became the winner in my list of the worst of the worst. I have never seen someone so broken, beaten, frighten, depressed, and at the end of the line as this young woman. She was on so many meds and had seen so many therapists and doctors that one would wonder if she was not just getting past off and past over due to her extreme circumstances. She has been abused and was unloved, and recently, an attempt on her very life was taken at knife point. Her throat was slit, and her side stabbed. She was underweight and looked malnourished. She had no money and was soon to be kicked out of her apartment. As she sat in my office, she simply trembled uncontrollably and wept nonstop. She was shaking so much that I had to turn off my air-conditioner to at least comfort her. Her face looked old and tired, much older than her actual age. She had such a fear of men that any look or touch sent her into a panic. Her words to me, among many, were that she "didn't even know who she was anymore." She felt like she wasn't even living in her own body, but through disassociation, she was outside of her own reality.

As I sat and pondered where to even begin, I thought to myself, *Lord, is this one too far gone even for you? How and where should I even begin, Lord?*

I thought of how empty even the gospel might sound to her, but I knew I must blindly trust the Lord. So I prayed, and then after some discussion, I went to the gospel. Even as I prayed with her and she asked Jesus into her heart, I still felt it was empty and hopeless; that was until the Lord moved me to take out the secret weapon, one that I forgot about. It was this simple yet clear object lesson that has broken through so many hearts in the past and one that would be the ticket today. It was simply a little four-inch-by-four-inch book-looking item. On the cover it said "Why Jesus Died." I took it out and showed it to her and asked her what the cover said. She read it and replied, "Why Jesus died." I said, "Okay, now open it and tell me what the answer is." She opened it only to find a mirror and her face looking back at her. She broke down in even more tears, but the point was made. After we were through counseling, I gave her some scriptures to read, and then she asked me, "Can I have that mirror book?" Well, I really didn't want to give it to her because I use it all the time, but when I asked her if she really wanted it, I decided I could always find another. She embraced that little book, even noting that she hadn't seen herself in years. I made some arrangements for where she could spend the night and got all her info.

Dear friend, the point of this long illustration is this: nothing is ever beyond the power and might of our Lord. I don't care how far you have fallen or what you have done, God heals, God saves, and Jesus is the lover of our souls. Yes, He can fix yours too.

October 14 - But I Need This!

Be not ye therefore like unto them: for your Father knoweth what things ye have need of, before ye ask him. (Matt. 6:8)

In my life here on planet earth, I have learned many things. One thing I have learned is the difference between wanting and needing. Now, I say that I have learned the difference, but that doesn't mean I like it or always follow the rule. I'm a gizmo guy who likes tools, gadgets, and novelty-type items. I'm a sucker for an AD on a new miracle wax or for a revolutionary new superwrench. When I go to trade shows and car shows, my eyes light up like a kid in a candy store. Just recently, a new major tool outlet opened up in my neighborhood. Walking through that megastore filled with tools and gizmos suddenly distorted my rationale on want versus need. Suddenly I wanted everything and tried to convince myself that I needed everything. Gladly, as I have grown, I am now able to fill my wagon with things and then when checkout time comes, I look at the wagon and say, "I don't need any of this stuff." I leave the wagon and go home. I had my cake and ate it too. I had the fun dreaming about the toys and gadgets and yet didn't have to spend a penny on them. Likewise with our Heavenly Father in relation to living a life filled with problems and pains.

I remember, when I first started fighting depression and anxiety, how I made up a list of demands for the Lord. "Dear Lord," I would say, "I want this, this, and this to happen. This is what I know I need to make me all better." What I didn't realize was that I was basically telling the Lord His business. I was telling the potter how to mold the clay. We must be careful when we are in a state of great need because we tend to pray for things not thinking or even being able to comprehend rationally what need anyway. Some people, when faced with depression, often think purchasing high-ticket items is the key. So new cars, motorcycles, boats, or jewelry are acquired. For a short time, it might even work, but quickly the new-car smell wears off, and we feel even worse than before because on top of being depressed, we now have a five-hundred-dollar-a-month car payment to make. All that glitters truly is not gold, and a happy heart cannot be bought at any price. Some try sex or affairs, long trips and vacations, yet none of them have sustaining appeal either.

Dear friend, it is the wise person who can look at their current situation and quickly determine that only a mind greater than theirs can unclog this emotional drain. It is the wise person who stops trying to unclog it and decides to call the plumber. God knows what's best, and when we pray to Him, we must always pray giving Him free rein to do whatever He deems best for our lives. It is crying out to God and saying, "Lord, I am but a man, and I know not what I need in this present state of despair, and so I trust in You, the Maker of man to do what you deem best for me." That might sound easy to do, and you might even be thinking that you already did that. My guess is that you did not because true faith in God is trusting Him to do anything, through any means, to bring about His will. It means thanking the Lord even if He chooses more pain or trials to be the vessel through which He feels best to bring you home to healing.

October 15 - If He Won't, We're in Big Trouble

For thou wilt light my candle: the lord my God will enlighten my darkness.
(Ps. 18:28)

Today I want to talk about the certainty of creation. Let's face it. There are some things that we never question, and by that affirmation, we are proclaiming that we have 100 percent faith in such things. Take air for a moment. We don't really give it a second thought. Will there be air to breathe tomorrow? Will there be air to breathe tonight? And will there be air to breathe in the next fifteen minutes? If not, then we're in big trouble. What of our heart? Will it continue to beat for the next few years? Will it continue to beat for the next few minutes? If not, then we are also in big trouble. Take the seasons. Will the fall come this year? Will the spring, summer, and winter come this year? If not, then something is very much wrong with our orbit and rotation, and we're in big trouble. What of the sun coming up tomorrow, will it happen? If not, then again we're in very big trouble. Now, you can laugh and say, "Yeah, I know what you're trying to do. Sure, I have faith these things will continue, but how does that help me?"

Dear friend, you just answered your own question by your answer. Everyone on planet earth, whether they are believers or atheists, all know that all these things will continue on. We do not wake up each day wondering if our liver will function or if our blood is still in our veins. We assume they always will be, and no matter how you cut it, that's called *faith*. Everyone lives by faith every day, and they don't even know it. For the anti-God people out there, I hate to be the bringer of bad news, but you live by faith every day. We all simply expect things to continue on, but we really have no proof that it will. That, my dear friend, is blind faith and nothing less. Now, I bring this point out today not so much for those atheists, but for those of us who trust in Christ by faith and yet are still suffering with depression and anxiety.

In Psalm 18:28, the same God who keeps all of our bodily functions working and solar systems powered up is the same God who also makes these promises: "For thou [*wilt*] light my candle: the LORD my God [*will*] enlighten my darkness." As our creator made all things and sustains all things, He also then must keep all promises of sustaining. In the case of our darkness, He says He *will* enlighten it, and in the case of the candle of our souls going out, He *will* keep it lit. That is a certainty as much as my eyes still seeing for the next few minutes. I will even go further and add this: even if the earth did stop turning, God will still lighten my darkness. He doesn't need the sun because He has the Son. As to my healing, it is not a matter of if He will, but when He will. It is coming, dear fellow sufferer, as sure as the sun will rise on the morrow. He is faithful in deed, word, and promise. All we need to do is grab hold of that promise and claim it as our own: "my Lord will lighten my darkness. And the only question of this certainty I see here is if He is your Lord. If not, then call out to Him by faith today and accept Him as Lord, King, and Redeemer of your soul. After that, the rest is in the bag. Only believe.

October 16 - The Problem with Rumination

Thou wilt keep him in perfect peace, whose mind is stayed on thee: because he trusteth in thee. (Isa. 26:3)

Today we will focus on a major problem, especially with regard to anxiety. Anxiety, by its very nature, is irrational fear. Kept in that state for too long, and it turns quickly into depression. One of the key factors of anxiety is the drifting of the mind into all varied and irrational conclusions. If you're a person who constantly thinks about things and overanalyzes them, then you are more prone to bouts with anxiety. When our mind runs to and fro from here to there and back again, we get into a fluid motion that in time will tip us.

An example of this is tanker trucks that carry large amounts of fluids. You see them on the highways and byways all the time. One thing a tanker driver knows is if he constantly changes lanes back and forth, from right to left, he risks developing a motion in the fluid compartment of the tanker. In time, the fluid moves back and forth so radically that it can take the tanker over with its motion. If you time that with a quick lane change, and catastrophe is a certainty. Now, what's interesting is what engineers have done over the years to combat this phenomenon. They built many compartments into that large tanker, but even more, they built baffles to keep that fluid motion from getting out of hand. It can still happen, but the odds are much less now due to this modification.

With regard to our minds, we can also develop this motion from too much back-and-forth motion with our thinking. It is called *rumination* in psychological circles and has the same effect as the tanker. What we need to do to stabilize our thoughts from running all over is to fix our minds on the Lord. In my worst days, I remember how rumination took control, and no medication or prayer could stop it. It is also called *projecting*, which means coming up with all kinds of worst-case scenarios of what could happen to you if this anxiety doesn't go away. Suddenly, the only thing we are thinking about is our anxiety, and our minds have no room to fit anything else. Thoughts of fear beget thoughts of fear. Like dominos, they take us lower and lower with each passing minute. It doesn't take long to get this motion rolling; sometimes it is just one random thought that jumps in from nowhere or sometimes is shot at us from the enemy. If our minds are not fixed on the Lord and His scriptures, they will take over again.

Isaiah 26:3 gives us the vaccination for this mind flu: "Thou wilt keep him in perfect peace, whose mind is stayed on thee: because he trusteth in thee." Notice the key components in this spiritual equation. 1) God will do the keeping of our minds in check when 2) our minds are ever focused on scripture and the promises of the Lord. 3) Peace of mind will be the result because we trusted in the Lord. In extreme cases of rumination, mood-stabilizing medications can be used, but for most cases, simply following Isaiah 26:3 is all that is needed. Ask the Lord to help you develop this skill for rumination control before your tanker truck tips over.

October 17 - When You Feel Better

Trust ye in the lord for ever: for in the lord jehovah is everlasting strength.
(Isa. 26:4)

How many times do I have to learn the same lesson until I stop making the same mistake? I have to admit that I stand in awe at the people of Israel from the Old Testament. Whenever I read of the supernatural wonders that they witnessed and then how quickly they fell away from the Lord, I have often found myself actually yelling at them as I read my Bible, "You dummies! You just saw the Red Sea parted. You saw fire from heaven, a cloud by day, all the plagues from the Lord, manna from heaven, birds for meat, water from a rock, what else more do you need to see?" Even today, it is common to hear people say, "If I would have seen what they saw in Bible times, I would never doubt God again." Well, in case you haven't noticed, things haven't changed too much in all of these years, and we still doubt even after seeing. We still see wonders in our lives and prayers answered and still we crumble at the next trail. Oh, and by the way, we still are living in Bible times. As long as time goes on, Bible times go on, so saying that God only did "that stuff" then is an excuse and a lie.

Dear friends, if I sound cross, I am, but not at you or anyone in particular, but at all of us, at myself, for forgetting and forgetting and forgetting again the wonders and faithfulness of the Lord. I believe the problem we all have is this: We have an emergency. We cry out to the Lord, we start reading the Bible more, going to church more, doing devotions more, serving more. Right away or in time, He delivers us. We feel better and happy again and then forget all about Him and go back to our lukewarm living. This is a syndrome I call bad-weather friendism or BWF; meaning, we are only close to the Lord when we need Him. As soon as all is well, we are back to our normal lives of pushing the envelope of sin, backing away from intimacy with the Lord, and delving right back into self-indulgent living. If people ever wonder why God doesn't just make our lives perfect the minute we become Christians, it is probably because He would never hear from us again. This is one thing that I get so angry at myself about because I never stop the circle of stupidity. I always say I am going to really stay close to the Lord this time even after I'm better, but the better I feel, the more I start compromising my time with Him.

I see this all the time in marriage counseling. People come to me in shambles. I tell them what they need to do, and so they do it for the most part. They go out to dinner, say they love each other each day, and have great romantic times of intimacy. Guess what happens next? Things slack off, old habits come back, and along with them come the old problems. Dear friend, if you are on an upswing today or when you do get to the place where healing begins and light begins to shine, *please*, keep trusting in the Lord. Not just in the bad times but all the time. Even on your happiest day, remember that in Him is everlasting strength. God wants us on our knees all the time in worship toward Him, so why not stay there all the time so He doesn't have to bring us there?

October 18 - Keep the Fire Burning

With my soul have I desired thee in the night; yea, with my spirit within me will I seek thee early: for when thy judgments are in the earth, the inhabitants of the world will learn righteousness. (Isa. 26:9)

Today we are going to repeat a bit what we spoke about yesterday. Why, you might ask? Well, because we need to be reminded again. Jesus first, God's will above ours, serving and yearning for His Word and truth. This needs to be a daily driving desire in our lives. Dear friend, as I write this devotional / book, there are things happening in the world that should be making our ears perk up. Now, I don't want to get into a whole debate about eschatology, but unless you have never read the Bible or today's news, things are a happening. Evil is growing stronger every day. The forces of darkness are on a rampage, and our full battle gear must be on. When the Bible says to put on the full armor of the Lord, it is not talking about cardboard cutouts but real spiritual shields and armor. We cannot afford one moment to go by without loading up on Bible wisdom and praying on our breastplate of righteousness. There are darts of fire being shot at us every day, and if we think we can just coast on through, we are sadly mistaken.

One of the most enjoyable things I like to do during the summer months is to sit outside on our patio around this little old beaten-up fire pit. My youngest son and I have the ritual down. We get paper, twigs, some light lumber, and then light the fire. But it doesn't end there; in fact, in order to keep that fire going so that we can all sit around it and feel its warmth in the late evening air, it needs to be fed. In the beginning, my little guy liked putting more wood to the fire, but once the novelty wore off, I had to keep reminding him. All night long that fire would consume an alarming amount of wood.

In our spiritual world, we need to remember that same principle. Sure, it's fun to read the Bible and go to Bible studies when we first come to know the Lord, but not too long after, time begins to dry up our desire for more wood. The result is the same as the fire pit; our fire becomes weaker and weaker until it gives neither light nor heat. All that's left is just some red embers and dusty white ash. It is sad to say that the reasons for our fires dying are similar to my fire pit fire: A) We get lazy in feeding it. B) We don't realize the fire is going out. C) We forget how great the heat and light of the fire are, at least until we get cold again and start yelling at everyone, "Who let that fire go out?" Our fire is our responsibility to keep lit. We cannot blame anyone else when the darkness comes again, and our wood supply is gone. Without light, there only comes darkness, and if you wait too long, it can get so dark that you can't even find where the matches are to light it.

The good news is this: even when my fire pit gets really neglected and there are only a few glowing embers left, all that's needed to stoke it up again is a fresh piece of wood. In good times and in bad times, keep the fires of Jesus Christ burning in your heart. It is not optional but mandatory. Then it won't matter how dark our world or our life gets, our light will already be roaring with spiritual fire.

October 19 - Peace for Us

lord, thou wilt ordain peace for us: for thou also hast wrought all our works in us. (Isa. 26:12)

Today in the news, there's the same old story about peace in the Middle East. It seems every year, for the last thousand years, someone has been talking about peace over there. It's funny how mankind thinks he can accomplish what only the Lord can do. That's like me trying to do brain surgery when I'm not even a doctor. One diplomat after another flies over there with the hopes of being the *one* who brings the Arabs and the Jews together. The world also watches and gets so excited that maybe this time it will be a lasting peace.

Dear friend, there can be no peace in the Middle East or in any part of the world unless the Lord Jesus Christ ushers it in Himself. Likewise in our troubled souls, neither can we make peace where there is only turmoil. We try everything in our power, and yet it fails. We listen to everyone's opinion, and yet that fails. Now, it's not that what we are trying or hearing is not good, but unless the Lord ordains it, peace will never come. At the end of the day, it must be the Lord who gets the glory as that's really the only reason we are here or even going through anything at all, that others would see Christ working in us and they too would desire to come to Him.

Peace is what the entire world wants. Peace is what all your neighbors, friends, and family want. The world has spent billions of dollars on peace projects that never work. Troubled communities have spent millions on midnight basketball projects, community-enhancement ventures, interfaith dialog, and hate-crime legislation. All of it has never worked, and it never will. All the politicians with the noblest ideals cannot do what only one man, Jesus Christ, can by changing hearts. I once heard it said, and I believe it to be true, that "you can't legislate morality, nor can you make people get along." All that you want is ironically found in an old laughed-at book called the Holy Bible.

Years ago, there was an elder at my church who worked for a national laboratory as a scientist. They were working on an atom-smashing collider for the sole purpose of finding out what happened at the beginning of time or something like that. While he worked there, he would always keep his Bible on his desk and jokingly say, "We are spending millions of taxpayers' dollars to find out what I already have the answers to in this little book on my desk." Sounds silly, but it is very true, and truer yet in regard to our quest for rest and peace unto our souls. With all the money people are spending on self-help books, clinics, studies, and research, in reality, all they really need to do is open up the living Word of God and find it waiting there all along. Have you opened up your Living Word Guidebook for the Human's Soul today? What are you waiting for? Peace awaits, and answers are at the ready.

October 20 - Other Gods That Rule Us

O lord our God, other lords beside thee have had dominion over us: but by thee only will we make mention of thy name. (Isa. 26:13)

In this current age of enlightenment, there seems to be a turning away from things in the spiritual realm. Well, let me rephrase that. There seems to be a radical turning away from the things of Christ. The secular spiritual world is running full-on and fast. It's only those who believe in the only true Living God who are expelled from all facets of life. What's dangerous even for us Christians is that we too can fall prey to these *other* gods. These other ways in the spiritual salad bar out there. So many times in our struggles with emotional issues, what we thought was a chemical imbalance or a true emotional condition might just have been simply the influences of spiritual forces not of God. Now, I know when we mention things like these, the world loses whatever little respect they have for us. But be that as it may, it really doesn't matter what they think. It matters what is true.

Friends, there are demonic forces out there all dressed up in pure-white apparel. They are leaders, gurus, and even preachers. Some call themselves motivational speakers; some call themselves life coaches. It doesn't matter what the title is; the demon behind the mask is all that matters. Today what makes it ever harder to detect is the hybrids of many pseudo-religious organizations, which appear good and godly but are far from it. From the New Age movement to Wicca to Scientology and Unitarian Universalism, they are all wonderful and glowing by virtue of their community outreaches and social engagement, yet that has never been nor will ever be the standard by which to judge if it is of God. We must be ever mindful of books we are given, DVD presentations we watch, seminars we attend, and new-fangled Christian idealism we encounter. The names change every so many years, but the people behind the masks never change. Some are simply out for your money, and some are even out for worse, your very soul.

Today in our age of extreme tolerance for all ways and beliefs, no one is brave enough to challenge these little gods for fear of persecution or being called a bigot or closed-minded Bible thumper. Fear rules the day, and questioning anything but Christianity is a politically incorrect no-no. What feels good for you should be your choice to make, at least that's what they tell us, but I hear another voice calling out in my heart. I hear the voice of truth, the voice of God. He tells me another story and warns me of the broad road of destruction.

Dear friend, I know that struggling with emotional issues can really push us to our limits, and the temptation to try some new healing clinic or mystic might seem very appealing, but if it is not of God, it is of Satan, whom Jesus Himself calls the father of lies. Try and test the spirits and see if they are truly of God. Settle for nothing less than God-ordained and Bible-confirmed counsel.

October 21 - I'm Afraid, Lord, Though I Know You're There

Like as a woman with child, that draweth near the time of her delivery, is in pain, and crieth out in her pangs; so have we been in thy sight, O lord. (Isa. 26:17)

One of the scariest part of going through emotional trauma is stepping out into the unknown. Face it. We have faced most other things in life but nothing like this. Broken legs, loss of a job, even loss of a loved one. They are hard and painful, and to some degree, we know what to do because so many others have gone through the same pain, and we can follow their lead. Even in sickness, we have dealt with much. I don't know anyone who doesn't know someone who hasn't had cancer or died from it. We all know even how to deal with that dark pain. If we have to face cancer ourselves, well, that's a terror of its own, but at least people understand why you are hurting. But of depression and anxiety, they are uncharted waters. It is a place that we have never traveled, and we don't even know many who have been there to get answers from. Of other people understanding, well, good luck with that as most can't or even don't want to understand what we are going through. Many even think we are faking it for attention or simply because we don't want to go to work. So if you are looking for sympathy, it is going to be a long hard search.

One of my son's friends is a young man in his twenties. Looking at him, you would think he is as tough as nails, and yet he recently lost his job due to too many days missed. Why? Because he suffers from extreme panic attacks that are so bad, he ends up in the hospital. Our biggest problem in dealing with depression and anxiety is knowing that God is there but still feeling afraid. It is knowing that God will heal us but still having to deal with an unknown monster, one we have never had to face before. It is interesting to note that most people who suffer from depression and anxiety didn't always have it. Sure, some are born with a predisposition to it and suffer all their lives, but many, like me, never had it full-blown until much later in life. To me, it was a shock, something that jumped up at me, which I never saw before. Hey, if I get a cold, I know what to do. I know how to deal with the pain, but I also know it will go away. Emotional issues have no time limits or end in sight. For all we know, this could be our lot forever (which it won't).

Dear friend, what we need to do is learn how to deal with these issues as with any other issues. Read about it, talk to others who have gone through it, and know that the Lord is still with us just as He is with us through any other type of trial of pain. Depression and anxiety are not something the Lord doesn't deal with as if it were out of His expertise. No, God fixes everything, and that's that. Trust Him just as you would trust Him in any other trial of faith. He is faithful.

October 22 - Sometimes We Just Have to Obey

Thou shalt keep therefore His statutes, and His commandments, which I command thee this day, that it may go well with thee, and with thy children after thee, and that thou mayest prolong thy days upon the earth, which the lord thy God giveth thee, for ever. (Deut. 4:40)

Today, with all the modern technology, it is amazing how life has changed. Technology has done a lot of wonderful things, especially in regard to health and medical needs. Even in our homes and with our new-fangled cell phones, the sky seems to be the limit. For the most part, it has all been good until you get your first electronic red-light ticket. Here where I live, they just started to install those all over the place. Roll through a red light or don't make a complete stop, and in a few days, there is a ticket in the mail with your face on it. I have gotten one so far, and it hasn't made me happy. I started to complain to my wife about all of these cameras watching us and invading our privacy. A law for this or a law for that.

Recently, the town-building department near our church told us our church sign was in violation of the building code. One sign had to be taken down and the other moved. All of these things cost money and fees and fines. When we put in our new parking lot at the church, the town stopped by again and said that our drainage wasn't right. After another thirty thousand dollars, we were up to code and paving our new lot. I must admit these laws, codes, and rules have made me very angry and bitter and caused me to even be in the flesh at times. I simply wanted to scream about what is expected of me and our church building. Well, as one of the elders of the church said,

"It's the law, and we just must obey, end of story." I really couldn't argue with that reasoning because it was true.

Friend, sometimes we go through issues and problems simply because we are not obeying God's rules. Sometimes our ailments and trials have nothing to do with medical conditions or emotional conditions, but they are just flags the Lord is putting up to remind us we are not following His rules for living. For some reason, we think because Jesus died for our sins, that we have a pass on how we live our lives. We say, "God doesn't really expect me to live completely holy unto Him." To be completely honest, righteous, hardworking, on time, loving, have a servant's heart, give my monies, stay away from R-rated movies and questionable people and places. Well, yes He does. He even says, "Be ye holy, for I am holy."

Dear friend, if you are going through any type of trial, be it depression or simply a work-related problem, always make sure that you are right with God before you look anywhere else for the solution or healing. It might be as simple as obeying the Lord's commands of holy living and nothing more. Obey Him and find peace to your soul. It's as simple as that.

October 23 - When People Wait for Your Destruction

All that pass by clap their hands at thee; they hiss and wag their head at the daughter of Jerusalem, saying, "Is this the city that men call The perfection of beauty, The joy of the whole earth?" (Lam. 2:15)

I remember growing up and driving to work with my dad. I started out pumping gas at our family-owned repair-and-filling station. The drive to work was a long traffic-filled one, and especially on the way home, my father would give me these tidbits of wisdom about life. Being a young teenager, I really didn't care what he said, but I had to listen. One thing he would warn me about was people who would wish your destruction. The people in the workforce who would do anything to take your spot or make you look bad so they could look good. I didn't believe that people were that bad until I entered the real workforce in the corporate world. He was right, and people were out to stab you in the back so they could move ahead.

In one particular place of employment, I had a rather well-paying and high-position job. I found out very soon that many were jealous of my position and questioned how I got there. Many also wanted my job and would stop at nothing to undermine me or destroy me. The more money I made, the higher I went, the more people made me believe they were my friends only to suit their own end. I also observed this throughout the upper management and the phony people and kiss-up attitudes they had simply to advance their own agenda. That was a hard lesson to learn, especially when people took advantage of your emotional struggle and used it to their advantage. I remember one time when my anxiety started to appear. It became so bad that I had no other choice but to tell my immediate supervisor that I was having some sort of breakdown. He accepted it well and promised to help me work through it, but I also knew I lost any respect that he had for me at that point.

As much as people will come up to wish you well and write you a get-well card, there are as many who are salivating to take your position if you fall. It is not an easy thing to accept that people wish you harm and, even more, that they wish you ill. Sad to say, I saw this even worse in the church, where a church split erupted soon after I took over my second church. When a large group of people left, you could feel that in their hearts they hoped I would crash and burn if only to validate their decisions to leave. People might tell you they love you and that they have your back, yet in their hearts they are hoping for your apocalyptic end.

In relation to emotional issues, there is no shortage of this same evil in the hearts of men. My advice is to expect it, trust no one, and keep trusting in Christ. They may laugh and clap in their hearts at your destruction, but the Lord always has the last laugh. Woe unto them who wish hurt on God's anointed child. Don't hate them but pray for them, knowing that the Lord is with you though every man has turned on you. Keep clean, holy, and pure and wait for the Lord's mighty hand to move.

October 24 - When He Says—It Is Enough

It is enough: stay now thine hand. (2 Sam. 24:16)

Sometimes we don't understand the Lord or why He does what He does. Sometimes His ways are downright confusing to the mind of mortal man, but would we want to have our Lord to have a mind of man anyway? I think not. In order to rule the galaxies and time itself, one would think that the controller of such things would have to be of infinite mind. I would have to agree, and I have no trouble with the Lord being far greater and wiser than me. I would go as far as to say that it would send chills down my spine if the Lord only had the mentality and IQ of me. Maybe some people feel different and think God should be more like us, but even if you feel that way, the system is not up for grabs, so it is as it is. God will always be higher and brighter than any man. If you can't accept that, then that's an issue you must take up with the Lord; but for those of us who have no problem with Him being higher and mightier, it actually brings much comfort to the soul.

If one is building a fine wooden vessel to sail the seas, I would then accept his expertise on how it is to be done. I would not dare offer my advice on something I know nothing, or even little, about. All I want to know is that when I climb aboard that ship, it is safe and seaworthy. The reputation of the builder's past successful vessels would bring me confidence for the ride. If a local shoemaker decided to build the ship instead, I wouldn't feel as confident, and I am sure I would never step foot on it. I make these points so we can apply them to our life in the Lord's hands. Our life is a creation of His; He tweaks and modifies us as He sees fit for the journey of life that we must take. Many times He might hammer or chip at our tender parts, and we might question His wisdom in doing so. But like the boatbuilder who takes that certain part of that wooden ship and bends it in a vise for months, we must accept his wisdom in doing so. It might seem odd and even bizarre at times, but He is the builder.

One of my many trades was a house framer. I worked with a master custom housebuilder who specialized in unique homes with rounded hallways. Not one part of the home would have any corners. When I first started working for him, I noticed many long planks that had hundreds of quarter-inch cuts made in them. These boards were soaked in water and then placed on a table with pegs, which would be moved each day. It seemed very odd until I found out that was how he made a house with no corners. If you were to just bend a dry beam, it would snap.

Dear friend, right now you might be going through the worst pain and emotional anguish. It might seem like the Lord is pressing too hard, yet one day when the soul is bent to His liking, He will say these long-awaited words, "It is enough. Stay now thine hand." Those were the words the Lord gave to the angel in charge of one of the Lord's projects. The Lord allowed the angel to do the bending of the people, and when the Lord felt it was enough, He commanded it to be over. One day, the Lord will say it is over, and you will be as He planned. The work is done, and you are now ready to serve in full capacity.

October 25 - Maybe This Is for That

And who knoweth whether thou art come to the kingdom for such a time as this? (Esther 4:14)

Providence is a part of God's system of doing things that always seems to amaze me. All through my life, I have seen it in action, and sometimes, not until long after a season of life has been passed. When I was a young man, I would never have been one for public speaking. Standing in front of anyone and talking was the furthest thing from my expertise. Yet in my later years, I took on a job at a certain employ. I never had any intention of doing anything more than I had signed for, but through the providence of the Lord, I was forced to fill an opening in doing something I hated and could not do. I was to teach a class of forty or so students, blackboard, desks, and all. I was persuaded that this was a good move in my career though I fought it long and hard. Well, it went from one class to two till I was teaching up to four different subjects. I was becoming a public speaker in the secular world. All the while, I thought it was to make more money and go higher up the ladder, but the Lord had other things in mind. He was training me to be a pastor and preacher one day, something that was not even an idea in my mind.

In my life, there have been many things that seemed very negative at the time but later ended up being all a part of the plan. As I have shared before, I also had a major struggle with pornography; and if I was ever going to be used by the Lord, it would have to be beaten. What I thought was going to be a problem turned out to be a blessing. I began to speak at men's groups about my struggle as a Christian man and lust. I ended up writing a book about it, and before I knew it, I was doing seminars, speaking on the issue and even being a radio guest host on the topic. I thought after that, the Lord was through and that was my calling, but lo and behold, this depression and anxiety thing popped up in my life. Again, I figured, well, that's it for me and ministry. I was a shaking bag of nerves thinking about taking my life. Well, before I knew it, I was adding this specialty to my counseling. I then became known as the go-to in my local area for depression and anxiety. Soon I was speaking about that at seminars, and even then I thought, *Well, that's that, back to my goal of being a pastor.* Years and years went by, and I am doing what I love, which is counseling and pastoring a small church. I see a rise in depression like I have never seen before. My counseling practice gets so busy, it triggers my old anxiety up again, and I fall back into depression.

Dear friend, I am writing this book today only because the Lord hit me again with depression and anxiety. Was He being mean? Or maybe He is concerned about so many people struggling with this and has to sacrifice one for the many. I think that's what He did with His own Son for our sins. My point today is this: What you are going through might not be what you think it is. It might be part of a major plan that the Lord has for your life. Don't fight it. Embrace it and prayerfully ask the Lord this question: "Lord, is this pain currently upon me for such a time as this, a time when so many are hurting that you need an army of depression-and-anxiety experts to comfort your hurting church and world?" He might just be calling you too for such a time as this.

October 26 - The Head Cheese

For I the lord thy God will hold thy right hand, saying unto thee, "Fear not; I will help thee." (Isa. 41:13)

There is something about knowing people in high positions. We all like to brag about who we know in a particular trade, business, or profession. When someone has a problem and we know a person who can help, we find great pleasure in saying, "Go to this certain place and ask for Joe. Tell them I recommended you." Even better than sending a person there is to have a trouble or a need and being able to go up to the counter and say, "Maryann Smith said to ask for Dr. Jones," then to have them say, "Oh yes, come right in. She told us you were coming." Suddenly we feel very important and comforted knowing that we are going to get special treatment.

I think the most exciting time that happened to me was when a visiting missionary was speaking at our church. He happened to know a friend of a friend who knew a person who was a bodyguard for a very big celebrity. We were told to drive to the city and go through the studio doors, and when we get to the front desk, ask for so and so and tell them who you are; it will all be arranged. Well, we did go there, and we did mention that name, and all of a sudden, we were treated like honored guests and shuttled up to the place where they shot the TV show. We met the star and felt great.

Sometimes when we are going through tough times in our lives, we would also like to have someone on the inside who knows someone at the top. Imagine being diagnosed with some life-threatening disease, sent to meet the chief of that department, who happens to be the top doctor in all the world, and being able to have a private meeting with him or her and getting that extra special treatment. Well, we have that same "in" with a Higher Up, and yet we take it for granted all the time. We are special, and we do have contacts that no one else has unless they too are a child of God through faith in Jesus Christ. We have access to the very throne room of the Lord. Now, I know what you are thinking. You're saying to yourself, "Big deal. What good has it done for me?" Friend, if that's the way you feel about that contact with God, then He is going to feel the same way toward you. The Lord deserves honor and wants honor and glory. Look at Him as a nothing and you will not get past the front doors of His holiness. Listen. We must understand what we have in Christ; it is not just a 50 percent-off coupon for dinner at the local restaurant. No, we have access to our Creator through His Son. We have an in, a big in.

People used to ask me years ago when I landed a very good job that was only gotten by knowing someone really important. When they would ask, "Who do you know to get such a position?" I would simply say, "I happen to know God personally." In Isaiah 41:13, we get a little taste of this privilege of being a child of God. We don't just get to talk to some angel or doorman of heaven; no, we get the royal treatment from a gracious God. Isaiah 41:13 says, "For I the LORD thy God will hold thy right hand, saying unto thee, Fear not; I will help thee." The Lord Himself, the Creator of time and space, He is the one who holds our hand, no one less but the Lord Himself. Yes, it is a big deal, and so we should look at it that way.

October 27 - Being a Good Soldier of the Cross

And they answered Joshua, saying, "All that thou commandest us we will do, and whithersoever thou sendest us, we will go." (Josh. 1:16)

Some of the hardest times in my life have been the times when I blindly had to follow. Following anyone takes faith, whether it is following them in a car or following someone in leadership. To follow one whom you have great trust sure makes it easier, but not necessarily easy. To follow a person or a way when that way and that person's choices seem logical is one thing, but a whole other thing when they look like they are leading you off a cliff. Today we have these new-fangled GPS systems in our cars and even our cell phones. If you have ever been lost and had to trust that mysterious computer voice, it's not as carefree as you might think. I remember the first time I used a GPS, and right off the bat, it was taking us on a route that I would never use to get to my location. It ended up taking me through New York City, a place that I hate driving through. I actually questioned if this little direction box was really working. I was actually yelling at it, "Where are you taking me? This is so out of the way." But since I was now really lost, I had no choice but to trust it even though it had me turning this way and that and heading through a bad part of town. It was either believe the GPS or be really lost. Sure enough, it did get me out of the woods, so to speak, and my fears and doubts of the directions it gave me were unfounded.

That episode reminded me of a lesson my father taught me in my youth while we were hunting up in the mountains. He was teaching me about compass reading and told me there would be a day when I would get lost in the woods, and the compass would point me home but I would doubt its readings. When lost in the woods, the first thing that happens is everything looking the same and panic setting in. You would swear that north was south and south was north. It was what my dad was trying to teach me as he said, "Don't doubt the compass. Follow it no matter how wrong the way that it is pointing looks."

It is a lot like following God and the people whom He has placed in authority in and over your life. To be a good solider or worker, you must trust your leader. With the people of Israel, they also had a compass-trusting problem. They had enough doubts following Moses, but when Joshua was put in charge, they really became unsure. "Is this man really of God like Moses was?" In time, they became more comfortable with Joshua because they found out that, like Moses, he was also faithful. He was a man that could be trusted. In Joshua 1:16, the people boldly were able to follow him: "And they answered Joshua, saying, 'All that thou commandest us we will do, and whithersoever thou sendest us, we will go.'" Notice they didn't say "some things" they would follow but all things that Joshua commanded.

Dear friend, during the dark days of emotional struggles, God is going to lead us down some odd, illogical dark roads. We will have no choice but to follow Him, and in following Him, we will have to do it blindly. It is when we begin to doubt the providence in His leading that confusion will set in. We cannot let that happen, and like good soldiers, we will have to follow our leader in full confidence, no matter how bizarre the path He takes us on may appear.

October 28 - Man Alone Cannot Help You

And he said, "If the lord do not help thee, whence shall I help thee?" (2 Kings 6:27)

In my years of counseling, there has been one thing I had to be careful about. There is one thing that any good counselor or therapist will tell you. It's the danger of thinking you are really the source of the people's deliverance. Being a counselor leaves your human, sinful nature open to many prideful tendencies. Sometimes you get hooked on people thinking you are great. Sometimes it is getting all puffed up with people depending on you. Sometimes the counselee becomes so dependent on you that they could actually fall in love with you as a father figure or even a romantic figure. It is a very dangerous place to be as many a young person looking for that missing authority figure, or a person going through a marriage problem looking for that perfect spouse, actually begins to think that you are it.

One of the reasons this happens is because you are simply the only one who is taking time to listen to them. You're the only one who makes them feel good and important. You seem to care when no one else does, and so they become so attached that they make up reasons not to get better so they can continue coming to see you. Over the years I have had to tweak my practice to avoid these pitfalls. One is never to counsel people too long. I won't counsel a person longer than six months, and even that is too long in most cases. The second thing and most important thing is to make crystal clear that you don't have any answers for them but only those which God does. It is to take yourself down a peg or two in their eyes so they don't look up to you but always up to the Lord. I am always quick to let them know that only Jesus can save them, that only God will never let them down, that *only* the Lord truly cares more about them, more than even themselves. In fact, one of the first things I tell a person when they come to see me is, "I cannot help you." Now, I know I have mentioned this before in this book, but I want to make it super clear. As I tell them I can't help them, I also finish that statement by saying, "But God can."

Dear friend, if anyone is going to help you heal, it will only be through the Lord's power. Unfortunately, the temptation to let people overtrust you is driven by another sin, which is the love of money. Many counselors will subconsciously lead people along for many years simply so they have a steady income based on their fees. Dear friend, I again want to make this clear. If God can't help and heal you, then no one can. Now, I am not saying the Lord doesn't use people, friends, doctors, counselors, and medication, but only the Lord can allow those things to work. If the counselor, medication, or friend is getting all the praise for their mighty work in your life, you can rest assured the Lord won't let their counsel work very well and / or for long. If you feel like you are getting too attached to your spiritual guide, pastor, and / or counselor, then quickly read Psalm 118:8. It will quickly remind you where salvation and healing truly come from.

October 29 - Let God Know Whom You Really Trust

And Asa cried unto the lord his God, and said, "lord, it is nothing with thee to help, whether with many, or with them that have no power: help us, O lord our God; for we rest on thee, and in thy name we go against this multitude. O lord, thou art our God; let not man prevail against thee." (2 Chron. 14:11)

I always think it is quite ironic that US money says "In God we trust." What's so untrue about that statement is we don't trust in God at all but in the money itself. One thing we must never forget is this: the Lord is not fooled or mocked, and He certainly knows if we trust in Him. I recently did a sermon on the popular scripture Proverbs 3:5 where it says to "trust in the Lord with all of our heart." It is an easy scripture to read and preach, but one that's so hard to live out. What's key in this attempt to trust the Lord is understanding the difference between trusting and believing. So often we get them confused, and so we think we are trusting in the Lord because we believe in Him. Again, God knows the difference. That is why the scriptures point out that even demons believe in God, but that doesn't mean they trust in God as Lord. Many times in our struggles with emotional pain, we wonder why we are not gaining ground in healing when the reason is simply that we only believe in God without trusting Him. Sometimes object lessons are the best way to illustrate an important yet difficult thought; and in the case of trust versus belief, it's a must.

Take, for example, an elevator at the end of a hospital hallway. You see it, and so you believe it is real. If people asked you about the elevator and what it does, you could also honestly reply with an intelligent answer: "An elevator is real, and it carries people up and down within a building." You again would be honestly reporting what you know to be true, and yet technically, you are lying because if you never used an elevator, you are then basing your knowledge only on hearsay. What is needed is the next step to confirm your belief. It would be to walk into it, close the door, and let it take you to another floor. This analogy really explains the dynamics of belief and more well. See, sometimes we can believe and even think we are trusting, as in stepping into the elevator, but never doing much more but stepping out again.

Dear friend, our Lord God doesn't just want belief that He is real, nor does He want trust that just steps in and out of Him without any chance for Him to take us anywhere. True biblical trust is to believe then enter through Christ then let the doors close and be transported to the next place where the Lord wants us to go. God is waiting for this movement on our part, and He is waiting for us to make it real in our lives by proclaiming this trust to the world around us. It is stating to us and the world that our God will carry, move, comfort, protect, and guide us to safety, and we trust in this with all of our heart.

Today if you are suffering in any way, you must stop believing God will get you through, but instead climb in, push the button, and let the doors of God's hands close in around you. It is only there that He can truly bring you to where He desires. Don't just believe. Trust in Him by living and working visible actions of faith.

October 30 - Remind Yourself Again

Art not thou our God, who didst drive out the inhabitants of this land before thy people Israel, and gavest it to the seed of Abraham thy friend for ever? (2 Chron. 20:7)

I'm not one for witty sayings and inspirational poems. Not unless they have biblical truth at their core. It is not hard to write corny love notes to ourselves and make them sound like truths to live by. Words like, "Just believe in yourself, and all your dreams will come true." That sounds wonderful and might even help you get past one bad day, but for the most part, they're empty words with no power behind them. In time, when real trouble comes, those words just become words and nothing more. Because there is nothing to back them up like gold to back up our currency, it simply becomes worthless paper; and in the case of flowery, bombastic wording, it becomes empty sentiment.

Pastors can also fall into this trap when they spend more time speaking their words in a sermon without including the Lord's. His Word is alive, and our words are empty. A sermon with no Bible to back it up correctly is fodder. Like the Word of God brings life to the spoken word, so does the actual workings of God in your life bring hope in a current negative situation. Like memorizing scripture makes recall for your present distress bearable, so does remembering God's past mercies bring strength for today's problems. What we need to do is keep track of what the Lord has done in our life and write it down on paper. Take note of the Lord's power in actual action and then you will have it to recall when trouble strikes again.

I like to recall very hard times in my life where the walls were closing in, and all seemed lost yet the Lord came through. As silly as it might sound, try reciting to yourself past examples of His deliverances. If you have trouble remembering things like that, then write them down. Whether in written or verbal form, get used to recalling God's mercies this way, so the next time trouble hits, you can say for example,

> *Oh Lord, when my bank account was empty last spring, you provided. When my mother fell and broke her hip, you gave her healing. When no one said I would amount to anything, you gave me that wonderful career opportunity. When I was alone, you provided a friend or a phone call just at the right time. When I broke down on a dark lonely street, you provided a policeman.*

Maybe even today, start keeping a journal of what the Lord is doing in your life and what He has done. Start by thinking back on your life when the Lord certainly kept you from great harm. Take note of those times where there was no other way to explain the help you received but by the Lord's own hand. If you can't think of a single miracle in your life, then something is wrong, and it might be time to make sure you are truly a child of God. If not sure, then call out to Him today in complete humility, confess your sins against Him, repent of those sins, accept Jesus's death on the cross for those sins, and declare Him Lord and King over your life. Ask Him to be your Savior, and by faith and in trust, turn to Him today. Then you can start keeping track of the blessings as they start flowing. So next time you are in a dark place, you can recall today's miracles and blessings.

October 31 - Hearing and Helping

If, when evil cometh upon us, as the sword, judgment, or pestilence, or famine, we stand before this house, and in thy presence, (for thy name is in this house,) and cry unto thee in our affliction, then thou wilt hear and help. (2 Chron. 20:9)

One of the most helpless situations I can find myself in is visiting a sick person at the hospital and not being able to do much but pray. As a pastor, you are kind of like a policeman who is on call 24-7. When the phone rings at my bedside at 3:00 a.m., I know there is someone hurting, and I must get up and get over to where they are. I hurry to get dressed, hop in my car, get to the hospital with my clergy ID flashing, and after hustling to sit by their bedside, I can do nothing more. It is the same thing in counseling when I get a suicidal person calling me at 3:00 a.m. and needing desperately to be heard and helped. In both situations, I really can't do much as their sickness and / or life troubles are what they are. All I can do is pray, speak words of comfort, and listen. Don't get me wrong. Prayer is very powerful and can move mountains, but more often, the present pain is what it is. Reading scripture is also powerful and can calm the broken, trembling heart, but again, it is more of me listening for that moment than anything else. The reason why I feel so frustrated at those early morning hours is because I can only hear when helping is what those people really need.

The good news is the Lord can do both and does both. He hears and then, in His mighty providence, He helps. Again, dear friend, I pray that you notice the constant theme I am trying to bring forth in this devotional book. That is, one of God-focused not man-focused. As a counselor and a pastor, I can hear and maybe even offer temporary comfort, but only God can actually help. If you are in need of healing, money, employment, a place to live, or a lasting companionship, neither man nor woman can really change that, only God.

Depression and crippling anxiety can't be removed by any man's word, but it can be removed by God's help. The less trust and hope we put in people, the more we can put in the Lord. The more hope we put in the Lord, the more He will help. When I say *help*, I don't just mean holding your hand while you steady to your feet, but help in the form of actual life change. God can change situations in your life; He can turn things right side up with the shout of His Word. What is broken can be fixed, and what is lame can be made new. There has been a few times in my ministry where, in anger and frustration, I had to speak these words to a perpetual problematic person: "I cannot help you at all. There is nothing I can do. We can talk for one hundred hours, and your problem will still be your problem. It is time you start talking to the Lord, for He alone will not just hear but will help."

Most people don't like when they hear those words from me because in reality, they truly want a tangible human touch to intervene on their behalf. Many times that is simply not going to happen, and that is why ultimate dependency on the Lord alone must be mandated.

November

November 1 - Even When You Don't See It

For we are saved by hope: but hope that is seen is not hope: for what a man seeth, why doth he yet hope for? (Rom. 8:24)

Ever have someone describe to you a place they visited and you start drawing a mental picture in your mind? Sometimes I have heard about the same place from a person so many times that I forget my mental picture of it is not really the place but what I envision it as. It's like hearing about a foreign land or reading about it in a book. No matter how much we read about it or hear it described, it is still not the same as being there. A young lady I knew went to Israel on a mission trip. When she came back, she did a presentation at church of what it was like. Though she had pictures, it was still not the same as being there. She was so excited and on fire with passion about her trip, but no matter how excited she was, we could never share in that excitement at the same level. To us, listening to her would only be a mental picture of what we think it would be like. It wasn't that she didn't do a good job describing it, but there were some things we just couldn't experience. Things like the sounds and smells and the people that made up her mission trip. Especially the special emotions that only the Lord can put in one's heart. Those are the things we can't see without seeing them or feel without feeling them.

Of Israel, I don't know if I will ever be able to afford to travel there, and maybe it's not such a bad thing for now. Maybe just hearing about it is better as the Lord puts that taste in my mouth so my appetite for it might grow. The Lord at times shows us things, and sometimes He tells us things in His Word. Sometimes the excitement of waiting for something is better than actually getting it or going there. Ever dream about something so much that it becomes an obsession, and then when you actually get it, the buildup was so much that it actually lets you down when you finally have it in your hands? It just wasn't as good as you built it up to be.

Sometimes we need to simply hope for what the Lord has waiting for us without obtaining it just yet, like being delivered from our depression or anxiety. If only five minutes after I fell into my first depression the Lord delivered me from it, I don't think I would even remember the deliverance being that big of a deal. I certainly would not have enough information and experience to be writing this devotional book. In my journey with depression and anxiety, the longer it took to be delivered from it, the more I grew and learned about it. Even more was how much closer I grew to the Lord as I looked forward to the day of deliverance. They say absence makes the heart grow fonder, and I believe it to be true. I couldn't wait to feel free again and to be alive in living joy in the Lord. I didn't have it at that moment of suffering, but when I finally knew that it would come, the joy of waiting for healing helped me not be so crushed by my present darkness.

Hoping in the Lord means trusting in what He *will do* sometimes. As I think of heaven, I know I can't go there yet, but I know it is going to be wonderful and surely better than I ever imagined. Let us hope in what the Lord has promised us and use that as our towrope to pull us home while we wait.

November 2 - Pain Can Lead Us to More Pain

Watch ye and pray, lest ye enter into temptation. The spirit truly is ready, but the flesh is weak. (Mark 14:38)

Pain is an interesting thing. Sometimes I wonder why the Lord made us to feel it as it would be so much better without it. But then I thought about stepping on a nail or a tack. If I didn't feel pain, I would step fully on it until it went deep into my foot. I could bleed to death and not even know it. Think of a person having a heart attack. If they didn't have those chest pains, they would never know to go to the hospital and have it looked at. No matter how we look at it, pain is a good thing because God placed the ability to feel pain within us. If He placed it there, then why would we want it gone? Even depression is a type of pain, and it also tells us that something is wrong and needs looking into. Now, with all things that the Lord has made to be good for us, Satan is also there to try to confuse us and take something that is for our good and make it for our harm.

Sex is one thing that comes to mind. It is a wonderful God-given experience but only to be enjoyed between a husband and wife. Satan comes along and, by taking it out of its proper environment, makes it ugly and dirty. In time, even the great feelings of sex can destroy us and then lead us to dark and sinful places. I remember when I first encountered my first person who was cutting. In case you haven't heard, cutting is a very popular fad among teens, especially female teens. They actually cut little lines into their arms, legs, or stomachs. They take a razor blade or any sharp object and scrape their skin until it bleeds. When I first heard of it, I immediately began researching it as it would become an epidemic in a short time. Today it is the fastest rising star of teenage pain management; unfortunately, it's a lie of Satan.

See, pain, like I said, is a warning sign from our bodies, but it should be a warning sign to fix the pain, not mask it. Cutting is just that, an attempt at replacing one pain for another. Teens who cut do so mostly because of deep emotional pain, and by self-inflicting physical pain, it temporarily displaces the emotional pain, temporarily! Is it by chance that these confused ideas come forth? I think not. Dear friend, depression and anxiety are surely pains of the worst sort. Getting rid of this pain is our body's greatest desire, but if our emotional pain is pointing to something, should we not first find out why we are in pain and then remove the source of it? Replacing pain to rid oneself of it does nothing for the healing of the original pain. It is like having an infected tooth and just living on painkillers instead of taking an antibiotic to kill the infection. I say this all to warn you of the temptations that Satan might place in your path to trick you into temporary healing. I have never felt so much temptation to sin as when I was suffering with depression and anxiety. The desire to just be rid of it for a moment was so appealing that Satan easily tricked me into his traps of lies. And to what end would Satan do this but to keep me in sin, which would keep me separated from my Heavenly Father. The longer we are separated from God through sin, the further we are from ever being healed.

November 3 - Focus

And if a house be divided against itself, that house cannot stand. (Mark 3:25)

It is getting closer to winter, and with the fall and winter come the difficult days for those of us who suffer with the pains of the mind. Thanksgiving, Christmas, and all the family gatherings that go with them sometimes can be a dark time. All the happy people bustling to and fro looking all jolly and gay, yet are they really? I wouldn't count on that, but be that as it may, these seasons, at least for myself anyway, are not my favorite. As I have gotten older, they have lost their glitter, and Christmas itself wears on my soul to get through it. Am I sounding depressed? Maybe, but I'm just being real, which is what we have to be. For me to tell you to smile through the holidays and just enjoy yourself are wonderful words, but I know the truth.

Dear friend, I am not here writing this book to tell you what you want to hear but what you need to hear. Holidays are tough sometimes, and the less time we spend thinking about how we will deal with them, the better off we will be. Will I get depressed? Maybe I will, but it won't last, and the season will pass. Hey, maybe we will be in great spirits this time around, and so we can rejoice in the Lord even more. The point I wish to make this day is one of focus, focusing on what is real and pushing away what is a lie. Having a happy-happy, joy-joy holiday season is a great goal to have, but I think it is better to focus on what is real—to focus on getting closer to the Lord this year, to focus on going over all I have learned through the spring and fall, and to get excited about what the new year might hold. These are all things that we need to focus on, not things that might or might not happen. Our minds are tricky machines, and if we run them into a state of conflict, we will end up in conflict.

Overthinking is one of the greatest downfalls of our emotional struggles. Putting too much thought into what we might feel next week, and what if we have a panic attack on Tuesday? These are conflicts of the mind, and something the mind has a hard time sorting out. In fact, sometimes these places of *overthought* often bring anxiety themselves. In Mark 3:25, Jesus speaks about a house divided and how it cannot stand. He doesn't say it might stand, but that it cannot. Too many thoughts, too many plans, too much contemplation can push us to a place of inner division. I have found that a big help to my OCD and my anxiety has been to not plan so much, to not have so many lists and orders to keep in check. The more I am able to let things be, let things just lay where they are, the more peace the Lord gives me.

So I don't go to that Christmas party that I am so worried about, no big deal! So I don't get done what I wanted to, so what? So I fall into a bit of melancholy around this time of the year, who cares? Everyone gets blue when the summer ends, when school starts, when the weather turns colder and darker. Sometimes we have analyzed ourselves so much that we miss the point that we are feeling not much more gloom than the next person. Sometimes we make ourselves into worse cases than we really are. Stay focused on one thing. Don't overthink many things. Expect a little blue time, and let's cut ourselves some slack. If we don't stop dividing our minds with too much thought, we will fall. Let us bite off smaller pieces of thought and planning and deal with them as if they were all we had to do for the rest of the year. Suddenly it isn't so bad, it isn't too much, we can make it through, and we're not that far off from everyone else in the world.

November 4 - Only if You Let It

No man can enter into a strong man's house, and spoil his goods, except he will first bind the strong man; and then he will spoil his house. (Mark 3:27)

In our quest for peace of mind, we must first understand that there is another one who is set on taking it away. Until I really understood the spiritual darkness that I faced each day, I didn't understand a lot of what was going on in my mind. I simply thought everything was cut-and-dried—"I'm going insane and losing my mind, and in time, I will be in a mental ward with drool coming out my mouth." Sounds extreme, I know, but if you have been to that dark place, you have had those thoughts too.

Letting thoughts rule you can be a dangerous place to hover. Not understanding the puzzle you are playing can leave you demoralized. Much of our problems are not due to our mental state but due to our spiritual one. No, not all emotional problems are spiritual, but I would say in my many years of counseling and suffering myself that most are. Much of the pain that we endure is pain that we allow control. We have opened the door and said, "Come in and consume me." Many of our fears are the ones that we let run rampant in our souls until they control our souls.

Dear friend, there is a gatekeeper of sorts in our minds. It is the will that is in us that wills to do this or do that. Then we have the outside forces that are trying to gain access and get past our gatekeeper. It is at that place where the battle really is. Who is going to cry uncle first? Who is going to fold under the pressure before the other one does? Satan and his cohorts are ever outside the door of our minds, and the gatekeeper called *our will* has the power to stop him. The problem with our will is its inherent weakness, which also was the demise of Adam himself. What was lacking and what is needed is the spring that holds that gate closed. That gatekeeper spring is the Holy Spirit of God who—*if we choose* to let control us—will.

Not to be too cliché, but our worst enemy is ourselves and deciding to stay where we are in emotional distress. No, I don't mean we want to stay there, but that we don't really want to try to beat it. As I have shared before, it wasn't until I woke up and said, "If I don't get out of bed and fight this, I will surely perish." No, it wasn't the Lord who had to make that choice, it was me. Did I have to go alone? Absolutely not, but I had to make that choice to fight on my own. We are strong in Christ, and the only way the enemy can overcome us is to bind our strength through fear and doubt. Once they bind that, then we are over, and the only way they can bind us is for us to let them. Don't let the enemy come into your home and take you captive. Remember the scripture—greater is He that is in you than he that is in the world. Let Christ rule by making the choice to be ruled.

November 5 - To Never Worry About a Leaky Roof

But Jesus said, "Suffer the little children, and forbid them not, to come unto me: for of such is the kingdom of heaven." (Matt. 19:14)

Children—there is something about them that the Lord Jesus Christ just loves. He speaks of them often and uses them as object lessons. He uses them as an example of the kingdom of God when speaking about faith. One day, while reading about Jesus and children and the account when Jesus lifts one into His arms in Mark 9:36, it made me ponder something—how old was that child?

I don't think God does anything by chance, and the specific age of that child was not an accident. Even though we can't know for sure that child's age, we can come close. After doing some research on the word *child* and the logistics of the event, I came to a conclusion that the child was between three years of age and six. I say this because a child any younger probably couldn't leap into His arms; neither could a man feel comfortable having them sit on his lap. An older child would simply be too big. Plus the age had to be critical because once a child gets too old, it loses that childlike trust and faith, which I believe Jesus is talking about. When Jesus chose a child for His example of faith, He chose that particular age group simply because it is the greatest faith we will ever have in our entire life. As an infant, there is not much faith because there is not much knowledge; and once we get to nine, ten, and eleven years old, reason and logic start to cloud our faith. No, this faith that Jesus is talking about could only fall within a small window of time. That age where your faith is working overtime, the age when whatever you tell your child, they will believe.

I know this to be true because when my two oldest boys were about four and five, I did an experiment. I had this fourteen-inch round electronic drum with many buttons and switches on it. And as was normal with me, I would make up stories and tell them to my boys. One day, I told my oldest, Jacob, who was about five, that if he sat on this machine, it could shrink him down in size so he could play inside the house of cards we were building. I said to him, "Do you want to try this machine so I can shrink you down real small, and you can play inside some of your toys and inside the cardhouse?" He said, "Okay, Daddy," and I sat him on the "shrinking machine" and said, "Are you sure you are ready?" He said, "Yup, I'm ready." So I pushed all the buttons and toyed with him for a few minutes and then told him, "I'm sorry, I was only teasing. Daddy can't make you shrink in size." Now, the point of all this is that God wants our faith and trust. If I were to tell my son that on Friday the sky will have pink polka dots, he would believe me. The question is why? The answer is simple: blind, 100 percent trust and faith in me.

Dear friend, with that type of faith, we'll never worry about the economy or the leaky roof. Daddy can fix anything, so I don't have to worry about anything. Remember being a child and feeling that way? That blind trust and peace in your heart, when all you had to worry about was looking forward to the next fun day to play? We can have that again, and the Lord wants us to, but it will take childlike faith. It's the only faith that works, and the faith we will need to get through this thing called life. Remember—perfect love casts out all fear, and when we know how much Abba Father loves us, we will trust Him like we trusted our dear daddy as a child.

November 6 - Do You Really Believe He Can?

And Moses stretched out his hand over the sea; and the lord caused the sea to go back by a strong east wind all that night, and made the sea dry land, and the waters were divided. (Exod. 14:21)

Sometimes I get lost in logic, not that I am that smart, but that I look at things, scratch my head, and ask the simple question, if we believe in this, then why do we fear that? As of the writing of this book, I have been a pastor for about nine years. Not long and probably still considered green by some. But I have been a pastor long enough to see a lack of logic in what we call Christianity. Not in what Christianity is, but what we believe about it. Take, for example, what the typical church and pastor preaches each Sunday. We open the Bible and speak of God's miracles and what God has done, is doing, and will do. We tell the people these truths, and yet no one really believes them.

Now, you might be getting mad at the statement I just made, and you might be calling me a liar because you feel you do believe all that the Bible says and all that your pastor says. Well, I would also like to think you do, but I don't think you, or I, really do, at least not 100 percent. Here is why I say this—if God said that He would never leave us or forsake us, if His Word said that Moses parted the Red Sea and that God is truly with us wherever we go, then why do we worry about so many things? If the Bible is true, and we say we believe it is true, then why are there so many of us afraid, doubting, questioning, and not running way out in faith to serve God? Why do we hold on so tightly to our money? Why are we so concerned about losing our jobs? Why are we so worried when our teenager is out late, and we can't reach them? If you are struggling with depression or anxiety today, and you're a child of God by faith in Jesus Christ, then why are you questioning if He will heal you or bring you through this? Now, don't get worried. I haven't lost my mind or my faith in the Bible. No, quite the opposite is true. I believe every word in the Bible, and I believe that God is very real. But I am also a sinner, and that sinful part of me, which will never go away on this side of heaven, will always question what we know to be true.

Dear friend, it is sin that is the issue and the problem to our faith. Sin uses reason and logic to feed itself. Like a dog will keep eating until it throws up, so will we keep sinning to feed our lusts. This is why confession is so crucial to truly walking and living by faith. If sin rules our minds, then faith cannot. The very fact that so many of us go to church, hear a great sermon, and then go home and want to end our lives proves that something is wrong. It can't be God, so it must be us. We simply need to desire righteousness more than we desire happiness. We need to only desire God and nothing else. When we do, then faith will have a place to grow; and when faith grows, trust begins to build. And when trust begins to build, then belief in what God says begins to become real to us. Only then will we really believe what the Bible says and only then will we be able to trust it. God will part the Red Sea of our broken souls. We just need to believe it. Do you believe Moses parted the Red Sea through God's power? If so, then you have to believe God will part your sorrow one day too—do you believe that?

November 7 - He Is Fighting for You

Exodus 15:3 The LORD *is a man of war: the* LORD *is His name.*

Exodus 15:3 is an odd scripture, and one that we might have trouble with. Is the Lord a man of war? This doesn't sound like the picture of the loving God we all desire and trust. Before we can toss a scripture away, we must also be willing then to toss other scriptures always. We can't just take the scriptures we like and deny those we don't—plus by doing so, we may miss the opportunity in seeing something that we are not seeing. Sure, calling God a man, person, or being of war sounds wrong, but why not dig deeper first before we run from it?

Let's step back today for a moment and maybe look for comfort in this scripture instead of fear. As with all scriptures, one of the biggest mistakes is taking one verse out of context. In this particular scripture, we need to understand what just happened before Moses said these words, which by the way are in song form. Well, God's people Israel were trapped at the Red Sea. The Egyptians were getting closer, and it looked like the end, but we know how it really ended. God destroyed the enemies of His people and did so in a very dramatic way. God's people were saved, and they were excited at that salvation and deliverance. On the other side of the Red Sea, they began to dance, sing, and praise God, and rightly so. God came through, and He, as always, did what needed to be done.

Yeah, sometimes He has to get tough and fight fire with fire. God is a God of love, but not as the world portrays Him as if He were some antiwar peacenik, a flower-power person who hands out roses at the airport. No, God is just and strong, commanding legions of angels, doing what needs to be done and always defending His people. He doesn't hide behind us as the enemy is coming at us. No, He stands out in front with power, might, and authority.

Dear friends, I'm glad that the Lord our God is love, but I'm also glad He is mighty and, if need be, a man of war. When trouble comes into our hearts, homes, and families, we don't want the pastor's pet poodle coming to our rescue, we want thrice Holy God in full battle armor with angels in their gear ready to defend. Hey, the enemy isn't using water pistols to shoot us, so we should find peace that our Lord is prepared for the real battle we face each day. In my days of depression and anxiety, in those days when Satan felt he had me under his cloven hoof, the Lord came with the right weapons to defeat him, and I'm glad He did.

Today find peace that the Lord we serve is a God of war as well as warmth. He knows when to tenderly hold our hand, and He knows when to get out His sword and cut off the enemy's head. God is always up to the task at hand, whether it is saving us from the dangers of life or the pains of depression. Like a Swiss Army knife, the Lord pulls out the right tool at the right time—always! He is fighting for us, not against us, and in that one truth, we should find great comfort and peace.

November 8 - And We Must Say It Again

If there be among you a poor man of one of thy brethren within any of thy gates in thy land which the lord thy God giveth thee, thou shalt not harden thine heart, nor shut thine hand from thy poor brother. (Deut. 15:7)

One of the hardest things to do is save a person who is drowning when you yourself are drowning. There are many risks involved in this, and the greatest one is that you will down that much faster. These are true facts in the real world, but in the supernatural world, it's a whole different story. Fact one: If God asked you if your life is more important than another's, what would you say? The answer is best found by watching what Jesus did. He gave His life for us. Fact two: In God's mind, if we risk our own life to save another's, would He not give us the means to do it? I say this all today because of what is written in Deuteronomy 15:7.

Dear friend, sometimes while we are in the middle of pain and sorrow, God might do the oddest thing, and instead of healing you at that moment, He may send someone who is in worse condition than you for you to minister. Now, I have made this point before in this devotional book, but I feel it needs to be mentioned again. We are here to be servants, not to be served. We are here to look past our circumstances and say to the Lord, "Here, I am, send me." Yes, I know what you are thinking. How can someone suffering with depression and anxiety help another? How can the lame aid the lame? Well, you can't alone, but in Christ, you can and you must. Even if it's just talking to a hurting person whom the Lord puts in your path, maybe an e-mail or a text, in some way reaching out and thinking about another besides yourself.

Dear friend, I would not be telling you to do this if I didn't do it myself. In fact, most mental healthcare providers would shy you away from helping others while you are hurting, but they don't know the Lord. In my struggles, the Lord forced me into so many hurting people's lives that I had no excuse but to help them. Even in my greatest darkness and pain, even in crippling anxiety, I was thrust into people's lives who were going through the worst of the worst. I could either say sorry and let them crash and burn, or I could step out of my self-centered dilemma and get involved in helping theirs.

See, the facts are in, and they are these: nowhere in the scriptures are our pains and problems an exempt ticket to serving, nowhere! Yes, it might seem impossible through your eyes to see how you could possibly help another, but how do you know that the very opportunity to help another or lead another to the Lord is the means by which the Lord is healing you? For me, that was part of the case—I led people to the Lord, counseled, and comforted. I even counseled people going through depression and anxiety while I was going through it. True, I backed down my workload to almost nothing, but I never completely stopped ministering to people. At the time, I didn't see it, but later I would. I would see the purpose in thinking of other's ills above my own. I would see the purpose in no longer whining about me all the time and start listening to others who were hurting. This is not a suggestion, friend, but something we must do—to care about another more than your own pain, that is truly of Christ. Yes, it will take great faith, but it can be done if we only believe.

November 9 - That It May Go Well with Thee

Thou shalt keep therefore His statutes, and His commandments, which I command thee this day, that it may go well with thee, and with thy children after thee, and that thou mayest prolong thy days upon the earth, which the lord thy God giveth thee, forever. (Deut. 4:40)

One thing I hate among many things is having a stomach situation and being stuck in traffic. If you have ever been there, you know what I mean. Just sitting there in cold sweat, longing for your own bathroom or any bathroom for that matter and knowing you can't move due to stopped traffic. I tell you, it is downright traumatizing. Now, that being the case, we know the thoughts that run through our minds, thoughts of just pulling over to the shoulder of the road and driving as fast as you can, or maybe even going through red lights and stop signs to get to that very distant bathroom.

I remember when we were expecting our second child. My wife went into labor about three in the morning, and the baby was coming fast. We lived far from the hospital, and so I drove very fast and did go through some red lights and stop signs. Now, the question that remains is this: Do situations such as a stomachache or a pregnant wife exempt us from the laws and rules of the land? Hate to bust your bubble, but they do not, and you can try it out on some police officer the next time you are pulled over for speeding while having to take a potty break. Besides, the laws that are broken there are also the very present danger to life, limbs, and property. It's just plain wrong, and yet for some reason, we convince ourselves that some situations warrant us taking matters into our own hands.

In Deuteronomy 4:40, the Word of God is clear about this. God doesn't suggest we follow His statutes but says that we *shall keep* them, and in doing so, great blessings will follow us and our families. True, by interpretation, He is speaking of His chosen people, Israel, but by application, the rules still apply. So the question is: What do we do with God's laws and systems and ways? Are they optional only for when we are feeling good, and life is running smooth? Or do they apply to all of us no matter what state our life is in? Again, it is another one of those inconvenient truths that we wish wasn't there but is.

Dear friend, because you just lost your job doesn't mean you are no longer obligated to give. Because you live far from the nearest church doesn't mean you don't have to assemble. Sure, there are certain circumstances when something just can't be done, but not when it comes to sin and obedience. As the scripture for today says, "That it may go well with thee." We all want that part of the scripture, but we cannot toss away the rest of it because we are not feeling well. If there is ever a time to be on the money with keeping our passions in check, it should be when we are in the grip of great trial. Does that mean that when things are going well, we can back off on the "Christianity"? Certainly not, but when you are in a deep trial, it certainly makes more sense to be closer to God than further away. Obey Him even when it's not the best time for obeying, and when you do, the Lord will declare, "It shall go well for thee."

November 10 - Fighting the Panic

Nevertheless he that standeth stedfast in his heart, having no necessity, but hath power over his own will. (1 Cor. 7:37)

Through this devotional book, I have kept to biblical values and concepts. I have done so because the Bible is the Word of God, and so it is faithful. Yet there are times when we can take a biblical concept and use it for something that maybe it wasn't designed for but where virtue can still be found. Now, you theologians out there don't get on an e-mailing binge to attack what I am going to say, but maybe let the Holy Spirit of God help us in a way we never expect. I speak of panic attacks and the powerful monster they can be. When one strikes you down, you know it's hard to pull out. It is like a plane that has just lost an engine and is descending toward earth at an alarming speed. You try to pull back on the controls, but no matter how much might you use, the descent is inevitable. Again, if you have had one, you know what I am talking about.

Well, today I want to give you a secular tip to stave off the crash while using a biblical concept. I choose as a starting point 1 Corinthians 7:37a— which is the first half of the verse. I know it is speaking about marriage and controlling sexual urges, but I feel the idea can also be transposed over to a panic attack. In the scripture, it speaks about standing steadfast and having power over our will. Now, sin is not the issue here, but being caught in the free fall of a panic attack. In this case, time is of great importance as the longer we wait to deal with it, the harder it is to stop. So certainly, we pray and cry out to the Lord for deliverance, but after we have prayed, I suggest we try this *panic control* quick fix.

For starters, if possible, find a quiet room, car, closet, whatever—what's great about this is you can do this procedure right at your desk, and no one will notice. Okay, so the panic is taking over, and your mind needs to be reined in from spiraling, runaway thoughts. What is needed is *mind distraction*, which is done by forcing your mind to focus on something else instead of the panic. This trick I learned can sometimes work if done correctly. Okay, begin by focusing on your right foot's pinky toe. Keep thinking about it until you can feel it and it alone. It is all about isolating your thoughts to one specific place. Next, move your focus up to your ankle, then kneecap, then upper leg. Also think from left to right, alternating the side of your body on which you are focusing. Work on up to your right arm then left arm, maybe your left thumb, then up to the back of your neck, then your right earlobe, and so on, even moving up to your scalp.

No, this is not a biblical technique, but it does teach us to control our will to some degree. By the time you have completed this task, your mind will have had to work so hard to focus that it must let go of the panic side. Expect to be a bit tired after this and take as long as you need, even going back down your body. It might not work the first time and might take practice. What is for certain is that your body is your vessel, and you need to be in control over its lusts, desires, and emotions. Do I fail sometimes? Yes, more than I would like, but they're baby steps. One day we will walk as adults yet with childlike faith. That is the goal—amen?

November 11 - Getting Better Can Be Your Work in the Lord

> *Therefore, my beloved brethren, be ye steadfast, unmoveable, always abounding in the work of the Lord, forasmuch as ye know that your labor is not in vain in the Lord. (1 Cor. 15:58)*

So many times we think of serving God as only set aside for pastors and missionaries. We see people in church running a Sunday school program or a children's church program and we think to ourselves, *Well, I can never do that with the condition that I am in.* When we begin to think this way, we become discouraged and feel that we are less than everyone else. It makes me think of Moses being called by God, and Moses complaining he couldn't take on the ministry due to a speech problem. Silly Moses and silly you and me. There is not one person created in God's image whom the Lord doesn't want to use and bless. Now, we might have some issues, true, but what if those issues are part of our ministry?

Listen to what I am trying to say. Let's say you are like me, struggling with depression and anxiety. You feel that your present condition is a liability to any further service to God. But what if the Lord wants your problems to be your mission? What if the Lord wants you to spend this time working on yourself? What if through this time of searching for answers, you are actually searching for a deeper walk with the Lord and don't even know it? With my life, my present condition was my ministry. If I didn't work through it with the Lord, I wouldn't be able to help anyone else with their similar problem. For that time and season, the Lord had me in personal counseling with the Holy Spirit. I was under His care and nurture, and all of God's focus was to teach me to better focus on Him. True, as I have said before, we are to serve others while in our condition, but sometimes we also need to make sure we are being repaired at the same time.

Think of this object lesson—if you have ever been in an airplane, you know about the safety class they give you before you take off. You know about the oxygen masks that drop down from above, and what do they tell you to do with it? Do they say to make sure your neighbor has his mask on? Or do they say first make sure yours is on so you can then help your neighbor with his? This is very similar advice that the Lord gives us. We need to make sure we are breathing and living so we can help others breathe and live.

Dear friend, right now your ministry and work in the Lord might be yourself. If that is the case, we can't move on to another ministry until this one is completed. It just might be a crash course in anxiety so you can train others. In 1 Corinthians 15:58, Paul says these words: "Be ye steadfast, unmoveable, always abounding in [*the work of the Lord*], forasmuch as ye know that your labor is not in vain in the Lord." Maybe our labor in the Lord is learning how to be healed. Maybe part of that training is also helping others in pain while we are in pain. Maybe that's the greatest step of faith, to be worked on by God while you are working on others for God, even while you feel like your whole world is falling apart—wow, our God is amazing.

November 12 - When Given a Dirty Spoon—Part 1

But He knoweth the way that I take: when He hath tried me, I shall come forth as gold. (Job 23:10)

Along with all of my quirks, which I have many, one of them is being a germaphobe. It seems to go along with our personality type: being nervous, worrisome, emotional, and extremely sensitive. Not the makings of a great pastor, I know, but the Lord proves out His scriptures once again by choosing the foolish things of the world to confound the wisdom of the wise. I am certainly one of the foolish things of the world, and yet the Lord saw fit to use me. That's good news, dear friend, for if He can use a worm as me, He can certainly use you. So back to my germ issues, I like things clean, neat, and certainly with no bugs or odd smells. When I travel, I am picky as to where I eat and sleep. In some cases, I would rather sleep in my car than a dirty, grimy, smelly motel. When it comes to eating at restaurants or any food establishment, I am even worse. Hand me a dirty glass or a half-washed spoon, and I am up and out of that place. I would never make it as a missionary as I couldn't take jungle life, and I certainly couldn't live without a hot shower once a day. I am truly the ugly American spoiled by the blessings of ease here in the USA. Though I come from a blue-collar, working-class family, I always had enough, including a clean bed and fresh food.

Be that as it may, the question of being given something less than you expect is something we must get used to. Being dealt the blow of depression and anxiety made me one unhappy young man. Sure, I worked hard in the trades as a young man, but I never really had any dramatic circumstances to deal with. So when the Lord handed me a dirty spoon of emotional turmoil, it was less than graciously received. I balked, murmured, whined, and complained. I cried until the cows came home (whatever that means), and still the Lord would not remove this dirty spoon of affliction. I became downright angry at the Lord and waved my fist of objection at Him. This attitude began to permeate all areas of my life as ministry became harder than I ever imagined. I complained about how hard it was, how mean people were, how small my church was, and on and on it went. The Lord would hand me a rotten apple, and I would complain again until my whole life was one of ungratefulness. No, I was not content; and no, I wasn't happy in Christ. I hated everything and was never satisfied. The emotional issues just made my immaturity even more recognizable. Bitterness can't be hidden, and you can't put on a happy Christian face to hide it. Like sunlight peeking through cracks in a wall, my unjoyful heart could not be hidden.

The problem was not the trials but my blindness to see their purpose. What I deemed as a destructive force of the Lord was really a furnace of purification. Oh, if I would not have fought Him so hard, I would have graduated from this class much sooner.

November 13 - When Given a Dirty Spoon–Part 2

> *Then said Jesus unto Peter, "Put up thy sword into the sheath: the cup which My Father hath given Me, shall I not drink it?" (John 18:11)*

This dirty spoon repulsion is really all about perception. I see a dirty spoon in my bowl of soup, but another person sees a bowl of soup that will fill their empty, starving bellies. When I was sixteen years old, I couldn't wait to get my driver's license; and as soon as I got it, I wanted a car. Back in the day, when I was growing up, parents didn't have the money like they do today in the USA to buy you a brand-new fancy auto. No, my father was a hardworking mechanic who owned his own shop, and though my first car was given to me as a gift, it was only a beaten-up junker my dad had lying around his auto-repair parking lot. It was faded red and did not run. As a gift, my father did a valve job on the engine so it would run and handed me the keys. Now, to some kids, that might have seemed like an insult; but to me, it was the greatest car I ever owned. I loved that car, and being dead broke, all I could afford was a can of paint, which I used with a brush and roller. The thought of a brush-painted car might horrify some, but it pleased me, and I drove that car for many years.

As I remember that car and the love with which it was given to me by my father, it can only remind me of John 18:11, when Jesus was given something that, to the world, looked horrible and undesirable to say the least. As I said earlier, perception is the key as we see Peter missing the blessing and only focusing on the thought of the soldiers taking Jesus away. God the Father was giving something to His Son. Peter thought it evil and ugly, but Jesus thought it an honor to receive. Jesus was given a cup of affliction, and He accepted it willingly. I was given a beat-up old car that some at school made fun of, but to me, it was a gift to be appreciated as it taught me many things about appreciating what you're given.

Dear friend, our cup of depression and anxiety might look like a raw deal to many. In fact, to you today, it might look like a raw deal; yet if it comes from the Father's hand, shall we not accept it? Notice in John 18:11 that Jesus doesn't just say He accepts what the Father has given Him, but He says, "Shall I not drink it?" To accept a lousy gift and then throw it in your closet is one thing, but to accept a (seemingly) lousy gift and wear it proudly is another. Jesus didn't just take the cup of affliction, but He willingly drank it. Was it easy? Did it taste good? Was it fun? No, not at all, but it had glorious purpose.

Dear friend, if Jesus didn't take the cup His Father gave Him, we would all still be lost in our sins; and if we don't take the cup of emotional pain the Lord gives us, we will miss the blessings on the other side. If God gives it to us or allows it to wound us, do we say that it is a mistake? If it is from the Father's hand, then it is good in some way or another. Let us accept the gift of sorrow and watch how it opens the door to a joy never before possible without it.

November 14 - Not a Curse but a Blessing

The meek will He guide in judgment: and the meek will He teach His way. (Psalm 25:9)

If you take an overview of history and the famous people in that history, you will find one similarity. Not that all famous people possess this similarity, but that those who have done great things for other people do. It is the characteristic of meekness, the gentle, compassionate, sensitive, tender soul that is you and me. Great writers, humanitarians, and missionaries all had a heart like ours. It is rare that you will find a mean, cold, loud, and overpowering person who suffers with anxiety or depression; and if they do, they don't feel that way after the depression and anxiety had a chance to work on them.

Anxiety and depression is the great neutralizer that evens the playing field and brings down the proud while raising the humble. Meek people are teachable, able to listen to instructions, honest, and able to see the beauty in a rose, where the cold and callous cannot. The meek take a deeper look at life; they walk slower and will crouch down to pet a passing puppy. We are not the norm, but we are also not abnormal; in fact, maybe we are even closer to what the Lord wants for all of mankind. Sometimes we tend to look at our hindrances as limitations when it might be the complete opposite. Because I'm not good at spelling doesn't mean I can't excel in math. Because I can't be a surgeon doesn't mean I cannot be a fine furniture builder. Hey, when on a sailboat, it's the short person who is less likely to be knocked overboard by the jib. When putting up lights on the Christmas tree, it is good that you are tall. Now, I know these might seem like insignificant limitations, still they are examples of the benefits of being different.

In our world today, meekness is certainly not a sought-after trait, but are we to seek what the world desires? We are to seek the things that are pleasing to our Lord, and meekness is one of them. It is not the proud whom the Lord will establish, nor whom He will guide. No, the many blessings of the Lord are laid aside for the meek of the Lord, those who are not filled with self but with Christ, those who seek not to rule but to serve. Those who are so in tuned with people and the world around them that any minor change in their surroundings are immediately noticed. Yes, we are the meek, the ones most likely to sit alone at the school cafeteria, the ones most likely to cry at a sad movie or feel the pain of a hurting friend. We are loyal and caring, loving and sensitive to the Lord's every tug on our reins.

Ever wonder why some Christians can just go happily along in their sins, and yet we are tormented by disappointing the Lord even a little? We are sheeplike, and that is why we are more prone to follow and depend on our Shepherd, Jesus Christ, and isn't that what Jesus wants from us all anyway? We are blessed, dear friends—let us be grateful for the special purpose the Lord has for us all. We are certainly more usable than most and, being so, more beneficial to the cross.

November 15 - Looking for Him—Not It!

That, according as it is written, he that glorieth, let him glory in the Lord. (1 Cor. 1:31)

If you were to take a poll of all the people in the world and ask them what they want the most, I am pretty sure most will desire one thing—

happiness. Sure, some would be more specific and say money, fame, sex, pleasure, things; but in the end, it all can be placed under the umbrella of happiness. It's what we all want, and we have all wanted it since the Garden. We can travel from a remote hut in some distant jungle to Main Street, USA, and still happiness is the goal.

If we have a pain in our side, we want that pain removed. Why? Because when the pain is gone, we will be happy, but with the pain, we are not. If you ask someone who has a real bad cold and lying in bed with a fever what they want right now, they will say, "Take this cold away from me." Ask them again why, and the answer will be the same—happiness. I can't be happy if I am in pain, and I won't be happy if I am in pain. Pain has one international common denominator, which is the desire to get rid of it. Now, we enter the Word of God and life in Christ, and we are told something completely abstract and different. We are told to rejoice in our tribulations, to count it joy, to suffer for Christ's sake.

Paul, when told his thorn in the flesh will stay, only replies with,

> *Most gladly therefore will I rather glory in my infirmities, that the power of Christ may rest upon me. Therefore I take pleasure in infirmities, in reproaches, in necessities, in persecutions, in distresses for Christ's sake: for when I am weak, then am I strong.*

We hear these words from great men and women of God and assume they are just words and not a reality but just some fairytale wordage. We conclude something is wrong because why would anyone want to feel pain or suffer? Why wouldn't Paul, Moses, and even Jesus, want to be happy like you and me today? Dear friend, the answer is simple, and it is found in this one biblical truth: "Happiness without holiness equals nothingness." Even above our personal joys and desires must be the desire first to please God and to find peace in simply knowing Him and being loved by Him. Until we can reach that place in our walk with Christ, we are simply walking the same road the world travels, which ends up at a dead end called selfishness. If we are to glory in anything, we must first be able to glory in Christ. God, and who He is to us, can't be a secondary consideration next to our primary consideration of being happy.

Happiness is fine, and the Lord can provide the true happiness that has eluded the world for centuries. But until Christ is all in all to us, we will never enter into the rest that Christ has prepared for us. If you are in pain and sorrow today, if depression has again reared its ugly head, before you seek to climb out of its snakelike skin, first make sure you are at peace with Christ by accepting this pain regardless if you are ever happy again. Tough words, I know, but we must lift the Lord to our lost world as our primary daily function and seek to be happy as only a secondary one. Little tip for you here: When you do only live to glorify the Lord, you will be happy even in your present pain.

November 16 - No Fear Is Not an Elusive Dream

He shall cover thee with His feathers, and under His wings shalt thou trust: His truth shall be thy shield and buckler.

Thou shalt not be afraid for the terror by night; nor for the arrow that flieth by day;

Nor for the pestilence that walketh in darkness; nor for the destruction that wasteth at noonday.

A thousand shall fall at thy side, and ten thousand at thy right hand; but it shall not come nigh thee. (Ps. 91:4–7)

I remember years back some company had as their slogan—No Fear. It was a craze that took over billboards and bumper stickers for a while. I saw it on T-shirts and tattoos. No Fear was the embodiment of a generation who truly believed they could live without fear. It was the season of extreme everything, from cycling to rock climbing to jumping out of planes. It seemed everyone wanted to beat their inherited fear of everything by going to extreme places of fear; and by somehow defeating them through some daredevil activity, it would remove all reality of life's fears. Fear is like getting cancer, going blind, losing a job or a loved one. Sad thing was it never worked because even though you could jump off a bridge with a bungee cord and not be afraid, the news of cancer would still bring you to your knees.

Today we still see the remnants of that short-lived movement. We see it in motorcycle riders traveling down Main Street at 140 MPH doing a wheelie. We see it in long boarders rolling down crazy steep residential hills with cars driving in and out of them. See, people are still trying to beat life's fears by substituting recreational fear. I think the only hope I saw lately was a bumper sticker that read—Some Fear. There is still hope, but only a worldly hope because you really can't eliminate fear on your own. That's a reality of this celestial life, but not if you bring in the supernatural life.

In Psalm 91:4–7, we find some of the most comforting words written in God's Holy Writ. Now, these are not simply bumper stickers or a company's slogan or gimmick. No, these are the true words of God, and if we have the faith to believe them, then, dear friend, we can truly live fearlessly! I know this to be true, for there have been times when I have caught that wave of being right with the Lord, and in that place, there is no fear. There is a trust, a confidence, a feeling of complete peace in the Father's hands. Kind of like that feeling as a child when your parent would carry you off to bed and you lay head over shoulder. It is sweet and alive, and if there was a bungee cord, I might even swing from it. But what's even better than a simple feeling of doing something reckless is a feeling of peace to deal with the unexpected. Things like death, sickness, and great loss. See, these fears are the real fears of life, and in Christ, in fellowship, fully trusting in Him, we can live with no fear of them. It is possible, and if it were not, then all the martyrs and missionaries of days gone by would never have been able to accomplish what they did against insurmountable odds. It's real, my friend, catch the wave if you dare.

November 17 - Seeds Watered by Tears Produce the Greatest Harvest

They that sow in tears shall reap in joy.
He that goeth forth and weepeth, bearing precious seed, shall doubtless come again with rejoicing, bringing his sheaves with him. (Ps. 126:5–6)

Well, it's still November, and if you live in a climate like mine, it is getting cold, and winter winds are on their way. Where I live, on the north-eastern coast of the USA, fall is a fun time, well, at least for the kids. Corn crops are now corn mazes, and pumpkin-picking and decorating season is here. I often marvel at the farmers here who don't waste a single shred of their farmland. In the spring, it's planting; in the summer, it's watering, and in the fall, it's harvesting. All through those seasons of growing, they are making a profit somehow. They sell their crops but also use the leftover husks and stalks to sell to people for decoration. Then, as I said, they take those dead cornfields, and before they cut them down and turn over the earth, they turn them into elaborate human mazes that can get a bit anxiety-inducing in themselves. They simply don't waste anything that the Lord has given them, and neither should we.

Each season of our emotional struggles is like growing seasons on a farm. Like a farm, the plants don't have any say in their lot but are simply used by the farmer to provide for his plan. Now, this doesn't mean they aren't cared for; on the contrary, they are diligently cared for and nurtured. Their seeds are planted at just the right time, in just the right soil, and given just the right water and fertilizer. Sometimes pesticides need to be introduced to ward off the pesky pestilences. Throughout that season, there are varied days—some with hot, dry sun, and some with driving wind and rain—where it would appear that the plants themselves are weeping under the strain. Yet through each stage, the farmer never takes his eyes off his precious crop as the Lord never takes His eyes off His very precious creation. Through each season, there is growth, and in some cases, plants need to be pruned. As the seasons march on, the plants grow big and strong, and then when they are at their biggest and strongest, the farmer does an odd thing. He harvests them, which is to cut them down, bundle them up, and haul them off to market. What a shock to those big and bold plants that never saw it coming. Was the farmer uncaring about his precious crop? Or maybe he saw a bigger picture than the plants could ever dream of.

Dear friend, we are growing in seasons, some painful and most glorious, and that's what is so hard for us to understand, those times when the Lord seemingly cuts us down in our prime, and we wonder what we did wrong to deserve such a fate. Dear child, most likely you have done nothing wrong but have come to the place where the Lord can now harvest you and make you ready for market, the place where all the effort the Lord has placed in us can now produce—for Him! Remember again Revelation 4:11: He has grown us for His work and purpose, and if we let Him use us in His time and way, we will find ourselves being crucial parts of so many very important things.

Ever see how many things corn is a part of? That corn plant feeds everything and everyone, from animals to people, and even makes fuel for our autos. That farmer had much bigger plans than that plant ever envisioned. It thought only of growing up from the ground, but the farmer was planning much further ahead.

November 18 - It's Fear, Not Problems!

In righteousness shalt thou be established: thou shalt be far from oppression; for thou shalt not fear: and from terror; for it shall not come near thee. (Isa. 54:14)

A famous politician from days gone by once said, "We have nothing to fear but fear itself." Well, truer words could not be spoken. Fear at the end of the day is what gets us, not so much the problems we face. With those who suffer with anxiety, it's a double whammy because we have fear of fear. If you have ever suffered with persistent anxiety or panic disorder, then you know how this works. We begin to fear, not so much what brought on the first panic attack, but the fear of the panic attack. In time, we really don't know what brought on the initial attack, and it doesn't really matter. What matters is that we now have fear of fear. It is a completely irrational fear, which is basically what anxiety is. Now, our Lord can bring deliverance from this fear or any fear. He first exposes the core of this issue by also pointing out what we need to really focus on. No, we are not to focus on the issue (fear), but the One who is in control of all issues.

Notice in Isaiah 54:14 that the Lord makes some rather clear psychological, cognitive conclusions. He first points out where our foundation of reality needs to be built upon. Righteousness is where we must stand—on God's righteousness and also on ours through Christ's imputed righteousness. That is step one in fighting fear. If we understand who God is, we understand that ultimately, everything is under His control, which results in—no fear. Next, the Lord promises for us to be far from the crushing weight of fear when we are supported by His righteousness. Continuing on in the verse, we see that we shall *not fear*, which is a command more than a result. And from terror or extreme crippling fear, it shall not come near you. Notice now an important point in that last statement. It doesn't say that terrifying things shall not come near you but that the terror of terrifying things shall not come near you. When we put all of these concepts together, we then have a leg to stand on in a scary fighting world. The fact that the world is scary, well, that cannot be changed. Evil, sickness, terrorism, and wickedness are constants, and there is not a place where they are not found. To search for that is to search for peace apart from the Lord, which is an impossibility, so searching for a peaceful world is not the answer to our fears. The answer is understanding that we have nothing to fear. No, not because there is nothing to fear— there is—but in Christ and under the Lord's wing, those scary things should not cause us to fear.

In Christ, and set upon His sovereign righteousness, we can look at the world, see the horror, and say, "My Lord has me in His hand, and nothing that this world can dish out can take me out of His hand. And because of that, I do not have to fear any longer. Christ is in control, and that is all I need to know."

November 19 - When I Get Better

For the lord giveth wisdom: out of His mouth cometh knowledge and understanding.
He layeth up sound wisdom for the righteous: He is a buckler to them that walk uprightly. (Prov. 2:6–7)

Dear friends, today I say again what I seem to say too often. I speak of deal-making and our relationship with the Lord. Listen, we all want to be better, happy, and back to normal, whatever that is. We want a good life, and if calling ourselves Christian helps, then we will do the Christian thing too. And there lies our eternal illusion of what life is really all about. We seem to think that in this world, there is ourselves and then there is everyone else, in that order. Then maybe we believe that there is God, and so we place Him somewhere in the picture, but because our knowledge of God is so lacking, we really don't know where to place Him. We think on it for a very short time and decide that based on what we know about God, He seems to be like some type of helper. Some type of social worker who has been placed in our lives to guide, help, and show us how to be happy. We see Him as a traffic cop who points one way or another. We see Him as a doctor whom we go to, be it reluctantly, when we are in need of healing. We figure, like with most life assistants, that all we really owe them is what they get from the taxes we pay. As with church and serving God, our taxes paid are our attendance and our few dollars in the offering plate. We basically make a god to our liking and to our understanding. In doing so, we basically create a god in our image and what religion is and needs to be.

Dear friend, we cannot be further lost than in that illusion I just explained. This is why when things hit us like depression and anxiety, we seem to run to God, but only in the same way we run to a fireman when our house is on fire. He simply becomes a means to our end. Once the fire is out, we really don't give the fire department a second thought. Maybe when they come around for donations or are trying to raise money, maybe then we toss some coins into the hat. Well, this is not God, or even close to how this thing we call life works. Dear friend, God is King and Ruler over all creation. He has made us for Himself, and so we are His servants who can become best friends and even His children through Jesus Christ. As family, and yet still willing servants, we are to live according to His house rules all the days of our lives. The problem is that, though we might understand this even a little, we still feel that we make the rules and choose the timing and way in which we believe we should serve Him. When it comes to walking uprightly, we simply say, "Okay, Lord, I will get around to that as soon as I am through or over with this current problem in my life. But until then I have bigger fish to fry, and Your Will, Lord, will have to wait." Dear friend, read Proverbs 2:6–7 and see how this thing really works. Get busy today living as a Christian should 24-7 with all of our heart and mind. This is not a game but our Creator's command. When we understand this, we will then find that He is more than happy to hold our hand and carry us gently home.

November 20 - Really?

Delight thyself also in the lord; and He shall give thee the desires of thine heart. (Ps. 37:4)

As I have said in the past, some scriptures are just so overread and used that they become sadly abused. Take Psalm 37:4, one which I have hanging in my office right where I can't miss it while sitting at my desk. I have looked at that scripture for many days and never really understood what it really meant until the Lord opened my eyes. Now, you may say, "How can you not see what it says? Doesn't it say that the Lord will give you the desires of your heart?" Yes, that is partly what it says, and if that part (b) of the scripture is really true, then there should be millions of happy Christians walking around with all their desires being met. And if we really take it to the *end-all* of it, then there should be millions of wealthy Christians driving around in fast sports cars, sailing in big yachts, and living in big mansions. Those who love music should all end up as famous musicians with the recording contract of their dreams. We should all have the perfect mate and be in perfect health. Laughing should be all we do each day as we get up in the morning. Well, unless you are living on planet Zion in the Nebula Galaxy, you know that, that is simply not happening.

Now if that is the case, then we must draw two conclusions: number one: God's Word is a lie and not trustworthy, or we don't understand what Psalm 37:4 really means. Well, since God is always true, then it must be our misunderstanding of the scripture or, better yet, our lack of desire to understand the scripture. I say this because if we truly looked deep into this scripture, we would see that the lack of its fulfillment is not due to the Lord's lacking but ours. For a moment study Psalm 37:4 and see what your eyes quickly focus on. Is it not on the promise part, the "desires of our heart" part? Yet why don't we carefully put as much effort into the first part, the "delighting ourselves in the Lord" part?

Dear friend, delighting ourselves in the Lord is a far greater feat to achieve than you will ever know. No, it's not found in placing a fish symbol on your car or owning a Bible. It is not found in going to church or calling yourself a Christian. No, delighting yourself in the Lord is to live, breathe, walk, and talk Jesus Christ all the time, every time. It is putting His Will above yours in everything you do. Notice what I just said—it is putting His will above your own in everything you do and say. Well, if that is the case, then what would happen to your personal will and desires? Wouldn't they no longer exist or at least become second to God's? And that being the case, then the desires of our heart would then be whatever God desires. Suddenly our desires become only what God would want, and suddenly having a speedboat no longer interests you but only what would be good for the Lord. Suddenly Psalm 37:4 becomes all about what God's desires are and not about ours. Suddenly we are back to the fact that everything we do and breathe needs to be for the Lord. Suddenly our desires of healing and joy become second to the Lord's joy and will for us to obey and glorify.

November 21 - Please Stop with the Truth!

Commit thy way unto the lord; trust also in Him; and He shall bring it to pass. (Ps. 37:5)

One thing I pray that you get out of this devotion is my intention of giving you the truth no matter how hard that truth is. I seek not to get you to like me as an author or praise me for this book. To some, there might even be anger toward what I say, and maybe even some will take the book and slam it shut and throw it in the trash. My calling in writing this devotional book on depression and anxiety in the life of a Christian is not to gain wealth or fame or anyone's approval. My intention is to bring to those who are hurting the healing and deliverance, which the Lord has given me. That being the case, I hit you again today with another painful truth of living the Christian life. To be where we need to be to ever find healing, we must first do what God commands us. It is being steadfast in pleasing the Lord before we please ourselves. For a certainty, this is extremely difficult and painful at times to reach, but nonetheless we must strive for it.

In our continuing study of Psalm 37, in verse 5, we see even stronger language from the Lord, a demand for our total obedience before any deliverance. Let us read it together: "Commit thy way unto the LORD; trust also in Him; and He shall bring it to pass" (Ps. 37:5). Notice the no-compromise approach to what the Lord demands. We are to commit, which is a place of total determination. Then it is laying our way and life out on the table and placing it into God's hands for evaluation. If that wasn't enough, we are then to also trust in Him, in such a way that we trust nothing else but Him. All people, means, and money become meaningless next to our dependence on Him. Then and only then will the Lord bring to pass that which He has promised us in verse 4. There is no highway option here, no loopholes to get around this strict demand. There is no other easier way or gentler path to find peace. The Lord gave His all on the cross, and He expects nothing less from us for Him.

Being committed to the Lord reminds me of the fear men have today who do not want to commit to marriage. They want a way of escape and freedom to bail if things don't go their way. They want their cake and eat it too, and so do we as Christians. We want all the blessings of the Lord with as little commitment on our part to Him. We want approval for the mortgage on our home without having to sign the papers or pay it back. We want a backdoor deal, an easy-to-swallow medicine that heals all our sickness.

Dear friend, our only problem is thinking that committing to the Lord is some type of punishment or some life sentence when in reality it is a joy and blessing. And when we start looking at it that way, the sooner the blessings begin to flow. Jesus is so worthy of committing to, and any strings attached are made of string candy: sweet and wonderful to have and be a part of. It is good to follow Christ, and it is better to want to.

November 22 - Why Would God Do Such a Thing?

Until the time that his word came: the word of the lord tried him. (Ps. 105:19)

If there was ever a person of amazing faith, it had to be Old Testament Joseph. Talk about trusting in the Lord and getting sand-kicked in your face for it. From his childhood, his brothers hated him, wanted him dead, and left him for dead. Then they sold him into slavery to a caravan of Ishmaelites, and then he was sold to Pharaoh's officer who showed favor upon Joseph. When the wife of Joseph's master asked Joseph to sleep with her, he did the right thing and did not sleep with her, and for his refusal, he was accused of rape, placed in jail again, all while praising the Lord. It seemed that no matter what the Lord allowed to happen in his life, Joseph made the best of it and even excelled in his place of torment.

While a prisoner, he decided to become the best prisoner. When asked to sin, he could only respond by saying, "How can I do this great evil against the Lord?" Did he have times of anger and doubt? Maybe, but we really don't know. All we do know is that he never lost faith in his God and never spent time moaning and complaining about his rotten life.

It makes me think about many of us today and how we are so *not* like Joseph. Often I hear from people this complaint: "Pastor, I don't understand God. I am serving, doing good for Him, living the best I can, making good, godly choices, standing up for Christ, yet all I get are problems." I think, to some degree or another, we all feel this way, though maybe we don't vocalize it. Nevertheless, God knows our thoughts and shakes His head in disapproval. We can almost hear the Lord saying back in reply to our complaints, "But you told Me you trusted Me, and that no matter what, you would follow Me."

Today, dear friend, maybe you are having a Joseph moment, except without the thankful heart. Maybe you are trying your best to serve and love the Lord, but it seems like you just get kicked down again and again. Maybe this depression or anxiety you are suffering is the straw that breaks the camel's back. Maybe you've had it with God and with things not going your way. Well, here is what you and I must do when we are in such a place: Do what Joseph did and serve Him even more, even as the ship is sinking, as the water is pouring in from every crack in your boat. Don't give up but bail faster and harder. God doesn't make mistakes, and if it seems like He has in your life, then you are simply looking at things from the wrong perspective. Maybe the sinking ship is a test of how much water you can bail; the depression may be a test of how much faith you have to stand tall and fight. Maybe the anxiety is a test to see if you can still march into battle even when you are petrified with fear.

God tried Joseph for a long, long time, and the result was a man ready for the blessings that were to come, from a prisoner for righteousness' sake to second-in-command over all Egypt. Joseph was raised to a place where he was above all in his family and in the nation and yet able to save his family because of his long trials and testing. What everyone thought was for bad, God was using for good. Your depression and anxiety will be for good if you can only see what God is trying to create in you. Until you do, it will seem wrong, and you will be bitter; but when you see the why and accept it, you will begin to get excited about the blessings that are on their way.

November 23 - Let Us Talk About Depression and Hear

Then shall the righteous shine forth as the sun in the kingdom of their Father. Who hath ears to hear, let him hear. (Matt. 13:43)

It seems like the Bible has a bit more to say about anxiety than it does about depression. There is certainly much discussion about fear, worry, and doubt in the Bible, and rightly so. Fear is the center hub that I believe all emotional issues circle around. There are some cases when depression is purely depression, but I feel that many times anxiety is misdiagnosed as depression, so wrong treatment and medications are given, only making the person worse.

Dear friends, I am not a psychiatrist or psychologist, and I don't claim to have their vast knowledge in these areas of mental illness, but I do know one thing: I have walked in the shoes of deep, dark clinical depression, and I have also walked in the trembling clutches of anxiety. I feel that gives me at least a little credibility, plus adding my knowledge of what God's Word says about such things, so I might know a thing or two about it. True, at the end of the day, I am simply a Christian counselor, and to some, maybe that is not enough. But what I have observed over many years in practice tends to lead me to this conclusion on depression: it has its roots around a core of fear. Depression comes in many forms and levels, of which we will discuss at a later date, but for the most part, I feel it is an "idiot warning light" that fear has secretly grown to control you.

Now, in case you don't know what an idiot light is, it is one of those lights on the dash of your car that pops up and says, "Check engine." Now, some of us see those warning dash lights, some in red, some in yellow, and our concern for that idiot light depends on how much the car is affected. Interestingly, the reason why they call them idiot lights is because by the time the light comes on, the damage is usually already done, as in the case of temperature and oil-pressure warning lights. Normally, there are symptoms that would have warned us ahead of time, which could have saved that engine, but only if we knew what the warning signs were.

Fear is a warning sign of coming depression. Anxiety, which is irrational fear, is the weed that grows around all that is joyful and pleasant in your mind and soul, and in time, it chokes out the joy until depression manifests itself. When that happens, we are already on a runaway course with disaster, and we don't even know it. Whoever has ears to hear what I am saying today will understand what I say. Some will not have those ears and instead refuse to listen to God's signals of a soul that is dealing with more stress than it was designed to process. Depression is an idiot light that points to a problem, or problems, that should have been dealt with long ago. Today, listen to the signals the Lord is sending and be willing to see what He is trying to show you before depression sets in. If you are already in that state of depression, then listen for the clues He is showing you to get out of it. More on this topic later.

November 24 - Don't Worry—Yeah Right

Peace I leave with you, My peace I give unto you: not as the world giveth, give I unto you. Let not your heart be troubled, neither let it be afraid. (John 14:27)

I am a realist, and I know that in the reality of living, there are two things that are a part of that living: death and worry. I would have added taxes, but they are just a cause of worry, so let us just stick with the top-two biggies. Jesus, being God in the flesh, knows something about what makes us tick, so He knows about our tendency to worry. We know this because He speaks about our worrisome heart quite often. In John 14:27, Jesus touches on this worry tendency again. Notice how He words His cure for our worry. Notice how He doesn't tell us how to remove the tick but how to live with it in peace until He chooses or does not choose to remove it.

Where I am from, ticks are a real issue and can cause serious health issues. I recently had a friend who found three ticks embedded under her skin, and after removing them, she quickly sought a doctor's care and also sought prayer. She was visibly shaken, and yet what caused her concern was not that she *was* sick from the tick bites, but that she *may* get sick from the tick bites. Isn't that what worry really is? It is worrying about things that *might* happen. Again, what does Jesus say and do about such fears? Notice again in John 14:27 that Jesus doesn't do much to take away fear as much as He gives us peace in that fear. Peace is something given by God, and worry is something given to us by Satan. Is Satan always the cause of worry? No. We do a pretty good job of finding things to worry about on our own, yet Satan does know what makes us tick (no pun intended), and he uses his knowledge of our fears to stoke them as one would stoke a fire.

In John 14:27, we see the word *let* not once but twice. Jesus here is explaining how we need to do something to get something. If a person is giving us a one-hundred-dollar bill, we must also take it. If our house is on fire, the only way the firemen can put it out is for us to *let* them on our property. Jesus also points out that being troubled in heart and being afraid are something we do quite easily. We are born with a tendency to worry and fret, so again Satan doesn't have much trouble snowballing that emotion. Is it easy to stop worrying about things? Certainly not, as I believe it is all part of the fall of man. With our rebelling against God, we also rebelled against His peace. This is why our "second birth" is so important to being freed from worry. The old stony heart must be replaced with a new heart that trusts in Christ.

As I look over my life of worry and fear, even before my trouble with depression and anxiety, I found this one fact to be true: For all the things I worried about, 95 percent of them never happened. Like I said earlier, worry is really a fear of what *might* happen, so instead, we need to focus on what *will* happen. This is where trusting in Christ comes in so perfectly because Jesus is already in the future, already dealing with the what-ifs and the will-happen things. We are really in error when we worry about something that may happen tomorrow when Jesus is already there.

November 25 - But I Want Money!

For the needy shall not always be forgotten: the expectation of the poor shall not perish forever. (Ps. 9:18)

Over the years, I have counseled some very interesting people. One that really sticks in my mind is a young man who came to see me for depression and anxiety. I didn't know him at all, so I had to start from scratch. I started as I always do by bringing him to Jesus Christ, and I thought he did come to Christ when we spent days praying and speaking about the things of the cross. He had me convinced he was sincere as he said all the right words and acted in all the right ways. He had some issues at home and problems living on his own. I tried to help and took care of some of the issues by simply making some phone calls and following through. After a few months, I started to see an angry part of him, a bit of annoyance when I always went back to Christ and prayer.

Then one day he left a rather nasty and threatening message on my office answering machine. It was so threatening that I have saved that message till this day. What he said to me was something that I would refer back to again and again in sermons and studies. It was simply the true heart of man when it comes to our fears and worries. In a paraphrase, this is what he said: "Pastor Scott, I don't want to hear about Jesus, about prayer, about heaven. I want money—give me money, I need money!" Now, I knew he had money issues, and I did try to help him get his money in order and taught him how to better pay his bills, but the root cause of his worry and concern was in the fact that he didn't have enough money.

Money is a funny thing, and again, something that the Lord knows much about. He knows how much faith we place in it by how much we worry when we don't have it. If you think back to many of our worries, not all, but most are somehow based on lacking money. At that place, we really don't want to know about Jesus or His promise of provision; we want money.

People, though we might not say it, will surely think it—*Jesus is great, but He doesn't pay my bills.* It's a sad state of affairs to even think that way, and even more, it is inaccurate. Jesus does pay our bills by providing the hands to labor and the means to attain it. When we truly cannot labor, then He will find a way to provide for our needs. Notice I said *needs.* Wants are not a given, needs are. Jesus will provide all that we need: a roof over our head, food in our stomachs, and clothes on our backs. What kind of food, clothes, and roof is up to Him. Once we understand that, all we really need will be provided by the Lord.

Then there is one last thing we have to worry about. Will we have the house we always wanted, the cell phone, or the latest in hairstyles? Maybe not, but the Lord will provide for His own. That young man sadly didn't want the Provider but the provision. The problem is that you cannot have the provision without having the Provider as your Lord and King. Come to the cross for forgiveness and salvation, and you will get the Provider. Strangely enough, His provisions will come too. Those in need shall never be forgotten, and those who worry about their needs will not have to worry anymore.

November 26 - The Hardest Choice You Will Ever Make

And the people said unto Joshua, "The lord our God will we serve, and His voice will we obey." (Josh. 24:24)

To obey God, why is that so hard to do? I wish I could tell you that it gets easier as we get older, but it does not. Our flesh, which is our old sinful nature, is a major monster we battle with daily. Sometimes we do get a handle on it, and we do have seasons of victory, but if there is one thing I have learned, that is to never rest in those victories. Satan is ever after our *wills*, and he knows our tendencies to sin. Once we are saved, there are not many other routes he can take to sidetrack us, so he goes after what is left: again, our old sinful nature.

I have been on megahighs of obedience and righteousness, thinking how far I have come; and within a month, week, or even a day, I am tripped up again, and temptation has me by the throat. One would think that a pastor would have reached a level of holiness that is far above sin or sinful thoughts. Well, think again, and also remember this: if Solomon, in all his splendor and holiness before the Lord could fall, what makes us think that we could not? Holiness is our goal, dear friend, but happiness is what seems to drive us. That might seem like a worthy goal, to be happy, but it is not. Holiness is what the Lord calls us to, and happiness is merely a by-product of holiness.

In our quest to be free from depression, anxiety, or whatever, the answer always lies in obedience to the Lord. One would think that if that is the case, then why not just obey God and be free? But again, the monsters of lust, greed, pride, pleasure, and money always seem to be bigger forces than our desire to please God. It is an undeniable force of fallen nature, and we must come to grips with it. The solution is the power of the *will* to do what is right. But how? We must have a desire to please the Lord, and that only comes from a true love for the Lord.

In Joshua 24:24, we see a people of God with a single voice: "We will obey the voice of the Lord and we will serve Him." They were a wise people, it would seem, and only the Lord knew if their words would be followed with action. But nonetheless, it's a picture of what our will must be. We must be stone set on fire and in desire for the things of the Lord. Only then is there any power to fight off the wicked world and the wicked one. I pray that you and I would both get off the boat of wanting to please the Lord and climb on the boat of actually doing it. We must ultimately look at both sides of the coin: a) the world and Satan's kingdom and b) God's kingdom, and from there make a continuous choice to follow Him. Sorry, there is no secret way around it but to confess our sins and desires and replace them with the desire to follow the Lord's will, full-on 100 percent; and in following Him, also choosing His will over our own. Lord, help us.

November 27 - A Picture of You and Me

Now the word of the lord came unto Jonah the son of Amittai, saying,
"Arise, go to Nineveh, that great city, and cry against it; for their
wickedness is come up before Me." (Jon. 1:1–2)

It is sad that historical accounts like that of Jonah, the Garden, Noah's Ark, and many others are tossed aside as fairytales. It is a shame because there is so much wisdom there, but wisdom left for dead. Dear friend, all of those accounts are true, and the sooner we understand that, the sooner we begin to really trust the Word of God. Jesus spoke of many of these events, and if so, then they must be true, or Jesus is a liar. As to the account of Jonah, it is one well worth looking into and gleaning virtue from. Take Jonah chapter 1 verse 1. Here, Jonah is given a direct command from God. Jonah hears, but like us, he doesn't want to do it. It is like when the Lord tells us "Fear not," but we say, "I cannot stop it, Lord, nor do I want to. Lord, I know you want me to follow You, but Your way looks dark, lonely, and painful. I will not do it!" Jonah begins to do at this point what we begin to do. We begin to make escape plans and try to convince ourselves that they are God's escape plans. Jonah didn't care about the Lord's plan, will, desire, and burden for the crying people of Nineveh. No, he only was concerned about his own crying. Sound familiar? It should, because we do it all the time.

I have this person from church who is often sick. What they want is people to help them, but they really do not care much for those people. It is all about them and nothing to do with God and others. As we have spoken about before, self-preservation seems to kick in whenever our world might have to face a challenge we don't deem worthy of our effort. All of a sudden, all kinds of harebrained schemes seem to pop into our heads. Running is one of them and probably the most common. Mostly it is running toward sin and away from the Lord. I can almost bank on this one as I have seen it in church people's lives over and over. A problem comes up, life gets a little harder, and the next thing they are doing is talking about moving far away.

Jonah, in about the same fashion, did the same thing. God called him to a place and ministry he didn't like, so Jonah decided to run to a distant location. Was it fear, lack of trust in the Lord, or just selfishness? Doesn't really matter, but what does matter is this: the Lord told him to go *this* way, and he went *that* way. If there was ever a defense for the free will of man, it is certainly found in the actions of Jonah. Let us look deeper into the mirror image of Jonah over the next few days and see how his mistakes can be ours—even in relation to our fight with depression and anxiety.

November 28 - Thy Will Be Done, Not Mine

So they took up Jonah, and cast him forth into the sea: and the sea ceased from her raging. (Jon. 1:15)

Poor Jonah, just a man wanting to be left alone, but is that what we really want? When we look back at our prayers, we seem to find symmetry to them all, a cry for usefulness, purpose, and significance. If you happen to be a person who doesn't want those things, then you are very selfish, and all you really care about is being left alone in the woods. Jesus didn't die on the cross to lock us away in a remote cabin but to set us free *for Him*. Remember again we are here for Him and His purpose. Revelation 4:11 points this out crystal clear, so the idea of just wanting to be left alone is antibiblical and never of the Lord. Getting back to our purpose and desire, is it not to do something, be something, be remembered for something? If so, then God has big plans for you, but plans that must be followed His way. So Jonah runs away from God's plans to hide. In that hiding, he ends up on a reclusive ship where he figures no one will know or find him. What's interesting is whom Jonah is really hiding from, God Himself, and it is so foolish for him as it is for us today to think that there is someplace where we can go where God is not already there. Hiding from the Lord of creation, what a silly thought. David himself knew about this when he wrote, "Where can I go from Thy Presence, if I go up on some high mountain or down to the bottom of the sea, You are there."

Dear friends, we might not like it, but it's a fact of Christian life. Once we are part of God's family, we become part of God's plan; and once part of that plan, there is no way to run from it. Sooner or later, what the Lord has ordained for you to do will be done. In some cases, it just might be that depression and anxiety are our lots and / or training for something very important to come. With that being the case, we cannot fight it, run from it, cry about it, or complain about it. Regardless of how we might hate our current lot, it will be done just as the Lord planned.

For lack of a better illustration, I think about eating some bad food. Our bodies are designed by God to reject that food, but no matter how much we desire for the vomiting to be stopped, it cannot. It must come. Though awful it might be, relief follows. As that bodily function is designed to save us from harm, so God's will is designed to save us from harm, but even more, to make us ready for service. For Jonah, God's will was ever present as he was tossed into the ocean. Was it a wonderful experience? Surely not, just as depression is not a wonderful experience. Yet just like Jonah ended up where he was to be in the first place by finally stopping his fight, so will we end up where we need to be when we end our fight. Jonah, I figure, didn't flail too much once in that ocean before that great fish swallowed him up. Hum, saved by a nasty situation. Can we also be saved by depression and anxiety? Let us read on.

November 29 - Custom-Made Depression?

Now the lord had prepared a great fish to swallow up Jonah. And Jonah was in the belly of the fish three days and three nights. (Jon. 1:17)

God truly does work in odd and mysterious ways sometimes. Let me rephrase that: He works that way a lot of times. As you look back over your life and how the Lord moved in your life, was it always through logical means? In my life, most of the great moving was through painful, odd, and, at times, bizarre means. I think about how the Lord answered my prayer for me to pastor the church where I am presently. Since the day that I walked through the doors of this church, I knew one day I was going to be pastor there, or at least I desired it for certain. How did I end up as the pastor? Through a very odd and unusual set of circumstances. Number one was that I had to move as far away from that church as possible. I moved three thousand miles away to California to take over another church. Yes, that was the plan for me to take over this one in New York. *Gee, Lord*, I thought, *what's up with having to move?* Yet I followed the Lord's lead, scratching my head all the way and finally deciding that the Lord never wanted me in New York but in California. So I packed my bags and went thinking I would never return. It was surely an odd way and plan He had in mind, but lo and behold, it worked.

The pastor who was in the New York church was getting on in years. He called me one day and asked if I would consider taking over in New York. Next thing you knew, I was moving back to New York, becoming the pastor of the church where I always wanted to pastor. Why do it that way? I don't know other than to test my faith and to also get me some real life training for New York by what I learned in California. Yes, our Lord certainly knows what He is doing, but unfortunately, He is the only one who knows.

In the case of Jonah, I am sure he never dreamed that his ultimate travel arrangements were to be inside the belly of a rather large fish. See, it is not so much the vessel that brings us to where the Lord wants us, but that we end up where and how He wants us. For Jonah, preaching in Nineveh was going to happen, and the best way to prepare him for it was to put him through some pretty scary situations.

For you and me, maybe depression is just a vessel and has nothing to do with the depression or anxiety at all. Maybe it is simply a custom-made training system that best works to bring us to a point of being the kind of person God wants us to be. My depression was, and still is, that vessel— constantly molding, breaking, and growing me into a better man of God. I don't like it, nor do I think it's a good way to train, but I surely cannot deny its effect on me. My depression and anxiety is custom made for my unique emotional makeup. For others, the Lord may use loss or financial problems, maybe even giving you lots of money to show you that money does not bring joy. Did I tell you the Lord did that to me also? Yes, I once made a lot of money and had all my desires, yet the Lord used those things to show me how empty and worthless they are without His joy filling me.

November 30 - Okay, I Get the Point, Lord

> *Then Jonah prayed unto the lord his God out of the fish's belly, And said, "I cried by reason of mine affliction unto the lord, and He heard me; out of the belly of hell cried I, and Thou heardest my voice.*
> *For Thou hadst cast me into the deep, in the midst of the seas; and the floods compassed me about: all Thy billows and Thy waves passed over me."*
> *Then I said, "I am cast out of Thy sight; yet I will look again toward Thy holy temple." (Jon. 2:1–4)*

Today we live in a world where everything seems to be based on efficiency. From our appliances to our automobiles, it all seems of the utmost importance that they do their most work with the least amount of energy used. Even on a practical level, we are finding new ways to do old jobs. Ways that are faster, better, and yield the most production per amount of labor used. Some people take this to an extreme as I saw this man once who used a power leaf blower to dust and vacuum his living room. I don't think his wife appreciated the gas fumes that ended up permeating the house. Efficiency—well, the Lord our God is King of it as He never wastes one word, breath, or movement in accomplishing His will. I simply stand in awe how He can be working in my life while using my problems to work in another person's life while that person is working in another person's life with what they see in that person's life. The Lord is the Master Chess Player, and every move is strategically planned, timed, and done for His ultimate *will* while blessing us at the same time—wow, amazing! In the case of Jonah again, we see this played out perfectly.

In Jonah chapter 2 verses 1–4, we see Jonah doing exactly what the Lord wanted him to do in the first place; that is, listen to what He was telling him. What did it take to get Jonah's attention? Well, a trip on a ship, being tossed into the ocean, swallowed by a large fish, and then vomited up on the shore of God's choosing. How long did it take to get Jonah to see the light? Not until Jonah was in that dark, dreadful place. A place that appears to be a lot like depression and leaves you feeling like you just had a massive panic attack. In verse 4 of chapter 2, Jonah finally got the point, which was, "Jonah, pay attention to My will, not yours." Jonah only then cried uncle and said, "Okay, okay, I will look toward Thy holy temple."

I must confess, after reading about the turmoil Jonah went through just so the Lord could get his attention, it came to me—gee, he could have spared himself a lot of pain and suffering if he just would have obeyed the Lord in the first place. But then I think to myself, *Would I have been able to escape all that I went through by just obeying the Lord the first time He called me?* The answer is probably no, and here is why: It was not just getting my attention or Jonah's attention that moved the Lord to put Jonah through so much, but it was what he would learn in the process, things that he could never have known even if he obeyed the Lord right off. Now, that really had me thinking, *So the Lord is so smart that He uses our rebellion and sin to His advantage sometimes.* To know the future so well that even though He knows we will blow it big time, He can still use that failure big time. Wow—that is a God I want to follow trust. How about you?

December

December 1 - When It's Just Too Much for You to Bear

Fearfulness and trembling are come upon me, and horror hath overwhelmed me. (Ps. 55:5)

There are good days, bad days, and then there are the worst days. If you have ever been in the grips of depression or anxiety, you know what I am talking about. Today I want to focus on the fear factor of our particular struggle. One of the debilitating factors of fear is its ability to drain all of your strength. They say after you have had a massive panic attack, it is just like stepping out of a boxing ring with a prizefighter. You are spent emotionally and physically, and you look like it too. Just getting up and accomplishing a single task can feel like trying to lift a hundred pounds of concrete. Some might see it as laziness, but it's not. It's a five-alarm fire being waged in your body and mind, demanding that all systems be on overload and for rest to happen now.

Sleeping on a bed of nails is no stretch as you could if you had too. Sleep is calling out to you through a bullhorn; this, my dear friend and fellow sufferer, is the place of being completely overwhelmed. For those who have never been there, it's almost impossible to describe it, but if you're reading this devotional book today, then I am sure you understand. It is at this place where you think and ponder how you ever arrived at such a condition. You think of bygone days when you were filled with energy and vitality, but that is just a dream at the moment. Next come the trembling and horror that travel through your body like an electric shock. You have done all the crying you can, and there is no one else left whom to complain. Sleep is all you can ever really look forward to or even have the ability to achieve.

Dear friend, I do not go over these symptoms to bring you down but to show you how far down you can be brought up from. Listen, I lived that private hell myself, and I am here and doing okay. As much as I thought I was alone in this struggle, I would soon learn that I was not. No, it wasn't so much the people who came to my rescue but what they did. Those whom the Lord sent to lift me did just that, but not of themselves. Sometimes it was knowing that others were praying for me. It's hard to ask people to pray for you without telling them what's wrong, but sometimes the Lord really wants us to humble ourselves and cry out to a few trusted prayer warriors. Go to them and tell them what's going on. Tell them that you are going to be okay, but without their fervent prayers, you won't. This will alert them to the fact that you are in a serious state, and their prayers, maybe even their fasting, are needed. This is a high-alert, all-bells ringing movement. If you are close to some church people in leadership, call them too. It's time to tell your pastors, elders, and deacons that you are in a bad condition. If need be, have them pray over you.

I don't say these things to alarm you but to explain that when you are bitten by a rattlesnake, you don't just skip along the road as if nothing happened. Dear friend, prayer is megacritical and oh so effective in these dark hours. I remember going through a very hard time when I took over my second church. Soon after I took the helm, a violent church split developed, and at a pastors' meeting with local pastors, they could see I was in a bad state. Thirty spirit-filled men gathered around me and prayed over me. I tell you it was real, powerful, and active. Godly people praying moves mountains, and when it feels like there is a mountain on your neck, it's time to call in the Calvary. Do it today and don't wait.

December 2 - This Is Getting Serious

> *I remembered God, and was troubled: I complained, and my spirit was overwhelmed. Selah. Thou holdest mine eyes waking: I am so troubled that I cannot speak. (Ps. 77:3–4)*

I don't mean to take you through days of downer devotions, but I know that there are days when they come in such a violent sequence. It's a steady slide to the rear, and gravity has the better of you. Here too I have stood, and also I have stood silent. There is a point when speaking is no longer profitable as you have said all there is to be said. There are days when you just stop talking because you are tired of saying words to no avail. Again, I will share with you some of these days. I do this again to give you hope from the ashes. Yes, I was this bad, and I was this dark.

One particular time, my anxiety was so ignited that it felt as if every nerve ending was being stabbed with tiny needles of electric voltage. There was no place to find rest or escape; it was as close to hell as I could come, and I wouldn't be surprised if a legion of demons were surrounding me—that's how tormented I was. My mother was over that day, keeping an eye on me as my wife was away. When she saw my state, she just fell to her knees and prayed for hours out loud. Maybe you are thinking that I am making this stuff up or that I should have been institutionalized, but this is not just an occurrence unique to me. No, this is common in the spiritual warfare of ministry. You should read of your missionaries and your great theologians like Spurgeon. Spiritual warfare is real, my friends, and you better be prepared for its onset if you ever desire to move up in ministry. Demonic oppression is not something for Hollywood movies but is a reality of serving God on the frontlines.

Now, not all debilitating anxiety and fear are demonic, but some are. That is why we must be very sure we are fighting the right battle with the right weapons. If it is clinical, chemical, and clearly nonspiritual in nature, then medication, therapy, and proper cognitive diagnoses is in order; but if it is spiritual, then we better have our full armor of the Lord on—our swords drawn, sins confessed, and our Bible quotations at the ready. Let me be perfectly clear in such cases. Satan is out to destroy you as he wanted to destroy Peter, as Jesus told him. Jesus even clarified that Satan *wanted* to sift Peter. Satan wants to get at those who are doing or will be doing the most for the gospel. He is good at what he does and knowing the best way of taking out a possible future liability. He will stop at nothing, be it with temptations that grab hold of you as if they had actual arms.

There will be thoughts that will overwhelm you as if you were hearing actual voices. Run to the Lord, run to scripture, run to your prayer warriors. I pray that no one reading this devotional book ever has to go to this dark spiritual place, but if you do, remember this: "Greater is He that is in you, than he that is in the world." Christ always beats the enemy every time! Remember that, but remember the clever devices of the cloven-hoofed one.

December 3 - Who Are You Really Wanting Help From?

Hear me speedily, O lord: my spirit faileth: hide not thy face from me, lest I be like unto them that go down into the pit. (Ps. 143:7)

Friends! I love having friends, but I have learned some great wisdom about them from the Lord. Friends are good, but God is better. Even family who you are sure will be there for you might just let you down. Funny thing about people, they love to speak great flowery words of "being there for you" but rarely do they follow through. I see this all the time at funerals and wakes. Yeah, I'm a big people watcher, been that way since I was young. I just like observing what people say and then weighing their words in my mind. As I said, at a typical funeral, as people are moving up the line to console the person who lost a dear loved one, what do they all say all the time? "Hey, if you need anything at all, call me." I just listen and smile because I make darn sure not to say that without meaning it. Sometimes I feel like asking them, "Really, so can you come over next Saturday and change the oil in my car?"

I know I am being mean here and a bit sarcastic, but I say this because the Lord is very clear on words. They mean things to Him, and He even says that we will be held accountable for every idle word we say. Does that mean that the words and promises of our friends will have to be accounted for? Could be, but the point I want to make is this: don't depend on those friends who promise to be there for you to *really* be there for you. They might, and they might not, but if you just assume they won't, then you will never be disappointed. Over my years of being a baby Christian and then moving up to ministry, I have been promised many things from many apparently sincere Christians. Promises like, "I have your back, brother, I'm there for you." Then the praises of how great a person or what a wonderful pastor I am. I tell you, a major hard lesson to learn was that those very same people whom I broke bread with would end up being my greatest enemies who would stop at nothing to bring me down. Many times I would be simply blown away and say, "Lord, how can this be? How can my dear Christian brother or sister now hate me so much?" I would also question the logic behind it and what the Lord was trying to teach me. Well, two things come to mind after many bitter, bloody battles, and that is, "The heart of man is desperately wicked who can know it?" and Psalm 118:8, which says, trust in no man but trust only in the Lord.

Dear friend, when things in our emotional life hit a snag, our first inclination is to call out to a friend for help, and we should, but—but we should always remember that at the end of the day, salvation only comes from the North. Expect to be let down, forgotten, and left on your own. Maybe it will be not on purpose as many truly do want to help you, but they just can't get around the hardness of their own sinful hearts. We are a selfish people as the scriptures declare, and when my ship is sinking, I will certainly save mine before I save yours. It sounds mean and cruel to say such a thing—well, maybe it's just Paul and I who are the chief sinners. I know man, and I know the Lord. Depend only on Him, for only He will never ever, ever, ever let you down.

December 4 - Good News for the Fallen

The lord upholdeth all that fall, and raiseth up all those that be bowed down. (Ps. 145:14)

December 4 already, and here in the northeastern United States, it's getting mighty cold. If you have ever had the pleasure of living through one of our winters, you know a thing or two about falling down. What's even worse is a phenomenon we have every once in a while called an *ice storm*. It looks like a winter wonderland but not for your derrière. It's when it rains and then the rain turns to ice over all the trees, power lines, grass, sidewalks, and even cars. Everything is encapsulated in a cocoon of solid clear glaze. No matter what type of shoes, snow tires, or chains you have, you just can't walk or drive. When you fall down, and you will, it's hard, and it hurts. For the elderly, it can be downright fatal. In our spiritual life, we do a lot of falling too. It is sad to say that many don't want to admit it as much as others, but we will leave them with the Lord. For though they might not ever admit to falling, God would make sure they do, spiritually, that is.

Dear friend, to think we can live in this fallen world and not fall is the same as thinking you can dance during an ice storm and not break your neck. Things happen; people get sick. People we thought were rock-solid Christians end up struggling with anxiety and depression. It is nothing to be ashamed of but something clearly to be expected. Whether it is falling into sin or simply falling through the trials of life, we will fall. Now, I am not promoting license to sin as some do, that we can just sin all we want because we are sinners, and Jesus always forgives. That is not what I am promoting as we are called to—"be ye holy for I am holy." That's what the Lord Himself proclaims, so running around calling ourselves sinners all day is not the route the Lord wants us to take; the road of seeking holiness is. What I am talking about today is this: we will sin no matter how you cut it, and so we better learn how to get back up again. We will fall into depression sometimes, and maybe anxiety and fear, but we must also know what the Lord says about that. Be it a voluntary fall into sin or an involuntary fall into life's dark days that leave us depressed, we need to know we have hope.

In Psalm 145:14, the Lord has something to say to us about any type of falling, even when we are pushed. "The LORD upholdeth all that fall, and raiseth up all those that be bowed down" (Ps. 145:14). I like that Psalm and especially how it says that the Lord upholds *all* who fall, and He raises up *all* who are bowed down through despair. Those are wonderful words, not just words but *the* Word of God Himself. If we fall, He will pick us up. That's not a maybe but a promise, and one we can take to the bank.

December 5 - Seen Thy Tears

> *Thus saith the lord, the God of David thy father, "I have heard thy prayer, I have seen thy tears: behold, I will heal thee." (2 Kings 20:5)*

Crying seems to be something most associated with children. As we get older, there seems to be less tears and simple sadness when pain comes upon us.

If you were to see a full-grown adult skin his knee and break into uncontrollable sobbing, it would seem a bit odd. But here is the thing, why is it odd for adults to cry? Who said that at a certain age, tears must stop flowing? Sure, our tolerance for pain is greater, and physically, we don't need to cry when we fall or burn our finger. But does that mean that tears are no longer to flow from our eyes? Interesting thing about tears, scientifically, there is no logical reason why we should cry when we have pain. Tearing when dirt is in our eye is something else, and that does have purpose, but what of crying when sad? If you wanted to refute evolution, tears would be a good place to start as they tell us that evolution only lets things evolve that have purpose. I'm sure they can come up with a reason for tears if you ask them, but it's very clear that crying when we are in deep pain or sorrow is for something much greater than a physical, natural purpose.

I believe tears are a type of pressure-relief valve system. It seems like we do feel a bit better (emotionally) after a good cry. The pain remains, but somehow the sorrow is cut back a bit. Now, if the Lord created our bodies with tear ducts and fluid that drains from them during sadness, then why should we suppress them? In my life as a Christian counselor, tears have shown me in people a place where there is a breakthrough. If I am counseling and I don't see tears, then I don't feel like I am breaking through. Tears are also a gauge that lets us know when we have hit a sensitive area. Tears show a breakthrough in the Lord dealing with a particular sin. Tears often follow a person's salvation experience and acknowledgment of their new life in Christ.

Now, with all of these positive issues for tears, there are some problems. Number one is that men seem to cry less, and it has a much greater stigma with it than with women. Tears are seen as a sign of weakness, which is something that men especially don't want to show. Tears are also a sign of humility, which again the world frowns upon instead of looking up to. Well, for all of you who refuse to cry, who cringe at the thought of someone seeing you cry, well, that's simply pride, and it is also holding back an important part of our healing through deep emotional turmoil. If you think that crying is beneath you, then you must think that Jesus is beneath you because He also wept.

No, my dear friend, we must cry before the world before the Lord will begin to work sometimes. In my struggles with depression and anxiety, whatever tears I didn't shed as a young adult, I surely made up for as an older adult. In those dark days, I cried until there were no more tears left. I would also leave a soaked Bible and sheets many a time. Dear friend, as we discuss tears over the next few days, let's not hold them back but let them flow. They have purpose.

December 6 - The Power of Tears

And Esther spake yet again before the king, and fell down at his feet, and besought him with tears to put away the mischief of Haman the Agagite, and his device that he had devised against the Jews. (Esther 8:3)

In Esther 8:3, we see an example of the power of tears to motivate. Sure, we can abuse tears to get sympathy and manipulate people for personal gain, but that's not what we are talking about here. True tears do have a power to them, a power for people to see your sincerity, true character, and passion about a subject. Tears have been known to sway votes in politics and also invoke deep trust in a person's pleas. With the Lord, He knows true tears, and He also can be moved by true tears. When the Lord sees a real broken and contrite heart, often that's His go-to sign to begin healing. Sometimes He waits years for us to feel the remorse of our sins, and only then does He trust our repentance. People can say they are sorry over and over again, but when we see that sorrow with tears, we tend to believe it more.

In the life of many people, I look for a moment of tears if I am to believe their true passion and love for Jesus Christ. If I don't see it, then I question it. Now certainly, tears are not mandatory manifestations to prove our salvation, but they sure do help. being forgiven for all our sins and given new life in Christ, one would think that would move us to tears. Tears after a great sin that has been controlling and directing our life for years is another good sign that it has finally been beaten, and we are truly rejoicing over it.

Speaking of rejoicing, I have seen people rejoice so much for what the Lord has done in their lives that they shed tears of joy. What triggers tears is always a mystery as sometimes it can be something as simple as a worship song that blows you over. I remember one Sunday before my sermon the worship team did a song that just happened to hit me while I was in a very sensitive and dark place. I began to weep so heavily that I couldn't even sing the words, and when it was over and I had to approach the pulpit, it took me a few minutes to gather myself together. The Lord's love for me in that particular song just blew me over, and only tears could process the dynamic feelings I was going through.

Dear friend, whether you are a man or a woman, I encourage you to really have a good cry fest, to get alone with the Lord if you must and let Him empty you of all that you are. Not to be gross, but not unlike a good vomit after a bad meal, tears are the sign that the pain is almost over. A sign that healing has begun, and new life is developing in you. We must also not discount the abiding of the Holy Spirit within us who convicts and tweaks our souls in a way that weeping seems to flow much easier than ever before. Be it standing or driving or getting on your knees at the altar, tears wash, and tears cleanse. They move us in a way that scares us sometimes, but they also help grow us. Without tears, there can be no true growth. Until you have wept over the Word of God, over Jesus at the cross dying for your sins, I find it hard to believe that you truly understand what was done for us.

December 7 - He Knows Each Tear I Cry

Thou tellest my wanderings: put thou my tears into thy bottle: are they not in thy book? (Ps. 56:8)

One thing we often do when in deep turmoil is to isolate ourselves. When we do this, we spend many hours alone and hidden from the outside world. If we are single, we really take this to its fullest dynamic and leave ourselves completely isolated from any help that might be waiting for us. For those who have placed themselves in this self-imposed exile, one of its worst side effects is feeling like no one really cares. Dear friend, to be going through some very hard time and be surrounded by family and loved ones is one thing; but to do it all alone is something else. Well, the good news for those who are in that place of total darkness and isolation is this: those tears you cried, though not seen by men, are certainly seen by the Lord; and even more, they are collected and counted. Imagine that! The Lord keeping track of every tear we have ever cried. That should be of great comfort knowing that the Lord of creation knows me. He knows you, and even more He knows the tears I cry and hears me when I call.

On this December 7, I want us all to consider why this is so important. I want us to take a moment to pray for the many people who are so much worst off than we are. To pray for those who truly have no one, not friend, family, or even coworker who cares. For those who belong to no church, have no church family, and live deep in the remote places of this world. For those who feel like they are lost in a sea of faces, just someone who is off the grid of life. For a person who feels that if they were to die, no one would ever miss them or care. That, my friend, is a deeper, darker place to be than most of us can imagine. Well, for those people I have a wonderful word of hope for you. God knows your private suffering; He knows what no one else knows about you. Maybe you can't afford counselors and medications. Maybe you have no one who truly is watching out for you. Maybe your money is just about gone, and you feel that you are not even worthy of God's attention. Well, He does care even when no one else does. He does know you are crying and hurting. He knows that you are afraid, alone, beaten down, and ready to give up.

Today, as you read these words, He is answering your prayers by acknowledging that you are very important to Him, and He is very concerned about you. Your prayers have been heard, logged in; tears have been collected and counted—He is on the case. Soon His deliverance and help will be coming, and you will not be alone again. Today, know that you are known, you are of worth, someone does care, and you matter greatly to your Father in Heaven.

December 8 - Without God, You Are Very Alone

> So I returned, and considered all the oppressions that are done under the sun: and behold the tears of such as were oppressed, and they had no comforter; and on the side of their oppressors there was power; but they had no comforter. (Eccles. 4:1)

Dear friend I don't know how clearer I can say this, but this truth is truth. Without God, you are very alone. In my years of counseling, I have stood by one rule, and that is this: I only do Christian counseling, meaning God must be a part of the counseling, or it has no value in it whatsoever. For me, to counsel without the Lord is like a surgeon doing an operation without a scalpel. It's a mechanic repairing your engine without wrenches; it's a dentist trying to fix a cavity without that horrible drill. I know this for a certainty because one time, I did bend my rule and tried to counsel without the God thing as the people didn't want anything to do with God. Well, it was a flop, and I will never do it again. And as I told that family, without the Lord, you are lost, and there will be no help for you. They took offense, but so be it, it is truth!

This brings me to you today, who are going through tears of pain or know someone who is. Maybe they or you really aren't into the whole God thing. You are not sure what you believe in and would rather just get some advice on dealing with depression and anxiety without the aid of the Lord. Dear friend, I have horrible news for you then. If you feel alone, well, you are alone. If you feel like there is no hope, well, there is no hope. True, you can get on a regimen of medications and see some therapist, who will ask you about your childhood and tell you your problems are because your mother dropped you on your head one too many times. That might make you feel good, and it might be a Band-Aid for your dyke that is ready to explode and flood your world. But it will not last, nor will you ever get to where God would like to see you. If you don't believe me, that's fine, but at least take a look at the world around you. Look at the world today, which has all but removed God from every facet of our society. How does that seem to be working? Is there less depression, less anxiety, fewer suicides, less school shootings, more morality, more order and decency in society? If you say yes, then you truly are in need of psychiatric help because you are delusional.

Dear friend, there is no hope in a world with no Savior. There is no peace in a world without the Peacemaker. There is no healing in a sick world without the Healer. Men are simply men, and they can make laws but can't change hearts. Jesus is the only way to fix us from the inside out. To change our worldview and see what the Lord wants us to see. If you want to go through it alone, then that is your choice, but please do not complain to the One you don't believe in. God is real, alive, abiding, and sovereign. There is no place where He is not there, so why should we try to repair what He created, without His wisdom about His creation?

December 9 - Either He Is a Liar or He Is Truth

He will swallow up death in victory; and the Lord god will wipe away tears from off all faces; and the rebuke of His people shall He take away from off all the earth: for the lord hath spoken it. (Isa. 25:8)

Sometimes we just have to get to the place where we ask this one question, is God a liar? Some may go further and ask, is God even real? That, my friend, is only a question that you can ask, and one that you must decide upon. It is not about what someone else thinks or believes, but what you think and believe. God is working on you, and He wants to know where you stand. Do you believe Him, trust Him, count on Him, and depend on Him? Do you trust His Word and believe that it is actually the Word of God Himself? That is a question that every man and woman must ask themselves while they still have breath in their lungs. And why is it so very important to you personally right now? Because what you choose to believe on this day will determine if you make it or you don't.

You see, if God is real, then Isaiah 25:8 is real. If that scripture is real, then you have a great wonderful hope for deliverance. But if you don't believe it, then you are wasting your time reading it. You are wasting your time praying, going to church, reading your Bible, and so on. God makes some rather bold statements throughout His Holy Word, and if they are true, then they are all the hope we need. But if we don't believe them totally, we are, of all men, most miserable. If it means anything to you, I believe with all my heart and with every fiber of my being that every single Word of God's Holy Bible is actual, literal, real, truthful, and anointed by God Himself. I know this because I have seen it, felt it, and know it to be true. What you need to do is ask yourself where you stand.

Take Isaiah 25:8. Look at all the glorious promises of the Lord. Imagine it being all true. Imagine how that would change so much about your life. Dear friend, it is true, and you only need to stretch your faith muscle just a bit to see it. The Lord is alive. His Word is alive; it is new and fresh every day. And if there is a liar, it is Satan, whom Jesus calls the father of lies. If you have been lied to, know where it comes from. If you have questioned God's Word, know what that is all about. Has there been doubts and fears placed in your heart about the Word of God? Remember who is trying to make you question it.

Dear friend, read our scripture for today over and over again. Place your name in it and apply those promises to your life. Then trust it, accept it, believe it, and wait patiently for it, for the Lord never tarries or is late.

He is just on time even if it is at 11:59. He will never forget those who trust in Him, those who also love Him and praise Him. All of these components are crucial to our relationship with the Lord. Understand them and embrace them all.

December 10 - Even This?

Whether therefore ye eat, or drink, or whatsoever ye do, do all to the glory of God. (1 Cor. 10:31)

Dear friend and fellow sufferer, I know many of these devotions seem to hover around this same ideal. If we have a problem, think about God first. I know this is contradictory to everything our hearts and minds tell us. It goes against everything our friends and the secular world tells us, but it is exactly what the Lord says. The whole concept of being in pain and then planning on helping a good friend move is almost bizarre to us, but it is not to the Lord. Today if you are suffering with depression or anxiety, I know your only goal is to not suffer with depression and anxiety anymore. If you have an earache or toothache, all you really can think about is that pain being gone and relief replacing it. You are not thinking about your neighbor who is having marriage problems or the person at the supermarket who lost their car keys. No, you and I both are thinking about us, end of story.

Well, in my many years of being a Christian, I have found out one important life fact: focusing on my particular problem has not lessened it one bit. For all my worrying and moaning about my current life calamity, nothing I do about it for myself changes it. If that is the case, then maybe it is time to try something new, to try what God's Word has to say about our present suffering, living, walking, and serving the Lord. In 1 Corinthians 10:31, the Lord's Word gives us this advice: whatever we do, eat, or drink, no matter what it is we are going through, we are to do it so the Lord gets glory. Now, why would the Lord ask of us such a difficult task unless, by following through on that task, it would be good for us? If we read that scripture and take it at its full-on literal meaning, it could then be applied this way: If I am suffering with depression today, then suffer with it as unto the Lord. Suffer with it so God would get the glory.

Some might ask of this significant request, but how? How can I struggle with deep emotional pain and do it so the Lord would receive glory? We might even ask, why should I be even thinking about giving God glory? I would rather curse God for what He is putting me through. In John 9:2–3, we catch a glimpse of what Jesus is trying to teach us about maladies:

> And His disciples asked Him, saying, "Master, who did sin, this man, or his parents, that he was born blind?" Jesus answered, "Neither hath this man sinned, nor his parents: but that the works of God should be made manifest in him."

Could it be that our current depression or anxiety has really nothing to do so much with us but everything to do about people seeing God through our pain? Dear friend, to give God glory through suffering is a major key to getting through it and be blessed even by it. It is to say to a person who sees us very down and knows we're hurting, "Yeah, I am going through a dark time right now, but God knows what He is doing, and when I'm through this, I will be better than before. Would you like to know about Jesus?" That's faith. That's powerful. That's a path to recovery.

December 11 - Worship Simply Because He Is Worthy

Saying with a loud voice, "Fear God, and give glory to Him; for the hour of His judgment is come: and worship Him that made heaven, and earth, and the sea, and the fountains of waters." (Rev. 14:7)

So here's a scenario for you and I both to ponder. We are driving down the road a wee bit too fast and get pulled over by a police officer. He then takes out his ticket book and gives us a hundred-dollar ticket for speeding. We then reply back to him in this odd way, which really isn't that odd if you think about it: "Officer, I just want to take this time to thank you for this ticket, for it shows me that you are watching over me and care about me getting hurt or hurting another by driving so fast. I also want to praise you for a job well done. I am just so blessed by you that I will be thinking about you all day and, even more, for the rest of my life. I will never forget what you taught me and showed me about myself this day." Well, I am sure that police officer would think you quite mad indeed, but in reality, he did do something that is good for us. We don't see it as clear as he does, but the fact remains that speeding is against the law, and we were breaking that law—should we be glad that we didn't get caught?

Dear friend, your reaction and mine to that scenario is why we don't understand this life and how the Lord works. We see things as always against us when we should see all things as for us. That is why our worship is so flawed, especially in the modern church of today. Most churches go to great lengths to insure that the worship experience is topnotch, but what are the people on Sunday morning really worshiping? Well, most, I guess, are worshiping God's love, power, and wisdom, but is there any worship of His judgment and justice? Are we worshiping His work of trials and testing in our lives? Are we worshiping Him for the pain He allows us to endure for the greater purpose He has planned? No, I think that most of us are all getting worked up to a hand-raising circus because we want God to show us favor and bring us blessings. We are forgetting the bigger picture by not also worshiping Him for the speeding ticket, the cancer that was allowed to teach us grace and faith, those things we don't see as benefits but as curses. And deep down inside, we hate God for them. We can't find a reason to celebrate those things because we don't think they have any virtue.

Dear friend, until you can thank that police officer for that ticket, we won't be able to thank God for our depression and / or emotional state of present blessed pain. Did you catch what I just said? Blessed pain. Can pain be blessed? Well, if it's ordained by the Lord, as He did in Paul's life and Job's, then yes. Can we curse Him for what we don't like and only praise Him for what we do? Should not our children love us the same when we buy them ice cream as well as when we punish them to their rooms for a week? Worship God today. Learn to worship Him always and in all things. By doing so, we show the greatest faith one can ever demonstrate. To love someone even when they say or do what we don't want to hear but what we need to hear. That is the true heart of worship.

December 12 - Fear Not Suffering

Fear none of those things which thou shalt suffer: behold, the devil shall cast some of you into prison, that ye may be tried; and ye shall have tribulation ten days: be thou faithful unto death, and I will give thee a crown of life. (Rev. 2:10)

I don't know about you, but I hate pain; I hate any pain. Burning a finger or anything that really hurts. I wouldn't wish it on anyone. As I think about pain and suffering, I begin to realize that I don't even like a bit of suffering. Over the years, my tolerance to any inconvenience for that matter has really been a weakness. The other day, we had some crazy cricket in my bedroom. It was the loudest darn cricket I have ever heard. What was amazing was how this little noisy bug was driving me insane. I was tossing and turning, getting up, and trying to catch him. I was so upset as if some great problem had entered my soul. Well, it didn't take long until the Lord convicted me of my pettiness of self and reminded me of the millions who suffer rape, torture, starvation, cancer, and so much more, and there I was, so upset by a silly cricket.

Suffering is not fun, and as I have learned, I'm not really into it on any level, but the Lord warns us of real suffering. In Revelations 2:10, we hear of a future time when there will be great suffering, testing, and even imprisonment for the gospel's sake. In our day today, we are to suffer at times and look at it as an honor for Christ. It is an honor to even share in Christ's sufferings. Yes, I know there are many TV preachers out there telling us that God has only happy times, wealth, health, and prosperity waiting for us, but if that is true, then why isn't that what we see? Is every Christian on planet earth somehow not doing what they are supposed to? Because according to what some of these tele-evangelists say, we should be dancing in the streets. No there is someone lying and it's not the Bible so it must be these fancy pants preachers with their $1000 dollar suits.

Dear friend, just take a stroll down the path of biblical history and examine the lives of the great saints and prophets of the Lord. Do you see any living a life of ease, health, and prosperity? If anything, just take a look at Paul. If anyone should be blessed into a life of beach-lounging and easy living, it should be Paul, but is that the case? Paul suffered more than most of us could ever endure, yet he did it in grace, peace, and joy, knowing he was doing it all for the King of kings.

Dear friend, if you are suffering today through some emotional torture, try looking at it as suffering for the Lord. Try to see it as a moment in time when lessons are learned, others are blessed by watching your faithfulness, and the Lord knows our suffering and will end it when He deems it best. As in the case of Jesus Christ, the Lord didn't end His suffering until the work of redemption was accomplished, and not one minute sooner. Should the Lord end our suffering one minute sooner than what's best? If you desire to know the end of your suffering, I will tell you. It's not at 11:59 p.m. but 12:00 a.m. Yeah, that one minute more can be a killer, but not if we focus on the one minute after.

December 13 - Fear Not Because I Am?

And when I saw Him, I fell at His feet as dead. And He laid his right hand upon me, saying unto me, "Fear not; I am the first and the last." (Rev. 1:17)

Sermon titles are a sport to me. I have made it a point since I started preaching not to have sermon titles like everyone else. I like my titles to be creative, provocative, and informative all at the same time. Sometimes, for fun, I like them to be an enigma wrapped in a riddle. I also like something else a lot, and that is calling the Lord by names that we are not used to hearing. I like calling Him the Creator for a few reasons: number one is because He is the Creator but also because it brings great power and authority to His name. I also like calling Him by the name He gave to Moses, the *I Am*! I often use the I Am in my sermons and titles because it causes great reverence for the Lord just by its utterance. Today I decided to give this devotion title a little flair by playing around a bit with it. At first glance, it appears to be saying, "Fear not because I really am afraid to," which makes no sense at all. But what I really want it to say is this: "Fear nothing because Jesus Christ is the Great *I Am!*" I think you get the point, and I hope it also gives you great comfort for today as it has given me great comfort over the years.

In Revelations 1:17, we see this title in all its glory by seeing what John saw facing God. John's first reaction was to be afraid, which is interesting because one would think that seeing Jesus in person would give great comfort. Isn't that what we all say we want? "If I could just see Jesus, I wouldn't be afraid anymore." Makes sense to me, but then why was John so afraid? Maybe because he saw who Jesus really is and what power He possesses. I would liken it to seeing some great celebrity, king, or president. We would be excited to see them, but being so close would also cause us to be in awe. Even more, it shows that we really don't know how we would react in the presence of greatness until we are actually there. To me, John's reaction gives me great comfort for many reasons. Number one is that he shows us how powerful Jesus really is. He is not some hippie love child handing out flowers at the airport but the Creator of heaven and earth. He is power beyond power, which means He has all the power He needs to fix, heal, and control our little worlds. Number two, I see something else. I see the love of God as He places His hand on John and says, "Fear not."

Dear friend, this same Lord, Creator, Comforter is saying the same thing to us today as we fear and tremble at life. We are trembling, but He is comforting us and telling us not to fear. So today, no matter what you might face, know that the Star Maker and Galaxy Breather is telling us the same thing: "Fear not, for I love you, and I loved you so much that I became a man, only to die for the ones that I love. I came to seek and save that which was lost, and that is you. Fear not because I am."

December 14 - Say What?

There is no fear in love; but perfect love casteth out fear: because fear hath torment. He that feareth is not made perfect in love. (1 John 4:18)

I have to admit, some of the renderings in the King James Bible are kind of cryptic. Some are even more like riddles than understandable instructions. In this devotional book, I have used the King James Bible exclusively, and some may wonder why. Well, first off, I am not one of those KJV-only people as I do use other versions in my preaching and studies. There are some great Bible versions out there that do make things a bit easier to understand. So why do I use the King James? Well, it is simply because that's what I was raised on, and I have a hard time reading anything else. I have read the KJV for so many years that I do understand it and even its archaic renderings at times. Be that as it may, 1 John 4:18 is a bit puzzling to the naked eye, but not so much to the spiritual eye. For today's devotion, let's spend some time breaking down this amazing scripture of truth and hopefully walk away with a little more peace about life and living.

First off is the introduction, which clearly states that, "there is no fear in love." What does that exactly mean? It means in God's love for us, it is impossible to have fear. If and when we understand how much God loves us, we would have no room for fear because His love would be all-consuming. Like a child being held in its mother's arms, that child has no fear, nor should they. With the same thought, part two of the verse explains how this is possible. It speaks of *perfect love*, which means a love lacking any faults at all. No selfishness, no anger, no doubt. God's love is like that, and if you are in the cradle of His love, there is no room for anything else. If there is something else in that cradle, it must be tossed out for God's love to fit. It would be like trying to mix oil and water in a baby-food jar. They simply can't mix, and something must go so the other can take over. If water is the equivalent of God's love, then the oil must go for the water to dwell freely. Next point is the description of fear and why fear cannot coexist with God's love. Fear is a tormentor, and by its very nature, it vexes anything it comes in contact with. It is like radiation; it contaminates whatever it touches, and so it must go or the love cannot stick.

Again, the oil-and-water example makes this clear. In the closing part of the scripture, it points to our dilemma and why we so often don't walk in God's perfect love. Fear can be the only logical reason, and until fear is exhumed from the soul, God's love cannot abide there. The question then must be how do we get rid of the fear? The answer is simple in description but difficult in execution. We simply must learn and focus more on God's Word than anything else. The more we study, seek, and desire to know of

God, the less time we will have entertaining fear. Dear friend, it's a choice, and one I have failed at often; but when I have succeeded, it has worked wonderfully. Seek God with all your heart, and in doing so, leave no room for fear to dwell.

December 15 - My Helper Because I Need Help

So that we may boldly say, "The Lord is my helper, and I will not fear what man shall do unto me." (Heb. 13:6)

As a man, I have this inherited repulsion to asking for help. When it comes to getting lost, I don't want to ask for directions. When it comes to putting something together, I refuse to read the directions. Over the years, time, experience, and the Lord God have opened my eyes to this foolishness. Companies spend a lot of money sending their products off with directions, so why would I not choose to use them? As always, the answer to most of our problems lies hidden under a cloak of pride. Right back to being a child, we are always repelling advice and exclaiming that "I can do it!" As a father of teenagers, I have to understand this and simply let my boys do it their way, watch them mess up, and still be there to kindly show them the right way back. I guess it is simply something about us humans that will never change as long as sin rules our hearts.

When it comes to depression and anxiety, we often repel the help we need, at least until we are so far gone that we have no choice but to ask for help. If I can get one thing of the many things across to you about emotional turmoil, it is this: Do not wait until you are forced to ask for help. Ask for it *before* you really need it. I'm always amazed of the double standard when it comes to getting help and emotional issues. If we have a lump or a pain, we go to the doctor. If we have a fever, we take aspirin. If we break our arm, we go to the ER and have it set. Not so when it comes to emotional issues as they raise the dirty little pride problem again.

Again, in surveys taken, men are almost certainly less prone to seek help for emotional issues than women. This is proven by how many men won't go to the doctor for testicular or prostate issues simply because they are embarrassed in comparison to women who will certainly go to the doctor at the first sign of a breast lump or vaginal issue. At the center of it all again is pride, but it is not just in men when it comes to mental concerns. Women, though not as prideful as men, still might hold off discussing depression or anxiety.

Regardless, the issue at hand is that we need help, and help is waiting. The Lord offers help and clearly tells us He is our helper, yet why do we refuse it? As we will talk about in depth, this issue is in not liking the form in which the Lord offers help. As people of faith, we only see God dealing with an emotional issue by simply removing it by prayer; other than that, we don't see how else or what else the Lord could do. We might dabble with counseling, but even there, we make mistakes. One is going to our pastors who, for the most part, are very lacking in this area, and the second is seeing a secular counselor who has no idea of the spiritual dynamic that a Christian needs to deal with. Then there is taking medications, which most Christians would not be caught dead with, which they just might end up being if they don't see that the Lord offers us help in many diverse ways. Stay tuned as we talk about such forms of help throughout this devotional and book (sold separately).

December 16 - Not Paul

For I determined not to know any thing among you, save Jesus Christ, and him crucified.
And I was with you in weakness, and in fear, and in much trembling.
(1 Cor. 2:2–3)

The longer you live your life, the more you learn about people, or should I say, the more you realize you are misreading people. I remember when I first became a Christian and entered my first Bible-believing church. I remember the awe I felt as I looked at all these wonderful holy, spiritual people. I thought that I could never be like them, so gentle, giving, and filled with Bible wisdom and truth. Well, that vision didn't take long to break into a million pieces. All it took was going to my first church business meeting or seeing people out of the church environment and seeing how they really act. When the Lord said in His Word that man at his best state is altogether vanity, He hit the nail on the head. Now, that being said, let's also talk about the apparent strong, bold people that we know. How many times do we misread them and assume that everyone is so much smarter, braver, and godlier?

As a person who knows about feeling afraid and being depressed, I also became a person who began to feel less than everyone else. The more depressed I became and the more anxiety took over my life, the more jealous I became of everyone around me. Even church people became idols to me as people who were so well-versed in scripture, so bold to share their faith, so take-charge in nature, so ready to go head to head with anyone. I would look at them and tremble even more. "Oh, Lord," I would say, "why must I be such a frail, weak, and trembling vessel? How can I ever be like these others of yours who know so much more than me, who are so much greater than me?" As time went on, I also started to believe that maybe I was loved less than these others. Maybe the Lord couldn't ever use me, and I was simply a mistake of nature to be tossed aside. All these types of thoughts are from a common source, which I call the SS factor; that is, Satan and self, which are our two worst enemies. They blind us from the truth that is found in Christ and about who we are in Christ.

Dear friend, you need not be a theologian, a Bible scholar, a bodybuilder with human strength, or even a great orator. No, all you need is what Paul and every child of God who came before and after him needed. We read about this in our scripture for today: "For I determined not to know any thing among you, save Jesus Christ, and Him crucified. And I was with you in weakness, and in fear, and in much trembling" (1 Cor. 2:2). Reading those words, dear friend, should send waves of joy and comfort through your very soul. Paul, whom I personally believe to be the greatest apostle, wasn't much different from you and me. He knew that all he needed was found in Christ, and he also knew that because of Christ living through him, he didn't need much more.

December 17 - What If God Said

> *"Go up to the mountain, and bring wood, and build the house; and I will take pleasure in it, and I will be glorified," saith the lord. (Hag. 1:8)*

What if God said? Today, as we get closer to Christmas and all the holiday cheer, we need to really prepare for war. As I have stated earlier, this time of the year, especially the Christmas and New Year holidays, can be particularly difficult for those of us who suffer with emotional issues such as depression. Be it mild depression, seasonal depression, or clinical depression, this is truly a hard time for us all. Not to mention the colder weather and the lack of sun, plus the knowing that a long winter lies ahead before spring. It is a lot to deal with. Yet that all being true, what if God said to us something that would change it all? Not that these hard seasons wouldn't come, but that He gave us something to do besides fret, ruminate, and ponder all day.

In the book of Haggai, God isn't too happy with the people who are more focused on their own concerns than the Lord's. Like many of us today, buying things for ourselves and doing things for ourselves seem to be an all-consuming affair of the mind. It is an affair that in some respect is an affair with ourselves. In some ways, depression and anxiety place us into a similar state of mind but for different reasons. We as sufferers often spend most of our time building our own plans, ideas, and ways of deliverance. We scheme and focus solely on being better, so nothing else has room in our minds to drive us. Back in Haggai again, as the people are building their own houses and dreams, God tells them to do something else: "'Go up to the mountain, and bring wood, and build the house; and I will take pleasure in it, and I will be glorified,' saith the LORD."

In case you and I have forgotten, when the Lord is happy with us, we are happy. As the Lord told the people to work on His house instead of their own, we should be working on God's plan instead of our own. How do we do this when all we can focus on is getting out of this funk? Well, we begin by thinking outside of the box (our box). We begin by seeking out the Lord this way:

> *Dear Father, it is a very hard time for me. My heart is heavy with pain, but I wish not to focus on this pain anymore. Instead, Lord, I request a mission for me, something to occupy my mind instead of my pain.*
>
> *Dear Lord, may You place in my path a person, family, or ministry where I can serve You,*

Lord, something that would please You and be part of Your will, dear Lord. May this holiday season be spent solely on Your desires and not my own. In Jesus name, amen.

Now, that might seem like a hard feat, but remember, it's not you doing it but the Lord. If our desire is truly His desire, then He will bring us something or someone to minister to, and before we know it, Christmas will be gone, and we would have made it through. And, who knows, maybe even a little closer to being healed at the same time. This Christmas, bring Jesus a gift instead of asking one from Him. Build Him a house of service and gratitude.

December 18 - Is of the Holy Spirit?

But while he thought on these things, behold, the angel of the Lord appeared unto him in a dream, saying, "Joseph, thou son of David, fear not to take unto thee Mary thy wife: for that which is conceived in her is of the Holy Ghost." (Matt. 1:20)

It is amazing how certain things scare us while the same thing doesn't scare another. It is also amazing how anything other than sin and God *can* scare us as we are children of the Most High. Well, the facts are in, and we all know that many things do scare us—some we know as they are obvious, and some we have no idea why they scare us. When it comes to anxiety, it's the same perplexing and vexing thing. Sometimes, for no reason at all, a spirit of fear will come upon me, and I cannot, for the life of me, figure out why.

One day, while feeling great, being in, I guess what you would call *emotional remission*, I took a wonderful bike ride with my youngest son to get some ice cream. It was a beautiful summer day, and all was right with the world, yet for some odd reason, when we arrived at the ice-cream parlor and sat outside to eat it, a flash of anxiety came over me. Now, if you are not a sufferer of such things, you have no idea that they happen, but for us who suffer with this thorn, it is all too real. As I sat there paralyzed for a moment, I prayed silently to the Lord, "Please, Lord, no, may this feeling pass, so I can enjoy this moment with my son." Well, it did pass, and the day went on.

Dear friend and fellow sufferer, sometimes we have to resign ourselves to the fact that *maybe*, in some cases, this may be our lot. For me, until the Lord says it is over, I will forever be walking with this dragon. And I am okay with that today, but for many years, I was not, and I refused to accept this gentle dragon of an emotional roller coaster. Now, I know there are some Christians in certain denominations—or flavors, if you will—of Christianity that will disagree with me. Some will say that if we truly believe and claim victory over our current ailment, then the Lord *must* remove it. And if He does not, it is your fault for not having enough faith. Maybe so, or maybe not. Paul was asked to carry his thorn for the rest of his life as ordained by the Lord. And if ordained by the Lord, how can it be bad for us and not good for God? And who are we to reject what the Lord has planned for us (John 18:11)?

In Matthew 1:20, the angel of the Lord appeared unto Joseph and said to him, "Fear not." Why? Well, according to the angel, this scary thing that just manifested itself in Joseph's life, Mary becoming pregnant with no intercourse was cause for alarm, let alone an angel speaking to him. Yeah, Joseph was afraid, frightened, if you will, by something that shouldn't have frightened him. Like anxiety, things that shouldn't frighten us do, and I believe the Lord gives to us the same words of comfort: "Dear child of mine, this season of anxiety and depression has come upon you, but do not fear it because it is from the Lord. It is conceived, ordained, and planned out especially for you."

Dear friend, what if the dragon we are given to walk on this life lease is a dragon given to us by the Holy Spirit Himself? Shall we refuse it? Should have Joseph refused what he was given to deal with? And by the way, Joseph had a lot to deal with being with a woman who was pregnant and wasn't married. Today, no big deal, but then, it was a very big deal. Yet Joseph accepted his challenge and accepted it with a proper heart. Let that be our story too.

December 19 - Of More Value than These?

Fear ye not therefore, ye are of more value than many sparrows. (Matt. 10:31)

Value is something that is very hard to put a number on. What's of great value to one person might be of little value to another. Many times, as children of God, we wonder what our value is. We read often in the scriptures of our righteousness as being as filthy rags and that there is none who is righteous; no, not one. We also read that the wages of our sinful hearts is death. All are sinners, we also hear. Sad to say, friends, it is all true, and because we are sinners, we are separated from the Lord, and that is a frightening reality, which means hell awaits us as nothing tainted by sin can ever stand before a thrice Holy God. It is a paradox of sorts and a conundrum, if you will. We are wretched and dirty, even called a filthy rag in the Old Testament, which in the day was a description of a woman's used sanitary napkin. Yuck.

As a person struggling with depression and anxiety, self-worth usually ranks in at about a zero on the worthy scale. Instead of making me feel better about myself, it is making me feel worse. Well, it would be true if it were not for another side of the coin: God's love for His creation. Dear friend, Satan has been trying all your life to get you to focus on your dirty little sin secret, and just as much effort he has put into keeping you informed each day of your dirtiness, he has also spent a lot of effort keeping us away from the knowledge of the love of God. He doesn't want us to know about that, which is also why Satan despises the cross so much. See, the cross will ever be the glass breaker that screams out, "I love you, dear child, more than you can ever know." Satan tells you of your worthlessness daily, which is probably why he created evolution in the mind of Charles Darwin, simply to further convince us that we are just animals, bad ones at that.

Sad to say that even in Christian circles, too many pastors and preachers hammer us all day on our filthiness that we start to think, *Why would Jesus die for us anyway then?* Maybe God was a fool to send His only Son to die for a worthless, valueless, filthy evolved ape. Dear friend, if you have any sense in you at all, you will quickly realize that God is brilliant to the thousandth power, so He doesn't make mistakes. He knows value, and by His own plan to save sinful man, He has demonstrated that we are of great worth. We are greater than the animals—yes, even greater than dolphins, Labrador Retrievers, and anything else you can think up.

In Matthew 10:31, Jesus Christ—God in the Flesh—tells us to "fear not." Why? Because we are worthless? No, but because we are of great value to Him. In fact, we are of greater value than all of creation. We are greater than the angels, the Heavens, and everything else. See, Jesus only came and died for mankind and nothing else. He did not die to save the seals (as cute as they are) or the whales (as glorious as they are), but He came to save us.

Now, if that all is true, and it is, then would He not also deliver us from our fear and things that go bump in the night? Fear not, dear friends, because God thinks you are wonderful.

December 20 - The First Panic Attack?

And for fear of him the keepers did shake, and became as dead men. (Matt. 28:4)

Christmas is coming soon, which means shopping malls and crowded stores. In the USA, it's a madhouse of money-changing and certainly not Christ-focused. If you are in another part of the world, I pray that your culture hasn't destroyed Christmas and its meaning like we have here in the USA. Regardless, the point I want to make this day is that of panic. Panic, anxiety, and fear are not all created equal. I have read where people have a separate designation for an anxiety attack as apposed to a panic attack. Call them what you will, it doesn't matter; they all have one similar characteristic—they ruin everything. Some people get them from being in large crowds; some get them for no reason at all. Some people get them only under great stress and tea-kettle pops.

I have treated people who end up in the hospital every time they have one. They go from mild to wild in symptoms. Some have trouble breathing; some become frozen and can't move. Some people claim they are having a heart attack while others get hot flashes and sweats. The list goes on and on, and it is not uncommon for them to affect our stomachs and thought processes. Yeah, it's a scary, scary thing to go through, and you might even think you might die.

Panic disorder, as it is sometimes called, is hard to treat if it is sporadic in nature as medication is often given, but the medication must be taken before the attack if you are ever to stop them. This would mean always being on medication. Yes, you can take medication when you have them, but they don't always work fast enough and leave you feeling like you were run over by a truck. In my own experiences with them, they normally set me back a few days before all the chemicals in my brain, which were released, got back to a normal level. Not to get too medical here, but a panic attack is simply a release of everything at once, from adrenaline to sweat glands going wild to pulse rate going through the roof. Your body is physically getting ready to fight off a rapist while you are actually sitting on a chair watching TV. It is chemical confusion at its worst. So what's the cure? What do we do? Well, for one thing, we must understand that they are a signal. They are a signal that our coping mechanisms have been misaligned somehow. Finding triggers that unleash them is a good step to take but never as good as taking it to the Lord, as we should do with everything else, and saying, "Lord, what does this mean? What am I to learn from this, and what are you trying to show me?"

Dear friend, the first mistake we make in our prayer life toward ailments like this is to immediately beg the Lord to remove them. This is wrong as we must first seek out why they are happening. The Lord does nothing in vain nor allows anything in vain. Find out why before you seek to find out how to make them go away. And by the way, they can go away, and in many cases, they can be treated to a very livable level. We will discuss some treatments for these in the chapter section of the book (sold separately).

December 21 - It Will Make Sense One Day

But as it is written, To whom he was not spoken of, they shall see: and they that have not heard shall understand. (Rom. 15:21)

Making sense of the senseless is not always easy to do. As a pastor, I am often left with the daunting task of explaining why God would take the life of a four-year-old child or why God would allow a young mother of young children to die of cancer. Early on in my ministry as a pastor, I was certain that I had to come up with some great theological explanation to every hard trial a family or person went through. That foolish pursuit died quickly as I realized I didn't have the answers, nor should I try to come up with one. In Proverbs 3, it tells us not to lean on our own understanding, so why should we try? Over the years, my new approach has evolved into simply being there to comfort and share in the pain. If asked why God allowed this or that, I would simply say the truth, "I really don't know, but God does, and one day we will too."

Dear friend, one of our biggest time-wasters is spending time trying to figure out why, instead of learning how to go on from here. If I lose an arm in an automobile accident, I can spend the rest of my life trying to figure out why the Lord let it happen, or I can spend those remaining years learning how to serve Him with one arm. Now, truth be told, sometimes we do find out why. Sometimes tragedy can be explained to some degree, and we might see why God did this or that. In my life, I have wasted many years trying to figure out why I had to deal with depression and anxiety when I could have been spending time learning how to live with it. Some might conclude that learning how to live with what the Lord has placed on your lap is the same as giving up and no longer walking in faith that the Lord may heal you again. I don't see it that way, and my study of God's Word over the years has taught me that sometimes, seemingly bad things happen, and nothing is going to change that.

For the most part, I know why God has allowed me to go through seasons of depression and anxiety. I know because I can see all the good that came from those seasons and how there was no other way for me to learn what I learned. Humility, patience, compassion, faith, and trust are just some of the things that the Lord taught me during those dark days. Today I am not 100 percent healed, and I don't know if I will ever be. Sure, there were some very long stretches of time when it was 100 percent, and I thought it was over for certain. But then the Lord would allow my pain to peek back in my life, again always drawing me closer to Him and using it as the catalyst for great blessings. I think the hardest part was accepting that this is just how I am going to be, and it is okay. I will struggle now and then, but if it is from God, then it is always good for me and, more importantly, for Him.

As for you today and finding out why you are suffering and when it will be completely over, well, we might not ever know in this life, but we will certainly know in the life to come. And that, my friend, has to be okay, That is true faith and trusting in the Lord that if He allows something in your life, He does it with purpose. End of story.

December 22 - As Simple as Jesus Sometimes

And the seventy returned again with joy, saying, "Lord, even the devils are subject unto us through thy name." (Luke 10:17)

Dear friend, as we discuss again the issues of depression and anxiety, I want to make sure we never diminish the spiritual element of emotional traumas. Though many come from many diverse physical / psychological conditions such as chemical imbalances, hormone instability, childhood experiences, loss, life's daily disturbances, heredity, low vitamin D, and genetics, we must not discount the demonic. In my own life, I believe that 10 percent of my issues come from my genetic line as my family has a history of fear, anxiety, and, in some cases, mental illness. But I still believe 90 percent of what I have encountered has been the dark spiritual side of things. The temptations, the spiritual teasing, the battles over good and evil are spiritual. They cannot be discounted, and even more so when you consider that my problems only arose when I went into ministry or even began thinking about it. From that point on, demonic forces have been haunting me, as well as taunting me. There were things and circumstances so bizarre and out of the ordinary that there is no other way to explain it. It has truly been a spiritual warfare of the greatest kind, and if it were not for the Lord and His warring angelic forces, I would be dead today.

Let's also not discount the personal spiritual equation. Many times, my anxiety also followed sins in my life. Depression would come upon me either pre or post the working of a great spiritual victory for the Lord. Lead many people to the Lord, great oppression would come. The harder you serve Christ, the greater the attacks and temptations. Of Satan, well, he's like clockwork. Whenever I would do a series or teach anything exposing him as a liar, I would fall into some emotional trial of sorts. In fact, the darkest depression and anxiety I have ever been through was set out of the blue after I did a series on false teachers and the occult in the church. It got to the point when I became more afraid of Satan than I was of the Lord. I had more respect for him than Jesus Christ. Not that I didn't love the Lord and trust Him, but Satan scared me so that I dared not speak against him for a while. I even cancelled a seminar that was going to take place, which focused on the occult and false demonic-inspired preachers. I was just too beaten down to stand up to him anymore. For a time, he won and I was in retreat, but not anymore.

Dear friend, with all the medications, therapies, and demonic dynamics, let us not forget the greatest power that exists, which is the name of Jesus Christ. So many times, simply at the mention of His name, and the casting out of Satan in Jesus's name, much supernatural deliverance resulted. When you are in the depths of pain, sorrow, mental or physical, let us never forget the name of Jesus Christ. For at His name alone, demons tremble, and dark forces depart; wounds are healed; and seas are parted.

December 23 - A Curse or a Blessing

And the angel said unto her, "Fear not, Mary: for thou hast found favour with God." (Luke 1:30)

Ever wonder about Mary, the mother of the humanity of Jesus? I don't think we give her enough credit for what she had to endure as a very young lady. Some accounts have her as young as thirteen while others have her closer to sixteen. Regardless, she was placed into a very awkward situation by the Lord, a situation where one could have been seen as a curse in most circles in that day. Also think about Mary's fear of what she was being chosen to be a part of. Being that we are getting very close to Christmas, let us think on young Mary, fear, and the will of the Lord. So Mary who has never been with a man physically and probably doesn't even know much about what that all means suddenly finds herself pregnant. She is going to have a baby, and she has no husband to account for it. Let us think of what could have been running through her mind at the time: "I'm pregnant. I'm not married. What will my family think? The townspeople? My friends? What of my future? Where will I live? Who will support me and this child? What of my reputation?" Here is pure Mary, a young girl of sparkling purity, who did her best to live a godly life. We can only imagine her girl friends snickering things behind her back, "Oh, sweet, pure little Mary, pregnant!" "Pure little Mary, who was always so good and holy, look at her holiness now?" We all know how cruel people can be, especially young teens.

Dear friend, what of your life right now? Are you facing some of the same questions in your mind? Are you maybe going through something that is causing your anxiety? Or is your anxiety causing you to go through something? Whatever the case, we all know the fear that can overwhelm us during these times of great trial. We sit and think to ourselves about what we will do to get out of this mess. We think about how we will make it in a future that seems uncertain. Be of good cheer because the Lord knows every single thought that has or is running through our mind right now, just as God knew every thought that was running through Mary's heart and mind. In Luke 1:30, after the Lord hears of Mary's concerns, present or future, He sent her an angel who said these supercomforting words: "Fear not, Mary: for thou hast found favour with God." Imagine the Lord saying that to you and me during our great times of fear: "Fear not, Joe, Bob, Scott, or Julie, for you have found favor with God."

Dear friends, we have found favor with God the day the Lord Jesus died on the cross for our sins. God doesn't just die for nothing but only for one who is of great worth. As you look at your life and feel like it has been one of cursing—well, what if it is not a curse but a blessing from the Lord Himself? For a time, Mary could have looked at her situation as a great curse, but once she understood that it was from God, she was able to rejoice and call herself a handmaid of the Lord.

December 24 - A Good Kind of Fear

And His mercy is on them that fear Him from generation to generation. (Luke 1:50)

Fear, a lot in this devotional is about it. From my story to your story, we all circle around a hub of one central emotion, which is fear. As we open the Word of God from Genesis to Revelation, we hear of fear, its terror and paralyzing effect on the human body. As I have stated many times before, fear is the axis from which most of our emotional pain and suffering emanates. From the fears of a child being eaten by the monsters under his bed to the fears of adults of losing a loved one to cancer—fear is the great equalizer. Be you a rich man or poor man, fear knows no boundaries. We have spoken a lot about fear over this past year, and for the most part, it has appeared to be a negative emotion, something that we would rather not have nor ever have to deal with again. But, dear friend, imagine a world without any fear at all. Now, at first thought, you might say, "Well, that would be great!" just like the cries for absolute freedom or the cries from a distant classic song that said, "Imagine a world with no religion, or even no God." They are all great premises at first glance, but taken to their extreme, they are horrifying.

Take a world with complete freedom. That would mean I could do whatever I want, but also could your neighbor. Think of a world without God—great until you realize how alone and dark things would be and death leaving you in a dark worm-infested grave. And what of a world without fear? "Oh, if I only had no fear at all, life would be so grand." Take that concept and again take it to its extreme, and we have a world where people would walk out into moving traffic with no fear. People would place their hands into a burning flame. People would walk out on a ledge and have no fear of falling, and people would walk up to a great beast without fear of being eaten. See, fear, like many other apparent negative things, also has many good aspects to it. Like the fear of the Lord, the fear of death without Christ, the fear of hell, and the fear of being alone for all eternity. These are all good fears that drive us into the arms of the One who loves us so much that He gave His only Son to die for us, so we would not have to fear those things—well, other than fearing the Lord and sin.

Dear friend, if we are to live this life in fear, let us choose to then fear only those two. Fear of the Lord and fear of sin, those fears open us up to receiving the gift of salvation, the gift of new life in Christ, and the wonder of walking in fellowship with our Creator. Oh, let us not be so quick to toss out the baby in the bathwater. And of our fears in the form of anxieties, well, if they have driven you closer to Christ, then how bad can they be? Maybe what we once dreaded so much was actually the tool that the Lord used to bring us to our great standing now or, for certain, our great standing in the future? Of the fear of the Lord—it is through that fear that His Mercy is placed upon us.

December 25 - Because of This Day, We Can Live Without Fear

And the angel said unto them, "Fear not: for, behold, I bring you good tidings of great joy, which shall be to all people." Luke 2:10

Oh, a day of great rejoicing as we think upon the wonder of our Creator becoming a man in the form of a babe, but we might be thinking—so what? Sure, I know that December 25 is probably not the actual day of Christ's birth, but the date really doesn't matter as the fact that He was born. Dear friend, I don't know how this Christmas day might find you. Maybe you are with many friends and family, or maybe you are all alone and left with only the clothes on your back. Maybe today this devotional book has been given to you as a gift from a friend or a loved one who knows you are struggling with depression and anxiety. I don't know your lot in life, but I do know the One who does and the One who certainly knows you right now wherever you are. Maybe today you are feeling very sad and alone, and Christmas only rubs your nose in the reality of your current emotional straits. If it helps, know that I have been where you are today. I have sat on a Christmas morn watching others rejoice, but their rejoicing only made my present pain that much worse. Of the joy of Christ being born, it brought me no hope or significance. Maybe this day only raised up thoughts of anger, anger at a God who would let you suffer so while others rejoice. I have been there too, friend, but I am there no longer.

As we read in Luke 2:10, we hear a word from an angel proclaiming these wonderful, wonderful words: "Fear not." Yet the words of comfort don't end there. They don't just tell you to stop fearing, but they tell you why you should stop fearing. It is because there is great joy coming, wonderful joy, and it's not just for some people but for all who will trust in its promise. The promise of our Creator being rejoined with His creation. Now, just as the angel proclaimed that this joy was certain, he also proclaimed a joy that really wouldn't be fulfilled until a later time, which is why he said "shall be." Listen, the Lord is telling you that maybe right now your sorrow is too deep to see past today, but soon after the pain, there will be rejoicing. Notice that the birth of Christ was wonderful, but babies are born all the time. No, it would be what this babe would grow to do that would really be the news that would change the world.

I often get in hot water with this statement, but I feel that Christmas isn't as important as resurrection day when death and the grave are defeated. So I am with you today. Christmas may be getting you down, and its glitter and fuss don't seem to do anything for you. Well, know this, dear friend, it is what will happen many years later that will bring us the great news and the great promises of God. News that you, who are dead in spirit, shall be alive in spirit. If you are under the darkness of night, you will be filled with the newness of day. No, it is not just some flowery words that I am pushing on you but facts from one who has been there. Trust Christ, and the future that He has prepared for you. Today might be of much gloom, but soon it will be of great joy.

December 26 - No One Cares Enough to Visit

That God hath visited his people. (Luke 7:16)

The day is past, and the celebration that had great preparation seems like a distant memory. Here in New York, it is not uncommon for many people to purchase live Christmas trees, and there is also a big to-do about making them all fancy and fair. But what baffles the mind is to see such a fuss made one day only to see them tossed to the curb the next. Yes, it's a strange ceremony: the setting up and decorating of the Christmas tree and then the unceremonious gloom of taking it down and dragging it out to the curb for the trashman to pick up. I don't know, but there is great significance in there somewhere. Maybe it's a picture of all the fuss we place on this life, thinking that when it is over, it is over, and we are tossed to the curb.

Dear friend, that could not be further from the truth as the Lord has great promises for us down here on planet earth. If it were not the case, He wouldn't have gone through such great lengths to come and visit us. I don't think we really ever think of the incarnation that way, as in God coming down from His glory to visit such an unglorious people such as you and me. If this day finds you thinking of what the new year might bring, thinking of what the next day might bring, think on this again and again—He came to visit you!

Many times those of us who suffer with depression and anxiety get much sympathy at first and many visits to follow, but unlike recuperating from a surgery, people expect you to be better eventually. They will only come and visit or sit by your bedside for so long. Soon they become impatient, and in that impatience, they become skeptical of your illness as if it has all been for show. I have seen this many a time as people really don't understand emotional issues, and their praying and concern for you has its limits. After enough time goes by, they can't figure out why you haven't healed and gotten back to living. Sadly their compassion is limited at best, but oh not so with our Lord. "He visited His people." I want to say that again and again. "He visited His people." Long after friends, family, and coworkers have given up on you, "He visited His people."

Oh, dear friend, the Lord understands this disrespected illness of ours. He understands deep emotions because He is the Lord of deep emotions. He understands deep passions for He is the Lord of great passion. He does not grow weary, nor does He grow impatient with our delayed healing. He knows us, friend. He knows our frame, that we are frail and weak. He knows us, friend, and how long some things take. He knows us with all of our faults, and yet "He still visited His people." He will visit you, and in fact, He is waiting at your door as it states in Revelation 3:20: "Behold He stands at the door and knocks." He will do the visiting, but we must let Him in. Let

Jesus in today, not just for a moment but deep within our very soul forever. Once in, He will never leave you or forsake you.

December 27 - Wish It Was That Easy?

Fear not: believe only, and she shall be made whole. (Luke 8:50)

To save, deliver, and protect. Sounds like the motto for some small-town police force. In actuality, it's the Greek meaning of the word for *whole* found in Luke 8:50. At the end of that verse, Jesus says these words: "Fear not: believe only, and she shall be made whole." So many times we read scriptures like this in the Bible and say to ourselves, "Yeah, I wish it was that easy." We see and read these accounts all through the Holy Writ and wonder if it is really even true. If it was, we conclude, "Then why isn't it working for me?" Fear not, Jesus says, only believe and we shall be made whole. Well, actually Jesus was speaking about a little girl. In fact, it was a dead little girl that had all the people weeping and moaning. Again, we think, "He raised her from the dead. All I am asking for is for this depression and anxiety to be lifted."

Dear friend, I think we need to take some time and look deeper into the Word of God. So many times we read the Bible with the enthusiasm of a person reading the warning label on cigarettes. It is always the same reaction: "Yeah, yeah, yeah. I have heard it all before, so what?" Dear friend, I implore you to take the time and dig into the Word of God as if you were mining for gold. Pray before you read. See what it says before the scripture you are reading and see what it says after. Find out the original meaning of the words and what different meanings they might have as compared to what we see at face value. In scriptures like Luke 8:50, we must understand that though Jesus can heal and did heal, it doesn't mean He will heal you in like manner. I haven't seen anyone raised from the dead lately, so obviously this scripture was for back then, to establish His authority as from God. Now, that doesn't mean that we can't apply this scripture to our lives today as in the case of the vast meanings of the word *whole*. Today we can take that scripture and take our pain and sorrows and plug them all in. Let us also notice the principles that never change, principles like not fearing, believing only, and waiting on the Lord. So many times we think we are applying these principles, but we only do so in such a way as we deem them applied.

To *not fear* in the face of present danger is to really *not fear*. To *believe only* is to trust in Christ and nothing else. It is taking these words and setting them on holy fire and holding on to them as if they were life itself—which they are.

Also, as we see, the promise in the word *whole* as in "made whole." What does that mean? It means a lot more than we think as we look at the original writings. *To save, deliver, and protect.* These are some forms of that word, so it is not just bringing someone back from the dead physically but bringing them back from the dead spiritually. The Lord is telling you today not to be afraid of your current trial, to believe and trust Jesus with all your heart. If you do, He will save you, deliver you, and protect you from the ravages of your emotional pains. He will raise you from the dead of lifeless living.

December 28 - He Just Wants to Make My Life Miserable

Fear not, little flock; for it is your Father's good pleasure to give you the kingdom. (Luke 12:32)

Ever wonder why God really allows pain and sorrow into our lives? I think it is just because He loves to see us suffer, or maybe it is just so He can have a power trip over us and control us. I think He really enjoys making us go through hell on earth because why wouldn't He want us to have all that we ask for? If He really loved us, He would want us happy, right? If you have ever raised children or have ever been a child or a teenager, then you know where I got these words from. Of course the Lord doesn't want us to be miserable. I have teens, and I have worked with many teens in counseling. I know how they think because I thought that way too. I remember when I was about seventeen, and I was shopping for a vehicle. Every one I found for sale, which I showed to my father, he didn't approve of. I was so angry at him as vehicle after vehicle, he said no. I actually thought he was doing it just to make me unhappy and cause me pain. I actually thought he just didn't want me to have what I wanted. Well, it didn't take long to learn that my dad, being a mechanic, knew a thing or two about engines and such. He saw a pile of junk that wouldn't last and might even be dangerous. I saw a glowing beauty with a great sound system that really looked cool.

Perspective is the key, friends, and it's the one attribute that we don't have simply because we are not God.

Do we really think that God wants us to live our days in pain and sorrow? No, certainly He does not, which is why when He created us, He gave us a perfect, carefree life in the Garden of Eden. That was the world that God had planned for us, and why wouldn't He? Do not all good parents only want the best for their children? But what happens when our parents give us the best, and we destroy, abuse, and corrupt it? Whose fault is it then that everything is falling apart? How many parents today buy their child a new car, pay for their college, and everything they will need? Parents buy them all kinds of toys and trinkets, and still the child curses the parent when their life doesn't go the way they wanted or when the parent says no to just about one thing. All of a sudden, they complain that the parent is just trying to steal their joy and take away their fun.

Dear friend, it is the Lord's good pleasure to give us all things. He desires only the best, but the world has fallen. We have taken it and destroyed all that was good and shook our fist back at His face. If there is pain, sorrow, cancer, and turmoil, it is not because of God but because of mankind. That's the result of the fall, but praise be to the Lord He still found a way to restore us again. He did that at the cross. It was there where we had our second chance at life and, more importantly, eternal life. All these things the Father has done for us, and yes, sometimes He must say no. Sometimes He must scold us. Sometimes He allows us to feel what it's like to be on our own, but only because He loves us so much. Instead of being so angry at the Lord today, let's try to see what He may be trying to show us. In the end, it will be good. It can only be good because God is always good.

December 29 - At the End of the Day

And fear fell on them all, and the name of the Lord Jesus was magnified.
(Acts 19:17)

As we are getting closer to the close of this year and waiting for a new one to start, I think it is time that we ask ourselves a question: what is life really all about anyway? Ever really sit back and think about it? I know, as I have gone through my deepest depression, it was the one thing that the Lord kept bringing to my mind. As I would sit or lie there in my great despondency, I would contemplate the meaning of it all. Depression does that, you know, and it's the one thing that's really so wonderful about it. Depression really does make you take inventory of your life and ask the hard questions about it. I remember looking over my possessions and all that I have acquired over the years, all my toys and trinkets and collections of things, and suddenly nothing glittered anymore. Nothing brought me joy, happiness, or peace. Not unlike King Solomon, I began to say to myself, "It's all vanity and vexation of spirit." It's all meaningless if it brings me no joy, or maybe that was the key right there? Maybe seeking to bring myself joy was the problem all along. Maybe in my pursuit of joy, fun, things, and peace, I have overlooked one very important person—the Lord God Himself. Was He just a second consideration in my quest for joy? Was He a disposable diaper that, once His usefulness has gone, I simply toss away? After all, weren't all my prayers about things for me, things for my family, things for my future, things for my children, things for my business? Sure, I had other people's benefit squeezed in there too, but at the closing of the day, the benefit was for me to be happy. For me to be happy that my children were doing okay, that my business was doing okay, that my family was all healthy. Again the *my* factor could not be ignored.

In Revelation 4:11, which I have quoted over and over again in this devotional and book (sold separately), the answer to it all screams out crystal clear: "Thou art worthy, O Lord, to receive glory and honour and power: for thou hast created all things, and [*for thy pleasure they are and were created*]." I don't know about you, but that scripture just can't be gotten around. It cries out for explanation, and it cries out to my selfish life. Dear Lord, have I forgotten why I am even here? Is this little error of mind the real cause for my empty and dark, depressed life?

In our scripture for today, we also see the apex of man's purpose: "And fear fell on them all, and the name of the Lord Jesus was magnified" (Acts 19:17). And the name of the Lord Jesus was magnified. Is He being magnified in your life and in mine? I came to realize that He was not, and the only one I aimed to please was myself. Sure, I tried to convince myself that I had nobler goals, but under the microscope of God's convicting Holy Spirit, I found myself to be a fraud. At the end of the day, it was me who was to be magnified, and if that was the case, then Christ was not. Dear friend, without Christ as the central factor in your living, you simply can't live.

December 30 - Take This Time to Mirror Talk

As in water face answereth to face, so the heart of man to man. (Prov. 27:19)

Well, we are almost there. Another year is coming to a close. Now, I don't know what type of year you faced. I don't know how heavy, light, mild, or intense your depression and anxiety were. What I do know is what lies before you, as well as before me; that is, a new year. That might scare you as you wonder if it will be more of the same, but, dear friend, we must also look to the other side of the coin, and it might be the year of change, healing, and new beginnings. Sure, it sounds corny, played, and old, but that doesn't mean it is not true. So with this thought and hope in mind, I ask you to look back. Look over your shoulder and see where you have been and if there were any virtue in it at all. Even go so far as to take out a pen and jot down what you have learned. Jot down what the Lord has shown you, what He has warned you, about and where He has led you. Have there been things that appeared negative but ended up being positive? Were there things that you learned you needed to stay away from, and things that you need to do more of?

In our scripture for today, we see a perfect picture of what we need to do before any new year—or day, for that matter—starts; that is, to look deep into our *soul mirror* and take inventory of who we are and where we need to go. Proverbs 27:19 says, "As in water face answereth to face, so the heart of man to man." As we look into a pool of still water, we see only our face, not our neighbor's or our families' but our face alone. Wonder why the Lord made water reflective anyway? Maybe it was simply for this one purpose. Before mirrors, it was the only way we could see ourselves, and I believe there is great significance in this.

I shared a while back the little why-Jesus-died mirror book with you and how I would hand it over to a person after asking them what the title said and then asking them to open it. The result was always the same. They see themselves, and it does something. It brings everything that's going on in their lives, past, present, and future, and makes them break down. They break down as they see what life without Christ has been like. So again—look into that mirror, and as you stare into it, don't look at the wrinkles, age spots, and bags under your eyes; they matter not. What does matter is why they are there and what stresses have torn you apart. Look deep into your own eyes and pray to the Lord, ask for guidance for this next year, for a better year, and also thank Him for the past year no matter how troublesome it may have been. Look at your face and remember that smiles will come again as certain as a new day will come again for planet earth. If need be, speak to yourself and get yourself ready for the wonders that the Lord has prepared. No, not a life without problems, but a life living and walking hand in hand with the Problem Solver. Thank Him over and over again for this new year and ask Him with reverence for the wisdom to see what He wants you to see. One more day, friends, one more day.

December 31 - Maybe It's God Talking

For it is not ye that speak, but the Spirit of your Father which speaketh in you. (Matt. 10:20)

You made it! Today is the last day of the year, and you are still breathing. The anxiety and depression didn't kill you, and that's no small victory, like a small village that was able to hold off an invading army twice its size. As they should be proud, so should you. Were there causalities along the way? Yes, there always are. Were there wounds inflicted by the enemy that almost took you out? Sure, and they were to be expected in battle. But, dear friend, you are a survivor! One of the biggest mistakes in warfare is not going far enough.

So many times future wars could have been averted if the leaders would have listened to its generals. How many times have famous generals said, "We are at the enemies' door. Let's take them out completely while we are here and have the manpower. We are so close"? Yet presidents and kings under political pressures would fold and say, "We went far enough. The war was too bloody. It is enough." Now, that might sound logical, but is it? Like a surgeon removing a massive tumor in your body and leaving a little section of it behind and declaring, "Well, we got most of it. It's been bloody enough and long enough. Let's close up the incision." Sometimes it is a tough call, but in cases of victory over depression and anxiety, too often it's the wrong move. It's the wrong move to stop forward progress when you are almost there. Maybe tomorrow is the day of complete victory. Maybe this new year is it.

Dear friend, sometimes the reason why we don't keep fighting is because we don't listen to the voice inside our head. Listen to me today. What if the voice of fear, pain, worry, and depression was not so much a voice of your heart calling out for help but the Holy Spirit of God's within you crying out to get noticed? Now, hear me out. If you're a child of God by faith in Jesus Christ, then the Holy Spirit of God Himself dwells within you. And if that is true, and it is, then some of those feelings and voices within you can also be from Him. Maybe the cry of depression is God telling you that something is wrong in your relationship with Him, and He is simply trying to get your attention. What if the fear, torment, and anxiety is not all from self but from the grieving of the Holy Spirit as it is trapped inside a soul involved in so much sin? It is having trouble comforting you.

Many people say they have never heard God speak, but I think they were just listening for the wrong voice. Remember the words of God come from that still small voice. Maybe the instructions we are waiting to hear are being spoken to our heart, and God is using the emotional trauma we are facing as the soapbox to stand upon to convey that message. Maybe all of these heavy emotions pouring out of us lately is the Holy Spirit spilling out His pain, turmoil, and deep sadness over where you are taking your life.

Dear friend, if you feel like you are being torn apart by two opposing forces, then maybe you are. Maybe there is God on the one side of your soul pulling east, and *your will* on the other side pulling west. Would you not feel torn apart? Let God tell you what He has been trying to tell you all along. Listen, do you hear His voice?

Make sure you pick up a copy of the companion book called *Depression, Anxiety, and the Child of God: The Book* also by S.R. Kraniak, which goes into deep details on fighting and winning this battle once and for all.

This devotional is based on the author's opinion and is not to be used to treat your ailment but to guide you into some suggestions. If you are in a deeply depressed place and thinking of taking your life, please call your local 911. This devotional does not necessarily express the views of the Centereach Bible Church. The people in this book are real, but the names have been changed to protect their privacy.

About the Author

S.R. Kraniak is the pastor of the Centereach Bible Church (www.cbctruth. com), a small church in Long Island, New York. He has been pastor there since 2006. Before that, he was pastor of a small church in Green Valley, California, the Green Valley Bible Chapel. While in California, Pastor Scott ran a counseling and youth ministry while running the little chapel in a bi-vocational status. He also authored a newspaper write-in Christian help column called "Ask Pastor Scott." After moving back to New York where he is originally from, he took over the Centereach Bible Church, which is also the church through which he came to know Christ way back in 1983, and in 1985, he began attending.

Back at the CBC, he continued his Christian counseling practice, which he had been doing back as far as 1990 on his own. He also hosted a live call-in radio show known as *The Last Call Radio Show*, another counseling-based call-in show. The show aired on two different local radio stations for about two years. Pastor Scott also occasionally writes in a local newspaper column on Long Island called "Ask the Clergy." Pastor Scott was also a frequent guest on a local radio show called *Iron Sharpens Iron*, plus a part of the *Pastors' Round Table* show on that same station.

For a while, Pastor Scott tried his hands at getting into local government where he chaired the local town youth board. He was a board member of two local civic-based boards and was outspoken at many town-board meetings with regard to youth-oriented issues. Back at CBC, he also ran a youth-oriented coffeehouse and numerous youth programs.

Pastor Scott also authored/published a book called *Spiritual Living in a Sexual World*, a book about and for Christian men struggling with pornography and sexual addictions. With regard to that book, he did seminar speaking about that issue at local churches, Christian-based venues, and also on local radio shows.

Currently, Pastor Scott is the track chaplain of a local racetrack where he ministers the gospel to race-car drivers and hot-rod enthusiasts through a ministry called Racing with Jesus Ministries (rwjm.com), see *New York Times* September 2013 article. Today, with regard to his counseling practice, he specializes in depression, anxiety, sexual addictions, teen cutting, and family counseling. He has a Masters degree in Christian counseling and a bachelor's degree in theology. He is also a member of the New York State Mental Health Counselors Association and a member of a local ministers' association called Suffolk County Evangelical Ministers Fellowship.

Yet with all of that, things have not always been easy or smooth-sailing. In 1997, he encountered his first bout with anxiety and depression, which was so serious that he almost took his life. Also extreme OCD haunted him, and sometime later, he would slip again into depression and anxiety. It was not something he ever expected but something that he knew he had to deal with. It was either give up or dig in and fight. Even till this day, there are times where those feelings pop up to remind him how trusting in Jesus Christ and having deep intimacy with Him is the only hope in a world with much pain and suffering. He began seeing his calling in this area and began being an outspoken advocate for discussion on topics of depression and anxiety in the church through seminar-speaking on the issues and joining a local Christian mental healthcare providers' group.

Pastor Scott is fifty-one years old as of this writing and married for over twenty-six years to his best friend, Julie. They have three boys—Jacob, Aaron, and their youngest, Luke, who were all homeschooled. Pastor Scott, besides serving Jesus Christ and being a part of the hot-rod ministry, also enjoys old Jeeps, of which he mentions often in this book. His dream is to be able to travel the country and speak on depression and anxiety in the church today. Some might not like his hard-nosed approach to life, his way of treating depression and anxiety, his gospel presentation, and doing what's right, but that's just how he is—old-school preaching without being afraid to talk about sin and God's justice, as well as His Love. His favorite authors are A.W. Tozer, Watchmen Nee, Dietrich Bonhoffer, David Wilkerson, Ray Comfort, plus many, many more old-school preachers.

Pastor Scott was raised a Roman Catholic, turned Atheist, dabbled a short time in the occult, and even played drums in the heavy-metal music scene of the 1980s before coming to know Jesus Christ as Lord. If you would like to have Pastor Scott speak at your church, please contact him at depressionanxietygod@gmail.com or on Facebook.

Depressionanxietygod.blogspot.com

Personal Note

CPSIA information can be obtained
at www.ICGtesting.com
Printed in the USA
FFOW03n1757030617
36237FF